—Winston Churchill
your courage
your cheerfulness
your resolution
talk
costs
lives.
TO
DEFEND
THE
RIGHT
TO BE
FREE
AIR RAID
SHELTER
SAVE
FOR
VICTORY
"we shall
not flag
or fail,
we shall
go on
to the end."
—Winston Churchill
If you
talk
talk
Victo
BILL STICKERS
WILL BE
PROSECUTED
BY JACQMAR
your courage
your cheerfulness
your resolution
careless
talk
costs
lives.
LEND
TO
DEFEND
THE
RIGHT
TO BE
FREE
AIR RAID
SHELTER

FEW EGGS
AND NO ORANGES:
THE DIARIES OF
VERE HODGSON
1940-45

Persephone Book Nº 9
Published by Persephone Books Ltd 1999

First published by Dennis Dobson 1971

Endpapers taken from a fragment of a
printed rayon headscarf called 'London Wall'
produced by Jacqmar Ltd. c. 1942,
reproduced by kind permission of Paul
and Karen Rennie.

Typeset in ITC Baskerville by Keystroke,
Jacaranda Lodge, Wolverhampton

Printed and bound by Biddles Ltd,
Guildford and King's Lynn

ISBN 0–9534780–8–4

Persephone Books Ltd
28 Great Sutton Street
London EC1V 0DS
0171 253 5454

FEW EGGS
AND NO ORANGES

A DIARY
showing how
Unimportant People
in London and Birmingham
lived through the war years
1940–45
written
in the Notting Hill area of London
by
VERE HODGSON

with a new preface by

JENNY HARTLEY

❀

PERSEPHONE BOOKS
LONDON

PUBLISHER'S NOTE

Vere Hodgson kept a diary in one form or another for most of her life. The earliest surviving volume is for 1924–27 when she went to teach in Italy for three years; she is known to have continued to write her diary until 1973. To begin with she wrote by hand in a small lined notebook but after 4 October 1940 began to type on filofax-sized pages. Later she used larger sheets of airmail paper. This was because she began circulating her diary around her friends and relations: it is not clear whether the surviving typescript was the original or was copied from the smaller pages which were then destroyed. What is clear is that *Few Eggs and No Oranges* is a heavily edited version of the airmail sheets. After the writer Leonard Mosley had drawn on the diaries for his 1971 book about London during the war, the Kensington-based publisher Dennis Dobson asked Vere to prepare them for publication. This she did, cutting by about three-quarters and editing substantially, and beginning the published diary on 25 June 1940, the day the war 'proper' began ('Last night at about 1 a.m. we had the first air raid of the war on London'). There were obviously wartime diary entries prior to this date – Leonard Mosley quoted 3 September 1939 and 7 May 1940 – but they cannot be found. The only wartime diary that has survived, apart from the handwritten entries for June–October 1940 torn out of a notebook and a few filofax-sized typed pages, was typed on the airmail-paper sheets sent round to seven or eight people; its final destination was Vere's cousin Lucy Hodgson in Rhodesia and it is this which is now in Kensington Public Library.

PREFACE

When war was declared in September 1939 many women in Britain began to keep diaries with a sense that they were recording private lives which had been dramatically disrupted by a wider public context. Some have found their way into print; some have been deposited in the Imperial War Museum or local history collections, and some still lie unregarded in attics and cellars. All these diaries are important because they make up the chorus of the People's War, they give us fascinating glimpses into what it felt like at the time, snapshots of daily lives that we ourselves might have led.

Vere Hodgson described herself as a recorder rather than a writer, and as a diarist of ordinary rather than extraordinary people. The point is made, almost defiantly, on her title page with its reference to 'unimportant people'; the first paragraph of the Foreword describes the diarist as 'an ordinary commonplace Londoner'. This emphasis on the ordinary is characteristic of the time, and of Vere Hodgson herself. Partly a modest disclaimer against being anything special, it is also a positive celebration of the nation at war, and of the recorder's place and role in it.

Again characteristically, the diary was pushed into rather than seeking the light of print. The writer Leonard Mosley advertised for diaries while researching *Backs to the Wall* (1971), a book about wartime London. Vere Hodgson lent him hers, and he quoted from it extensively, praising it as a 'remarkable record'. Reviewers of his book agreed enthusiastically and singled her out for comment. *The Times* noted that Miss Hodgson 'documented brilliantly the war years'; *The Times Literary Supplement* considered her diary 'the richest mine of all'. When the diary was eventually published in 1976 reviewers again applauded the 'treasure trove', the 'evocative details' and the 'human touch'; the book was particularly successful in Commonwealth countries. As well as inspiring a band of devotees in Britain (flowers have been laid on her Aunt Nell's grave), the book has been used fully by social historians such as Angus Calder (in *The Myth of the Blitz*, 1991) and Philip Ziegler (*London at War 1939–1945*, 1995).

For them Vere Hodgson represents a reliable source of information, a recognisable London type, and a version of Englishness. Her diary comes from the heart of the myth of the blitz as well as contributing to it. We must, of course, be clear that 'myth' does not necessarily mean falsehood or untruth. Here it points, rather, to elements of national identity and standards of behaviour which were fostered by propaganda, and which in turn helped people to get through difficult times. The middle-class well-educated Vere Hodgson could not speak for the chirpy Cockney, but she could and did exemplify other aspects of the myth: the comradeship and sense of 'we're all in it together', the good humour and stoicism, the public-spiritedness. She is also a classic wartime Londoner in her enthusiasms and affections: her feelings about the City of London and St Paul's Cathedral for example, and her near-worship of Winston Churchill.

During the Blitz of 1940–41 London was bombed heavily for seventy-five consecutive nights (with one exception in November, when bad weather intervened). What was known as the 'Little Blitz' returned in the early months of 1944, and from June 1944 V1s (pilotless planes) and then V2s (rockets) bombarded Britain, aimed mainly at London and the South East. In the words of the war historian Richard Titmuss, 'London was on duty for most of the war . . . Between the first and the last incident the alert was sounded on 1,124 occasions. If these are averaged, it may be said that Londoners were threatened once every 36 hours for over 5 years.'

Winifred Vere Hodgson (1901–79) came from Birmingham and was proud of the Hodgson family tree, which included bishops, mayors, Vice Admirals and Major Generals in the Bengal Army – the stuff of England. Researching one branch in 1979, Vere Hodgson characterised them as 'public-spirited people, who worked hard, loved their families, and left a good name behind them'; she could have been describing herself. Vere was the middle child of three; her elder brother died young. Her father died in 1907, and to provide for her children Mrs Hodgson ran the family house in Edgbaston as a boarding house. The two girls, Vere and Catherine, both did well and went to Birmingham University, where Vere read History. In the mid-1920s she taught English for three years in Italy, which she adored. Later she taught in

England, and in 1935 she took up welfare work in Holland Park in West London.

Vere Hodgson was, according to her friend and literary executor Veronica Bowater (who, as Veronica Thackeray, writes highly enjoyable books about the Welsh Marches), a woman of terrific energy. 'Brisk' is the word that people who met her use; the voice that we can still hear on tape comes over as that of an active and alert woman. She was well-informed, warm-hearted, loved animals, birds and children, and had, in Veronica Bowater's words, 'an enthusiasm for living which never left her'.

The diary was started, typically, as a generous offer to keep her cousin Lucy, newly departed to Rhodesia (Zimbabwe) in touch; it was also circulated round family and friends at home. This would not have been unusual at the time, nor would her inclusion in the original (which is now in Kensington Public Library) of newspaper articles and photos. She also included poems by herself and others, and cartoons, which were for her and many others a vital ingredient in morale-boosting.

For Vere Hodgson the war undoubtedly came at first as an excitement. She refers to 'thrilling experiences' and 'the adventures of the night'. Always ready to volunteer for some new training or experience, she might find herself being bumped down a flight of stairs as a pretend casualty or nearly knocked out by gas. She has been used by social historians to express the spirit of England; the excitement is her positive response to the world turned upside down, where she eats her lunch on a battlefield and walks, clad in her dressing-gown, up Ladbroke Road in the dawn.

If she occasionally takes her role as 'England under fire' a bit pompously, thanking the Canadian soldier in hospital 'on behalf of England for what he had done' and standing to attention alone 'in my little room' while the Marseillaise plays to celebrate the liberation of Paris, this is also the woman whose healthy curiosity sends her up the road to Olympia, where she has heard the French officers look 'most impressive in their cloaks'. Her documentation of the changes brought about by the war make her a gift to social historians. When they refer to the new flexibility, it is the detail in the diary which brings this to life: for example the raw cabbage which Vere has 'long read about' but not previously tried. The egg and orange index running throughout the diary gives the material side of wartime life; she also gauges changing attitudes, such as the increased indifference to unexploded bombs – 'we are an adaptable race!' Her own behaviour illustrates this well. By the 'Little Blitz' of early 1944 she has become so inured to bomb danger that she cannot resist going out on the roof to enjoy the 'amazing sight' of a night-time air raid.

Air raids are at the heart of Vere Hodgson's war experience. Newspapers at the time carried few details: her local paper, the *Kensington News*, offers general columns about how well Kensington is bearing up rather than the facts and figures of the damage, and radio broadcasts often annoyed listeners by their vagueness – this was presumably in the interests of national security. What Vere Hodgson likes best are first-hand accounts of bombs and their aftermath. Second-hand bombs and rumours are also appreciated, and her own response is unhesitating: 'At the Mercury I was told bombs had fallen again in St Charles' Square, so I took a bus there.' Sometimes she would run in her haste to get to the scene, and she was not alone, 'A policeman came to drive us away.' This taste for bomb tourism may strike us now as ghoulish, a thought which seems to have bothered Vere herself in July 1944. She has gone to investigate reports of Doodlebug damage to a crowded Lyons Restaurant at the corner of Earls Court Road and reports: 'Went to look – shop unrecognisable. I make these full records, because people are undergoing a great test here.' The responsibility of the recorder justifies what might seem like insensitive voyeurism.

Vere Hodgson's London walks and bus rides often took her into the City, where she surveyed the damage done to her beloved old churches. The diary keeps a sad and faithful tally of the terrible destruction, accompanied in the original manuscript by newspaper photographs of the bombed churches. She clearly knew and loved the City well, as did many Londoners with whom she shared her Sunday pilgrimages. As she 'went along Bread St into Cheapside, and saw poor Bow Church still looking down sorrowfully on the ruins around', she would have known that she was following in the footsteps of an earlier diarist, her favourite Pepys. Nearly three hundred years earlier, in September 1666, he had gone to see the Great Fire and commented: 'But Lord, what a sad sight it was by moonlight to see the whole City almost on fire – that you might see it plain at Woolwich, as if you were by it.'

In the London Blitz of 1940–41 Vere Hodgson was, unknowingly, also in the company of other women who were moved to write about what they saw. Lamenting the destruction of 'my city churches', Virginia Woolf wrote to her friend Ethel Smyth in September 1940:

> And then the passion of my life, that is the City of London – to see London all blasted, that too raked my heart. Have you that feeling for certain alleys and little courts, between Chancery Lane and the City? I walked to the Tower the other day by way of caressing my love for all that.

In early 1941, not long before she died, she went up to London to 'walk among the ruins', as she told Ethel Smyth:

> D'you know what I'm doing tomorrow? Going up to London Bridge. Then I shall walk, all along the Thames, in and out where I used to haunt, so through the Temple, up the Strand and out into Oxford St, where I shall buy macaroni and lunch. No. You never shared my passion for that great city . . . Its my only patriotism.

Elizabeth Bowen, whose novel *The Heat of the Day* (1949) is a masterpiece of the period, had first-hand knowledge of the blitzed streets as an ARP warden. 'Walking in the darkness of the nights of six years (darkness which transformed a capital city into a network of inscrutable canyons) one develops new bare alert senses, with their own savage warnings and notations' (Preface to *The Demon Lover*). Another novelist, Rose Macaulay, was dashing round London in her ambulance; her version of the ravaged city, haunted and enlivened by its many ghosts, appears in *The World My Wilderness* (1950). For the American imagist poet H. D. (living not far from Vere Hodgson in Lowndes Square) bombed London takes on some of the mystery and magic of ancient Egypt, as she recreates it in her *Trilogy* (1944–46). For all these women, London besieged becomes a powerful source of inspiration, and Vere Hodgson's faithful records provide an essential accompaniment to their work.

Vere Hodgson says little about the work she did for the Greater World Association; we know that it was welfare work important enough to exempt her from conscription. She describes herself as practical and level-headed, inclined to identify with the Biblical Martha; her employer, Winifred Moyes, was quite a different sort of person. For more that thirty years she was the leading light of the Greater World Christian Spiritualist Association, and acted as a medium for the teachings of her spirit guide Zodiac. Accompanied by a band of helpers, she would regularly go round the country to address meetings – and this at a time when all were asked if their journey was Really Necessary. Vere Hodgson doesn't mention going to spiritualist meetings or seances – and according to Veronica Bowater she had no connection with such things in later life – but she was, like many during the war, interested in prophecy and astrology, referring to them frequently.

The period between the wars had seen a great increase and proliferation in the number of spiritualist sects and societies. Parents wanted to contact children who had died in the Great War, or seek comfort in their bereavement. After the Battle of Britain Air Chief Marshall Lord Dowding, who attended one of Miss Moyes's meetings, tried to make spirit contact with the RAF pilots for whose deaths he felt responsible. Vere Hodgson's local newspaper carried advertisements for many such meetings, as the war, according to Angus Calder, 'promoted a wide interest in spiritualism'. A Mass Observation study, *Puzzled People* (1947), reported on attitudes to religion during the war, and commented with surprise on the extent of belief in reincarnation. 'Among the interview sample about one person in twenty-five *spontaneously* went into enough detail to show that they held some such belief', a figure which the Observers felt was 'almost certainly an underestimate'. Astrology also had a strong following, up to 50%, especially when news was bad.

In her diary Vere Hodgson describes herself as 'inclined to be flippant and disbelieving on the subject of prediction and I get disapproving looks'; nevertheless she is interested enough to 'study', record and pass on prophecies and predictions from newspaper and word-of-mouth sources. She also preserved newspaper cuttings of predictions for the year ahead. In editing her diary for publication she cut out several references to the circle of mediums which centered on Miss Moyes. One incident in February 1941, cut from the published version, suggests mixed reactions: 'A little medium for whom I have a great respect was resting in the office to-day before the Meeting when she began to "see" things in the office, and standing by me she saw an Indian lady of aristocratic bearing in a rich silk sari . . . I record it for what it is worth . . . It seems to me in the nature of a warning.' Her attitude was, however, robust enough to enjoy Noel Coward's *Blithe Spirit* in 1943. The play starred Margaret Rutherford as Madame Arcati, a comical and inefficient medium, and was a great hit. Vere Hodgson found it 'extremely funny', and commented, 'Spiritualism can afford to laugh at itself as long as it is accepted as genuine'.

Much more uncomplicated was her attitude to Winston Churchill. 'A statue in gold would not be too much for what we owe him.' What we owed him, according to Vere Hodgson, was nothing short of salvation: 'The one thing that kept us going was Mr Churchill's indomitable courage.' She likens him to national heroes such as Nelson and Alfred the Great, listens enthralled to his broadcasts, and reads his speeches carefully as well as biographies of him. It is Churchill the orator – 'the spell of that wonderful voice' – that she responds to so strongly; his speeches rather than his action inspire her devotion. His presence was constant and reassuring, in contrast to Hitler's low profile in the years after 1940, leading to speculation, rumour and political jokes at Hitler's expense. Vere Hodgson appreciates the high visibility of her leader, worries about his health, and sympathises with him when he has bad news to announce – 'poor Mr Churchill felt it dreadfully'. She also admires his straight talking: 'Churchill did not try to minimise it [losses at sea]. I like that about him. The news is bad – and he admits it.' From the diary we can see that 'ordinary' people like Vere Hodgson were better informed about events in Europe and at home than some historians have thought. In 1941 her blood runs cold as she listens to a 'recording of Nazi cruelty in a Concentration Camp', and in 1942 she comments, 'The massacre of the Jews is awful to read of.' She also hears on the news about the 'terrific shelter disaster at Bethnal Green'.

Sixty years after the events Vere Hodgson describes, we are in a position to compare her experiences with those on the other side of the battlefield, as she could not. Recently released documents about the German home front reveal more similarities than she might have suspected. Her views on retaliation, giving the enemy 'a taste of their own medicine', were shared by German women, but so too was her experience that a community grows stronger under fire. The campaign of mass bombing of civilian targets by the RAF began with Lübeck in early 1942. Vere Hodgson comments: 'We are all heartened by the terrible raids of Lübeck and Rostock. It is dreadful to be so glad – but we cannot be anything else.' She herself, however, was in a good position to realise that bombing can have the reverse effect on civilian morale to that intended, as was the case in Lübeck where an observer reported: 'Never before has the sense of community and sense of belonging been so clearly demonstrated as during that night.'

We cannot afford to ignore the testimony of recorders such as Vere Hodgson and many others; from them we get the strongest sense of what it is like to be in a city under fire.

Jenny Hartley

FOREWORD

This is a very unpretentious work. It is the diary of an ordinary commonplace Londoner during the war years. The writer had no spectacular job. She just did her daily work regardless of bombs and sleepless nights – just like everyone else who remained in the capital. There were times when it meant a great effort to keep the diary going, owing to intense fatigue. We all did any useful work that came to hand, and it often meant carrying on far into the night.

The diary begins on 25 June 1940, with a few quiet entries written in longhand. We were all stunned by the Dunkirk evacuation and the fall of France. Later I was able to type it, and it records fairly accurately the hopes and fears and daily drudgery of an ordinary person during many weary springs, summers, autumns and winters.

The writer was never bombed, but heard distinctly every bomb that dropped within range during five long years. The emotions and fears of those years are recorded at the time. Thousands of Londoners must have felt the same.

The events of those years seem like a forgotten nightmare, but they were terribly real at the time, and I am thankful I made the effort to keep these records. They may interest another generation – if the world survives at all.

I was attached to a community which did both religious
and philanthropic work. Its headquarters were in Lansdowne
Road, Holland Park. The head of the organisation was
Winifred Moyes, a woman of dynamic personality and
determination unbounded. She knew no fear. She used to
say: 'If a bomb drops on us we cannot continue; but until
it does we carry on.' My main interest was welfare work. At
first in connection with the Night Shelter for Homeless
Women in Lambeth, established many years before the war.
Then with families in Notting Hill. They loved to come to the
Sanctuary and tell their troubles, where they had instant help.
It was before the welfare state came into being, and the
need was great.

The Community had its own printing works in the basement of a very large house. A weekly journal was produced
which disseminated religious teaching. One page, however,
was devoted to the philanthropic work of the Association.
Money and clothing were sent from all over the world.

I lived in 56, Ladbroke Road, quite near, and later – in
1941 – I had my own flatlet opposite in no. 79. My mother
and sister lived in Birmingham, where I had been educated at
King Edward's High School for Girls, and at the University.
In earlier years I had taught English at a school in Florence,
called Poggio Imperiale. But at the time of the diary my
interest was in social work – hence the fact that I was not
called up during the war. The authorities considered that
the welfare activities of the Association were sufficiently
important.

Vere Hodgson
Shropshire, 1976

FEW EGGS
AND NO ORANGES

A DIARY

showing how

Unimportant People in London and Birmingham

lived through the war years

1940-1945

written in the Notting Hill area of London by

VERE HODGSON

Few Eggs And No Oranges is a 600 page diary of the war years kept by Vere Hodgson while she was living in Ladbroke Road and working in Lansdowne Road. This beautifully produced book is No 9 in Persephone's much-acclaimed series of reissues with uniform grey jackets, cream 'labels', and endpapers reproducing contemporary fabrics – in this case 'London Wall' 1942 by Jacqmar.

All our books cost £10 including P&P.

PERSEPHONE BOOKS LTD
28 GREAT SUTTON STREET · LONDON EC1V 0DS
phone 0171 253 5454 · fax 0171 253 5656
sales@persephonebooks.co.uk

To
my cousin
LUCY VERE HODGSON
the original recipient of
the diary
and the sender of innumerable parcels of food
from Northern Rhodesia
throughout the war,
and
to
my sister
CATHERINE DUFFELL HODGSON
this diary
is
most gratefully dedicated

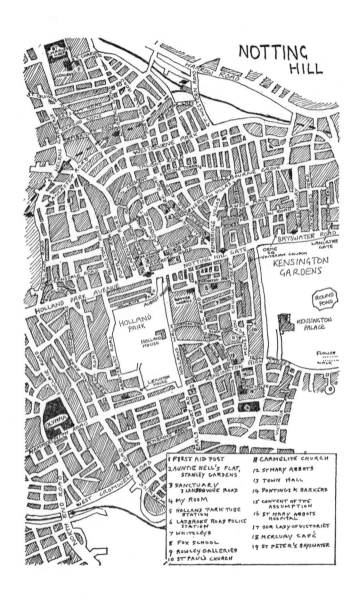

NOTTING HILL

1 FIRST AID POST
2 AUNTIE NELL'S FLAT, STANLEY GARDENS
3 SANCTUARY 1 LANSDOWNE ROAD
4 MY ROOM
5 HOLLAND PARK TUBE STATION
6 LADBROKE ROAD POLICE STATION
7 WHITELEYS
8 FOX SCHOOL
9 ROWLEY GALLERIES
10 ST PAUL'S CHURCH
11 CARMELITE CHURCH
12 ST MARY ABBOTS
13 TOWN HALL
14 PONTINGS & BARKERS
15 CONVENT OF THE ASSUMPTION
16 ST MARY ABBOTS HOSPITAL
17 OUR LADY OF VICTORIES
18 MERCURY CAFÉ
19 ST PETER'S BAYSWATER

WHERE THE DIARY WAS
WRITTEN

⋯⋯✻⋯⋯

The Sanctuary. This was at 3, Lansdowne Road, Holland
Park. There was a chapel in the building; but the whole house
was referred to as the Sanctuary. It belonged to the Greater
World Association Trust, founded in 1934 and administered
by a management committee of men and women, about ten
in all. The property had been bought by a wealthy manu-
facturer, Mr Alfred Morris, for the use of the group of workers
who surrounded Miss Moyes. There were residential quarters,
offices, and a printing works in the basement, fully equipped,
with a staff of about eight. It was considered that if the work
were concentrated under one roof the publication of the
weekly journal, *The Greater World*, and the dissemination
of the spiritual teachings given through Miss Moyes would
be facilitated. Mr Morris also bought no. 1, and later the
Association purchased no. 5. They were all large handsome
houses with gardens.

Miss Moyes had been interested in the social work of Mrs
Cecil Chesterton for some years, and she determined to
found a Night Shelter for Homeless Women. By chance, Mrs
Crookes, daughter-in-law of Sir William Crookes, called to see
her, and instantly gave £100 towards the project. Other

money followed, and in 1933 she opened in China Walk, Lambeth, a place where fifty women could have a bed, a hot-water bottle, a good supper, and breakfast in the morning. There was a warden in charge. Voluntary workers also helped in the evening. Later a convalescent home at Leigh-on-Sea was given by another donor, where Miss Moyes sent women for a holiday. A second night shelter was opened at Leeds in 1935.

But after the outbreak of war the welfare work was gradually built up at the Sanctuary itself. Clothing was received and sorted. Tins of food and money were given in the Notting Hill area and elsewhere. The Association was on the Lord Mayor of London's List for goods coming from U.S.A. and other parts of the world.

The basic idea of no. 3 was *service*; and many people, unconnected with Christian Spiritualism in the formal sense, like myself, worked there. I joined the staff in 1935, after teaching for about ten years in Italy and parts of England. I felt I needed a change from the academic atmosphere in which I had always lived. I had it!

I wrote the diary at my office desk in the evenings when I came down on fire watch. So when I write 'came down here', I mean from my little flat to the Sanctuary.

PRINCIPAL PERSONS IN THE DIARY

Lucy Hodgson My cousin, an Education Officer in Northern Rhodesia. When the diary opens she had just returned there. She left us with grave misgivings. I promised to write frequently. This is how the diary began. Afterwards it was sent round to other relatives and friends before going abroad.

Auntie Nell A beloved aunt, who lived at 27, Stanley Gardens, W.11. She is one of the chief figures in the diary until her death in 1945, a few weeks before the war ended. She made endless jam for us. She was always full of concern and ready to help in any possible way.

LEADING PERSONALITIES AT THE SANCTUARY

Miss Winifred Moyes This remarkable woman, around whom the work revolved, came of a journalistic family. She gave up her work on the *Daily Telegraph* because, quite by accident, she discovered she had psychic gifts. She had attracted round her many men and women who considered that the spiritual addresses given through her guide, Zodiac, should reach a wider public. So the Association was formed. In 1935 I answered an advertisement in the *Telegraph* for someone interested in philanthropic work. It was worth trying. I was there for seventeen years !

One page of the weekly journal, called *The Greater World*, was devoted to welfare work. Often I wrote up some of our cases, or I supplied Miss Moyes with the material. Money came in from all over the world. The three leaders travelled to public meetings every Sunday. A Zodiac address was given and taken down in shorthand for publication the following week. She worked herself to death – and was prepared to work everyone else around her! She died in 1957, some years after I had returned to Birmingham.

Mrs Margaret Hoare   A lifelong friend of Miss Moyes. She was head of the office, and note-taker at all meetings. She lived in a top flat at no. 3 with her mother, Mrs Cox. She died in 1963.

Mrs Cox   The Little Old Lady of the diary aged about 80. The moment the Warning went she used to come down to me, when her daughter was away. I loved her – she was very forthright.

Mr H. F. Bendall   President of the Association. He was in the Civil Service. He came in every afternoon about 5 p.m. He travelled with Miss Moyes and Mrs Hoare every Sunday, and took the chair at all meetings.

Mr A. H. Hillyard   He is often called The Chief Workman in the diary because he was so clever at mending things. He was a Customs and Excise Officer in the City. He worked every evening in our office, was a member of the management committee, and a devoted reader of the Zodiac addresses. He lost his right arm in the First World War. Therefore I used to help him by typing his letters in the evening. He went to his family in Parkstone for the week-end.

Miss Rose Mackay   An elderly lady who lived at the Sanctuary. She was a member of the management committee. She was a very cultured woman; had studied art in Paris. I loved her dearly. She was an angel to the staff.

Major and *Mrs Osman Gabriel*   Members of the management committee. They held a healing service in the Sanctuary on Thursday afternoons. Major Gabriel was a highly cultured man, and a very old friend of Miss Moyes, whose work he admired tremendously. He died in 1975. He had devoted all his latter years to the Lifeboat service and had presented them with two fully-equipped lifeboats costing £60,000 each.

MY COLLEAGUES IN THE OFFICE

Barishnikov   A well-educated Russian who had lost everything with the fall of the old régime. He had been an interpreter in our activities against the Bolsheviks. Then he worked in London at the Russian bank, until all the staff were summoned to Moscow ! He joined the office staff of the G.W. about 1935.

Mr Recsteiner   Known as Resti. A Swiss. He was the chief accountant for the entire work of the Association – printing works, as well as the religious and philanthropic work. There were separate funds for every department. He was a delightful colleague and friend.

Miss Ashton An accountant for smaller items. She was an old friend of Miss Moyes. Elderly and very precise, but a dear little soul.

Mrs Fisher and *Mrs Smithers* Both worked in the office at various times.

Mrs Francis A widow with two small boys. She was a wonderful part-time worker on the welfare side. She was my principal helper on the Caledonian Market at the Fair.

Miss Cameron Sister of the above. She worked in the City but later joined the office staff.

Miss Jones A part-time worker in the office. She managed the small items of the philanthropic work. A devoted follower of Miss Moyes.

The cat His name was Scamp. This little animal was very popular in the house and the office. Alas, he was killed on D-Day. A marmalade kitten then took his place.

OTHER COMMUNITY WORKERS

Mr and *Mrs Harry Johnson* Mrs Johnson was the matron at the Night Shelter in Lambeth, which did such wonderful work before the war and up to the blitz. Then the women slept in the air raid shelters and came to Mrs Johnson for breakfast and supper. Mr Harry Johnson helped with the work of his wife but was also a missioner for the G.W. He travelled abroad; and also accompanied Miss Moyes and Mrs Hoare on their lecture tour of U.S.A. and Canada before the war.

Miss Marjorie Rowe A member of the Community. She had a flat in the house and did spiritual work of her own.

OTHER FRIENDS OF MISS MOYES MENTIONED
IN THE DIARY

Chief Os-Ke-Non-Ton He was the head of the Canadian Mohawk Indians. He came for some months every year before and after the war to give lectures on Red Indian life to schools, and to be the Medicine Man in *Hiawatha* at the Albert Hall. He had a glorious singing voice, and was a delightful personality. He was a great admirer of Miss Moyes both for her religious and charitable work. His visits to the Sanctuary always brought excitement and pleasure to us all. 'The Chief's come!' went round the office. I helped him write the memoirs of his life.

The Pig-breeder A very kind eccentric admirer of Miss Moyes's philanthropic work. He would never divulge his name, but he was always ready to produce churns of milk for the Fair, invite us to gather his fruit or even bring an occasional sack of coal for us to give away where needed. He lived at Hounslow.

Dr Bell She was a retired lady doctor and a voluntary worker at the Sanctuary. She had a flat in Church Street. A personal friend of Miss Moyes.

Ivy Croucher A teacher of elocution. At one time she had been a leading member of the Macdona Players, who toured in Bernard Shaw's plays. Interested in the philanthropic work of the Association.

The Stick-up This took place every Wednesday afternoon. Voluntary workers came in to help us pack and despatch the weekly journal. There was always tea for everyone, and what cake could be found during the war!

PEOPLE WHO LIVED IN THE HOUSE WHERE
I HAD A FLAT

The Old Dears This is what I called them collectively. One was a Miss Lambart, a very kind soul and an enthusiastic British Israelite. The Misses Brown were two others.

PEOPLE IN NOTTING HILL GATE

The Old Pole He kept a greengrocer's shop. Quite a character. Had come from Poland years before the war. He was very kind to me in those difficult years.

Mr and Mrs Booker They ran the Mercury Café. I often had lunch there. Situated at a corner in Pembridge Road. The Rambert Ballet from the theatre also lunched at this place. Mr Booker was a Warden, and part of a Rescue Squad. He died of TB. Next door was a shoe repairer – also a friend of mine.

The Police of Ladbroke Road Police Station My near neighbours and often mentioned in the diary. It was from this station that the siren screamed out, and also the welcome All Clear.

MY PERSONAL FRIENDS IN LONDON

Dr John Remy A distinguished Frankfurt lawyer. He was known to my family before the war. He came to this country in

1939. His wife, Carola, and two little daughters, Ilsa and Helga, remained in Germany.

Mrs South An old lady and beloved family friend of many years standing. She was bombed out of her flat in Earl's Court, but returned towards the end of the war.

Kit Sauvary A very dear friend. I met her first when we were both on the staff of Sleaford High School in Lincs. Her home was in the Channel Islands. So I had first-hand news of Guernsey.

Mrs Marie Idiens Often called in the diary, Marie. She was a very old friend from Birmingham. At times she shared my flat. Her son was in the R.A.F.

Mrs Jean Tuckwell and *Miss Mary Bewley* Both were former pupils of mine at a school in Folkestone. Both were trained nurses. Jean was married during the war. Mary and I attended the wedding.

Miss Anne Aird She lived at Radlett where I went sometimes for week-ends. We had done educational work together.

Mr and *Mrs Ellis* and daughter, *Margaret* The latter had been a pupil of mine before I left teaching. They lived at Wimbledon. I visited them often, and I detail their bombings. Very dear friends.

Miss Mabel Lucy An elderly second cousin of mine. She lived in London, but at last was compelled to return to Stratford-on-Avon to her niece.

My mother and *my sister*   Lived at 73, Francis Road, Edgbaston, Birmingham, our home town. My sister, called *Cath* in the diary, was a science specialist, and taught at a school in Holly Hall, Dudley.

Dr W. T. Hillier   He was pathologist at the General Hospital in Birmingham. He had made his home with us since the early 'twenties, when he returned from the First World War.

Beryl   A youthful resident home help. She came from my sister's school.

Annie   A poor old soul who had been bombed out. My mother took her in. She was, however, more a hindrance than a help!

Ariel and *Cecilia*   A mother and daughter. (Ernest, the husband, worked at the Midland Bank.) They lived near Sutton Coldfield, and were very old friends.

Elsie and *Neville Roberts*   Elsie was an old school friend. We had both been pupils at King Edward's High School for Girls. It was in New Street in our day. Former members of the King Edward Schools in Birmingham, boys and girls, are always alluded to as *Old Edwardians*. Her husband was an estate agent (Messrs. Bright Willis and Co.). He was Divisional Warden for the Selly Oak Division.

Mrs Paula Symes   Also an Old Edwardian. We had known each other from the age of ten. Her husband was *Jack*. She had two boys. *Elizabeth* was her devoted help.

Bernard Sleigh He was a well-known Birmingham artist who had retired to a cottage at Chipping Campden in Gloucestershire. He usually came to us for Christmas, complete with his cat. My mother and I spent several holidays at his cottage.

In addition I had two aunts, who lived at Brede in Sussex. They were younger sisters of Auntie Nell. *Aunt Mollie* was one. *Aunt Winny* the other. The former broke her thigh and I visited her in the London Hospital during the war.

SOURCES OF QUOTATIONS

Unless otherwise stated these are from *Hymns Ancient and Modern* and referred to by italic numbers:

p.1, *358*, Bishop Heber; p. 1, *676*, John Bunyan; p. 7, *214*, P. Pusey; p. 13, 16, *193*, Charles Wesley; p. 18, *337*, A. Midlane; p. 21, *225*, J. M. Neale; p. 25, *685*, Ada R. Greenaway; p. 27, 'Locksley Hall', Alfred, Lord Tennyson; p. 33, *240*, H. F. Lyte: p. 36, *685*, Ada R. Greenaway; p. 39, *375*, J. Hampden Gurney; p. 40, *29*, H. Kirke White; p. 43, *677*, S. C. Lowry; p. 46, *276*, J. Anstice; p. 48, *250*, Sir H. W. Baker; p. 49, *738*, Jane L. Borthwick; p. 51, *3*, Isaac Watts; p. 53, *391*, S. Baring Gould; p. 55, *346*, S. Baring Gould; p. 58, *724*, Charles Wesley; p. 59, *685*, Ada R. Greenaway; p. 61, *777*, Catherine Winkworth; p. 63, *501*, From the Latin; p. 64, *274*, S. Baring Gould; p. 67, *4*, John Keble; p. 70, *200*, Isaac Watts; p. 71, *393*, E. H. Plumptree; p. 74, *393*, E. H. Plumptree; p. 78, *60*, Charles Wesley; p. 79, *269*, Charles Wesley; p. 82, *291*, H. Kirke White; p. 83, *437*, Bishop Walsham How; p. 86, *678*, Elizabeth Wordworth; p. 88, *274*, S. Baring Gould; p. 90, *Hamlet*, W. Shakespeare; p. 92, *682*, Isaac Watts; p. 93, *95*, W. J. Copeland; p. 94, *225*, J. M. Neale; p. 97, *412*, H. Alford; p. 99, 'Little Gidding' from *Four Quartets*, T. S. Eliot; p. 102, *493*, From the Latin; p.103, *66*, J. H. Newman; p. 103, *676*, John Bunyan; p. 241, *735*, A. C. Ainger; p. 339, *197*, Sir H. W. Baker; p. 339, *738*, Jane L. Borthwick: p. 439, *437*, Bishop Walsham How; p. 439, *Isaiah*, Ch. 21. v. xi; p. 551, 'Journey of the magi', T. S. Eliot; p. 551, *225*, J. M. Neale; p. 551, Ed Morrow on the photograph taken by Yussuf Karsh; p. 551, *634*, F. W. Faber; p. 587, *135*, From the Latin; p. 587, *228*, J. M. Neale; p. 590, *166*, W. Kethe.

FEW EGGS
AND NO ORANGES:
THE DIARIES OF
VERE HODGSON
1940–45

❧❧❧❦ ✻ ❦❦❦❧

THE YEAR
1940

'Waft, waft, ye winds, the story'

'Who would true valour see,
Let him come hither'

THE MAIN EVENTS
OF THE WAR
IN 1939 AND 1940

1939

Neville Chamberlain Prime Minister

September	1	Germany invades Poland
	3	Britain and France declare war on Germany
	17	Russia invades Poland
	27	Surrender of Warsaw; end of Polish resistance
	29	Germany and Russia partition Poland
November	30	Russia invades Finland
December	13	River Plate naval engagement
	17	*Graf Spee* scuttled

1940

February	17	*Altmark* incident
March	12	Russo-Finnish armistice
April	9	Germany invades Denmark and Norway; Denmark capitulates
May	3	British evacuate central Norway
	10	Germany invades Holland, Belgium and Luxembourg

Winston Churchill becomes Prime Minister

May	13	Bombing of Rotterdam
	14	Dutch army capitulates
	19	Germans take Amiens
	28	Belgian army capitulates
June	4	Dunkirk evacuation completed
	5	Germans attack remaining French armies
	9	Allies evacuate Narvik
	10	Norwegian resistance ceases
		Italy declares war on Britain and France
	14	Germans occupy Paris
	17	French ask for armistice
	22	France capitulates
	25	Japan occupies bases in Indo-China

DIARY BEGINS HERE 'WE ARE ALONE'

July	3	British attack French fleet at Oran
	21	Russia attacks Baltic States
	10	*The Battle of Britain begins*
August–	8	*Attacks on Ports and Convoys*
September	6	*and Aerodromes*
September–	7	*Big blitz on London begins*
October	31	*and ends*
August	19	Italians capture British Somaliland
	20	*Churchill's speech on 'The Few'*
September	2	Britain leases West Indies bases to U.S.A.
	15	The decisive battle
	27	German-Italian-Japanese mutual assistance pact

October	28	Italy invades Greece
November	14	*Bombing of Coventry*
	20	Hungary joins Axis
	23	Rumania joins Axis
December	9	British offensive opens in North Africa
	29	*Great fire raid on City of London*

GENERAL NOTES

Air raids It should be remembered that when bombs fell on London during the blitz, owing to its size only those dropped in one's own particular district could be heard. But when they fell on a small town every single one was audible to the whole population of that place. Even in Coventry, which is not small, this applied.

In the countryside it was not the German bombers heading for their target which they feared, it was later in the night when, driven away by the R.A.F., those same bombers just dropped any bombs they had left indiscriminately, in their flight home. It might be in the fields, where huge craters and dead cattle could be seen in the morning, or even just on a single farmhouse where the family was at rest for the night. Nowhere in their path was any person or place really safe. Details of such cases are given in that wonderful compilation of events called *Front Line, 1940–41*, from which the preceding notes are taken.

Churchill At this time ordinary people such as myself did not realize the greatness of Churchill. I had always connected him with the Fall of Antwerp in World War I, when the Royal Naval Brigade were all taken prisoner before they had had time

5

to do anything. Then the Gallipoli affair. Again his misunderstanding of the general feeling of the country during the Abdication Crisis. Even the Munich Crisis had not really opened our eyes. But we were thankful to have him after Chamberlain's ineptitude. Gradually we came under the spell of that wonderful voice and inspiration. During the awful days that came so soon his stature grew larger and larger, until it filled our sky.

Postscripts These were ten minute talks following the nine o'clock news on Sunday evenings. J. B. Priestley began them in June 1940, after Dunkirk, but from mid-October on they were given by a wide range of people. A huge audience listened to them and their generally high quality did much to encourage and inspire the country.

Quotations The quotations used at the head of various pages in the diary of the year 1940 are, for the most part, from *Hymns, Ancient and Modern*. I was sitting one day in church waiting for the service to begin, and idly turning from one hymn to another, when suddenly lines here and there reminded me of our feelings during the blitz. Death often seemed near in those days, and thankfulness for escape was constant. One was back at basic emotions. Such thoughts seemed to be expressed in many of the simple verses I was looking at. That is how the quotations were chosen. A few, however, came from other recesses of my memory. Details will be found on p. xxxi.

JUNE 1940

'See how our foes their banners are unfurling'

Tuesday, 25th Last night at about 1 a.m. we had the first air raid of the war on London. My room is just opposite the police station, so I got the full benefit of the sirens. It made me leap out of bed half way across the room. I shook all over, but managed to get into my dressing-gown and slippers, put my watch in my pocket, clutch my torch and gas-mask, and get downstairs first. Incidentally I forgot the skylight which is not blacked out, and was rightly reprimanded for showing my torch upwards. I have now covered the light with blue paper and I hope I shall not forget again.

I found myself in a little corridor in which Mrs Gray was rearing two mattresses against the door. The others gradually assembled. I did not know them and it was dark. I passed round my few bottled sweets. The people chatted and joked.

We could hear no sounds of firing or bombs, so after about a quarter of an hour most of them returned to bed. The two top floorers (myself and another lady) hesitated a few minutes and then we did the same. I looked out of the window. The moon was clear and lovely. Not a sound anywhere. I thankfully sank into bed, and eventually fell asleep.

7

<u>London.</u>

Tuesday, June 25<u>th</u>. 1940.

Last night at about 1 a.m.
we had the first air raid of.
the war on London. My
room is just opposite the
police station so I got
the full benefit of the
sirens. It made me
leap out of bed. half way
across the room. I shook
all over but managed to
get into my dressing gown
& slippers, put my.
watch in my pocket,
clutch my torch +
gas-mask & get down
stairs first. Incidentally
I forgot the sky light

I was awakened by the sirens giving the All Clear; but it is as terrifying as the Alarm, and again I leapt out of bed and donned my dressing-gown. I heard the birds beginning to sing. I saw movement at the police station. A car drove in. At last I realized all was well. I fell asleep once more.

Of course we all had our tales to tell at the office, and many had slept through it. It is a dangerous thing to do, and could be done once too often. But how lovely to be killed asleep!

The news is steadily worse. The French Fleet will probably do as it is told, and be used against us. The bright hopes of yesterday!!!

Listened to Noel Baker on the French news. He was trying to buck them up. I am tired and must go to bed, as I have worked at the office until after 9 p.m. I like my [new] room and my [hired] wireless is a joy. If I live on bread and cheese I must keep it. Shall we be disturbed again, I wonder? I wonder how the family is.

Wednesday, 26th   No alarm last night, but I did not sleep well. The police station opposite seems full of activity all night. I lay awake very depressed, wondering what I had better do – go or stay.

Handled a splendid gun in the office, taken by a British soldier from a parachutist in Norway. Not too heavy for a woman to use.

Went to see Auntie Nell tonight. Found her rather depressed over Lucy going. Seems to think she will go to Eardisland as there is nothing to keep her in London if the Brede Aunts evacuate to Devon.

Convalescent Home is to be closed.

Listened to Anthony Eden's speech and felt a little better, though he has a melancholy delivery.

Auntie is not very enthusiastic about General de Gaulle as we have trusted foreigners too often.

Discovered the whereabouts of my refugee [Dr Remy], but I don't think he is allowed to write, and I feel I ought not to trouble the censor.

No news from home. I think they should send me a postcard to let me know how they are standing up to the strain – short of a German march through London one feels the news cannot be worse. So it may be the darkest hour before the dawn. Our boys are doing magnificently in bombing Germany. But what a day it will be when we hear some really good news. We seem to have forgotten what it feels like to rejoice over anything.

Thursday, 27th   A peaceful night. A card from Kit says she is in England. Met her in the dinner hour. The Channel Islands evacuated at the week-end, and we are not going to defend them. All the military have gone, the aerodrome ploughed up, and anything likely to help the Germans has been destroyed. People were given twelve hours to leave. What a scrimmage for everyone! Kit's father would not come. She got on a little boat, and looked after a baby who was sick. She slept with it in her arms, rolled up in a rug. There was no milk on board. They were twenty four hours crossing. The people of Weymouth were marvellously kind, and Kit drank seven cups of tea right off!

She has now put her name down to escort children to Canada or Australia. Then to begin nursing. The trip is no sinecure. They average twenty children to one adult – and this on board a ship!

Received a letter from home [Birmingham]. They have been in the Anderson Shelter and found it quite good. They hope to make further improvements in it. Cath sounded cheerful, and Mother not too bad. I have just guided a lost Belgian to the bus. He had been searching Notting Hill Gate for someone who could speak French. He told me his wife and he had escaped from Brussels the day before the Germans entered. They reached Paris, and then when the Germans arrived she decided to remain with her sister and eleven children. He came to England alone. I put him on a 31 bus, and the Association gave me the 2/6 given to him. He was most grateful.

Friday, 28th Did not sleep well. Heard General de Gaulle. Magnificent personality he sounds. I hope he will be able to rally some Frenchmen, but it does not look very promising. His voice is thrilling, and his answer to Pétain made me shiver in my chair. Such tragedy too in his tones.

A few raids on Britain but nothing of importance. We are, however, to be conquered by August! That is just a month. We shall see.

Saturday, 29th Another peaceful night. Heard the Channel Islands had been bombed, though there were no military objectives left.

It seems the French Empire is not going to fight. Incredible that General de Gaulle's impassioned call can go unheeded.

Read a lot of John Gielgud's autobiography. He is no writer but it is interesting nevertheless.

The sun is shining. My room looks nice but I do miss the trees.

At last received a letter from my refugee. He is in the Isle of Man, and wants me to send him some food.

Sunday, 30th   I find it difficult to decide whether to send stuff down to Brum, or risk my precious winter clothes being destroyed by the blitzkrieg.

Heard Chamberlain tonight. I wish he would just say nothing. It is the same old stuff about our wonderful advantages. We don't know what we are really made of. We may be quite soft. We have not been tried, so it's best to keep quiet until we've something to show.

End of June 1940

JULY 1940

**** ❋ ❈❈❈❈

'While the gathering waters roll'

Monday, 1st Apparently the blitzkrieg is due this week! Guernsey and Jersey have been occupied by the Nazis. Kit says a lot of women and children left there. That damnable raid was just to terrorize them.

I went to Kensington Town Hall for a Respirator drill practice. I am not a warden, but I thought I might pick up something, so I went through the drill and passed the second time.

Tuesday, 2nd Raids over England, but not here. I have a feeling they will go to Ireland first. They will soon polish them off, and then try here. They seem to be building shelters all over Kensington, surface ones.

There are now new orders out about work continuing until gunfire is actually heard. I suppose that is due to there being raids all the time in various parts of England.

The *Scharnhorst* hit again. Splendid. I wish they could sink it. All these attacks must be delaying the blitzkrieg. General de Gaulle again last night. Such a glorious speech.

13

Wednesday, 3rd Lunch with Kit. A lot of her friends stayed, the reason being that, as they think England will be occupied anyway, they might as well be occupied in their own homes! Well, well, we shall see. While there's life, there's hope. A platitude helps sometimes.

Thursday, 4th We seem to have seized the French Navy. Who would have thought the war would have taken such a turn! What a world! I feel if ever we come out of this, I shall never leave England again. I have finished with foreigners. French sailors are said to be arriving in London in great numbers.

Heard the *Arandora Star* had been sunk with German and Italian internees on board. Germans behaved badly. I bet they would. I knew them so well in Italy.

Friday, 5th Further news about the French Navy. We seem to have most of it. What a relief! Went to A.R.P. lecture. Saw the baby gas-mask. You have to keep pumping it. Also saw the Mickey Mouse one. There are lots of children going abroad – so many they cannot cope with more. All children are being moved from the Northern Coast. It looks as if the attack may come from Norway. But it is no use being prophetic about anything until a few months have passed. If we were one hundred per cent British we should be all right. It is the Fifth Column we fear!

I must make arrangements to go to Incendiary Bomb practice.

Saturday, 6th No blitzkrieg as yet. We continue our good work over Germany and also have bombed some warships of the Italians. They don't seem to be doing too well. I am very relieved. I was afraid they might. There have been air raids on South Devon. London is the safest place there is no doubt! Lucy must be in Africa by now.

Sunday, 7th Went to First Aid Post, and joined the new shift. Found them very nice. Put my name down to go through the gas-room, and also for Incendiary Bomb practice. News is good so far as it goes. Recruiting for Frenchmen opened at Olympia. That is just down the road so I must wander along and see them. People say the officers are most impressive in their cloaks.

I wrote to my refugee friend to buck him up; but apparently letters take a fortnight to reach the Isle of Man. More bombers brought down.

Monday, 8th No raids on London yet! We seem to be bombing everywhere. A very healthy sign. It is to prevent them starting. But Eire still seems to me the weakest spot. Nice bright day. Went to see Auntie Nell in the evening with glass jars for making jam. Also to tell her the good news that I could get two pounds of preserving sugar for her. We listened to the news, and heard the bombshell about tea! Two ounces per head, per week! However, it will do for me. I don't like it strong; but I like to have some to offer other people a cup.

Listened to General de Gaulle on sinkings at Oran. He was deeply moved about it; but said how dishonourable the Pétain Government had been, and that he would rather the *Dunkirk* were sunk than that it should be manned by Germans.

JULY 1940

'While the tempest still is nigh'

Tuesday, 9th Worked late at the office, but just heard a bit of the news which said we are to have six ounces of butter cum margarine, and two ounces of cooking fat. *Ugh*! Also that the war is costing six million a day, or some such fantastic figure. Some of us had better take a mortgage on our places in heaven – otherwise I don't see how it is going to be paid. Just upset a jug of milk – most annoying.

Mr Hicks spoke to the women of England. Sounded sincere. Nice to get a little appreciation some time. Cartoon on Ireland excellent.

De Valera blindfold in chair, guarded by two blindfold soldiers . . .

[Beginning of the Battle of Britain, though we did not realize it.]

Wednesday, 10th Rather a busy day. Kit Sauvary came to supper. Full of news about her war nursing. Fifty hours on trial. She had been ticked off by one Sister in the usual heartless manner. She had had to escape from a blood test, as she felt herself fainting. Kit with nerves of iron! What should I be like?

Auntie Nell came to put rings on my black-out to stop flying glass. Kit was there and said she feared the Channel Islands would freeze or starve during the winter. Auntie feared Kit was blaming the Navy for not defending the Islands. But Kit with her father and so many friends there feels strongly. It will be hard for them, but I think they will worry through.

No news yet about children leaving for Canada. I expect the Navy cannot spare the ships in the circumstances.

Thursday, 11th Went through the gas-chamber today. It was C.A.P., a non-persistent tear gas. We had to don gas-masks and go in with an official. Two solid crystals were heated from beneath and vapour given off. I found I had to breathe from my boots to keep going, but this was probably nervous reaction. I got calmer. When we were out in the air I felt a slight pricking of the eyes – it was gas in my hair. Next Thursday to go through the smoke room.

No stirring news. No blitzkrieg yet. I feel our coast towns are having a nasty time. In London all is peace.

Friday, 12th Went to the Gas Lecture. Little bottles of them passed round. Had a good sniff at Lewisite. Strong smell – like geraniums. Then the lecturer broke a capsule of phosgene. You can call it Musty Hay. It is like decaying vegetation. Then BBC, which is supposed to be bitter-sweet. This I did not consider so clear a description. But Mustard seemed to have a definite smell – but I could not say of what.

Anyway it was a great help. On Monday we go to the Cleansing Stations. Came back along Holland Walk. Listened to French News. A Polish officer said how amazed he was to find the British Fleet in such full command in the Mediterranean – and his voyage entirely uneventful! Everywhere Britain still ruled – Gibraltar, Malta etc. – there was peace and security.

Saturday, 13th Went to Hammersmith Broadway this afternoon, and looked with great interest at Olympia, garrisoned by the French. A few soldiers and officers about. It all seemed impressive and historic – not the thing itself, but the thought behind it.

Returning along Holland Walk encountered various refugees looking for Aubrey House. I decided to lead them there, as it is difficult to direct people round those little turnings. They seemed to be refugees from Danzig. One girl had no news of her family.

Sunday, 14th Thought of General de Gaulle and the French Legion up in Whitehall. I should love to have heard him shout – Vive L'Angleterre! Vive la France!

Heard the Prime Minister at 9 o'clock. He sounded as if he had got over all the shocks the French had given him, and was once more in command of the situation. Listened to a recording of the Fight over the Channel. Jolly good! But, oh, how I wish we could hear of the Italian fleet being sunk; or Libya taken. Should love to give them a drubbing for their impudence.

'Up in the bright blue sky'

Monday, 15th Went to the Gas Cleansing Station at Earls Court. Saw the wardens in protective clothing. Afterwards they had to have an eye douche, and go under the shower. It poured with rain all day.

Kit came for supper. She was weary after seven hours on her feet in hospital. Had attended an operation, and gave me a minute description. I should have fainted, but she was splendid . . . She tells me that it was the fault of the Channel Islands authorities that the position was not explained to the people. The British Government said the Islands would not be defended. Her father would have come had he realized.

Tuesday, 16th Still raining. This will probably hold up the blitzkrieg, which is due at the end of the week, according to Gayda! Great shortage of eggs in London. I shall have to switch over to baked beans.

Worked late at the office. They don't seem to have found at the B.B.C. an alternative time signal to the 'Tramp of the death-watch beetle'. Also called a 'Ghost in Goloshes'. Someone suggested we have 'Drake's drum'. The idea is sound. No Germans here yet. One man said that the moment they got here every Britisher should put up a Union Jack on his chimney pot, and it should not be hauled down except by a Nazi climbing up over the dead bodies of the household.

Wednesday, 17th Blitzkrieg due to begin on Friday as the constellations will be favourable! It is a full moon, and we shall see.

Priestley's broadcast is in for criticism because he lifted the veil from a certain famous Kent resort. I was surprised when I heard him name the place. I don't think, however, it is fair to blame Gardiner for his Channel Flight broadcast. It is a game to these Boys – a deadly game – but if it were not, it could not be borne.

Hope to go through the Smoke tomorrow. Have borrowed a beret, and shall go in an old coat and dress. Dr Remy sent me some money to send him food to the Internment Camp.

Thursday, 18th Up early to go to my Fire-Fighting. Pouring with rain. Paddled down to Kensington Square. Found the Convent of the Assumption. A nun came to ask me my purpose. She was aged and gnarled like a Rembrandt picture, with her immense hat. Wandered round to the back. I was early. A few more arrived, including Commandant Ellis of my First Aid Post. Also the pleasant little woman I met at the Gas Cleansing Station. We had a lecture on Incendiary Bombs, and then were taken out for the practical.

First part was the Stirrup Pump. Having used this before I earned a Very Good, from the instructor. Next the corrugated iron hut. One by one we had to creep through a door, work our way on hands and knees through the smoke with a fierce fire burning in the middle of the place. We were asked to stand up, and when we choked got down to the floor again. Jolly glad to get in the open air. We were all in men's overalls and gum boots, much too large for us.

Next episode was the bomb. The side of the hut was let down, and a rough room created with the fire still going well, in the centre. In the room was the bomb – old furniture spread round and sprinkled with petrol – set on fire. We had to use the stirrup pump and cope with the Bomb and Fire at the same time!

Then the walk. We had to climb a ten-foot wall and then drop from it! Men showed us how it should be done. It looked so easy. I hated trying, but in the end enjoyed it and landed better than some of them. I had been taught by Miss Jaques at King Edward's School to land from the parallel bars. Lots of people watching us. Finally we practised dragging an insensible person down a flight of stairs. I volunteered to be the person, and though I was dragged by The Expert, the stairs being iron, I can still feel the effects! Felt exhausted and hungry. Returned to office and worked until 9 p.m.

'And now we watch and struggle'

Friday, 19th Day the Blitzkrieg is to begin! I am well-sprinkled with bruises from yesterday. About 4 p.m. there arrived in the office a N.Z. soldier, connected with the Wellington Church. Very young and simple – knew nothing of London – he had thoroughly lost himself during the morning. We tried to find some man to take him round, but in the end I did it.

We tramped for two and a half hours all round. He kept saying: Gee-whiz! Bai Jove! It nearly took his breath away to see all the places he had read about over there. He came from a ten-thousand-acre farm of Sheep, and was an excellent horseman. Twelve miles on horseback to school every day. He had advanced his age to join up.

We went to Lyons Brasserie for a meal, which he was under the impression was a Night Club. Fixed him up at a Y.M.C.A. Hostel opposite the Abbey for the night. He was far too inexperienced to be wandering round London alone. We had our pictures taken in Trafalgar Square, feeding the pigeons – with the sun out. So that will be sent to a mother and sister at home. Miss M. wants an article about him, so I have been struggling with it.

An Italian cruiser sunk. Excellent. Going to Ballet at King's Theatre. Hitler has offered his final ultimatum. His speech. Gee-whiz, as the N.Z. soldier constantly remarked. How often I think of Mr Chamberlain saying: 'Words for Herr Hitler bear a meaning different from those usually associated with them.'

Sunday, 21st Went to First Aid Post. Was able to practise a few splints. Tried the thigh one. Went to St Charles' Hospital to watch dressings.

Monday, 22nd Very busy morning at office, as Miss Moyes is off to Leeds to see about our Shelter there. Ran here, there and everywhere to get her off.

Tuesday, 23rd Nice free day. A fine message from General de Gaulle on the French news. He seems delighted that French pilots are helping to raid Germany.

Wednesday, 24th Sent the paper off with a full crowd of voluntary workers. Mr Hillyard back with a Stirrup Pump. We are well equipped now to cope with fire and casualties. Hope we may not have to, but it is well to be prepared. The Germans may decide to do a little concentrated bombing on London when the Blitzkrieg really begins, as I fear it will.

Thursday, 25th Miss M. back, so had to fly in all directions. She had had an awful time at Leeds Shelter, owing to a burst pipe. Mr H. has brought buckets back from the City, so as soon as we can get a moment we must practise with the Stirrup Pump.

Air Marshal Joubert was well worth hearing on the subject of ladies who collect German Parachuters. As long as there were no more than six, he advised, they could go ahead; but if we see seven we had better phone the police!

Friday, 26th Always more bombers brought down. I don't like the Italians occupying a corner of Kenya. I don't want them to have any success whatever. Uncle Wykeham out there is now a parashot with a gun. Tried the Stirrup Pump in the garden.

Sunday, 28th Read the *Observer*. Garvin pleased about the American aeroplanes, but rather worried lest Mussolini, strengthened by the Germans, should attack Egypt and the Sudan. This seems to be a likely occurrence, and we are not too strong out there. I hope S. Africa is doing something. Heard the broadcast of Dorothy Thompson's magnificent speech to the Canadians. It reduced me to tears. I wish we could have it in full. Took a walk in Kensington Gardens . . . what peace and beauty. The balloon was just going up.

Monday, 29th The first batch of children has sailed. U.S.A. comment is that Hitler would sink a shipload of angels if he thought it would be of any military advantage; but the writer could not see any advantage because it would finish alienating the Americans.

Mr Ogilvie, Director-General of B.B.C. alluded to the innocent tick-tock time signal that had caused much criticism. Another description of it is: March of the Gestapo.

There were eighty planes over Dover. Sounds as if concentrated bombing is to begin. I shall go down to Brum for the week-end and take my Venetian glass. Great shortage of eggs. South Africans are in Kenya.

End of July 1940

AUGUST 1940

**** ❋ ****

'Seek not for rest until the day is done'

Thursday, 1st Went to see Auntie Nell last night. Found her with all her treasures out again. The House Cushion was there, and Merlin on the wall. Because at the moment London is the quietest place in England. So, as I tell her, if we are to be bombed and burnt, we might as well enjoy what beauty we can to the end!

Friday, 2nd Auntie Nell came last night and tried to fix up my black-out better. I had to stand a considerable time at the window this morning in my nightgown, drawing it up into folds. The policeman on sentry duty opposite seemed much interested in what I was doing.

Hope to catch the 6.10 p.m. train. It will be interesting to see the countryside. Hitler dropped leaflets over us last night. I would like to see them – to explain his speech. Just as if we had not heard it!

Saturday, 3rd Arrived in Brum in good time. Dr Hillier [pathologist of the General Hospital] on the station to meet me. Very full train. We had the Air Force and the Artillery in our compartment. We saw the remnants of a German Bomber being carried away, this side Banbury. Ground was all charred. Also we were told that a German bomber had come down and surrendered in the North; this sounded too good to be true. The countryside looked normal, except that no stations had a name, and you could not tell where you were.

Mother very glad to see me. Plenty of food in Brum. Lovely to have so many eggs!

Sunday, 4th Spent the morning dodging about. Lay down on the sofa half in the garden when I felt tired. Examined the vegetable plot and the Hans Anderson Shelter. Really topping. They have paved the floor with wood blocks from Broad St, so it is dry as a bone, and put a screen up to the door. Steps go up to it, and others go down. They are going to get some hammocks. I feel it will be quite safe. It seems the Blitzkrieg is to come quite soon. We had a warning from the Government not to relax and think the danger is over.

Went over to Boldmere in afternoon. Tea in the garden. We discussed a Shelter for them. Ernest said ours was the best he had ever seen. Elsie and Neville came to supper. So nice to see them. Neville [of the firm Bright, Willis and Co. Estate Agents] is in charge of 50 warden posts, and has to go round every night and week-end. It takes him ten days to do it all. This is in addition to a full day at his office, where he has not a man left! He is managing with what he calls a beauty chorus! The women have done marvellously well, he says. He could not have believed it possible.

Monday, 5th A full day. At 10.30 a.m. had to tear off to the General Hospital. Found Dr Hillier's Laboratory after a bit. He showed me a few things. Then in my super-clean white overall I descended to the Casualty Ward, and was put under the care of a nurse. I was on the Men's side, and the dressings were all for septic accidents. A long queue of men – old and young, and even small boys. Several were munition workers, suffering from over-fatigue. I do hope the long hours will be knocked off. The people cannot do it. Their spirit, however, was wonderful. They wanted to help the boys, and replace our losses in France. I felt humble before them. They had done so much! One can see how they have accidents. A man had fallen and cut his elbow open. The doctor let me see the stitches put in. Then he sent me along to the Casualty Theatre, and I was kindly invited to stand behind the man giving gas. A finger was being lanced by an Indian doctor. I was much impressed with everything. The doctors and nurses so good to everyone.

Dr Hillier took me to a nice lunch at Barrows. I wandered round the shops, and since in the ordinary way I never have time to do this, it was grand – and to have them open. Dr H. was on duty with the Hospital Home Guard, so he could not see me off. But with chocolates and cigarettes I set off for London. We were due at 11.25 p.m. Actually arrived at ten minutes to one. I had missed the last tube, and just caught the last 27 bus. In bed at 1.30 a.m. very exhausted.

> *'The nations' airy navies grappling in*
> *the central blue'*

Tuesday, 6th Very sleepy, but managed to get to the office. The feeling is that the invasion is about to begin. Barishnikov and Dr Bell had a bet on it. Sixpence to the Shelter Fund. He said: 'No raids before next Tuesday.' She said: 'Blitzkrieg on London before next Tuesday.' We shall see. Miss Moyes said that she felt like a cat on hot bricks.

Wednesday, 7th Despatch of our paper. My article and photo with the N.Z. soldier and pigeons in Trafalgar Square in this issue. Went to see Auntie Nell. Bob and Beverley had been to lunch. According to Beverley the War is already won, and the Germans defeated. I wish I thought so!

Don't like this invasion of British Somaliland, and everybody leaving Gibraltar and Malta. A lot of these refugees are in Kensington. Whole blocks of flats have been taken over for them – the original tenants turned out.

Thursday, 8th There was a big air battle on all day over the Channel. Our Boys did wonderful deeds of Derring-Do. We heard that 50 German planes were down to 16 of ours! Mr Churchill seems to be inspecting defences every day. Jerry is hourly expected . . . I wonder . . . how I wonder.

Friday, 9th Jack, our caretaker, called up and gone on the land. Very busy day and much dislocation of life without him. Not easy to get another.

More news of the air battle. We brought down 60; and 15 Italians over Libya. They are, however, still mopping up in Somaliland.

Sunday, 11th Went to First Aid Post at 11.30 a.m. Did a bit of typing for Matron. Also some bandaging. Practised Splints.

Got back at 3.30 p.m. and prepared tea for Miss Mowbray. She is from Dublin, and volunteered in the last war for service. Found herself at Winchester on the land early on. She had to sleep in a van. There were bunks, but only of wood, no straw or coverings of any kind! The men in the party had to sleep under the haystacks and hedges! Her job was to stand on a haystack and pitch the hay down, as she was the only one who could use a Fork. This for hours on end! Van was moved from place to place and rattled along as if filled with bones. She was with two other girls. In one place she found a bed for them; but for herself the landlady made the following suggestion: 'My son is on night work, so you can have his bed at night. He only needs it in the day.' This marvellous idea was not received with rapture by Miss Mowbray; but for a few nights she shared the young man's bed! She added that it was wonderful what you can do without if you have to! Then she became ill with lumbago and had to return to Dublin to be nursed.

However, she returned – though refusing the van again. They made her a Supervisor. She did not know what she had to supervise, but discovered it was the billeting of men, girls and horses. The horses were the easiest. I think she was splendid. She also worked at Dublin Castle on her return, doing the files of suspected persons. When you left the Castle at night you never knew whether a bullet would find you, as the place was full of spies.

A good story about the war. Three Scots escaped from the Germans. They were recaptured – so they talked hard in

Gaelic. Five or six interpreters were fetched, none could understand Gaelic. Finally a map was brought, and they were asked to point to the place they came from. So one pointed to the extreme north of Russia – and the Germans let them go!

Monday, 12th More Germans brought down. Great battle on all day. By evening we heard that 39 planes were down!

Tuesday, 13th On the 8 a.m. news we learn it was 60 planes brought down yesterday. The Boys are marvellous. Is poor old England going to emerge at last? What cheered me was the fact that one German pilot who was down said if the R.A.F. went on bombing Germany like they were doing, the war would soon be over! Several others expressed joy at being taken prisoner, and said the English were too good for them. Is all this the preliminary to Invasion? That is what we all want to know.

People seem hopeful about Egypt; but I feel Egypt would not fight very heartily for us; though we know our own people out there will do the best they can. These successes of the R.A.F. are so joy-bringing that we are in danger of forgetting the darker side of the picture.

Heard General de Gaulle again last night. I believe he is getting stronger every day.

Wednesday, 14th Went to see Auntie Nell. She was busy making jam. I heard that bombs had been dropped on Sutton Cold-field, and also in Herefordshire near Eardisland. Blitzkrieg seems to have begun. Mrs Loder was telling us about her relatives on the cliffs over Hastings in a bungalow, with no Anderson Shelter. They get under the dining-room table!

Wonderful Fights in the Channel. I understand there is tremendous betting on the Stock Exchange as to the numbers brought down.

Auntie gave me a lovely pair of mittens she had knitted. We sent them to a man on *H.M.S. Orion* who writes to Miss Moyes.

Thursday, 15th Our First Daylight Warning! Had just got in from the dentist and was having supper. I knew they must be near, so seizing my gas-mask and watch, I went downstairs with the other top floorer. The landlady came in to rescue her birds; also the daily help. I produced my little brandy flask for the landlady. Gave sweets to the Daily Help. The All Clear went in about half an hour. We heard nothing. It seems it was on Croydon Aerodrome. Went down to the office, and found Notices on the gate telling anyone to take shelter in the house. The Stirrup Pump was in the hall, and buckets of water ready.

Worked until 9 o'clock, and then returned home for the news. Great battles all day.

Friday, 16th Two warnings in one day! I was half-way up the road for lunch when it started. Returned to office as I could get on with some work. It lasted three-quarters of an hour. Went to Mercury café, and they had been carrying on as usual. This afternoon at 5.10 it went again, and lasted an hour. A letter from Mother this morning rather worried me. They had had a bad raid on Brum on Tuesday night. The noise, she said, was awful. Just off to take sugar to Auntie Nell in case another begins!

Saturday, 17th We learned from various sources that the raid at teatime yesterday was Wimbledon way. A lot of damage to houses and people. Just sheer wickedness, because as far as we know there is nothing down there. I was due to go to the Ellis family, so I had first-hand information. Mrs Ellis and dog sat in the cellar while the house rocked to its foundations, and the noise was indescribable. Apparently it was either side the railway line they attacked. New Malden booking office was destroyed. South Wimbledon suffered, as it is a closely populated area. This bears out the Government's contention that while nowhere is safe, it is better to scatter people. The children could have been evacuated.

One electric train had a bomb explode in front of it and another behind it! Time bombs were used. One went off Saturday morning, and lifted Mrs Ellis' house from its foundations. Fortunately Margaret was away in the country. People were constantly ringing up to find out how they were. Mr Ellis was at Molesey when the raid occurred. Two men in the Canteen refused to come down to the Shelter. Suddenly they saw a German plane seem almost to approach the window – they turned and ran like the wind for the Dug Out. Just as the door closed behind them terrific bursts of machine-gun fire burst forth.

Sunday, 18th Such a warm and beautiful day! Lunch at the Mercury. Warning went, but we decided to stay put unless we heard gunfire. Two wardens begged us to take cover, as only a few minutes ago they heard planes above. We went to a Shelter. It was cold down there. After a few moments the All Clear, and we took a bus to the City. Alighting at St Paul's we walked towards London Wall. At once we found the Church in which Mr Hillyard is interested. It was shut. We contented ourselves with noting the Roman Bastion which forms the vestry. Continued along and found the Church of St Alphege with the real Roman Wall visible. We reached Charterhouse Square, and decided that a flat there, looking on the trees, would be nice. Sat beneath the Mulberry Tree in the Court-yard. Half dead with thirst we made for Holborn, and found an orangeade. Just as we reached home and were drinking a cup of tea the Siren went again! Thankful to be in . . .

'On they go from strength to strength'

Monday, 19th Auntie Nell seemed very bright. She had received a letter from Lucy in Mufulira. Mr Eden spoke on radio. He seems rather a disappointing Minister of War. I feel he is too suave and elegant, better at diplomacy.

Tuesday, 20th Very busy morning at King's Cross with Miss Moyes. Great running to and fro. Lots of soldiers and sailors. Leeds train very long and full.

Mr Churchill's speech in the House of Commons. I listened to the summary of it on the 11 o'clock news: *'Never in the field of human conflict was so much owed by so many to so few.'*

How well he puts things. Wonderful tribute to Churchill by Garvin on Sunday. It seems he excels at everything he touches. An Orator for great moments and a master of light banter. A man of action and a literary artist.

Thursday, 22nd Not too well . . . nearly fainted twice trying to get myself a cup of tea, but finally managed it and reached the office. It is cold and autumnal. Not many raids. I learn that two of the German pilots brought down at Croydon were in commercial aviation, so they knew the place. Well, they have paid.

Miss Loder at Fairlight [Hastings] had to lie flat on her tummy in the garden while a German plane circled overhead. In the *Daily Telegraph*: Irate Mother to daughter in one of the raided towns: 'For goodness' sake put that book down, and listen to the Air Raid!'

The black-out is getting earlier each night – oh, those long dark evenings. America nearer to war.

Friday, 23rd Warning last night about 3.30 a.m. I am beginning to get used to them, and did not shake all over. Went downstairs and we all gathered in the gloom. Just as our landlady was making a cup of tea the All Clear went so we hastily returned to bed. What joy! Barishnikov had been awakened by the thud of bombs long before the sirens. He had seen the German planes caught in the searchlights. Raids seem to have been on Harrow and Wembley. They were looking for Northolt aerodrome. A cinema was hit, but not many casualties. No warning during the day. Better then than at night!

Saturday, 24th Air-raid warning just at 8.20 a.m. I was reading the *D.T.* in bed, and just thinking about going down to bath. Anyhow decided to go to the basement for a few minutes to see if there were guns or bombs. After about five minutes returned and dressed and breakfasted. Not a sound anywhere. Sometimes the stillness was uncanny. All Clear at 9.15.

Sunday, 25th Roused last night at 11.30 p.m. Downstairs until 1.20 a.m. We could hear a Nazi plane snooping above our skylight, and thought every moment a bomb would fall on the house. It was, however, dropped at London Wall – a screaming bomb. Fires broke out, but hundreds of fire engines were on the spot in seconds, and it was put out.

Felt a bit queer when I awoke. It is the result of shock, but after a cup of tea felt better. Went to First Aid Post. Everyone lifeless with lack of sleep, so I could not practise anything.

No further raids up to now. I am wondering how Miss Moyes got on at Portsmouth. It must be rather in a state of confusion today. Two warnings – one at 10.30 p.m. for an hour. Went back to bed. Again 12.30.

Monday, 26th Heard Miss Moyes' experiences in Portsmouth. For the first time she could not hold her Service. Her hall was in the bombed area and had lost the roof and most of the contents. A warning went while they were there. On their return they saw the German flares lighting up the country-side. They reached London just in time for our warnings. It took them until 1.30 a.m. to reach Holland Park.

I see it was St Giles' Cripplegate that was damaged. Milton's statue in front has gone, and some of the Church windows. Also some of the Roman bricks fell to this next Barbarian! I learn with amusement that the fact that the Nazis are dropping bombs in fields is because they have our ordnance survey maps, on which CAMP is often written. They think these are Military Camps, whereas in fact they are ancient British earthworks! This is the theory put forward – it is ingenious, and possibly true.

'Fight till the fight is won'

Tuesday, 27th At 9.30 p.m. last night Wailing Winny started up. Went downstairs, and we could plainly hear the Nazi snooping overhead. Remained there until 12.30. I even went to the front step and heard guns in the distance. Returned to my room and the searchlights were a wonderful sight – forty or fifty trying to catch him! German or no German I went to bed. Very broken night. Many people had been caught at 9.30 p.m. and had spent the night in shelters!

Worked at the office until 8.30 p.m. Had supper, and was just in bed when Old Snoopy sounded again up above. Went downstairs with my pillow and crept on to the sofa in the kitchen. The landlady let me stay, and put a blanket over me. Lucy's dressing-gown is a godsend at a time like this. All Clear went as I was dozing. Came to bed. Half an hour later Wailing Winny started again. Thought I could hear thuds and guns. Dozed again. At ten All Clear once more. Slept – and nothing but a bomb in my ear would have roused me! They have had three terrible nights in Brum – each worse than the last! Not a great many casualties, but a lot of noise. The Market Hall has gone – and there were many fires. It is 9 p.m. – and Snoopy has arrived.

Wednesday, 28th Slept all through the night in spite of Snoopy. Woke several times and heard him, but was too tired to bother. Felt better in the morning. Learned they had been over many districts. Went to see Auntie Nell. She is going to buy me a mattress which I can take down and spread on the basement floor anywhere, so that I get some sleep.

Thursday, 29th No Warnings last night. I heard Snoopy though. The authorities seem to have decided not to rouse seven million people. Bombs were dropped but not many. News of our big raid on Berlin. Three warnings during the day; but these don't matter. We just carry on. Sounded like him overhead in the afternoon, but he did not drop a bomb on the Sanctuary.

Friday, 30th More Warnings in the day. Heard him at night, but did not go down. A woman came to the Sanctuary for clothes. She was going hopping. Then the Warning went, and she began to cry. Snoopy sounded close. A bad night – went down to basement with mattress. Gunfire very close. I thought all Ladbroke Road must be in ruins. Expected a bomb at any moment. Curiously did not feel frightened. Went up to my room for a drink of water. The sky was glorious – such stars. The Police opposite were chatting cheerfully, so I knew there was not much destroyed in the district. All Clear at 3.45 a.m.

Saturday, 31st Felt pretty second-rate this morning. Everyone at office the same. I am to go home for a week on Wednesday. Shall be glad to see for myself how they are. Went to see Auntie Nell in the middle of a raid. She was having tea in the corridor! Lent me two blankets. We expect an onslaught tonight.

End of August 1940

SEPTEMBER 1940

❋

'Endless months the same'

'Dangers, like a stormy sea
Beset our country round'

Sunday, 1st We've been a year at war! How well I remember that Sunday and being awakened by the sirens and Mr Chamberlain's speech.

Saturday night I spent mostly in the basement. There were three Warnings. By 3.30 a.m. I came up to bed, not knowing if the raid was on or off. I fell asleep, and was awakened by the All Clear. Being Sunday I could have a lazy day, which I much enjoyed. Read the *Observer*. Garvin still writing about the Air Force. Barishnikov came in the afternoon and we had tea with Mrs Fisher. She has twice been caught until 2 a.m. in a public shelter.

Tuesday, 3rd Long letter from Birmingham at last with full account of their thrilling experiences. They sound, however, calm and collected. Various warnings during the day. Worked at office until 9 p.m. Slept all night notwithstanding a

Warning. Hope to get home to Brum without being stopped by Sirens, just as I am on the way to Paddington. Glorious weather!

Wednesday, 4th   Left office at 4.45 p.m. and scrambled to Paddington, where I had an hour to wait; but was glad to be on the spot. Reached Snow Hill promptly. Cath met me. I gather that the very noisy Sunday night they had was due to our A.A. Boys banging away for dear life all through the night. They never hit anything, but it sounded, it seems, like the Battle of Waterloo! Since then they have not been able to enjoy themselves quite so much.

Thursday, 5th   This morning a short warning at 9.30 a.m. Have since heard that a raider was brought down at North-field by A.A. guns. Pretty good. Mother and I are off to Sutton Coldfield to see Ariel and Cecilia. Hope they will come with us to *Pinocchio* tomorrow. It is warm here. All theatres in Brum are over by a quarter to nine, to let people get home before Warnings.

I must record that Miss M. got ticked off by the Ministry of Information for mentioning Portsmouth in her article.

'Oft in danger, oft in woe'

Friday, 6th   Cath and Mother slept in the shelter. I preferred the house and bed. They came up at 3.30 a.m. with the All Clear. Trees in the garden are lovely. Another warning at 9.30 a.m. . . . unusual for Brum. Cath went on duty at Five Ways. Heard a plane had been brought down, but we never had it confirmed.

Went over to Sutton to see Kathleen Evans. Have not seen her for ten years. She looked just the same. Has taken a job at Dudley Grammar School for boys. Was rather nervous about it.

Apparently some of our Fighters have been sent to Brum to deal with the Visitations. Kathleen gave me a bag full of William pears, some of which I bestowed on the driver and conductor of the bus. They were pleased. They gave me news of Pipe Hayes, which has had pretty well of trouble – being near Nuffield's factory.

Warnings and All Clears sounded all through the night, until we did not know t'other from which! We slept on.

Saturday, 7th Went and toured the damage in Stratford Road with Cath. Saw the gas main which was struck, and the road had received an aerial torpedo. All pretty grim, but, of course nothing to what we expected, and they seem to have got them taped pretty well. Much enjoyed *Pinocchio*. All came back to tea. Going to Coventry tomorrow for the day. It feels somehow safer in Brum than in London. I suppose it is being at home. Cecilia was thrilled with our shelter, and kept running in and out and on top.

Sunday, 8th Saw the damaged cinema in Coventry, but nothing of military importance had gone. The cathedral looked lovely. They are asking for watchers for incendiary bombs. We came back early to be in before a raid.

Heard the news of London's big raid. Very upsetting. Passed the Market Hall again. Lots of people looking round.

More details about London on the 9 o'clock news. Rotten! No warning in Brum. First night without sirens here for a long time. But now they have adequate defences things are not so bad. Did not sleep so well. Very cold.

Monday, 9th Very cold. Cath had to be at school at 9 a.m. instead of 10. I think she rather wanted a Warning! Elsie came over and described the A.R.P. organization in Brum. There are eight Divisions, and one in the Centre. Neville is a Divisional Warden, and the University comes into his.

More news at 6 o'clock. Another bad day yesterday in London, but not so many killed as anticipated. Mother very much against my returning there! *Daily Telegraph* did not arrive until the afternoon.

Tuesday, 10th Still those bad raids on London. Very difficult to get accurate information. Not so many killed. Londoners have learned wisdom and are taking cover.

Went up to Lightwoods Park with Mother, and sat in the Shakespeare Garden for a while. Talked with a working woman. Such a chatterbox, but interesting to listen to her reaction to the raids. She was very cheerful. Had a Warning in the evening as we were playing Bridge. No bombs, so I slept well. Talked to the Norwegian lady from next door who had lived in Brazil.

Wednesday, 11th Caught the 3 o'clock train to London, hoping to reach Paddington by 5.20 p.m. and be in for the Prime Minister's broadcast. Alas, for human hopes! There was a Warning on the train, and we had to pull all the blinds down. Then they told us there was a Time-Bomb on the line, and we must all get out at Ealing Broadway. We crawled slowly there until 7 p.m., but did not stop. Inch by inch we crept on. At 7.30 p.m. we stopped for a few seconds at Westbourne Park, and some of us took the opportunity of slipping off the train, and taking a bus to Notting Hill. Arrived 8 p.m. very hungry.

I had just made myself a cup of tea and had some soup when the Sirens went and the bombardment began. Went downstairs and spread my mattress. Came up to eat my supper. But the noise was terrifying. Leaving everything I grabbed my pillow and went down again. It lasted all through the night. I believe a Shell a minute! Scarcely slept until after 5 a.m. when All Clear went. How thankful I was to get to bed. Saw all the people returning from the Shelters. But everyone said: 'the noise was ours!'

> *'Bind us all as one together, weak and*
> *healthy, poor and wealthy, sad and*
> *joyful, young and old.'*

Thursday, 12th Felt very second-rate. Arrived at office at 10.15 as I overslept. What a night! It seems that now we have mobile guns on Lorries going about the town, and we can also hear guns from destroyers in the Thames. According to Mr Churchill Invasion is Imminent. Hitler has it all ready from Norway to Boulogne, and we must be on our toes for the next two weeks! Felt better as the day proceeded. Warning in the afternoon. Began to hear details of the damage. Very upsetting. Bow Church seems badly hit; St Thomas' Hospital; Gt Ormond St Hospital; Holborn – but not Staple Inn.

Friday, 13th Rather better night. I slept because I was so weary. Definitely a bomb fell. It seemed to whiz past my ear. I learn it was on 40, Ladbroke Square. Quite near. I nearly took a room there some months ago! Otherwise the gunfire was not so terrific. But how awful these nights are! The people at no. 40 were mercifully rescued. I don't know the details, except that all day they were trying to get the caretaker out. But they don't know if he was alive.

Every night one's only prayer is for the morning!

More bombs on Buckingham Palace today. They are trying to drive the King out of London. Auntie Nell has left. Mrs South has been bombed out of her house, and is now safe in Essex. But I feel desolate without them.

Saturday, 14th Seemed to sleep better in spite of gunfire. Did not hear any bombs. When the noise died away it was uncanny. Could not sleep for a couple of hours after. Came up to bed on All Clear. It was nearly dawn. One lovely bright star still shining. Fell into a doze until 8 a.m. All day we had Warnings. Planes sounded uncomfortably near, so I went downstairs once or twice. Weather cold.

Invasion is expected this week-end. Apparently they tried last week-end; but this news has only come to us via America. Let us hope this tension does not go on for long – it is most unnerving.

September 14th, l940. London.

My dear Lucy,

Another chapter of my Blitzkrieg diary. I wonder if any of it is reaching you. We are having a fairly un-nerving time, but are trying to keep our chins up. I went down to Brum for a welcome week, and then returned here much against the will of the family. But I did not feel I could give up just like that. We must all take our chance. However, everyone is relieved to see the morning. Perhaps soon we shall be able to keep them out. Warnings on and off all days. Another one as I write to you, and it is barely 8 o'clock!

Auntie Nell has left London, and Mrs South has been bombed out of her house! Cheerio.

Vere

Sunday, 15th Remarkably good night. Went to First Aid Post. Two warnings while there. Went into shelter. Bombers very low. Later heard that one had been brought down. It drifted to Victoria Station.

Mr and Mrs Watkins arrived in the evening from their house. They told us how they had watched the water rise in the cellar, having no idea at the time that the house was cracked. They spent the night in the Tube trying to get across London to the Sanctuary. They have now taken a room in my place. I am glad to be able to help them temporarily.

Monday, 16th Not such a good night. In fact – awful. I was in the basement with my neighbour, and we thought every moment would be our last. I kept saying: 'This is ours!' as

Swish down it came. I slept about an hour, and crept upstairs with the All Clear. I looked out, and expected to see London in ruins; but strangely enough the landscape looked the same.

'Sudden wild alarms'

Tuesday, 17th As my landlady was very nervous, and said everyone in the house must come down into the passage, I asked Miss Moyes if I could come down to the Sanctuary. She was quite agreeable. Mr and Mrs Watkins have been over to Peckham to fetch their cat. Their house seemed to be filling with water, and they could not leave the little animal there.

Last night not too bad. I slept down in the Printing Works and got my fill of Printer's Ink. So determined to try upstairs on the office floor tonight. Felt very second-rate all day.

Miss Edwards gave me full account of her awful experience at Shepherd's Bush – an aerial torpedo a few doors down, and a time bomb in the road! We gave her some clothes. Then Ivy Croucher came into the office. She had been out to dinner with a Polish officer to whom she is teaching English, and she walked back through the bombs to her Club. I am in the office. It is now 11 p.m. and the brutes are above and the guns are going. Do we live to see the morning?

Wednesday, 18th Well, we lived through the night; but it was pretty bad. Such awful swishings through the air. I believe they were some distance away, but they sounded immediately above my head. I felt every moment I should be buried beneath the ruins.

More warnings all day. Could not get to lunch until 2.30 p.m. Damage everywhere pretty bad. Mr Resti, our accountant, nearly bombed out again – the house opposite him collapsed with a deafening crash. Mercifully the people were in the basement and were saved. Oxford St shops caught it. Busy day and did not feel too good.

They arrived again at 8 p.m. prompt. Earlier every night! What a prospect for the winter.

Thursday, 19th Very bad night! As I lay in my own bed at ten to eight enjoying a little comfort and rest, Ivy Croucher burst into my room, bag and baggage, having been bombed out of the Three Arts Club at Marble Arch. She had run into the street for the wardens. The gas main broke. They could have no light. She was put in charge of 56 people. First they were led to a public shelter. Then sent back. Then as dawn broke they were told to evacuate the club, as a time bomb had dropped near!

A Special Constable, who lived opposite, begged her to take care of his typewriter. So, staggering along with her own cases, she struggled to friends in Nottingham Place – only to find they were evacuated! So she decided to come to me. I am so glad she did. I made her some tea and let her rest. She came down to the Sanctuary with me, and we made arrangements for her to go to Dr Bell's for the night. I put her on the sofa where she slept a bit.

It poured with rain all day. No warning much. I believe the weather is keeping them away. The brutes arrived at 8 p.m. Letter from Lucy to say my diary is arriving in Africa. She has sent me some tea.

'Out of the deep of fear'

Friday, 20th Not too bad a night for guns. Things sounded bad at 5 a.m. with bombs. All Clear at 6 a.m. I quite enjoy walking in the early morning up Ladbroke Road to my room, and seeing the police tearing off on their bicycles. A quiet day. They have arrived again at 8 p.m., but it is fairly quiet. Sounds too good to be true, and we hardly dare to comment in case a landmine comes dropping down on Lansdowne Road the next minute. I should be glad to be back on my nice Divan, instead of lying in a straw mattress on the floor! However, I am glad enough to have it.

Saturday, 21st Feeling very second-rate. Have a heavy cold from sleeping in the Printing Works. Mrs Watkins woke me soon after 8 a.m. to say she was very worried, as there was someone in the house with a Morse Code Receiving Set, which they were using during an Air Raid. News indeed. My landlady thought a lot of the young man concerned.

Full morning, and was glad when 1 p.m. came. Did some shopping, rested and listened to radio. Ivy Croucher came at 5 p.m. She was very happy sleeping at Dr Bell's. The warning went. I passed the young man's door and heard his radio blaring out. He opened his door, and appeared to watch me go along the corridor, and then wait for me to go up to my room! I stood for a moment and heard him shut his door, and start the Morse Code for dear life! It all sounded terribly suspicious! With Nazi bombers actually over London, and nerves unstrung from all we were going through we leapt to the worst conclusion! Without stopping to think of the consequences, Ivy, in her impulsive way said she would fetch the police. She rushed across to the Station. They came at once and collided with the landlady on the step . . . who went into hysterics. The police walked straight into the young man's room. Well, it is a Morse Code set, but apparently, he is only practising to go into the Fleet Air Arm! So it is all in order!

But one can risk nothing in these terrible times. I knew I should have to pacify the landlady. She was most upset, especially with Ivy. But I explained that our nerves had gone after ten nights without proper sleep! I apologized to the young man, but I told him that to be using a Morse Code set in London with a Warning on, was liable to misunderstanding.

Went to see the damage in and around Church Street. A few houses down, but some were empty. Down to Sanctuary at 7.30 p.m. Finished some letters. Bedded down on office floor as usual. Fell asleep and nothing could wake me. All Clear at 4.40 a.m. but waited until 5.30. Went up Ladbroke Road to my room. Lovely moon and stars.

'No arm so weak but may do service here'

Sunday, 22nd Slept like a log until 10 a.m. It seemed like heaven! A lazy morning. Lunch in Church St . . . rather dear . . . 1/9d. Met Ivy coming back from her lunch at the Grosvenor with her Jewish pupil. Barishnikov came to tea. Also Mr and Mrs Watkins. They brought a huge piece of shrapnel from out of their kitchen at Peckham. Down at Sanctuary at 8 p.m. Guns soon began. Things sound pretty hot outside! Just heard a nasty whistling sound though the air. Let us hope we all live to see another day.

Monday, 23rd   After midnight I knew no more. I just slept. All Clear and then another Warning; but I did not wake until five to six. All Clear followed. I must have slept for six hours.

Returned up the road, and slept another hour. So far as we can tell no damage very near to us. Mr Bendall [a Customs Officer] came to the office this afternoon, and said that last night an incendiary bomb dropped on his doorstep. He found the house three doors from him wrecked. So the wardens made them all evacuate to a School. He collected his household, which included a niece whose baby is expected at any moment. School was full, so someone took them in. In the morning it was discovered the bomb had wrecked the house next to his, but it did not explode, so he can return to his own house tonight. This is in Victoria.

The news of the sinking of the children's ship nearly finished me, this morning. The thought of those little creatures being swept overboard is heart-rending.

The young Morse Code naval boy came up to my room tonight to apologize. He never thought of what other people would think! The police have asked him not to use it during a Warning, as those in the street might hear him and report it. He was very charming, and immensely pleased that he had caused two C.I.D. men to come across and investigate what he was doing!

Blitzkrieg on as I write . . . it is 10.45 p.m. It would be

lovely to be somewhere else, and able to sleep in peace. But it's no good – it has to be faced. And so to bed.

My dear Lucy,   *September 23rd, London*
I am so glad you are getting the diary, and that it interests you. I am still alive at this particular date, but whether I shall be when you receive it is another matter. However, everyone in London is in the same state of questioned animation. The devils are here as I write, and the guns booming. It is all horrible. But it cannot be helped. The Abbey is still whole . . . Thank God!

I received the tea . . . food is the least of our troubles, but perhaps one day there will be some good news. Those poor children!

Much love, Vere

'*Live this day as if thy last*'

Tuesday, 24th   An awful night! I thought we should never live through it. I don't think I slept more than a couple of hours. I knew there must be much damage near us, because of those awful swishings through the sky. Up in my own room with the All Clear I dozed for a couple of hours.

Back at the office found Miss Jagoe. She had been bombed out of Elgin Terrace by an aerial torpedo. At the time she was descending the stairs because of the din, a wardrobe fell over and all the pictures fell off the walls. She almost fell down the stairs, and shouted for the wardens – the stairs half gone. I don't know what happened next, but the houses next door were down, and the people buried in the basement. We gave her sal volatile and breakfast. She slept on the drawing-room floor at night with the rest of us, and began to recover.

There was much damage, I understand, at St Charles' Square, my First Aid Post. I am anxious to go on Sunday and see. Felt so tired all day that I was unable to exert myself. Poor Mrs Booker, at the Mercury Café, had had all her windows blown out. I felt I should sleep tonight whatever happened. There is a lovely coal fire in the office. Postcard from Cath to say they expect me in Brum at any time, in any condition! I only hope they get me in a recognizable form!

Wednesday, 25th   I believe it was the foulest night so far of the blitzkrieg, but I was unaware of much of it. Thank God, I slept! When I awoke at various times, these awful roars filled the sky, followed by violent explosions – and I knew hell was loose. At 6 a.m. All Clear, and I went up the road. What a lovely moon and clear sky!

We gather damage was in Central London. A land-mine struck T. Court Road. There was not a pane of glass left in Oxford St, Regent St or T. C. Rd. I wonder how long it will be before London is a heap of ruins! St Clement Danes was struck . . . but so far not the Abbey. People go to the Tubes at 3 p.m. and stake their claim outside. There does not seem any hope of stopping the raids; and how we shall escape I do not know. That is – unless we fly the place. I do not want to do that, though I feel all this must eventually affect our health. We go to Berlin and bomb our worst – but that does not bring our own folk back to life. Eight million people are all facing the same – and yet no one talks of running away. I expect the Sirens to go at any moment, and, once more, commend my soul to God!

'We are not divided –
All one body we'

Thursday, 26th   Worst night on record! Yet I slept the best since I returned to London into the blitz. I got so drowsy with the lovely fire that when I spread my mattress at a quarter to twelve, I fell asleep before midnight. I was aroused at 1.20 a.m. by the whole house shaking to its foundations and terrific explosions rending the air. Slept again, but was roused by still more horrible sluicings through the sky, with bangs, plonks and rumblings. Miss M. came down from her room to say there was an incendiary in the garden. We ran to the window and could see one burning in the next garden – ours seemed to have gone out. Really awful to listen to the sounds in the sky. We felt no stone could be left standing on another. We made tea – then all lay down again. All Clear at 5.30 a.m. I walked up the road under a glorious moon.

On investigation in the morning, we discovered a house in Lansdowne Rd., nine doors from us, was gone inside. The walls were standing, but it was burnt-out inside. Walked to Clarendon Cross. Every pane of glass had gone, and several houses down. A pretty bad night! It does not bear enquiring into too much! There seems no end to it. Our incendiary had put itself out against the Rockery.

Heard Mr Bourne of Bourne and Hollingsworth speak. Their bomb fell on Wednesday night last. They re-opened to the public on the Monday. I don't know what John Lewis are doing.

It is 10.30 p.m. Blitzkrieg on again. What the night will hold we cannot tell. Guns are going. We are all round the office fire. I have written Mother and Auntie Nell tonight. We may see another morning – here's to hoping.

Friday, 27th Not such a bad night. I slept. We turned in about 11.30 p.m. Seven in the Drawing-Room, and two of us in the office. It was so warm that I slept after midnight. Wakened by noises at 1.30 a.m., but slept again. At 4 a.m. All Clear. Miss Mackay went up to her room and slept, but another Warning sounded, and it was not until 6 a.m. that I walked up the road, and slept again. It seemed a miracle! On enquiry we found that other parts of London have had it. So there is not much consolation for us. Air Battles over us all, but these are not so terrifying as the night ones. We could hear dozens of German planes overhead.

Bad news everywhere. Dakar failure. Japan joining the Axis. Military divisions of Germans going to Spain. I do not expect such another happy night as last. It will be incendiaries, or time bombs – which? So I close my diary for tonight, and hope the morning will come with me alive to see it . . .

Saturday, 28th A very exciting night! Four basketfuls of Incendiaries dropped all over the houses here. We heard them come down like rain. I seized my torch and made for upstairs, not quite sure what it was. Miss M. shouted that some were burning next door near the house. She tore out of the front door, and I followed her. Found her scrambling over the wall. She had gone by mistake to no. 1 whereas the bombs were at no. 5. In the darkness I lost her. She shouted to bring the Stirrup Pump. I shouted back: 'Not necessary if the bombs are outside.' I ran for a bucket of sand. Mrs Hoare dashed up the road with another as bombs were burning in great numbers up the road. Wardens were running up and down putting them out. Found Miss M. at no. 1, and people with a Stirrup Pump working at a bomb. We took over – and I handed the bucket of sand to a man to tackle another.

Fortunately the bombers were not overhead, or it would have been horrible. Then it was discovered that one incendiary had fallen on the house opposite. It was burning inside – and we did not know if it was occupied or not. A fire-engine was found somehow, and they put it out. After all this excitement it was difficult to sleep! However, we felt we had done our bit. We heard that Holland House had been burned to the ground. We could not believe it – but, on enquiry, discovered it was Essex House on Campden Hill.

The Beasts arrived as usual at 8.15 p.m. A tremendous amount of gunfire, and a few swishings. But I was so warm I slept, and did not wake until ten minutes to nine on Sunday morning.

'Shadows of the evening steal across the sky'

Sunday, 29th Went to the First Aid Post about 11.30 a.m. What a scene of Desolation met me! All round St Charles' Square I could see the windows broken – and then I got round to the Post. The little half-made Surface Shelters on the outer wall were cracked and split . . . the wall a crumbled mass. Went a few steps further, saw the Post itself – every window broken. I scarcely recognized the entrance. Trod over a broken wall, and found the Shelter where we had been the previous Sunday. That was standing – but the houses at the end of the road were gone – a huge crater was there instead. I climbed across the Convent grounds and spoke to a man. 'Yes,' he informed me, 'the First Aid Post is unusable, and the folk on duty are in the Convent.' I crossed the grounds under the beautiful trees, and made my way with difficulty into the building. The remnants of the staff were round a fire, and they told me the adventures of the night.

They had been bombed three times; but Monday was the worst of all. They had been sleeping in the School Hall – it was just midnight when an H.E. crashed just outside. Miss Scott informed me that she just turned over on her tummy, covered her head with the blankets, and waited for the place to fall in on her! Every window broke into a thousand pieces, and these blew into the building. Every door blew off its hinges. One landed straight on top of her. The place was a mass of debris, glass and dirt. They got up – about fifteen in all – not knowing if they were alive or dead. Two men of the staff rushed them across the grounds. The Nazis were zooming overhead, and they all took refuge in the Convent basement.

I had dinner at the Hospital, and saw the room in the Convent where the incendiaries fell on Tuesday night. Fortunately St Charles' Hospital has escaped. Were they aiming at the Hospital, or at the Gasometer a few yards away, which we are told is not in use?

I was told there was a stable at the back of the blitzed houses. The man was able to get his horse out safely on that awful night. I went into the stable, and there, in a manger, lay a black and white mother cat with a black kitten! The children around were feeding her. It was such a sweet and pathetic sight among the desolation!

Returned home in the afternoon. Went down to the office and lit the fire. Mr Hillyard returned, also Miss Moyes and company from their meeting. A very gunny night, but mercifully I slept.

Monday, 30th Felt all the better for a good night. On enquiry found that no bombs dropped on us, plenty, however, on Ealing. So it is not that we are getting the better of them, alas. Several warnings during the day. Did some shopping. Shops are open except when guns are going.

Down at the office. I wonder what part of London they are devastating now. One can only go to bed and trust to wake in the morning.

End of September 1940

OCTOBER 1940

'Bursting peals of thunder'

Tuesday, 1st   Not a very happy night. There was a deep under-current of trouble all through my sleep. I woke occasionally. The gunfire was continuous all night. But I can sleep through that now, so long as there are no swishings. I felt it was nearer to us than the previous night. Perhaps at Shepherd's Bush. All Clear at 6 a.m. I seemed spirited up the road through the air back to my bed, and slept for two hours.

On enquiry it seemed to have been Ealing again. There were many deaths in *Daily Telegraph* from enemy action. I learn there have been no bombs on Kensington for three nights. Makes me feel horribly nervous. It will soon be our turn again. Blitz began at 8.10 p.m. but things are fairly quiet. Only distant guns.

Wednesday, 2nd   Lots of noise all night. Felt sort of un-comfortable. No bombs on Kensington for four nights ! Do they do it in alphabetical order? It was round Lambeth last night. Windows at our Homeless Women's Shelter were broken. Blitz began early tonight, but All Clear has actually gone now at 9.15. No further warning, and it is 9.45 p.m. I wonder what has happened. Has the blitz begun to slacken? Or are they invading somewhere? Auntie Nell wrote and approved of my staying in London. She sent £1 for the Shelter Fund to comfort us in our trials.

Thursday, 3rd Blitzkrieg began again, of course, last night. Cannot remember the hour. I heard some frightening cracklings rending the air, but I slept notwithstanding. We had a great Battle over us this afternoon. Terrific gunfire, and what sounded like a bomb. It began tonight at 8 p.m. Three ghastly swishings. They were in Kensington, because this house shook to its foundations. It brought back all the old sick feeling again. One sort of wishes for the Final Bomb to end it all, and then one can investigate the never-never land in peace!

I cannot bear to listen to the News. There is nothing in it. We bomb them . . . they bomb us. That is all. Life is a miserable affair. Miss M. is away for the week-end, and we have to guard the property as best we can. We are persevering with preparations for the Christmas Fair. Just imagine! Well, well . . . we face another night!

'Ready to face the danger'

Friday, 4th I slept badly, though All Clear went at 2.30 a.m. They did not return. I heard the clock strike two, three and four. Stillness uncanny. At 6 a.m. went back to Ladbroke Road, where slept until ten to nine. On enquiry we discovered that bombs on Kensington last night were just behind High St station. One fell on an empty house; but a salvo was dropped. It was said to be near the stables of the United Dairies Horse Stables. Poor things! I thought it was the turn of Kensington – they go in a rota system.

Yesterday afternoon they were all over Brixton. Bombs in the daytime; also today. They have been here this afternoon. Guns fierce. Weather is foul, and you would wonder how they can see anything. Very nasty just now – a salvo dropped. Guns at top speed.

Dr Remy is in Canada. What a surprise. I thought if he could put the Atlantic Ocean between him and the Nazis he would do so. He sounded much happier than in the Isle of Man. We are short-handed in this house if we get a bomb. However, if it is a direct hit – we shall not want any help! Good night, everybody!

Saturday, 5th Heard bombs fall about 10 p.m. last night. They were in Kensington, but not N.H.Gate. Fearful racket overhead until midnight. Then seemed to die down for a bit. Urged Miss Rowe, who has a room at the top, to rouse me if she heard anything like incendiary bombs. I am getting so accustomed to the blitz that I shall sleep through the bomb that gets us, I think, and arrive peacefully on the other side, without knowing it! I had no idea the body could get used to sleeping through such a din. But I shall make a soldier yet!

Went to dinner with Marie in West Cromwell Road. On my way had a look at the R.C. Church – Our Lady of Victories in the High St. What a ruin! It must have been an oil bomb. It happened the same night as Ladbroke Square. Walked down

Earls Court Road, found the flats that caught it. Marie was without gas. Everyone cooking on fires. What a game! Earls Court Station not caught, but some flats there had. One road had an unexploded bomb reposing in it. A Warning went while I was walking. But I have become so blasé that I persevered; and though I could hear Nazi bombers overhead, I had a feeling they were not going to drop bombs just where I was. Two or three weeks ago my heart would have been pounding away, and I should have rushed apprehensively into the nearest Shelter. Such is education!

'Death may come – or tarry yet'

Sunday, 6th Went up with the All Clear. Tremendous wind and heavy rain clouds. Reminded me of *Wuthering Heights* – only I was not walking over the Yorkshire moors. So lovely to go on sleeping. Lazy morning. Read *Observer*. We have got to look after Egypt, according to Garvin. That will be the next. We must save it at all costs. Hitler has failed in our little island itself, but will now try the Empire piecemeal. Well, I only hope we can save it. But I have not much faith in our powers in that direction. We shall send an Army, but it will be short of all the things they need . . .

Bombs last night on Kensington High St again. Burton's the Tailors just opposite the Underground. Also Shepherd's Bush again. Had lunch at the Mercury, and in spite of Warning went on to the West End. Along the Bayswater Road a block of flats facing the Park at Albion Gate had caught one. At Marble Arch too. Hundreds of people about. Walked down Oxford St. Windows at Selfridges had gone. As for poor old

John Lewis – they had got it good and proper. Whole length unusable! Also Peter Robinson's. These can, of course, be built up again, but they represent a tremendous loss. I was too tired to go further. Returned on the bus. People were lined up for the Tubes as night sleepers. This at 4 p.m.!

Monday, 7th   Well, they did come last night, but not for long. All Clear 9.30 p.m. and no return. Our little office cat, who sleeps on my blanket on the floor, decided he wanted to go out at 3 a.m. and see why the Nazis had not come! It was clear then, and the stars were glorious. So it was not the weather. Seemed to be something to do with the Brenner Pass Meeting . . . Blitz called off for a moment. Judging from Garvin, perhaps they will suddenly develop an interest in Alexandria, and leave London to lick her wounds a bit!

I learn one of the Bastions of the Tower was damaged on Saturday night. Also the House of Lords. Though that may have been some time ago. Richard Coeur de Lion's statue had the Sword bent – when a bomb dropped beside it. Well, they have come tonight, as I write. I doubt they will go away so easily. A very nasty one has just come down. You could hear it swinging in the air for several seconds, and then plonk. The house shook in its socket – though the bomb must have been a mile away. I was beginning to cheer up, but I fear we are in for it tonight. Last night the silence was uncanny. One felt in the midst of a primeval forest! In fact being so accustomed to noise, I could not sleep for the stillness. How difficult it is to satisfy the human race!

Wednesday, 9th   Quiet for the rest of the night. All Clear at 6.45. But I heard the news of last night round here. Five houses were struck at the far end of Lansdowne Road. No wonder we felt it. Some people saved – others buried. All round Oxford and Cambridge Gardens, and Ladbroke Grove Station – houses and shops were down. Also Pembridge Place and Chepstow Villas. Mr Booker [owner of Mercury café] told us the story of two men who were told by a policeman to take cover. They walked on – and were terribly injured. First Aid Parties had to turn out and face the bombs through their foolhardiness.

I gather bombs were all over Hammersmith. Cherry Blossom Boot Polish Factory and Pascall's. Some say Harrods Depository. But I don't know. It seemed nearer . . . also Olympia. Does not bear thinking about. The devils have come with the night – before 7.30 p.m. . . . I have hardly had time to eat my supper. Frightful noises! Moon is getting fuller.

'Rise, for life with death hath striven'

Thursday, 10th   Well, we lived through another night. Many horrors came down before midnight, and we were pretty well shaken. But it was a shade less bad than on the previous night. One funny incident . . . Miss Rowe and I were talking in the office. Mr Hillyard was in the Drawing-Room. We heard a sudden whistling sound. I leapt half across the room and murmured in tones of awe: 'That's a new kind. It must be a whistling bomb.' Then Mr H. came out with a broad smile as we were gazing towards the front gate. It was the Sideboard Cupboard – he had been opening it and it requires some oil on the hinge! Cowards die many times before their deaths!

Pretty quiet all day. Had news that the High Altar of St Paul's had caught a bomb this morning. Also the Grosvenor – badly. A bomb dropped in Fetter Lane this afternoon after the All Clear. Rotten! We must reconcile ourselves to the loss of a good many of our beloved buildings. A good thing Lucy saw them when she did – goodness knows what will be left for her to see next time she comes to this country.

Went to see the houses in Lansdowne Road that caught it. Just heaps of rubble . . . several people killed. It is nearer Auntie Nell's flat than this house . . . right on the corner of Ladbroke Grove – a stone's throw from Stanley Gardens. It is 9 o'clock. A nasty sound is getting nearer . . .

Friday, 11th Well, my last words were prophetic! They did get nearer – and it is a miracle that I am here to write this diary tonight. By the Grace of God we have been spared this time.

Awful swishings filled the air, and fool-like I was just about to remark that they seemed further off, but restrained myself . . . when . . . something like an electric force tore through the air above the house. The office, despite wooden shutters and thick curtains, was filled with an uncanny light. Mr Hillyard and I dropped to the floor. He had just been preparing to dictate me a letter. Our hearts stood still. We expected the end. I could see the bomb passing over the house – though there was a ceiling and several floors above me. Then the tension passed. We were not dead beneath the ruins. It was a ghastly experience.

'Nights of doubt and sorrow'

Mr Hillyard picked himself up and said to me: 'You are all right. I must go and see about the others.' Miss M. had been sitting in an easy chair. Her glasses were blown off her nose right across the room. The question was – where had the bomb fallen? I thought it was Portland Road – so what of Barishnikov? Everyone went into the road to look. I went on to the roof, and heard water cascading down like a waterfall. They said it was in Ladbroke Road, on two empty houses – a stone's throw from us.

I admit I was very shaken, but if I had been called on to do something I could have done it. We knew there had been other bombs, but could not locate them. Rescue men were soon on the spot. A water-main had been struck. We learned that a Stick of Four Bombs had been dropped – only one of which had struck an inhabited house – in Lansdowne Walk. People were buried in the basement. There was nearly a panic in Holland Park Tube Station, crowded with sleepers, when the bomb fell. Barishnikov had been blown to the floor, chair and all. They nearly had to vacate their house owing to the burst water-main.

After all this we slept a little. Planes over us practically all night. I wondered if my own place was standing. It was. Have felt queer all day.

Saturday, 12th   They are here again. It is 8 p.m. How we are all going to escape I cannot imagine. I have a strong feeling that one night they will get us. Unfortunately, I am something of a prophet . . . anyway, they say the Spirit World is a good place.

Sunday, 13th Forget what time All Clear went. I ran up the road just as Miss M. and the others were getting up to travel to Lincoln. It was 5.30 a.m. Lovely to stay in bed. Did not try to rouse myself. Decided not to go to First Aid Post. I never do anything now when I get there, and really I need a few hours to myself. Read the *Observer* . . . not too cheerful. There is nothing to be cheerful about! Ivy rang up, and we went a walk in Kensington Gardens. Saw the ruins of a house in Orme Square . . . had happened in the night. Went and had a look at Ladbroke Rd bombs. The old ladies in Lansdowne Walk were killed.

Listened to Princess Elizabeth on the radio. Lovely! She has such a sweet voice. At 7. p.m. went down to Sanctuary. Lit the fire and Mr Hillyard returned – to my amazement. He did not like us being alone. I began on some work because I cannot bear just to sit and hear the bombs fall. Did a lot for the Fair.

Miss M. had not come by midnight, so we turned in. At 2.30 a.m. they arrived, having had an awful time. Hours late at King's Cross. Then they had to walk through the blitz along T.C. Road, which had had two bombs. All littered with débris and fallen glass. At Oxford Circus Miss M. was done up – they managed to get a taxi . . .

Monday, 14th and *Tuesday, 15th* [*dates mixed up*] The Devils are here now at 7 p.m. . . . we shall have to endure this until 6 a.m. The Moon is full . . . so God help us.

What an awful night we had. They never ceased until after 5 a.m. We could not count the bombs we heard. Dozed vaguely between – because one must sleep some time. Then in the morning the radio announced that the raids were less intense! Everyone we have met says it was worse in this district than they can ever remember! So much for the Ministry of Information – I should think they live in a cottage in the country.

I tried to trace our bombs, but happily, though many came down near us, they nearly all fell in gardens or roads, and not on property. Hearing there was an Oil Bomb in Stanley Gardens, I hurried there after lunch. Found the hole – plonk in the middle of the road – grease spread everywhere. Curtains flapping in the air from broken windows. The Miss Coombes had felt the shock in the Shelter, but their windows and Auntie's were undamaged. Others fell in Holland Park Avenue. A rumour of one on Kensington Palace. St James' Church, Piccadilly is said to be badly damaged. The Corner House in Piccadilly caught a bomb . . . St Thomas' Hospital, too.

'Through sleep and darkness safely brought'

We are all speechless with fatigue. I shall sleep if bombs fall round my bed! Blighters are here again, but not quite so active. They must have worked Holland Park out of their system, and are making for somewhere else. But there are a good few hours ahead before daylight comes for them to remember us. I was invited away for the week-end, and how gladly I would have gone, but I cannot leave as I am part of the Home Defence of this property. Good night everyone . . .

Wednesday, 16th Well, in spite of it being the worst night of the blitzkrieg so far, I slept a few hours. From 11.30 to 1 a.m. Then I was awakened by frightful gunfire and numerous earth tremors. The house rocked like a cradle! So it went on all night. Dozed a little, and then had to get up as I smelt burning, or thought incendiary bombs had fallen. Then the cat wanted to be let out. It was all awful – and no use going into long descriptions. At 5.30 All Clear. I hopped up the road. No sooner there than the Warning went again . . . I slept on until the house swayed like a ship at sea. But I slept on.

A lot of damage round us . . . landmines or H.E.s in Archer St and Campden Hill. Marble Arch and the City. No use going into it. Church of Austin Friars has been demolished, I believe. Mr Bendall had a packet at Victoria. Has been obliged to send niece and baby out of London. I shall have joined the great majority before those slacks arrive being sent by Auntie Mollie. Lucy's dressing-gown is my salvation. I wrap myself in it, and sleep for two hours. Devils are here again. Raining hard, but that does not seem to deter them.

Thursday, 17th Last night it poured and poured, and as far as our little plot was concerned we had no bombs. We slept. But there was activity in some districts. It is 7 p.m. and the Blighters are here. Have not felt too grand all day, so I hope they will let us down lightly.

Friday, 18th Half a dozen horrible swishings about 9.30 p.m. not far from here. But I have not heard where because

Mr Booker [Mercury Café] was not on duty. Holland Park is to have a rest for a night or two . . . But they are here now. A few Woofs Woofs, but those are our own dogs barking.

Saturday, 19th Very quiet night and slept well. Did not hear a single bomb – but this does not mean none were dropped. They were – but not here. Went and had a look at the land-mine on Campden Hill. It took nine houses . . . and I should not think anyone could have survived in them. Four people were killed. I found Holland House – big gates are down and the wall. Shell of house is still standing, but rumour has it that it is burned inside.

They are here now – and guns are going like hell. Have just heard a bomb . . . and a shell.

Sunday, 20th Last night was bad. A lot of beastly stuff came down. Twice we thought we heard incendiaries in the street; but could only see the moon. I toured the house in case of fire. Went to bed at 11 p.m. Gun fire terrific. I think they were trying out some new ones. Lots of damage, but not in our roads. Went by bus to Oxford Circus in the afternoon. Big crater in Bayswater Road – so the bus went round some side streets where also a lot of damage – some last night. Saw the refugees from Gibraltar – I don't wonder they were frightened.

Marble Arch looked a bit messed up. Walked from Oxford Circus. Academy Cinema has one – and lots of places along there. T.C. road closed and looks pretty derelict. Along New Oxford St to Holborn . . . many shops out of action. At

Southampton Row the Warning went. I persevered along . . .
High Holborn, heard gunfire, and saw people pointing to the
sky and saying: 'There they go – they've just turned 'em.'
Saw curls of smoke in the sky. Since Holborn seems to have a
fascination for them, and I was in an unfamiliar district, I
went into a shelter. No one else there. I read the *Observer* until
the caretaker arrived. We had a little chat. He said about 15
people came and slept there at night. He considered Holborn
had caught it most – barring the East End.

With All Clear I continued my walk. Very bad. From
Kingsway to Staple Inn on either side of the road . . . I don't
think there is a shop doing business. Mercifully so far it has
stopped at Staple Inn. I turned back. Another Warning, but
continued towards Kingsway and the Strand. It has caught it
here and there. I was tired and went to Lyons for a cup of tea.
There I read somebody's *Despatch*, and Madame Tabouis said
ominously that things would get more dark for us, and that
the Nazis would continue in the Mediterranean. Went for the
bus – saw a bomb had fallen between King Charles and
Nelson. Glad to be returning to Kensington. Nice to have had
some fresh air . . .

'Moons that wax and wane'

Monday, 21st We had to dive under the table once, all of us. I
went first, Miss Rowe followed me, and then to our astonishment the Little Old Lady dived out of her chair and under
my desk – only to encounter the cat on the other side. When
the five horrible swishings had passed we got up and laughed
so much that I am sure the old lady was saved a heart attack.

She was so amused at finding the cat under the desk, and the expression on his face at her undignified conduct!

It was, however, nothing to laugh at . . . they caught the Waterworks on Campden Hill, very near to us – and lots of houses. Mr Booker had to help dig the people out. After that it was fairly quiet. Mr Bendall rang from Paddington to say they could not get through, but would come as soon as they could. We went to bed. At 12.45 I heard the taxi. Miss M. had stayed in Brum. Mrs Hoare [who was the note-taker for the address] and Mr Bendall had had an awful journey to Birmingham – six and a half hours in the train. They had arrived too late for the Meeting. The first time this has happened.

Tonight we have listened to Churchill broadcasting to the French people. He was in great form; but I expect The Narrrzis will sink a battleship as a result. He does enjoy giving them one; but I feel we ought not to allow ourselves these luxuries yet. It is good to know we shall be supreme in the air by 1941. I should like to live to see it after all we have suffered!

'Still march in firm array'

Tuesday, 22nd Slept very well. A wonderful night. I don't know where the Narrzis went. I am afraid Brum had a bit of a pasting. All Clear at 4 a.m.

Blighters here again. Soon after 7 p.m. – and some very nasty stuff has come down near here. The house rocked like a cradle – very un-nerving. Auntie Nell is returning on Wednesday. The night outside is as black as pitch. They cannot see anything they are aiming at . . . dirty dogs. Our own dogs don't seem to be barking much either. Can't think where they all are.

Our Musical Box, given us by a stranger to sell for the funds, is lovely. Its sweet melody is in contrast with the odious noises of the Merry-go-round in the sky! Br . . . rrr . . .

Wednesday, 23rd Very peaceful night . . . no bombs or guns. On enquiry found there had been a disaster at Whiteleys. Two bombs had fallen straight on the building through to the shelter, and exploded there. Forty seven people said to be killed or drowned, as a water-main burst. Must have been ghastly. We heard the bombs fall. The Freemasons Arms was destroyed in Portobello Road – also a bomb on Addison Road, but no great casualties. Had a letter from Mrs Clive to say bombs had fallen in her garden at Brympton D'Evercy in Somerset. She wants to know how we all are. How lovely of her to write.

Auntie Nell called to see me, and took me out to lunch, and thoroughly spoiled me. Bought me apples and Ovaltine. Also she will knit me a cape of cream astrakhan wool. It will be for Christmas – if we ever reach that epoch. Letter from Mother. She sounds depressed. They have had raids on Brum – and she does not like it.

Thursday, 24th A still more peaceful night. We did not hear any bombs at all, at all, at all . . . They all slept in their beds at the Sanctuary like Christians – the first time for five weeks.

Auntie toured Westminster Abbey, and was worried about the windows. But the fabric so far is intact. I hope to go on

Sunday and see Cheapside and some of the ruins. It sounds uncommonly quiet tonight – only hope it continues. The stars are bright, but it is very dark. I understand some bombs fell in the Serpentine and the Round Pond the other night . . . all to the good!

Friday, 25th Another peaceful night. They all went to bed, and I slept alone on the office floor with the cat. Did not wake until clock struck 8 a.m. First night for six weeks that I have had a really unbroken night! Went up the road in my dressing-gown and a coat thrown over my shoulders. Felt rather odd in broad daylight; but no one took any notice. We are used to anything in London now.

A Warning at 9.15 a.m. while I was in the bath. Heard them overhead and guns began to go. Another at lunch hour. Bombs dropped in Piccadilly and Paddington. These we heard. All in Mercury Café were ready to drop to the floor. I learned from someone that in Whiteleys people screamed. Well they may. The terrible bomb dropped through the glass dome. Nothing to stop it until it reached the ground floor.

Brutes are here and zooming around. Heaps of guns!

Saturday, 26th Not such a good night – but no bombs. Everyone in the office departed to their own bed at 5.30 a.m. as it was quiet. So I ran up the road. Still dark. A bomb fell about noon . . . they say in Knightsbridge. People shopping were killed. At the Mercury I was told bombs had fallen again in St Charles' Square, so I took a bus there. The Square was a scene of complete desolation. Roof of the convent had gone, and every house was derelict. First Aid Post was finished. Came back and spoke to a bus man who had helped there last night. One hundred incendiaries had dropped on the convent and grounds. The girls at the Post were trying to put them out – but with so many it was awful. No one was hurt – but the First Aid Post is moving out today.

Did some shopping. Raid on all the time. In my room the gas pressure has returned, so I was warm. Turned on radio and dozed. Came back here at 6 p.m. and did black-out. Some bombs have fallen this evening – two about 7.45 and more at 9.15 . . . some distance away. I am listening for incendiaries all the time.

'Still lift your standard high'

Sunday, 27th Not such a bad night. Slept pretty well. The cat was the chief nuisance. Miss Rowe waked me at 6 a.m. and though the raid was still on I went up the road in the dark, and got into bed. Dozed until 10 a.m. So lovely not to have to get up at 8 a.m. Lazy morning. *Observer* not too cheerful. Ivy rang up and we arranged to lunch together. Said she had been bombed out again. Found it hard to believe! This is the third time.

Ivy is staying in Binney Street and it appears that last Sunday morning a bomb fell on Kings Weigh church – 100 people were taking communion. The vicar's wife was killed and the vicar badly injured together with many people. Ivy's room adjoins the church and now is declared unsafe. We took a bus to Marble Arch, passed Whiteleys and saw the mess. Only fourteen people were killed – not forty-seven. But it was bad enough. Walked along Binney Street, and she was quite correct – the inside of the church had gone. That was 10 a.m. last Sunday.

Walked along Bond St – a lot of damage. A shop called Gieve's was a complete ruin. In Piccadilly found St James' Church – it is just standing, nothing more. The Water-Colour Painters is badly damaged. The Fifty Shilling Tailor is a mess – just a heap of rubble. Walked on to Leicester Square. Badly hit. The one big Cinema has gone and other places – also in Coventry St. Then I took a bus to St Paul's. Found the place where the Time Bomb was – just in front of Queen Anne. Went inside – the Altar is railed off. Along Cheapside – much damage, but Bow Church and steeple still stand. Though quite how I don't know, for all around it is in ruins. Gamages etc. Scarcely a business premises that is habitable, though a few more than in Holborn.

Came back along Fleet St. Tried to get into the Temple, but it was shut. St Clement Danes looked derelict, though the walls are still standing but it is a mess. Wandered down Whitehall – more buildings caught it since last week. Very tired and took a bus back. Raids on and off all day. The devils are here again – but so far no guns or near bombs. For this I am thankful. It is black as pitch outside, and I fear it is only the absence of the moon that is keeping them away.

Monday, 28th   Very quiet night. Slept fairly well. At the Café I discovered that the two bombs I heard on Saturday night were on Shepherd's Bush. I thought they were near. On a little pub called The Telegraph. Many people were gathered there, having a social evening. The bomb fell right on the place, and it is said forty were killed.

Just to mention something that made me laugh. The wireless announced a tune called Imagination, saying it was one of the season's better songs. I listened and began to wonder what the worst were like . . . It was followed by one called – The Pessimistic Gentleman with the Crab Apple Face. This struck me as having a good title – and my hopes of the English reared again.

Not such bad raids here last night. I suppose they were in the Midlands. However, at this moment the guns have begun in a big flurry. Italy has begun to invade Greece. What the Greeks think they can do, I cannot imagine. I expect they have two and a half aeroplanes . . . We offer them help . . . How? We shall send a handful of soldiers – and they will be bombed out . . . There will be another masterly evacuation . . . we know it all so well.

Tuesday, 29th A quiet night. The others slept upstairs. Went up the road at 7.15 a.m. Had a chat with Mrs Watkins about the bomb that fell on the tramcars. It passed right over her office . . . and made a mess of cars and people. She told me the Carlton Club had been bombed, but no one hurt. They sent a cheque to another club, and there the members went. A rumour that a bomb has come down at Lancaster Gate at 11 a.m. . . . a district with a fascination for raiders even in the daytime. They are here tonight, but so far not too bad. I gather Brum has had it with bombs in Broad St, and time bombs all over the place. Poor Mother! She will be agitated.

Wednesday, 30th Quite a quiet night as far as we were concerned. But at the Café learned that on Monday night there was a bomb on Walworth Road and St Peter's Church, where lots of people were sheltering in the crypt, many killed. They say the Italians are bombing us. Gun-fire has gone off now. Pouring with rain.

Thursday, 31st Last night as we sat in the office there was suddenly a ping on the roof of Miss Moyes' office, and a sort of crash. We could not locate anything out of order, and concluded it was shrapnel. This morning I found a large slate on the lawn, but in the Circle Room there was the headpiece of a shell – a round heavy disk. It had bounced on the office roof, then gone through the window. It would not have been nice on one's head! Fairly quiet all day. They came early this evening . . . but All Clear at 9 p.m. It seems uncanny without the noise. I could almost go up the road now, but I fear to trust them. Lucy had had four instalments of the diary. I seem to have been in London for years!

End of October 1940

NOVEMBER 1940

»»»» ❀ ««««

'Join the triumph of the skies'

Friday, 1st All clear at 9.30, so at 11 p.m. ventured up the road to my own bed. Slept on it all through the night. This is the first time for seven weeks! Warning went again – but I did not heed. Guns went – but I dozed on.

Tonight, however, things are not so good. Warnings at 6.45 p.m. and soon two bombs came down fairly near here. Near enough for me to dive under the table. Very nasty. More down later. Planes zooming near. Have been working hard all the evening addressing envelopes for the Christmas Fair. Felt rather tired.

Saturday, 2nd [This was the 57th night of continuous bombing of London. Sept. 7 – Nov. 2nd.]

First All Clear at 2 a.m. so I ventured up the road. Dark, but with stars. Various Warnings and All Clears followed through the night, but I slept on and felt better in the morning. The location of the bombs last night was Brunswick Gardens, Church St. But they fell in the garden of the Warden's house, and though the blast caused a shindy, no one was hurt. The other fell in Westbourne Park Rd apparently near some buses, and nine people were killed.

It has poured with rain all afternoon and evening, but I went out. Though my feet got soaking wet I did not care. Lovely to be out in the fresh air. I could hardly keep my umbrella up – the wind was so strong. Anyway, it kept the Nazis away. Took a bus to Chancery Lane, and walked up. An immense block of buildings called the Safe Deposit Co looked as if it had had at least half a dozen bombs on it. They were clearing it away. Saw that I could walk to the Temple. All the gates were open, so I went in . . . it is terrible. The Church is not damaged, but the rest is just dreadful. I walked in all the courtyards, and it seems to have had bombs in all directions.

Took a bus to Aldgate and walked along to the Tower. It was teeming down, but I struggled on, glad that I had not to keep one eye on the sky for chance bombs . . . certain amount of damage. It is the Bastion on the Curtain Wall . . . right down in the moat; but I think it could be built up easily. The rain nearly swept me away, but I turned down Gt Tower St and Eastcheap . . . quite a lot of premises had bombs. Bus to Victoria, and saw the immense craters by Blackfriars Bridge. On past Waterloo station. The Palace Theatre had caught a bomb – but outwardly not the same damage as in the City.

It is a wild night – but they have come all the same.

'Seek not yet repose'

Sunday, 3rd　All Clear just after I had bedded down in the office. I woke about 3.30 a.m. and padded up the road. Lovely to have a long night in bed. Read the *Observer*. Garvin thinks if we make use of the Greek opportunity it will be a great help. It is, however, if if . . . another masterly evacuation . . .

Invited the new young man to have a cigarette with me . . . he seems to think I do not approve of him, so thought I had better do something about it. Up to the Mercury for lunch . . . the bomb last night was on Colville Terrace – fairly near us. Poured with rain all day. The new young man is doing ARP work on Campden Hill, but I gather in peace time he is some sort of actor or writer. He was quite agreeable. I told him that when I recommended him to our landlady I did not vouch for his personal character, but had said that he looked all right. He was much amused.

Listened to Mr Herbert Morrison . . . very good. A few guns began this afternoon. Barishnikov came to tea. We came down here at 6 p.m. to do the black-out. All Clear at 7 p.m. . . . a record. It is raining hard and I am sure they cannot tell if they are over London – or the Black Sea!

Monday, 4th No warning at all through the night. Marvellous! I wended my way up at 11 p.m. It was pitch, and I kept colliding with corners, but eventually reached my room. I learn, however, that some bombs were dropped on Chiswick. Mrs Horton Smith came in today, full of her experiences of Friday night. A bomb near them. Someone asked her how she felt. She replied that she just ceased to feel during that awful moment. That is all I can say about our bomb of Oct. 10th. Part of Miss Linde's ceiling came down, but otherwise they felt only shock. Just as I was coming down tonight at 6.30 p.m. guns began to bark out, and great flashes filled the sky. Plenty of shrapnel – so I waited. Intense for a few moments. Then a lull as the sirens screamed out. I ran down here. No bombs so far.

Tuesday, 5th Guy Fawkes Day! Went up the road at 11 p.m. as it sounded so quiet. But half way up flashes filled the sky . . . guns began to roar, and I could hear the raider coming nearer. I did not dare to run, as it was pitch dark, and I was afraid of falling over something. Managed to find the house, and put the key in the lock. Just as I got up to my room there was real barking from all our dogs. It went on intermittently all night, and shook the house – but I dozed in between. Felt better for sleeping all night in my own bed. Did not hear any bombs near us, but parts of London had it. Wireless said it was more intense than on previous nights. It is very wet tonight, and I think they have been drowned again – serve them right. Just going up the road. Churchill spoke tonight. He offered us nothing spectacular as usual – but he sounded solid.

Wednesday, 6th Slept in my own bed, but it was far from being a quiet night. In fact it was awful. At about 3 a.m. was awakened by two screaming bombs coming down not far away. Others followed. Gunfire terrific. I slept and dreamed all about bombs until I could not tell which was dream and which reality. Then I plunged into a nightmare – in which I was in a long room, a German and an Italian soldier walked in and said: 'I must inform you that England has lost the war.' I think I spat at them, but cannot be sure.

At the Café was informed that a bomb had fallen on a Police Station in Salisbury Rd – near Harrow Rd, and killed

20 policemen and injured many more. Poor old Shepherd's Bush had it again. I felt some were nearer, but could get no more information. Spoke to Mr Bendall about Bow Church. He said the walls were still standing, but it was badly damaged. He suggested I walk down the Minories and round St Katherine's Dock!

Blighters came at 6 p.m. Bombs and din fearful ever since. Shall have to sleep here tonight.

'Bear the toil, maintain the strife'

Thursday, 7th   A terrible night! Guns never seemed to cease. Many bombs. No chance to go up the road. Slept at office until All Clear after 7 a.m. Not very refreshing to sleep in one's clothes, but the lovely bath helps a bit. Every district of London got it last night. Near us it was Campden Hill again, though no confirmation. But Maida Vale, Kilburn etc. Later we heard that Gerrard St and the Swiss Club, where some of de Gaulle's men were supping, got it. French Church near Leicester Square was destroyed. Tonight not so bad so far; but the moon is climbing, and I do not trust it.

Very difficult to get any eggs . . . almost impossible. Not a kipper to be had for a long time. Can't think what they have done with them. We are still persevering with Fair preparations.

Friday, 8th   Did not go back to my room last night. Office was warm. Jerries kept zooming back. All Clear went, but I felt too comfortable to move. Managed it at 7.45 a.m. Very dark – at least murky. Later in the day heard that bombs had fallen on St Quentin's Avenue near Mrs Fisher's. Some killed.

In the news tonight Mr Chamberlain is reported to be gravely ill.

Have been looking out some fancy dresses today . . . just imagine in the Blitzkrieg! Felt rather tired. Have been reading about Mrs Perugini, daughter of Dickens. One advantage of London being so depopulated is that one can get books. Read Noel Coward's *Present Indicative* . . . very interesting.

Saturday, 9th   Went up at 10 p.m. so tired I felt I must get to bed at once. There was a lull, so sprinted up. Lovely for the second time in two months to be in bed. Terrific plonk at 4.30 a.m. But felt refreshed in the morning. Miss M. off to Oxford to stay the night. No rooms booked, and I feel the place may be full of evacuees. Barishnikov got me two eggs, for which I am most thankful. Mr Booker at the Mercury is not too enamoured of the demolition men . . . thinks they go off for a drink when they might be doing some more rescuing. Have heard this before, but one hesitates to believe it. He would welcome the Welsh miners, as they are used to the work. It must be terribly hard – and in the dark, too. Mr Booker has got into trouble for not waiting to put demands for the ambulance through to the right quarter. Instead he has gone to fetch it himself . . . this is most reprehensible, it seems. He seems a conscientious sort of man, and I hope if I am buried he will be near to try and dig me out . . . Guns are going grimly now!

'Hearts are brave again, and arms are strong'

Sunday, 10th All seemed quiet so went up the road about 10.30 last night. Into bed with great thankfulness. Warning went about 4 a.m. Terrific gunfire overhead for half an hour. Got ready to bury my head in the pillow. Then slept uneasily. Dreamed there was trouble at home. Woke again at 9.30 a.m. and thanked God it was Sunday. Blessed day! Garvin fairly cheerful. Greeks have done better than we expected, but he thinks the Italians will try harder.

Lunch at Mercury. Heard Neville Chamberlain had gone. The best thing. I shall never forget the Sunday just over a year ago when he said we had declared war. He did not think he would go so soon . . .

Pouring with rain, but decided to get a little fresh air. Goloshes a great help. Went along the Bayswater Rd where the buses could not get. Tremendous craters in front of the Palace hotel. So much so that it may be here they are building a bridge across. Anyway men were working for dear life in the rain. Turned down the Edgware Rd which is now partly open to traffic. The end near Marble Arch is badly damaged. Messrs Cozens does not seem to know how to hold itself together. Great block of mansions behind the Pavilion Theatre, which is a ruin, is uninhabitable. Turned along Upper Berkeley St. Rather battered looking. Got to Gt Cumberland St and at the end could see a big bomb had fallen. Persevered to Bryanston Square, where there is one great mansion down to the ground. Others have lost windows and doors.

Into Baker St which I was anxious to see. The side streets have caught bombs, but though the whole length looks torn and weary, there was no great damage on the surface. Turned into Marylebone Rd and reached Madame Tussaud's. Damage is extensive there. Obviously aimed at Baker St Station. Cinema behind suffered grievously. For the sake of Auntie Nell though very tired, I trudged on to the Dispensary to see if it was still standing. It is – and with the exception of a few windows seems intact, but the building beside it – whatever it is – is not there! Men were running a special truck up and down clearing the debris. Mansion opposite has had a heavy bomb.

Queen Charlotte's Hospital is uninhabitable. It must have had a very bad time, though the walls seemed to be standing. Got bus to Notting Hill. Sat by the fire and read the Ranee of Sarawak's biography. Cannot think why she had such awful daughters. Barishnikov came to tea. Ran down to do the black-out. Guns began. Hope Miss M. gets back from Oxford tonight. We have not had a Warning all day today . . . A record!

Monday, 11th Armistice Day Did not feel too good all day. Miss M. arrived back without adventure. Trains are running faster now. They had had no raid on Oxford.

Tuesday, 12th Several raids during day. On printing works yesterday at Victoria about 5 p.m. Workpeople still there – many killed and trapped in masonry. Very cold. Moon full tonight. Came down at 6.15. Planes are here now. One bomb very near. It may be Campden Hill. It shook this house and gave me the jim-jams for a few moments. Guns going strong. However, we all keep on working and it takes it off.

Wednesday, 13th Feeling better this evening. Pouring with rain and All Clear went a few minutes ago, about 10 p.m. They have been drowned out – and thank goodness for that. I shall be able to use a torch to get home. That's a mercy as the gutters are like running rivers and in the dark one goes splash-in.

The bad bomb last night was in Phillimore Gardens – the end near Kensington High St. Don't know if it was the Waterworks they wanted. Three houses demolished. A doctor, his wife and 2 children were killed. It is about half a mile, as the crow flies, from us. Raids were general.

The Naval Victory is very heartening. Good news for once. But it shows how short we are of ships that we had to entrust one enormous convoy to a small ship, which could only die defending itself. Bless them!

Raids are definitely better. We all held our breath last night. But we do not have it hour after hour – bombs falling all the time – as in September and October.

'Our crafty foe still strives to work us woe'

Thursday, 14th No sound from the enemy all through the night. Very busy day. Getting ready for the Fair – a few parcels coming in, so we may make a pound or two. Letter from Brum to say nothing very bad there since October 24th–26th. These were their bad days.

Friday, 15th Guns came on full and strong. It sounded unpleasantly near my roof. Could hear the shrapnel dropping – ping, pong – on Ladbroke Rd outside. Every moment expected something through. Could hear the raider well overhead, but no bombs. Felt cold. Turned on News at 8 a.m. and was alarmed to hear a Midland town had had a bad raid with many casualties. I was terrified it was Brum. But at lunch time heard it was poor Coventry. The Cathedral destroyed – a 14thC. building. Mother and I walked round it when we visited Coventry last September. They have not got Tubes to go to like the people here. My poor cousin – hope she is all right. I felt there was some fresh devilment abroad, because they left us so quiet in the early part of the night.

Saturday, 16th Truly ghastly night! We lost count of the bombs that came down. Guns and sticks of bombs falling well into the evening and night. Mr Hillyard and I began to notice doors rattling about 8 p.m. At 11.30 four came down, and it was obvious I could not venture up the road. Lay down on my little mattress on the floor, but at 2 a.m. was wakened by awful drivings into the earth, and swishes through the sky, planes droning and guns going.

After about half an hour of this Miss M. came down saying that as we could not sleep should we make a cup of tea. I don't like it in the middle of the night, but this time I was thankful. Dozed off uneasily. More bombs. At 7.45 a.m. wandered up the road and made myself another cup. We all agreed that it had been as bad as September . . . that is hell.

I read about poor Coventry. They say it is like Warsaw – not a street undamaged. People were pouring out of the town which is all cordoned off. Mr Herbert Morrison went down there at once.

'A night of gloom and terror'

At lunch time heard at the Mercury there had been a landmine last night in St Helen's Gardens. Immediately took a bus. Walked along Cambridge Gardens. Saw all windows gone and St Helen's Gardens roped off . . . not a house habitable on either side. No 89 looked the worst of the lot. A policeman came to drive us away. Asked if anyone had been killed. He relieved my mind by saying no. Could get no further, but I felt if Mrs Fisher had been in bed when the landmine struck the tennis court, she must have been seriously injured. Decided I must find out if she was in hospital . . . but how? Went to ask Mr Booker . . . and there, as large as life, drinking coffee, was Mrs Fisher relating her experience!

It seems that by a miracle she was in her little lobby doing some ironing at 8 p.m. when it struck. Everything went black. She found herself choked by cement and debris, and hit by falling masonry. She could smell hissing gas escaping. Heard no sound of breaking glass – though for half a mile around every pane had gone! She heard voices calling and crawled through what she thought was the door. It was part of a fallen wall. The road was full of screaming people. Twenty wardens were rounding them up and taking them out of twenty houses – none were habitable. Rain was pouring down. They were walked to St Charles' Hospital, where the Casualty Ward windows had gone. They all had to sit in the dark and cold, suffering from shock. Then someone nailed down the black-out. Mrs Fisher was bleeding but not much.

She then joined a few others, and they were taken to a house where three of them got on to one bed under an eiderdown. At 6.30 a.m. as soon as it was light, they got up and rushed along to the ruins. No one was allowed to move a door or touch a beam, but only to salvage a few personal effects. Mrs Fisher found her handbag and money; but not her suitcase with documents and policies. Whole flat was smashed. She felt she must say goodbye to everything. She is very plucky over it. I took her back and helped her collect her suitcases; gave her a good tea and a warm, and arranged to see her again tomorrow. She rested all the afternoon in my room.

Came down to office. Spent evening preparing for the Fair. Devils are here, but fairly quiet. I hope to go back up the road and get a long night in bed.

Sunday, 17th Quiet night. Had a field day preparing for Fair. All of us up and down the stairs, polishing, decorating, ironing and arranging. Glorious sunshiny day. Soon after the News Mr Hillyard called us to see what he said was a flare descending. It got larger and larger. Then we saw it was a balloon on fire. It seemed to be coming straight on our house, and I ran for a bucket of sand. But it fell in blazing bits the other side of Ladbroke Road. Pouring with rain. Plenty of wonks and plonks going on intermittently through the night. Black-out does not end until 8 a.m.

Monday, 18th Felt very tired. Far too busy. Shall be glad when the Fair is over. Checked up about the balloon. The Wardens'

Post were watching it come down and thought it was dropping in Westbourne Grove. The cables were dangerous, so they went running after it. Mr Booker considered it much nearer. He jumped over a wall, and found it was burning itself out in the convent grounds. Six others came down soon after. It was an electrical storm. No damage . . . pouring all day. I think we shall have a quiet night. Poor Coventry! The more one reads about it the worse it gets . . .

'For this relief – much thanks'

[*A few days are left out here as I was too busy to write my diary.*]

Sunday, 24th Too busy all the week to write anything. Was working to midnight more or less most of the week. The blitz behaved well for our Fair, and gave us no trouble; but we scored at the expense of other towns. Tuesday night they had it in Brum. I can get no news, but I am afraid there was a lot of damage. Now they talk of a West Midland town, which I think must be Wolverhampton . . . heavy casualties. Friday night Penberthys was damaged . . . took a slice right off it; but everywhere caught it that night.

Made over £350 at the Fair. I think it was splendid. Better than last year. When Miss Moyes had the handbills printed this time we thought she was mad – as the blitz was then at its height. Her faith is justified . . . bombing was at its lowest ebb during the Fair since the Luftwaffe began on London. I sold £28 of stuff on my Caledonian Market Stall. It is a stall that pleases everybody – and people gave no end of stuff for it.

Guns are going faintly in the distance. The Government treated Mrs Fisher well. She got £17 down for immediate expenses, and put in her compensation claim for after the war. She cannot move anything from her house, as it will collapse if she does!

[*My diary for the last few days of November and beginning of December was lost on its way to Africa.*]

End of November 1940

DECEMBER 1940

⟶⟶⟶ ❋ ⟵⟵⟵

'Put a cheerful courage on'

[*It was during this period that Miss Moyes fell and broke a bone in her foot. At the time she treated it as a sprain.*]

Monday, 9th Last night was very bad indeed. Began soon after 5.30 p.m. Barishnikov and I had to run from my place to the Sanctuary as the barrage was working up. It never ceased until 2.30 a.m. Many bombs came down . . . some in our district. On enquiry today I find it was around the Sion Convent, Chepstow Villas and Dawson Place . . . people buried.

Miss M. arrived back at 8 a.m. I got her fire going, and made myself and Mr Hillyard a cup of tea. We had not turned in until 2 a.m. and had slept little. She had managed York there and back, by being carried in a chair. Got her nice and warm and settled. Then back to my place, had a bath to freshen myself up. Worked hard all day – but felt very cheap. Doctor came and rather sobered Miss M. She is not to put her foot to the ground for a fortnight – not even a toe.

Thursday, 12th No time to write my diary. Miss M. being upstairs has made extra work. There is the selling of goods left over from the Fair. Found the day a struggle, but got through somehow. Learned that Brum had a bad raid last night. We had pretty well of noise, but no bombs near us, I understand that Victoria Station was struck, and other places. Rumour goes that the Tower had it last Sunday – and the Governor injured. Greeks doing well, and we in Egypt.

According to Mabel Lucy who passed on the prophecy, we are to have one more big setback, and then we shall turn the corner. Good . . . Blighters are here tonight. I hope my people in Brum have a roof over their heads.

'Quiet nights – from troubles free'

Friday, 13th Lovely letter from Lucy. I like the note outside: 'We realize in Rhodesia that the safe arrival of this letter is due to the British Navy.' She has begun to receive the really bad part of my diary – September – and is appalled. I am not surprised; but I hope she realizes it is not like that now, else I should not be here to write it. Anyway I am glad it is interesting people out there.

Letter from Brum at last. Mother does not say much, but it was written before the Thursday raid. She talks of rows and rows of shops, houses small and large all down . . . it has to be seen to be believed. A man in the Mercury was telling me that from the railway Brum looks pretty bad: and if the Queen sent them £200, the King [who had visited it] must have told her it was not too good. Anyway I shall see for myself at Christmas.

The better news in Greece and Africa cheers us up more than anything. I am glad the stuffing is being taken out of Mussolini at last.

Sunday, 15th   Last night All Clear went early, so I could go up with a tranquil mind. Friday night I chose the wrong moment. Guns were going strong. I kept close to the wall to dodge the shrapnel. Got in without adventure. Too tired not to sleep. Woke once or twice and heard a lot going on, but it failed to register and I slept on. We have to keep the Black-out until 8.30 and it is going to be 8.45 a.m.

Very busy packing up parcels for the Poor Folk – some few toys also that we have collected for the Shelter and Tube Parties. Indeed how to get through the work before Christmas, I don't know . . . it is formidable.

My nice warden, Mr Booker, has gone into Hospital. He has T.B., a legacy from the last war. He told me that to resign from A.R.P. was one of the hardest things he had ever had to do. I fear he will not get better. It is terrible. No Germans all day. A bit blitzy this evening, but not much. Miss M. got there and back to Chichester. News interesting. Garvin pleased about Egypt; but another correspondent thinks Hitler is planning a new sort of Luftwaffe on us.

Queer doings in France and Italy. Dr Remy is released from Canada, and can return here or remain over there.

'And now we live in hope'

Monday, 16th No warning all day – but on and off this evening. They are trying to break through, but have not succeeded. Heard the bad news that All Hallows, Barking by the Tower, was damaged the other Sunday. Bomb came through near the Altar. I understand Sheffield had it again last night.

Good news from the Greeks – and the Desert. Most heartening. Been working hard all day – it is nearly 11 p.m. We publish the paper tomorrow and again on Saturday. An awful struggle with all the Christmas things – but I suppose it will get done.

Tuesday, 17th Very busy. Packed the paper – and ran in all directions at once this afternoon. Missed the Desert news – but I think it was good. The Boche is preparing something else with these quiet nights. Just read Lord Lothian's last speech.

Wednesday, 18th Had a terrible fright this morning. Was with Miss M. taking down some letters, when a telegram was brought me. Tore it open and read: You must arrive by daylight. I jumped to the conclusion that the roof had been blown off the house in Brum, or that Mother was ill. Went all sick and put through a call. Was in a thorough panic. Then the others in the office said if it was a case of illness the message would have said: Come at once. So I thought again and became a little calmer. Then Mrs Hoare produced a letter for me from Cath explaining that when I came for Xmas I must arrive in daylight as often soldiers on short leave had been left in sidings all night – because of bombs on the line! Anyway this all helped in the end, for Miss M. decided I must stay at home for the rest of the week – and go early on Tuesday – just what I wanted . . .

Saturday, 21st No time to write up my diary. Very very busy. Miss M. better. Rather a blitzy night now. Something nasty seemed to come down. A new sort of noise. Guns busy. Liverpool had a very bad time the other night. My cousin writes from Coventry: 'Old Palace Yard is down to the ground. The Cathedral is gutted – only the spire remains. Hertford and Smithford streets, West Orchard and Broadgate are flat. Terrible damage on the outskirts also.'

Have sent off lots of parcels of clothes; and we are giving toys to all the children in the Public Shelter opposite our Shelter in China Walk, Lambeth. Miss M. is giving the people a hot supper on Xmas Eve . . . hot pies and mince pies. Then in our own Shelter the women will have a good dinner on Christmas Day. From here we have given many women 10/- to help them, also clothes and toys if there were children. It was so nice finding things to fit them.

Sunday, 22nd Slept well, but woke very cold in the early hours and expected snow. Came down to Sanctuary. Heard that a bomber had come down on Victoria Station the previous night at 7 p.m. That was the queer wonk I heard. It descended with all its bombs on Ebury Bridge. The Station is unusable today, and everyone had to go by bus to Clapham Junction to pick up trains. Guns are working away outside. *Observer* is very emphatic for us to watch for invasion this Christmas. I don't know about getting down to Brum . . . there are no extra trains, and I fear they will be full. But Fred, our caretaker, is coming to the station with me, and perhaps as I am only one I shall wedge in somewhere.

Monday, 23rd Very busy day. Just listened to the Prime Minister's magnificent speech to the Italian people . . . in the dramatic style that suits him, alluding to Garibaldi, Mazzini and Cavour – and all we did for them. He alluded to Mussolini . . . It was a thrilling speech and made me think our Prime Minister is really the greatest man we have ever produced in all our long history – except perhaps for Alfred the Great. We have never been so near defeat as we were in June, nor so near invasion on our actual soil. It was just touch and go – and he saved us. A statue in gold would not be too much for what we owe him.

Must get ready now to go to Brum, and will write diary on my return.

'Peace – and lively joy'

Sunday, 29th Got to Paddington in good time – I was taking one of the Fair Prizes for someone who had won it. Train left late and was full, but I had a seat. I looked up at the glass roof of the Station and marvelled that in spite of all the raids it was still there.

Reached Brum an hour late. Dr Hillier waiting for me and amazed I was so early. Cath was not setting out for about three hours! As we came out of Snow Hill station I saw the Arcade opposite black with fire and closed. Broad St had had some hits, but not Hagley Rd; and so far no bomb on Francis Rd. Cath and I went down to the Market Place. Not much to buy. Apples were 1/4d a pound and oranges difficult to obtain. I got four from a Jewish trader by spinning him a yarn. This was better than N.H. Gate where I was allowed one! Saw New St Marshall and Snelgrove's is like John Lewis' – only the damage is on a smaller scale. Smallbrook St and John Bright St are a mess. However, New St has not gone on both sides.

Christmas Day was nice. We had a goose which Cath had obtained. Also a few nuts and chocolates – though all are very scarce. We thought of last Xmas when we were short of nothing. In the evening I rang up Elsie, an Old Edwardian school friend, and Neville, her husband. He came and fetched me, and showed me his Divisional Warden H.Q. of which he is justly proud. He sleeps there every night and has the phone by his bed; often he is roused whether there is a raid or not. All a great strain as he has to carry on his business as usual. Wonderful maps he has of every street in his area. I think A.R.P. is very good in Brum. In Cath's group the Divisional Warden located the streets of three bombs quite correctly from a distance. Very difficult to do. Cath has to cower in doorways away from shrapnel. She has had her particular Broad St bomb to cope with. Had to take charge more or less – but the shops were empty, and she only had to look after distraught people living either side.

We drank to a Happier 1941! I phoned the Clives who said they would be pleased to see us. Mother and I went by the first train. Changed at Kidderminster and Wofferton, and slow all the way. Sun shining and country looked lovely. Travelled with another Old Edwardian going to Leominster. She told me about King Edward's being evacuated to Cheltenham, and how difficult it was in billets. How they returned to the new Bristol Rd School. Then the blitz began in earnest. So they went to Kidderminster; but the boys stayed on in Brum. Arrived in Hereford, and since there was no one to carry Mother's bag, heavy with food, I hailed a Coal Cart, and persuaded the boy to take it to the Square for me! We caught the bus. The Clives were sweet. We talked of Lucy and Auntie Nell, and how peaceful it was in the village of Eardisland. Mother was enraptured, and I am sure she will be happy for a few days. After lunch had to catch the bus back. The place looked more like a picture postcard than ever. Saw a small Tank pelting along, and the Boys in it very pleased with themselves. Train to Shrewsbury. It was pitch dark – but I shouted I wanted a train to Brum, and was hoisted into one without delay! No blitz in Brum.

> *'With flame of incandescent terror*
> *Water and fire shall rot*
> *The marred foundations we forgot,*
> *of sanctuary and choir.*
> *This is the death of water and fire'*

Dr Hillier and Cath came to see me off. They had given me some eggs – most acceptable. Reached London at 3 p.m. and took a taxi – great luxury. Came down to Sanctuary. Familiar Sirens have gone and the guns are on once more. Have not heard a bomb yet, and I hope they will soon go away.

Monday, 30th   After I wrote my diary last night there were Terrible Fires in London. We went up on the roof to look. At Shepherd's Bush flames were leaping, and towards the City they were gigantic. As I walked up the road I could see the smoke. A great red glow filled the sky – I had no need of a torch – I could see every step I took and could have read a book if I had wished. The police said it was Waterloo Station, but the taxi man told Miss Moyes that the City was on fire, and they were trying to save St Paul's. These were her first words to me as she arrived, and I shall never forget the horror of them.

This morning we heard it was a great attack on the City. Mr Bendall rang up to say his office was down to the ground. When Mr Hillyard came back it transpired that his office in Finsbury was also gone. From Mrs Whittaker we heard that part of the roof of the *Daily Telegraph* had gone. Everything was so hot no one could go near. The fire went up Fleet St across Ludgate Circus to St Paul's, and then along Cheapside. I did not think this part could be ruined any more – but apparently there is now less of it standing. It took Guildhall and went along Moorgate into City Road. All this is a line of fire with true German thoroughness.

St Katharine's Dock was gone; much damage to warehouses. No great loss of life, except the poor Firemen. Difficult to get food in the City today. No gas to cook by. Half the people could not get into the remains of their offices, because they were still burning. All very crushing.

I shall never bother with Germans or foreigners again, except the Greeks who have helped us. It makes you want to give other people a taste of what we have had.

No Warning tonight here – and I should think not! I do hope they are not pasting Brum the same.

With regard to news on the Home Front, as if there is not enough to do, the Cat was taken ill! He was ailing before Xmas – could not jump on a chair. I fetched the vet. He found it difficult to discover the cause of the intense pain. Between us we poured some liquid paraffin down his throat. We wrapped him in a blanket to do this. The vet left a pill for him night and morning. I put the little animal up on a shelf near some warm pipes. He seems better. A sheep and a cat are the two most difficult animals to treat, the vet said.

Tuesday, 31st   We had further news of the damage to the City – and all through neglect! Always the same . . . no one wants to take responsibility . . . let others do it. Common sense should tell us that it is madness to leave buildings to one caretaker, or to no one at all, in times like these. We don't leave this house – nor the one at home. It serves a lot of them right – but it has caused harm to many beautiful Churches. Our postman looked at me this morning and said: 'It doesn't bear thinking about. I wonder if those that done it reflected on what they had done.' I leave it at that.

Mrs Starmer came in from the City. She had rescued her records, but the offices are doomed. No food in the City. She looked worn out with the sights she had seen . . . they must be seen to be believed, she said. I boiled her an egg and made her a pot of tea, for which she was most grateful.

The Cat is better, and even asked to take a walk in the garden. But I had to carry him back. Poor little thing!

However, I think he will recover. I have never seen a cat so ill.

Mr Herbert Morrison says that it will now be compulsory for every building to be guarded. I should think so indeed!

On the Postscript they gave us some of the phrases of 1940. All the best are by Churchill. We shall never forget them . . . Blood and sweat and toil and tears . . .

Description of the result of the Fire Raid on the City:

'The largest area of continuous air raid desolation in all Britain.'

End of 1940

'Begone, ye powers of evil'

THE YEAR
1941

'Amid the encircling gloom'

'Who so beset him round
With dismal stories
Do but themselves confound,
His strength the more is'

THE MAIN EVENTS
OF THE YEAR
1941

January	5	British take Bardia
	20	invade Eritrea
	22	take Tobruk
February	7	take Benghazi
	18	invade Italian Somaliland
March	1	Bulgaria joins Axis
	11	U.S. Congress approves lend-lease
	24	Yugoslav government joins Axis
	27	overthrown by neutralists
	30	Cape Matapan naval engagement
	31	Rommel attacks in Libya
April	6	Germans and Bulgarians invade Yugoslavia and Greece
		British enter Addis Ababa
	17	Yugoslavia capitulates
		Greece capitulates
May	2	Pro-Axis rising in Iraq
	18	Italians in Abyssinia surrender
	20–31	Germans capture Crete
	27	German battleship *Bismarck* sunk in Atlantic

| | 29 | Rommel halted at Egyptian frontier |
| | 31 | British suppress rising in Iraq |

Russia in the war

June	22	Germany, Finland, Hungary and Italy attack Russia
July	7	U.S. forces relieve British garrison in Iceland
	16	Fall of Smolensk
		British invade and occupy Syria
August	25–29	Anglo-Russian forces occupy Persia
September	19	Fall of Kiev
October	24	Fall of Kharkov
November	16	Fall of Kerch
	18	Second British Libyan offensive opens
December	5	German drive on Moscow halted
	7	Japan attacks U.S.A.
		British and Dutch in Pacific. U.S. Fleet largely put out of action at Pearl Harbour

U.S.A. in the war

	9	Tobruk relieved
	10	Battleships *Prince of Wales* and *Repulse* sunk off Malaya
	11	Germany and Italy declare war on U.S.A.
	13	Fall of Guam
	20	Fall of Wake Island
	25	Fall of Hong Kong
		British retake Benghazi

JANUARY 1941

****** ❊ ******

The first day of the New Year. Wednesday, 1st Slept well and said white rabbits on waking. This is a good start. The cat much better. He was able to walk without groaning. He ate and drank, and so seems to have turned the corner – like the British Commonwealth.

Devastating news from Mr Bendall about All Hallows, Barking by the Tower. He seems to think it is quite destroyed. I knew it had had a bomb, but I thought it was only on part. I must go and see on Sunday. They say still how awful everything looks. The whole of Finsbury St, where Mr Hillyard's office was, is flat.

The doctor called and said Miss Moyes' ankle is fractured in three places, and if she does not go carefully she will have a permanent limp. There seem to be a few more eggs and oranges in the shops.

Thursday, 2nd We learned this morning that all the ledgers of the Association probably perished in the fire. They were at the accountants' and had not been returned. His office was in the burned-out area. Our accountant is wild, as it took him seven years to make that Ledger, and the Balance Sheet was finished some time ago. Had the books been returned to us, it would not have happened. Everything of reference to the Association could be turned up in seconds in that book – and it has gone.

So much of the damage seems the result of carelessness. Now everyone is a fire-fighter. Fancy leaving the City of London unprotected in days like these! I hear today that there was a land-mine on the Temple last night, but I can hardly believe it. However, one gets beyond feeling. They seem to be making a dead set at the City.

The cat continues to improve. He was so funny. He wanted to get back to his warm perch, but could not jump. We helped him on to a chair, but still he demurred . . . Mr Hillyard kept urging him – and he replied as plainly as anything: I can't. Then he looked me straight in the eye: You do something. So I lifted him up. It has been snowing, but he went in the garden and lumbered back up the steps with encouragement. So he is recovering strength.

Saturday, 4th   The blitz was on Cardiff on Thursday. Poor things! We have had nothing, except that they are dynamiting parts of the City. We could hear the distant explosions.

We have been trying to trace the genesis of a remark made by Queen Victoria, which is much quoted now: 'There is no depression in this house. We are not interested in the possibilities of defeat. They do not arise.' I felt it was meant for foreign consumption, and that the old lady said it to one of her foreign relations. It seems, however, that it was said to Mr A. J. Balfour at a dinner at Windsor in 1899 during the

Black Week. Persevering further at the Library I discovered that the Kaiser was at Windsor then. I feel she made the remark for his benefit. Apparently the country had gone hysterical to some extent; but the Old Queen was as calm as a rock, and Mr Balfour was very pleased with her self-control.

Sunday, 5th Before I start, let me say they are here again! I have just heard a big bomb fall not too far away.

I went up to the City about 1 p.m. Managed to get a bus to Ludgate Circus. It is the first day, I think, that a service has been restarted here. It was gently snowing. Walked up Ludgate Hill. I was by no means the only person in the City. There were hundreds and hundreds there. Firemen were still about. The Church on Ludgate Hill is undamaged, but above that it began. Everything is a shell . . . all burnt out inside. Smoke was still coming from one building. All Ave Maria Lane was closed to the public. I just looked down . . . burnt out. So I believe is Paternoster Row. On the right Debenham's big building – burnt out. Lots of men working on it.

We had to file through St Paul's Churchyard. Cheapside is closed, so went along Watling St. On left only remains of buildings. Friday St . . . just vistas of destruction wherever one looked. Went along Bread St into Cheapside, and saw poor Bow Church still looking down sorrowfully on the ruins around. Went along Coleman St – it has pretty well gone. St Stephen's just has the walls. I found Guildhall . . . roped off. Union Jack was flying bravely above it. Men working hard and no one allowed near. St Lawrence, Jewry, the Church that caused Guildhall to ignite, was only a shell.

Reached London Wall, but no one is allowed along. Cranes and engines were working on the ruins. Fore St also closed. Got back to Moorgate, and the left side took part in the blaze. The station closed . . . just one mass all behind of charred walls. Ropemakers and Chiswell St were blown up in part – I just arrived to see some of the walls falling. It is like a battlefield. Walked back to the Bank and tried to find Austin Friars. With great difficulty found the little curved lane, and was standing in front of what was once the Church, when I heard a familiar drone overhead . . . Felt I was not in a healthy spot. Sirens went and thought I had better move from that part of London in which so much interest has been taken. Saw a bus labelled Victoria and got on it. Saw a good old Wonk in Victoria St – quite near the Abbey.

I like the American comment: 'Hitler and Churchill both have a wonderful mastery of words: the one fills the air with poison gas . . . the other wields a broadsword.'

Monday, 6th   Some bombs fell last night after I had written my diary. One at 7.15 was said to be at Wormwood Scrubs, and another, round about 11 p.m. I understand was a large Time Bomb at St Charles' Square. That unfortunate Square seems to get it every time. Don't know any details because my Warden is ill in St Charles' Hospital.

Many warnings today, and some bombs. Could hear the guns. Good news of Bardia on 8 a.m. . . . Excellent! A few victories at last!

Wednesday, 8th   Plenty of warnings on Tuesday in the day time. A plane came very low as I was having lunch in the café

– but my heart did not miss a beat! I never thought I should get used to having my lunch on a battlefield . . . Anyway, I understand people in the streets ran for cover, which is unusual.

Felt second-rate all day. Baden-Powell has gone. Well, he has done a great work. No warning so far, but the snow may be keeping them away. The sky is heavy with it.

Friday, 10th Very blitzy indeed last night. The guns never ceased from early on in the evening. Could not possibly go up the road, so sat and read *Antony*, by Lord Lytton. About 11.20 Mr Hillyard let old Scamp in. He had not been enjoying himself out in the blitz. I never saw him so pleased at being by his own fireside. He couldn't tell me enough how it was outside! Just as he was in the middle of all this – and I was sympathizing with him – a terrific bomb came down and rumbled beneath our feet. Mr H. went on the roof, and I was listening for incendiaries all the time.

Guns did not cease until about 12.20 – by which time I was all in, and as I had not slept well the previous three nights, I decided to risk it and go up the road, while it was quiet. The moon was high and it was a good night for a raid. I was mighty glad to be near my habitation – that length of road had never seemed so long!

The guns began again, but I was too tired to bother. About 4 a.m. felt the whole house sway like a poplar tree – and I was in a nest at the top! Heard terrific bangs and falling masonry. All this weaved itself into my dreams, so you can tell I was tired. When I awoke I was not sure if it had all been a dream.

But going down to the Sanctuary about 9.30 a.m., to my horror found the road barricaded, and for a second dared not look at the house in case it had gone! But it was standing – so I walked up Lansdowne Road to find the damage. Apparently the bomb we felt at 11.20 was a Time Bomb, which had landed in the garden of no. 36. People all round had been hurriedly evacuated, and it went off at 4 a.m. It was a large bomb – it took the whole house and a half. Those either side are not worth much. But how awful for the two girls in whose front garden it fell! Another bomb fell in Lansdowne Crescent – but I have not seen the damage there.

Well, it was a lucky escape for us. Curiously enough it fell in exactly the same place as the previous little bomb which took the back of 38 Lansdowne Road. Miss Moyes said it sounded as if each brick was falling one by one. She thought it was next door – it seemed so close. I took her up in the afternoon to see it in a three wheeled chair for invalids. A bit awkward, as it is not made for the street. She much enjoyed the jaunt.

Good news from the desert.

Saturday, 11th Rather blitzy tonight. This afternoon I went to see the other bomb in Lansdowne Crescent – it fell just in front of the house. People were inside, but the house stood. Remarkable. It churned up all the gas mains, and men were hard at work doing repairs.

Guns have been going. Mr Hillyard reports lots of incendiaries. I went up on the roof. A huge fire in the distance. I thought it was the City again, but he said it was nearer Notting H. Gate – just by Kensington Palace. I hope not. Could see volumes of smoke streaming up and a great light filled the sky; but in an hour it had gone.

Sunday, 12th Woke late. Learned the big fire last night was in Church St. It was the Rowley Galleries – all burnt out. Great pots of paint and varnish on the top floor – went up like fun! Ran along to see it – the nicest shop in Church St. Remains of beautiful furniture and pictures all in the street.

In the afternoon Ivy and I took Miss Moyes in the Invalid chair. When I think of all the Tan Sad chairs she has provided for other people – and then when she needs one herself there is not one in the place. Most aggravating. Anyway, we were a funny procession – no springs and three wheels. She had to get out every time we crossed a road. We took her a tour of the bombs she had not seen. The moveable sides of the wretched thing kept coming unscrewed with the vibration. She saw the fire and enjoyed the outing, though my heart failed once or twice on the way back.

Tuesday, 14th Met Mrs Horton Smith. Her flat is near the fire. They felt the heat of it, and had to stand with suitcases and coats in case of evacuation. She said Mr Rowley was negligent and the police were very angry. He lived at Richmond and no one had the key. The wardens had to borrow an axe to smash the plate glass windows. There was not a bucket of sand or water in the place! The timber yard behind caught fire and burnt out. Sir John Ellerman's house near Kensington Palace was on fire; but there were people there to deal with it.

In fact showers of incendiaries fell on Notting Hill and Bayswater Road. Wardens had to run in all directions at once. The shop owners did not leave until late at night when the attack was over. Fires all along Bayswater Road.

They went last night to Plymouth. I liked what Miss Wilkinson said to the American people: That though we felt we still had to suffer much – deep in the subconscious mind of the tribe, we felt the tide had turned.

I understand the Mayor of Kensington was wild with the man of Rowley's Gallery because it was lighting up the whole of Kensington – if they had chosen to come back and bomb us.

We seem to have had a victory in the Mediterranean.

Thursday, 16th No warnings until late last night. I did not think it was anything, but we hear from our people at Lambeth that a bomb fell on some workmen's flats near Lambeth North Tube station.

The bomb which fell on the subway of the Bank Underground the other Saturday night was a terrible affair. It is said the blast blew many people on to the live rails, and they were electrocuted immediately. This was from an eye-witness. He also saw two children blown under an approaching train, and a Jew crawl under and rescue them! At the peril of his life.

Saturday, 18th We have snow. Been blowing a blizzard today. The poor people who have no windows must feel the cold terribly. Mrs Johnson [hostess of our own Night Shelter in Lambeth] was telling me what they felt like last Saturday night when the blast struck the place. They crouched on the floor, and could hear bricks hurtling through the air and bunging up the doorway. However, the wood partition that had been made for the front door black-out saved them from injury. The blast lasted two minutes, but it felt like two hours! They are still digging the poor men out from the flats.

It seems we are enjoying a little respite now, so that we may be prepared for the spring. About March, it seems, the Americans think the assault will come. If they think of lending us some of their Navy things must be pretty grim. I don't like the look of it. We have got to put up with a lot more bombing of our towns, Mr Churchill says. As soon as the weather improves, I suppose, those horrible all-night raids will start again.

I was talking with Mr Murray, the cobbler. He is quite a character in his way and well worth talking to. I was saying that he might invade us from Ireland – and had we guns at Liverpool and Bristol? Mr Murray thought it would be just as difficult on that side, and that if Hitler had failed in the autumn when we were not ready, there was no question of his succeeding when we were more prepared. However, he also thought we were in for another two years of war.

Have just read *The Kaiser and his English Relations* by Benson. Most interesting. Strangely enough once when he visited England to be friendly and all that, he met Joseph Chamberlain, who was most struck with these expressions of friendliness. He made a speech later expressing the opinion that 'England and Germany were natural allies; that every cause of difference had been eliminated and that the way was clear for an Anglo-American-Teutonic Entente.' Strange how history repeats itself. Joseph and Neville both being deceived in the Germans. Lord Salisbury took a much less optimistic view of the Emperor's protestations. He knew him.

Sunday, 19th Walked up last night in the snow about 10 p.m. Lights kept flashing in the sky. Strange how at one time the Warning made my heart beat faster. Now it affects me no more than a dinner gong! This extra fire-watching may cause Mr Hillyard to stay in the City sometimes, but as he has only one arm they may let him off. I do mine here. Tonight there is really only me able to do anything in this great big house until nearly 11 p.m. as Miss M. and Mrs Hoare will not return from the meeting until very late. However, there is a stirrup pump and many buckets of sand and water, and rakes and long shovels. I shall just stand at the front door and shout for help if necessary.

News seems very ominous still – perhaps I have been a little too optimistic. As soon as spring comes Hitler is to make a tiger spring at us. But what form it will take no one quite knows. That victory in the Mediterranean was not a victory at all – they sank one of our cruisers and damaged two others. Not so good.

Barishnikov took Mrs Fisher and me to the Brasserie for lunch. We had half a bottle of sauterne, and drank to our final victory. I have not done anything so adventurous since the blitz began in September.

Rather slushy in the Park as we walked back, but there was a breath of spring in the air.

Monday, 20th Stayed up until party returned at 12.30 last night. They brought with them a woman whom they had met in the train. She was on her way to St Albans from Durham to see her son, who is ill with pneumonia. The train was three and a half hours late – and she would have been stranded. We put her by the office fire, and I made them cocoa. The woman was full of gratitude. Mr Hillyard to take her to St Pancras this morning. She got scared of our big house in the night and eventually slept in a chair by Miss M.'s fire. I got to bed at 1.30 a.m.

Had trouble with the wardens last night. Someone had left their gas fire full on with no black-out, and light was streaming down the Drive!

Tuesday, 21st Three Warnings and an explosion or two. We are advancing on Tobruk. They have met at Berchtesgaden – I don't know what that portends for us. So glad General Wavell is getting on before the full German onslaught begins.

Thursday, 23rd No warnings. I wonder what it all means. Meanwhile we drink in the victories in N. Africa, and since we are rather parched in that direction it is all very agreeable.

Weather has been milder, and the Pioneers are getting on with clearing up the debris. The City now has gas again, and is beginning to pick up. Our Accountant was in today discussing a fresh start for all the books. Twenty years of work has perished. He was carrying all his office today in a black bag. Did not dare to leave it anywhere.

Saturday, 25th What does all this peace and quietness forebode? I wonder! We are beginning to forget what an air raid is. Weather has been dreary. But snow has gone. I am less tired, for which I am truly thankful. I hope to build up a bit in case we have any more shocks to meet. News from Africa is very heartening. So glad the Italians are copping it at last – for their audacity.

Nice letter from Dr Remy in Canada. He remarks about my not wanting ever to visit Germany that he certainly does not! He adds – it was his misfortune to be born there – that is all!

Tuesday, 28th Today we have had so many warnings that we have lost count. A good deal of gunfire and planes over us. Here they were very high, but low over the City. It is now night – rain is pouring down and has been for hours and hours. I don't know what they are up to. Sandbags are reposing on most doorways all over London.

We like Mr Wendell Wilkie amongst us. I must not forget to record that a rabbit was found running round and round Piccadilly Circus! It was discovered to be a Regimental Mascot, and was restored to its regiment.

The news tonight that General Metaxas has died fills me with dismay. He organized the Greeks to victory and there may be no one to take his place. My bulbs have nice long stems now, and I can see the little buds in the sheath. No oranges to be had. I do miss them. They are the one fruit I can afford, and they are unobtainable.

Friday, 31st Yesterday there was much going on above us and gunfire. Mrs Starmer came back full of news of incendiaries in the City at Moorgate. The people rose out of the ground in droves to put them out! Everybody was laughing at the fun. She said it was like a football match and all enjoyed themselves. Fortunately no high explosives came down as well – else it would not have been so funny.

Mr Johnson brought news from Lambeth that about 11 a.m. a terrific shock struck our Shelter. He found a bomb had fallen opposite the Lambeth Baths – some shops were down.

I hear that bombs fell on Middlesex Hospital and Dean St in the middle of the day. According to rumour – doctors and nurses killed. I don't know. It seems that people in Oxford St had to throw themselves on the pavement when the stick fell on Middlesex St . . . A lady in the Mercury café told me she was having lunch in Oxford St. Suddenly a terrific wonk shook the place; all the cups and saucers danced and rattled about on the table. The man opposite her said calmly: 'That was a bomb, wasn't it ?' She replied: 'I'm sure it was.' And they all continued to eat their meal.

End of January 1941

FEBRUARY 1941

ᘙᘙᘙᘗ ✿ ᘗᘗᘗᘗ

Saturday, 1st Found my landlady very cast down because the Wardens had made a grand schemozzle over the lights. The lady in the room below me went out and in broad daylight left her light on. It was still on after Black-out, so the Ladbroke Road police came across, and Mrs Gray found them wandering round the house!

There is an unholy stillness in the air tonight.

Monday, 3rd No raids of any sort. But the grocer tells me their head office in Hampstead caught a bomb pretty badly last Friday afternoon. A P.O. and an oil shop and warehouse were destroyed. A Mother and daughter in the P.O., all the people in the oil shop and several in the warehouse were killed. This was at 2.30 p.m. I thought it sounded blitzy when I went to the post. A time bomb went off this morning in Goldhawk Rd, Shepherd's Bush.

Wednesday, 5th Warning on Monday night – up at the café they said incendiaries had been dropped in Ladbroke Square and Kensington Park Rd.

Tonight the news from North Africa is still good.

Thursday, 6th No raids all day. It was snowing hard when I went up the road last night, but so quietly that I did not realize it until I got outside. Gave the poor mendicant cat on the steps his fish and bread; he retired to some shelter of his own. News from Africa – we are still advancing . . . who would have thought it a few months ago!

Friday, 7th Fall of Benghazi! Really it is splendid. Who would have thought we should have pulled up so well! Mussolini must be gnawing his best tunic with rage. It seems like the march of a forest fire – so swift. Poor Italians!

No raids today. Snow nearly gone. We have a second stirrup pump in the house now. We are agitating for the key of no. 5. This is empty and locked up and if it burned it might involve us, so we have written the owners.

My daffodils have grown very high. We are watching them with great agitation in case they forget to bloom.

The last time I concentrated on Madame Tabouis in the *Despatch* she seemed to say the Spaniards would come in against us, and that the situation in the Mediterranean would deteriorate. Just the opposite seems to have happened. I cannot understand this Colonel Williams in U.S.A. saying he thinks Britain will not win. Of course, we are only fighting the Italians in N. Africa – but we are sharpening our swords. I like the sound of the U.S.A. Ambassador, and I am glad he is not a great talker.

Sunday, 9th Bought a pound of apples yesterday for one shilling . . . what a price. No oranges at all, at all. Very annoying.

Quiet morning with the *Observer*. Apparently the full blast will be on us at Easter. I am full of optimism – don't know if it is ill-placed. But I do not feel we can ever have the blitz quite so badly on London as last autumn. Nor do I think the invasion will stand much chance. We have bombarded Genoa, and are tearing beyond Benghazi. I am just trying to imagine the demoralized Italians scurrying along the coastal road, hoping to reach Tripoli. The R.A.F. and everybody else on their heels. It does not seem they will get there.

The P.M. speaks tonight. God bless him!

Monday, 10th No raid all day. Just heard it is said 80,000 businesses were destroyed in the City on the night of the fire. Mr Hillyard says they have cleared a great deal of débris now and you can see the ruins – walls standing with nothing inside. Everyone in London wants a typewriter – 50,000 were burned that night. The oldest models are brought out again and used – especially legal ones.

I can see the danger to French Tunis now. They fear Goering's parachutists. Perhaps Wavell is sweeping on to try and be in a position to help Tunis. It looks as if he will get to Tripoli. The British minister leaves Rumania. So it looks as if it is occupied by the Nazis. I hope they do not fall on the poor Greeks. I fear they will be swept right back if the Germans march through Yugo-Slavia and Bulgaria. We shall see . . . we shall see.

Tuesday, 11th No raids all day. Mr Churchill's speech has rather sobered me. I was beginning to be a little optimistic. I even began to think there might be no Invasion . . . but he thinks there will, it seems. Also I had a feeling the end might be soon in sight; but he seems to be looking a few years ahead! So I don't know what is going to happen to us. We seem to be waiting – waiting, for we know not what.

I like Rulers of States who exchange lines of poetry.*

Wednesday, 12th I liked the story in the *Telegraph* yesterday that a young British officer in Egypt was awakened in the middle of the night because one hundred Italians wanted to surrender. Being annoyed at this disturbance of his sleep he is reported to have answered: 'Tell them they can't. The battle does not begin until tomorrow. They must come again.'

Thursday, 13th One alarm tonight – window rattled badly – like a landmine in the distance . . . but it may not have been.

Have just finished some recollections of Kipling called *Something of Myself*. I am horrified at his sufferings as a child. When not with the Burne-Jones family he was boarded out with some terrible people . . . and he never complained.

* Wendell Wilkie brought a letter to Churchill from President Roosevelt. In it were some lines from Longfellow's 'Building of the Ship'. They ran:

> 'Sail on, O ship of State!
> Sail on, O Union, strong and great!
> Humanity with all its fears,
> With all the hopes of future years
> Is hanging breathless on thy fate.'

Churchill's comment on this letter: 'These splendid lines were an inspiration.'

Now I am about to read Mrs Roosevelt's autobiography. Apparently she was a very shy child, and everyone said she would never draw attention anywhere!

Friday, 14th, St Valentine's Day A certain weariness of the spirit seems to assail me. The News is pretty bad. I was very alarmed when I read the paper this morning to find that Australia was likely to be attacked.

There has been a blitz this evening, and because I wanted some fresh air I have been standing on the step watching the light from the guns. When I heard a plane zooming very near I hopped inside – and the little cat with me.

Saturday, 15th Heard the news of Thursday night's damage today in the Mercury. I could not understand why one bomb should cause such a considerable amount of damage. A lady explained to me that her son was on Hendon aerodrome with two W.R.A.F.s, and they saw the thing come down. It is a new kind of bomb. Had a flare attached to it. It fell on High St before the Warning. People were out and so did not stand a chance. It destroyed five streets of houses and spread damage for three miles – so the lady said. Many killed and injured and made homeless. It was a working class district of Hendon. The three young people on the roof found themselves tied in knots, and did not know if they were dead or alive.

Last night bombs on Wembley. Slipped over to Barkers. Lovely to see the shops. Bought some lingerie material – the kind free of tax. Walked back through the Park. Army lorries and tins of sand all along. But the Round Pond is still round, and ducks and gulls were basking in the first sunshine of the year. Have not found the snowdrops yet, but I believe they are out near Peter Pan.

Dr Remy sent me news of his release and said he was returning to England. This is good – for I have missed him. I think he, too, will be glad to be among friends again.

Am just longing for some fruit. I went out with the firm determination to pay one shilling per pound for apples, but to my horror there was not one in any shop in N.H. Gate at any price whatever. The windows seemed full of turnips.

News yesterday not good. Australia involved perhaps – it made one's heart stand still. Every morning I expect to hear the Germans have invaded the Balkans – it all points to the poor Greeks getting it in the rear.

Had some of Auntie Nell's nice jam for tea. It did taste of fruit. Ran into a tall thin lady from Auntie's flats. She is most amusing about her fire-watching. She had been doing so much night patrol that the night the Oil Bomb actually fell – she was asleep. She leapt up and saw the flames five feet high in the street . . . and the wardens dealing with it. She shouted to the other elderly ladies and they replied they were all right. The night the bomb fell on Archer St she was in a corridor, and she declares she saw the two walls of the corridor almost meet – and then the house right itself. The one on Lansdowne Road three weeks ago made her bed leap in the air and the floor heave up!

Sunday, 16th Slept soundly. Felt lazy. Was doing my bits and pieces when I heard a plane zooming low over the house. Tore to the window and the policeman opposite was looking up into the sky – then the Warning went. Barishnikov told me he was at N.H. Gate and he saw it quite clearly – had never seen one so low. Fortunately they dropped nothing and either went or were chased off.

Mrs Fisher and I went into the Park and found the snowdrops. They were under the trees and round Peter Pan. An agreeable day for early Spring – soon the trees will be in bud. We found what we thought was a gun emplacement – though no gun visible. The policeman beamed at us and said it was his Little Grey Home in the West.

Mr Bendall informed me that the Tower Bastion which was smashed was the home of one of the Beefeaters. He was killed, but his daughter in the same room was unharmed.

Mrs Gray was so sorry for me when she heard that I was longing for an apple that she sent me up a Bramley which I ate with relish. Mr Booker was saying that though he hates onions, when once more we can get them he will sit down and really enjoy one. I think we shall go in for onion binges when the war is over.

Monday, 17th They are here tonight. We can hear Jerry zooming about all the time. The parashots seem to have done well in Southern Italy. I often wonder what happened to my friends there; Major de Bernardi, his wife and the Falorsi family. I hope Signora Falorsi died years before all this happened. The Plane is getting very near and our guns are cracking out. I fear it is a big raid.

Tuesday, 18th Last night it was rough in some parts. I heard Westminster mentioned, but no details. Also Willesden and Kilburn.

We had Gas Mask drill in the office. Mr Johnson and Barishnikov did a good bit of larking about in theirs, but I could only sit tight – it was all I could do to breathe but they are not so bad.

Wednesday, 19th The *Observer*'s comment on the Invasion . . . 'It is like a blind man in a dark room looking for a black hat that is not there.' It seems about that.

Learned at the Café that the damage to Hendon was result of a land-mine. The parachute failed to open and it dropped like a stone – and the authorities thought it was a new type of bomb . . . 104 people killed that night – in addition to wounded and homeless. The Shelter business in Westminster seems to have been bad on Monday night. Or perhaps it was Tooley St.

We have the right to go now over no. 5, the empty house next door. So my fire-watching on Saturday night will have to be extensive – if there is a blitz. The house is nearly as large as this.

Had gas-mask drill again. I tried going upstairs with it on. Did not like it much – no breath, but it could be done. We were glad of cups of tea afterwards. The Printing Works manager came up and lent us some anti-dim and gave us a few hints.

It seems if cheese is rationed we shall be entitled to about a one inch cube per week, per person. It is quite unobtainable here at the moment. I fear we are going to be short of many things before next Winter is out.

Mrs Hoare has found a Whistle among her treasures. It is now hanging in the office. If incendiaries fall on the house you just blow for all you are worth and fire fighters will start out of the earth to aid you! Seems a sound idea. Some incendiaries fell half an hour ago on Ladbroke Grove. We are getting quite neighbourly in this part of Lansdowne Rd now. We tried the whistle in the office – the cat streaked under one of the desks. To have the blitz on his own hearth was too much – and gas masks too.

They've gone all good and quiet outside now.

Thursday, 20th   Good bit of damage last night. I hear Fulham Hospital was hit – for the third time. The terrible disaster which took place in Kennington Park at the beginning of the blitz happened like this. Numbers of people were sheltering in the Trench Shelters there – they flooded with water – the earth fell in and the people were drowned and buried. It is said they never got everyone out – and now they have concreted it up. Dreadful to think of.

Proper Gas practice today. Our works manager suddenly appeared up the back staircase and shouted Gas! We had to scramble into our masks. Barishnikov was first with 15 seconds. I second in 16. Much fun out of it.

Good news from Singapore. Lovely to feel we have regained our ancient push and are not just elbowed out of everywhere as under the Chamberlain régime. Concerning our Fire Whistle Mr Hillyard looked at it and remarked: 'Another nail in Hitler's coffin!'

Saturday, 22nd Managed to get a few eating apples yesterday to my great joy. I treated myself – they are one shilling and one penny per pound. I carried them home as if they were the Crown Jewels. Also had some luck over cheese. Went for my bacon ration and while he was cutting it had a word with the man about the Cubic Inch of Cheese. He got rid of the other customers and then whispered, 'Wait a mo'.' I found half a pound of cheese being thrust into my bag with great secrecy and speed!

Then going to the Dairy for my butter ration I was given four eggs and a quarter of cheese! Had no compunction in taking it, for I went straight to my Mercury Café and gave it to them . . . they had said they did not think they could open the next day as they had no meat and only a morsel of cheese. I could not resist, when I got in, cutting off a hunk of my piece and eating it then and there. I always sympathized with Ben Gunn when he dreamed of toasted cheese on that desert island.

Heard the blitz in the far far distance last night as I went up the road. But it seems Swansea has had three nights of it in succession, poor things.

Sunday, 23rd No blitz, so my fire-watching was easy last night. These blissful Sunday mornings! There is nothing like them. I must record the description in the House of Lords the other day of the Civil Service: 'A seething mass of gentlemen of leisure . . .' Not true, but rather delicious.

In the *Daily Telegraph* they say Coventry Cathedral would have been saved if there had been more help. The clergy risked their lives to try and save it. The walls have to come down.

Went in the Park with Mrs F. Many people about. Sun shining and to our joy we found dozens of golden crocuses out. So pretty among the snowdrops. The seagulls were there in dozens round the fountains. Walked along the Long Water, and then to the Albert Memorial. Not perceptibly damaged. We could well have spared it and kept Guildhall and All Hallows. Along the Flowery walk there was nothing, of course, now, but at the Children's Playground we found it full of Maltese and Gibraltar children enjoying themselves. They live in those luxury flats near Lancaster Gate and sleep in the Tube station at night. I believe it is a babel of foreign tongues.

Listened to Mr Menzies – full and rich voice – the accent quite pleasant. I liked the impressive way he said we were not to think we were alone. I understand Lord Haw-Haw's father has died of a broken heart. I am not surprised. All quiet so far tonight.

Monday, 24th I was speaking to a woman in the Mercury today who had been buried for eight hours. She was living at Lancaster Gate and had just got into bed on the 2nd floor when the bomb fell in the middle of the road . . . she saw the window simply cave in and felt herself shot out of bed on to the floor. She lay beneath the other floors – how many I know not – for eight hours . . . conscious all the time. She could hear people getting to her. What saved her was a big radiogram which fell across and prevented all the stuff burying her. They gave her morphia. She seems to have recovered, but felt cold all over when she heard a plane overhead. What an awful experience!

Asked Mr Murray, the shoemaker, what he thought of Mussolini's speech. He is rather good at polishing off the Italians. He thought the best part of the speech was where Mussolini informed the U.S.A. that they had nothing to fear from Italy! He said he just hugged himself over this.

Very bad job about Swansea. Mr Bendall's family have moved to Tenby. They had a time-bomb near their home. Miss Cameron heard from her people there that if they had had a fourth night – they could not have coped with it. There was not enough water to fight the flames, and they had to let the houses burn. I can imagine this . . . if a bomb hit the water-main outside us, and incendiaries were burning, we could do nothing.

Italians seem to be scurrying up from Calabria after those parachutists landed. They thought hundreds more were coming, I expect, to march on Rome. The Turks seem to be standing by us. I do hope so.

Gas-mask drill today. I did it in nine seconds. I understand they are having a street one in Pimlico.

Wednesday, 26th Warning early tonight. Stationary flares in the sky. We are responsible for Tuesday night. Night is divided into four shifts; you change it each Tuesday. You are on for two hours – then you phone the next squad. Not so good when your shift is 2 a.m. to 4 a.m. We are all getting alarm clocks. Very difficult to obtain – and they cost £1.

Received a nice box of apples from the aunts at Brede. Ate one during the lunch hour and an important visitor caught me – so I explained my longing for an apple.

We seem to be advancing in the Somalilands. Much interested in the Graziani news. What a row there must have been in Rome. I wonder the Duce did not go to Libya and lead the armies in person! He cannot have any Generals left – they have all been sacked.

Thursday, 27th Heard a land-mine had dropped on East Ham last night. Must have done much damage. More news of Swansea. His sister had written Mr Bendall. On those three awful nights the houses in their road went down one by one . . . out of 32 sixteen were bombed. At last they just sat on the cellar steps waiting for the end. Their Mother is eighty. Her three daughters and the housekeeper were with her. The house next door was alight and the firemen were struggling with it. Nowhere to go for safety! The next morning one daughter set out for the garage to find the car – a policeman stopped her and said there were three time-bombs round about. She went some back way – garage door jammed – she climbed on the roof and got in somehow. Got the car out, put all the family in it – and drove past the Time Bombs! What an experience!

I think Swansea must be worse than Coventry. They have no drinking water. All dreadful – and it is a foretaste of the Spring and Summer for us. However the African successes seem to be going on – and that is something.

End of February 1941.

Saturday, 1st Too tired to write Diary last night. Better today. Set off up the road last night, and that awful howl began. It felt like a violent internal pain which rose and fell – but inexorable. I knew it would rise again and again before it died away. It has not gone through me like that for a long time. Last Monday, I was told that fourteen bombs fell on Peckham in four minutes. Only small ones – but to anyone listening to those Swishes – I know just what it means. Peckham is the second worst district for bombing. Presumably the worst is Dockland. The woman who described it to me said the shops had no one to sell to – everyone had gone.

Went to see *The Dictator* today. How I enjoyed it! Superb satire! For all its tomfoolery written with a profundity of serious purpose. The speeches of Hynkel, half-German, half-English are there. People who understood German were even more convulsed than I was. How Dr Remy would enjoy it . . . and Aunt Emy too. The palace scenes, where Hynkel did not waste a moment, were all in the spirit of German thoroughness. But Mussolini in real life does not smile so much. All done by an East End Jew! How Hitler would writhe if he could see us laughing at him – and the Italians would flash with fury.

Last speech was good, but Chaplin has not the magnetic elocution that Charles Laughton had for that kind of appeal.

Sunday, 2nd   Up the road last night just as a Second Warning went. Could hear the German plane zooming very near over my head, and the road seemed very long. Great flashes filled the sky – the guns boomed out . . . I knew the shrapnel would begin to fall, so hastened my steps and fell up the little flight of steps to the front door. Once in the porch I watched in case incendiaries fell – and I must run back to Sanctuary. Guns again and again, then ping, ping – down came the shrapnel.

A nice restful Sunday. Took Mrs Ellis of Chichester into Kensington Gardens. She had not been to London for thirty years – and remembered it last with horse buses! Her son is a pilot in R.A.F., so felt it my duty to look after her for the sake of what he was doing for us.

Tuesday, 4th   Slow inexorable tramp of events in the Balkans. So like last year . . . as the Winter draws to a close moving on to the time when Kings Go Forth to War. Only the day of kings is done – and we have something worse. Cardiff got the blitz. Seems they are going for the ports now. Fed the poor mendicant cat on the step. A pity he does not settle down – cats are in great demand in London now, since so many were killed off and mice are getting a nuisance.

Thursday, 6th   We packed the paper this morning. P.O. came in person to ask us. Much better – not such a scramble as in the afternoon.

Mr Hillyard could neither sleep before nor after his fire-watching. I want to do it next week, as with only one arm it is difficult for him to dress quickly. He says, 'Certainly not,' to me. We shall see. The blitz ended before 11 p.m. but our fire-watch goes on. It saved Cardiff. No blitz tonight. Lots of stray cats – we seem like a monastery gate where the beggars congregate.

The Americans seem rather slow. Blow them! I hear the news to the Italians now. The speaker concluded with an impassioned appeal to them, telling them the British had never hated them and never would. Quoted a speech of Mussolini in 1926 about the traditional friendship with Britain. A man from Genoa spoke of how industry had been ruined there by the war – which was all Mussolini's fault. The Germans are massing on the frontiers. Only a day or two it seems before the Balkan cauldron will boil over.

Friday, 7th Raider brought down off the Norfolk coast on its return from London. Good job, too! Dr Remy came over with the last Canadian troops. May go to see him in Cambridge in a week or two, if there is no invasion, and I can dodge the fire-watching for a bit.

Wish there were some apples somewhere and that I could get at them! But we shall have to go without more than apples, methinks, before next Winter is over. The poor mendicant cat was taken away today. I made him comfortable last night with bread and milk and a nice bed in the wood cellar. When I peeped at him about 10.30 p.m. he was cosy and asleep. Now there are two more on the step!

Saturday, 8th   No blitz last night. Delightful story on News of the smiling faces of the Italians surrendering – beautiful teeth all shining!

Was introduced to the Marmalade cat taken in at the Mercury. He has been bombed out of somewhere, and looked it, poor mite. He seems unable to miaow – just opens his mouth and no sound comes. In my room from time to time I have heard a mysterious cooing sound – could not understand it. Now I find it is a pigeon on my chimney pot – such a pleasant sound.

Went to see Mabel Lucy in her new quarters. Near Archer St where quite 20 shops are out of action. Her house seems short of windows. She has two good-sized rooms and a kitchen – plenty of sun. She has ceased to worry over the blitz . . . does not think it can ever be as bad as last Autumn. We talked of Florence and all the Tedeschi prancing about; of our little café in the Duomo Square and its wonderful omelettes, and the dear little waiter, and how I smoked there my first cigarette in public!

I am at the Sanctuary on fire-watch. If there is no blitz I shall go back to my own room. Firemen came today to inspect our top rooms. They commented on the vast amount of inflammable material in them. It was at our own risk. There are plenty of fire-escapes. Seems nowhere else to keep the stuff . . .

Sunday, 9th   It is curious how one can be misled into a sense of security. Miss Rowe, one of the resident community, looked in at the office last night saying: 'I think I shall just go up the road to the cinema for an hour. We shall be out before nine – if you can wait. But I will not go if the Old Lady is to be left alone.' I replied airily: 'Oh, yes, do go. I shall wait. Besides I don't think there will be any blitz. They are too busy in the Balkans.' I settled down peaceably to some sewing, put the cat out and – just before 8 p.m. the Warning went. It developed into one of the most fearful raids we have had. For two hours the Racket never ceased. Planes roaring overhead – guns thundering out – glass breaking – bombs screaming through the air.

The Old Lady, aged 80, put her head round the door and asked if anyone was in. I begged her to join me. She said she would if it got bad. About ten minutes later a stick of bombs dropped almost on the house, I dived under the desk, expecting the walls to cave in. It sounded as if tons and tons of heavy stones were dropping on the roof. A landmine, was my thought, which must have taken off the top of the house. One ceases to function in those awful seconds. In reality there were six bombs. I heard flying feet down the stairs. I rushed to the door to catch the Old Lady. She almost tumbled into the room . . . shaking all over, as I was too. She is so tiny – like a Jenny Wren. I don't believe her feet had touched the stairs. She just flew through the air down two flights of stairs, and announced that the whole house was filled with smoke!

I gave her some brandy. I was shaking so much I could hardly pour it out – so I conceived the remarkable idea of having a little myself. This calmed me down. Then from under the desk out came the little cat, whom I had previously let in. He was just warming his paws before the warm hearth when the bombs fell and he streaked under the desk beside me.

So we passed the next two hours laughing at ourselves and the cat. The Old Lady and I dived under the desk hand in hand. The little creature was there also, looking at us and saying clearly: 'What you do, I do. When you go under, I go under.' He looked most comical – his toes tucked up on the mat. Once we heard a terrible whirring sound – and we grabbed one another and dived. It was only the clock making up its mind to strike 9 o'clock!

I did not count the bombs we heard. They screamed in the distance. From time to time I ran up on the roof as we heard the Fire Engines go by. A big fire Hammersmith way. The moon was gloriously clear and bright – an ideal night for them. At 10 p.m. it died down a bit, and Miss Rowe returned. She was just returning down the hill, and had reached the Flower Shop, when the bombs fell. One behind them. I know how awful she and her friend must have felt. They cowered in a doorway, clinging to one another and a strange woman with them. They could not tell if they were being transported to the Next World or not! A warden came and hurried them into the Coronet Shelter. Poor Miss Rowe was worried to death about the Old Lady and me – imagining me coping with incendiaries all by myself!

They had had a very narrow escape, for the Blast took the length of Holland Park Avenue. Dozens of shops with glass entirely smashed – and if they had been opposite one when the glass blew out . . . well . . .

No All Clear. By midnight I was tired, but could not leave.

Made myself a bed on the chesterfield in the drawing-room. The Old Lady went upstairs. Then Pussy came padding round and plonk, jumped straight beside me . . . and settled down on my feet and ankles. I lay like a mediaeval statue on a tombstone. I dozed a bit, but got cold, so at 3 a.m. I decided, as all was quiet, to go home. The police man at the Station flashed his lantern across at me suspiciously. Got into bed at 4 a.m. hugging my hot-water bottle – very thankful I had not been bombed out.

This morning I sallied forth to inspect. Behind the Coronet, in the little streets, two bombs had fallen. Mercifully one family had gone to see their Mother just before. All windows gone. A bomb fell on the Corner Restaurant right through the flats on top. One man killed, and also a Warden from the Campden Hill Post – another seriously injured. At the Mercury I learned of bombs on Chepstow Crescent. Mr Booker had helped to dig people out. Went along to see – it was bad. Three large houses down. He is not a warden now, but he could not rest, so joined the Rescue Squad. After getting out two people it was thought there was no one else. But he said he was going back to make sure. The others joined him. After a few minutes they heard tapping – three had fallen with the house – one a customer from the Mercury!

Went a walk in the Park to see the lovely crocuses. Barishnikov came to tea and told us his adventures. He was at his Firewatching H.Q. when the Blast swept the Avenue, turned his corner, caught the shop and split the glass – it just missed him.

At the Café de Paris in Leicester Square there were 500 people last night. A bomb fell straight on it. Here we are tonight. Blitz has begun – so far not so bad as last night. I pray it will not be.

Tuesday, 11th   Out early in Notting Hill this morning a little girl stopped me. She asked me to take her across the road, which I did. I enquired where she was going. It appeared to school – but had never been alone before. She did not know if it was this way – or, pointing in the opposite direction, the other. Here was a conundrum. She was about seven, the dearest little thing. It was her birthday, she said, and she was to have a party, and she had received five picture postcards. The School was called The Fox School, she explained. We went hand in hand to the ironmonger and consulted him. Yes, it was in Kensington Place and was probably bombed. With this information we set off for Church St. There we met a police-man and told him the story. He looked at me and I at him . . . we both had the same thoughts. She cheerfully set off hand in hand with him, doubtless explaining in fuller detail her birthday and why Mother was not able to take her to school as usual . . . I have never forgotten her.

At the Mercury arrived the Doctor's secretary whom Mr Booker had helped to dig out. We were amazed to see her. She said she still felt awful, but described to us her sensations as the first two bombs came down and knew in her bones that the third would strike her home. She had the presence of mind to turn off the gas. She was in a basement and it dropped in the garden. When she came to she found herself a prisoner. She could see a window, but both doors were jammed. She shouted for help, and a woman came out of the Mews near, and called all right. Then the wardens broke the windows and dragged her out. The others were buried deeper and it took some hours to release them. This woman was cold and I brought her down to the Sanctuary, found her a nice coat, suit and dress. We had no suitable underclothing, but I know others would help. She had a talk with Miss M. and went away much cheered.

It is considered a landmine exploded in the air over Holland Park on that awful night. That is why I thought the roof was off, and accounts for the terrible roaring. It is the only theory that accounts for the blast breaking so many windows in Shepherds Bush. Indeed we had a lucky escape.

Wednesday, 12th Miss Linde has taken refuge here with her two dogs! There were 38 bombs on Kensington last Saturday night, she says, during two hours . . . in addition to the landmine. No wonder we were kept diving under the table. Mr Major, head Warden on Campden Hill, is very badly injured. He fell into a bomb crater, broke his arm and is paralyzed from the waist. Saw the secretary again. She has worked twenty years for the same doctor, and mercifully had put all his records in the refrigerator. Hopes they are safe. She looked as if shock was beginning to tell.

Walked along to Kensington Place. It is a mess. All the little houses have been struck in one way or another. Kit Sauvary had lunch at the Mercury with me. They are nursing a casualty from Church St. They had terrible cases from Hendon. One man lay there for five days before he was claimed – he died eventually.

Miss Jones [a part-time worker] attended an investiture yesterday at Buckingham Palace. Her sister is a big swell, being Matron-in-chief of the British Army. She had an award in the New Year's honours. The Palace had been bombed again on Saturday, and they were dealing with the debris. Scarcely a window left. The King in Air Force uniform. He spoke to everyone. The Queen not there.

Sunday, 16th No raids yesterday. Nice restful morning. Listened to a bit of Roosevelt. Took Chow for a walk in the Park. The crocuses are a carpet of gold, purple and white, and all the daffodils are in bud. The sun shone and it was perfectly lovely. Not a breath of wind. Chow is aged 13 and decided she had had enough.

Admiral Muselier, I think it was, on the French News gave it Darlan hot and strong. Could not get it all, but there was no mistaking he was in a tearing rage with Vichy. Just read Roosevelt's speech . . . jolly good. He is a great man, but not so great as Churchill – though if he had to face the same thing, he might be. His speeches are wonderfully heartening to us – but they lack the touch of magic Mr Churchill gives.

Found some little spring onions at the greengrocer's. Asked if they were a thousand pounds a bunch. But bought them for three onions a penny. Had them for my tea as a sandwich with some nice bread – and some of the extra butter ration in which we are wallowing this week. Miss Linde and dogs have departed. They and our cat had a private blitz at the end. A funny gramophone record this morning, called

The Village A.R.P. They had one tin hat between eleven – and that is what most people have.

Tuesday, 18th How joyful they must be in Berbera. I liked the story of the lieutenant going in a little skiff to find a landing ground, without being observed. Reminded me of taking of Quebec.

The Cat Meat shop is the joy of N.H. Gate. All the old ladies go up to get the favourite 'steak' of their favourite cat. They nearly drive the man crazy suiting all these animals. He sells out every day. Ours was ramping round this morning until, in desperation, Mrs Hoare sent Barishnikov up to buy him one.

No blitz tonight, but the damage to Clydeside and Mersey-side is published. In the Mercury people said it was bad. Clydeside had not had one before, and it was a nasty shock. Bristol, too, has had a bad time. The bad incident at New Southgate made Mr Smithers really ill – he was in the thick of the rescue parties.

Story of Hitler and Goering flying towards England: Hitler seeing flames and devastation thought he was over London and gloated accordingly. Goering put his finger on his lips and whispered: 'Hush, Adolf, it is Bremen.'

Wednesday, 19th Very blitzy tonight. A thundering number of Germans over us at this moment. Windows have been rattling. Poor old Puss has just slipped in and seems mighty glad. Nothing to be seen but the stars – and to hear, but this determined whirring above our heads.

Mr Churchill's speech at the Pilgrim's Dinner stunning as usual. Wonderful to have a man of action who can put our emotions and longings into such deeply moving phrases. He is in the heat of the conflict, and yet he can speak as if he were a hundred years in the future, appraising our conduct. I like the way he faces the worst. I hope we deserve him. I think we do.

Thursday, 20th   Very bad blitz last night, but only guns for us – but they were whoppers. Shook our windows and doors and the vibration ran all round the room. At 11.30 p.m. a lull, so put on my bonnet and ran. Guns seem often to bark out when I am just half way – and the walk seems interminable. I fear I was not made to be a hero.

This morning shrieking headlines of The Big Blitz Back Again. It was East End. Ilford, Stratford, Bromley Gas Works. Pressure very bad. At the Mercury they could hardly cook the dinner. The Remington man came to collect our typewriters, and he had come through the East End. West Ham Hospital hit – just missed The London. But Stratford Broadway, Bow and Bromley were badly hit. Remington factory had lost 9,000 typewriters – not to mention their customers', too.

Blitz has begun again, but, so far, not very loud. We do not know how many miles more they have advanced into Abyssinia. What a day it will be when they enter Addis Ababa!

Mrs Horton Smith gave me a first hand account of the N.H. Gate Bomb attack. Fortunately, she had her little dog in her arms – and she was blown on to the landing. All lights went out – windows were gone, of course. The Wardens called her, and she had to go down just as she was. She nearly fell over the body of the man who was killed at the door, going out to look. The First Aid people were trying to do something for him, but he was dead. They pushed her and the dog across to the Unitarian Church. It was very cold. Miss Linde, meanwhile, was frantically searching for one of her dogs who was lost in the scrimmage and darkness.

Apparently the poor people in Kensington Place had double trouble that awful night. One bomb fell on the Garage and another on the Reservoir. Water came pouring down the street – so they were bombed, homeless and nearly drowned in the dark, with the blitz raging. No wonder several did not survive until morning. This is London in war time . . .

Friday, 21st Quiet night and day. We seem to be pushing on here, there and everywhere. To have sunk a few Italian ships! But I wish they were German.

Had one of Aunt Winnie's apples last night – felt all the better for it. It is good news the Americans are going to send us some food.

[Diary missed for a few days owing to Cambridge visit.]

Monday, 24th With Saturday morning off I launched myself into the West End. At Selfridge's found one floor devoted to war weapons, so felt bound to study these Horrors – went up. There was an immensely long, pointed, wide metal container. This was part – only part – of an aerial torpedo. Did not like the look of it at all. There was a Bren Gun on a motor-cycle – it was a ladylike little creature, and small boys were queueing up to fire it. The Tommy in charge looked a very benign being. There was a Collapsible Dinghy. Seemed immense to me, and looked as if it could ride the waves – but not too big ones. All this I saw and lots more.

Betook myself to Liverpool St. This is the first time I have travelled by Tube since last September. The bunks looked all right – and with something spread over them, you could sleep.

Train was very full, but I was lucky and got a good seat, not being impeded with baggage. Raining hard. I was fortified with sandwiches, apples from Brede, some knitting and a Wilkie Collins novel. All mist and gloom through the window. Lovely to be going out of London for a few hours. Dr Remy met me on the platform at Cambridge, all smiles, and very happy we were to meet again. We reminded each other of two Easters ago when Carola [his wife] came. [She was still in Germany.]

The hotel was The Red Lion in Petty Cury. Very old fashioned and respectable. Mostly officers and their wives. Unpretentious. Streets were crowded with soldiers. Thousands of evacuees there. Army and Air Force in large numbers. In spite of the rain we padded round the colleges. To my surprise I got tired first. Then I saw a notice – *Tobias and the Angel*. He was quite agreeable to go. We had a nice meal at the Friars Restaurant and then to the theatre. I have seen the play twice already, but I love it. Dr Remy enjoyed it too.

It was still raining when we emerged. Dr Remy did not know where he was in the black-out. Wandered about looking for a taxi – not one. I suggested going back to the hotel and asking the porter. Easier said than done. Had it not been for our linking up with other people, also looking for the same hotel, we should never have found it. It had a large stable door closed right up – and I should have imagined only horses inside! This was typically English, Dr Remy remarked: He supposed the door had been there since the days of Queen Anne!

Inside little encouragement. Cashiers packing up. No taxis in Cambridge at 10.45 p.m. Then we remembered Dr Remy should not be out after 10.30! Horrors! He looked really troubled. He dared not stay the night in the hotel, and how to reach that wretched Madingley Road in the dark, he did not know. However, having great faith in porters if properly approached, and leaving on one side the damsels going to bed, I seized a man in buttons and began to explain. Dr Remy, behind me, with the magnificent offer of half a crown forward in his hand, asked if he would go out and find a taxi. All ended happily. The porter sped like the wind, and in five minutes the only taxi on the streets of Cambridge was at the door.

Slept well – but awoke to find it snowing! This depressed me. I longed for my customary cup of tea, and the *Observer*. It has, alas, become a great hardship for me to have to get up without drinking at least two cups of tea. However, with a superhuman effort I did it. My luck was in. All the Sunday papers were spread out. I collared a seat by the fire and prepared for the exceptional luxury of having someone to wait on me. The breakfast was delicious. I ate it all – grapefruit, porridge, halibut, toast and tea.

Dr Remy arrived about 10 a.m. Had reached his lodgings without trouble. In the rain and snow we set forth for King's College Chapel. Have long heard of this lovely place and wished particularly to see it. Windows were boarded up and glass removed. The Choir was on vacation. We sat in the Choir Stalls and loved it. But I want to see it again in its glory . . . we could hear a Sergeant-Major drilling hard outside.

There came a gleam of sunshine and my heart rejoiced. We explored the Chantries and the Library – very cold. Then we walked. How lovely were the crocuses! Sun shone and the puddles began to dry up. Dr Remy continued with his adventures in Canada. Another sumptuous meal at the hotel – soup, sole, cherry pie. I wished to see the Grantchester meadows. We did not get there quite. I took him to a milk bar for a cup of tea. The tea was cold, and to Dr Remy's intense surprise, I sent it back again! It was time for me to go. No blitz in London. A very enjoyable change. He is very charming and sweet-tempered. I know the refugees suffered many humiliations and indignities at the time of their arrest – but it was understandable in the danger of the moment. I enjoyed doing things '*à grand seigneur*'.

Wednesday, 26th Such quiet nights. We do not know what to make of them. The general feeling is that some devilment is being prepared for us. The Doctor's secretary says it is curious what has been saved of his equipment. Some of the most delicate bottles with expensive drugs are intact – things one must always handle with the greatest care! Yet heavy wardrobes have been cracked to bits. She could just see her wireless set protruding out. But it began to rain, which she did not think would improve it.

Thursday, 27th   Such exciting news! Mr Bendall brought word in the afternoon that the young King of Jugo-Slavia has declared for us. That Prince Paul has fled, and the signers of the Treaty are under arrest. Marvellous! Mr Churchill announced it – how pleased he would be to have such good news.

Mr Hillyard says the City has been cleared a lot – but the space vacant is sometimes a quarter of a mile in depth. All round St Paul's it is marvellously clear and you get a wonderful view of it.

Began to clean the filing shelves with a vacuum. Have never used one before. Mrs Hoare and I both had a go. Old Scamp did not approve of our goings on – he seemed to think the Germans had come! He turned and fled in terror – his eyes rounded with amazement. This is the lighter side of London life at the moment.

No blitz again! There's something in the wind.

Friday, 28th   The Nazis have forgotten us. News last night was prodigious. All those victories on one Bulletin! Keren . . . Harar . . . and revolution in Jugo-Slavia . . . the first one of all the Peoples whom we have been expecting to rise against these minorities – and never do. Dr Remy and I had talked about it. I said the British mind was constitutionally unable to understand these overbearing minorities who bossed the majority. We had tried it once with Oliver Cromwell – and never again.

Read Churchill's two speeches right through – just as right as ever. How like him to hug the good news to himself until the end – and then throw it at the people. Those who knew him well suspected he looked more than ordinarily happy. I wonder how he will attempt to settle Europe afterwards – and whether he will be so omniscient about peace as he is about war – and the events leading to war . . .

Cannot understand the Priestley controversy. I am anxious to meet one of those diehards who foam with rage when he speaks, and learn what they don't like about him. He makes you think. You may not always agree with him, but I should not have thought it possible his views could create so much furore. He might be Stalin himself – the fuss that is being made. He seems to be a man of good judgment in most things. Travelled and well-read – but not over intellectual. Gives simple things their right and proper place and keeps to the eternal verities. Besides his voice is full of power, colour and conviction. One does not feel in contact with a little mind.

Letter from Mother today. They are all right – but have no marmalade!

End of March 1941

APRIL 1941

＊＊＊ ✻ ＊＊＊

April, 10–15th, Easter Have been to Brum for Easter. Left early on Thursday. Indulged in a taxi to Paddington, as I cannot carry a heavy case far, struggle with gas masks and pots of marmalade for a marmalade-less family. Found train not too full. Asked the porter if he knew where the Raid was last night. I had a bad feeling it was Brum . . . he thought not. Two damsels got in – they had come over from Euston post haste as no trains were running into New Street. Then I knew there was damage.

At Snow Hill we were aghast to find the platform an awful mess. A bomb had fallen direct on it – the whole place was all churned up. Fortunately not on the line, but they were mending the platform for us to get out. I was met, and heard the story of the big raid. An awful night! Bombs and landmines everywhere. The Great Western Arcade had looked pretty bad before; but now it was a ruin. Had to walk a long way before we could find a bus . . . in fact to end of Broad St . . . as the gas main in Victoria Square had been struck. The flames had reached as high as the top of the Council House. Still burning as we passed. Pressure bad everywhere. Mother was struggling to cook a meal over the sitting-room fire.

Mercifully they missed the Town Hall, the Hall of Memory, the Municipal Bank and the Hospitals. A delayed action bomb in Loveday St and the General Hospital had been evacuated to the Queen Elizabeth. It was a treat to reach the Hagley Rd.

Mother was not too well with no sleep. Sirens went again. Cath had to rush out and report to her Post. I determined to go to bed, as I was not particularly on duty. Guns began and the sky was lousy with Germans. Backwards and forwards they ranged for hours just above me. I dozed. Cath kept coming in and out, getting a snooze and off again. Woke at 8 a.m. She was asleep but not undressed. I set to work on breakfast. It was Good Friday.

We went over to see Elsie – telephone not working. A notice outside the University saying that there were delayed action bombs in the grounds. King Edward's School looked all right. Elsie far from well, but would come over on Monday. Incendiaries in Bristol Rd. Walked back up Edgbaston Park Road – all well. Took bus in Church Rd and were surprised to pass a bomb crater in Highfield Rd – in a front garden. Slept well.

Saturday, we went to town. Considerable damage in shopping centre – about two-thirds had gone. What remains is: New St from Town Hall to Corporation St. But the Dolcis down to the ground . . . the Theatre Royal with a bomb inside – and the Prince of Wales in Broad St. In Corporation St the C & A shop had been burned out; Donne's next door – all glass gone the length of the street. Lewis's and Gray's still stand; but that is about all. Lower end of Martineau St gone, and trams not running. Poor old High St closed. Kunzle's in Union St had gone. Outside a tailor's in Union Passage was a large Union Jack over a broken window: We do not make suits of this material, but it is the finest covering in the world.

Midland Arcade a ruin in all directions. Round to the Bull Ring. Worcester St closed for a delayed action bomb. Many firemen still playing hoses on smoking ruins. St Martin's Church had had a good slice off. We had seen enough. We realized there was plenty more. John Bright St railed off – ruins everywhere. Saw a biff near the Queen's Hospital.

Easter Sunday afternoon Mother, Dr H. and I went over to see Ariel and Cecilia. Found them full of excitement over the landmine in Erdington. It had taken all glass the length of High St and about 50 houses. Many people killed in Goosemoor Lane.

Monday Cath arranged a coffee party. Such preparations were made for it we might have been expecting all the Royal Families of Europe. A lovely fire and plenty of conversation. I was only required to receive guests.

In the afternoon I prepared for my party – perhaps eight more or less. Neville had one day off from his Divisional Warden duties, so he came with Elsie . . . very nice of him. He takes a class of men in Rescue Squad work on a Sunday morning, and is teaching them what parts of a house to take down. Says they were all Crossing Sweepers before the war. He told me two good stories: A certain poor old soul had been well bombed out. When Neville went to see her the roof was off. He climbed over what had been the porch and the hall. The water main had burst somewhere and the place was swimming. But the dear old thing, aged 83, came forward with: 'Oh, good morning, Mr Roberts, do come in.' Neville began – 'I'm so sorry to see you in such trouble, Mrs . . .' The old lady replied mystified – 'What trouble?' Neville waved vaguely round at her ruined home swimming in water. 'Oh, that,' she replied, 'there's plenty worse off. Will you have a cup of tea. I've got the spirit kettle going.'

Neville was left dumb.

Then there was a man who kept a fish and chip shop in the Horse Fair – had had it all his life. He had been bombed out more than once, and always came along to Neville, who deals with such claims. 'You see, Mr Roberts, I must open again somewhere. My customers need their fish.' Last Thursday he came to Neville for the third time, explaining that he was opening in some other street and would Mr Roberts come along and see if the shop was all right. Such a splendid spirit!

Our little cat resembles the Lincoln Imp, and I am not enamoured of him at all. He lifts up his throat and demands from morning to night.

Left home at 8.30 a.m. reached London about 11.30. Very full train. Sirens have just gone.

Wednesday, 16th The air above me, as I write, is just thrumming with Germans. They have come over in dozens tonight. Have heard one big packet drop. It is our night for a Big Raid – guns are biffing away for all they are worth.

In my diary of the last few days I have said nothing about the war, because I did not have time to write. But we are going through dark days and it is difficult to imagine how the tide is going to turn. We are just in need of a miracle to help us. Before me as I write are a few predictions. Since these are in the *Daily Telegraph*, I give them: April 26, Hitler will experience a serious defeat. Italy will seek peace soon. Ceasefire in middle of February, 1942. May 26 also a bad date for Axis.

It is curious how the papers are filled with these prophecies. There seems an unlimited public for them. I suppose it is that in our own minds we can see no way through the wood, but to break it down twig by twig; and so we look to the stars for aid – and hope a miracle can be worked for us. It is amazing how swiftly the whole scene has changed since we had victories every night . . . That poor Belgrade with Germans tramping around the ruins. It is 11.30 p.m. and a salvo of whistlers had just come down – at least six. I was under the table by the last one. The Old Lady is here – but Mr Hillyard does not seem to mind them at all.

I have some primroses on my desk. They look very sweet.

Thursday, 17th Well, last night was a fiendish raid, and no mistake. All night long they thrummed over our heads, and what we heard coming down is more than can be put into words. It was like one of the worst nights of last Autumn, and even then I don't remember hearing the sky so full, incessantly, hour after hour, of bombers zooming overhead.

At 12.30 I asked if I could lie down on the drawing-room couch, as no one else seemed to be using it. The others stayed up all night round the office fire, patrolling the place. I was glad to get away, because as the night wears on the human face becomes less and less attractive, and by 5 a.m. you are prepared to hate your brother man . . . if you have been sitting up all night listening to the bombs coming down. I did doze a little from time to time, but sleep was impossible. I covered my head with the cushions when I thought the windows were coming in. Sometimes I went and looked down the drive, and could see fires in the distance. It grew quieter – but we knew awful damage had been done.

I walked up the road, and saw the sky red with the biggest fire I had ever seen – larger than when the City was on fire. So I judged it nearer – it was like fairyland . . . All through the day news trickled in. Barishnikov saw a land-mine coming slowly down by parachute. Thought it was falling on him direct, but it was in Moscow Rd Bayswater; one fell straight on Kensington Town Hall. It did not go off, however, and was successfully dislodged. Had it done so – St Mary Abbots Church would have gone with it.

Miss Moyes' friend at the *Daily Telegraph* rang up to say she had had to walk from Fleet St at 6 a.m. *Daily Express* had had to evacuate in the middle of the night, as there was a land-mine sitting in front of them. As she walked along Strand and Piccadilly broken glass was being swept up in mounds. From the postman I learned that the Big Fire was from the Great Central Goods Yard in Marylebone Rd; Paddington station also hit.

At lunch time we heard a bomber had been brought down on Campden Hill. So Miss M., despite injured foot, set off with me to find it. It had fallen near what I think is part of Bedford College, and did not injure anyone. One of the Germans, baling out, got caught on a high building in

Kensington, and had to be fetched down. Remains of bomber were being carted away. Mr Bendall came in and said Victoria station and coach place were both hit. He saw a landmine fall near his house and the blast blew him across the room. He looked shaken and upset. Holborn had caught it a bit more. Oxford St is closed . . . What a catalogue . . . bad business.

The Church in Hart St, where Pepys used to worship is badly damaged. Also three theatres in Shaftesbury Avenue. Everywhere . . . Sometimes I think it will end for me like that girl in Liverpool who wrote a diary. The blitz was going well overhead, and she sat writing about it . . . The diary was eventually found – she never was.

Friday, 18th Slept marvellously last night. The papers give fair details of that night. Particularly interesting is the Fight over Our Roof. I am glad I did not fully understand what was going on . . . It would have been no joke to have that bomber come down in our garden, nor to have a Nazi bale out on our doorstep. Barishnikov was lucky to follow it while it was happening, and to hear the machine gun from our plane chasing it!

Saturday, 19th They gave out some of the damage on wireless this morning. All the world knows now that St Paul's has had a big bomb, and is closed to the public. It is on European news too.

I much enjoyed the way the announcer gave out the Government statement that if Athens is bombed so would be Rome. 'This is what Churchill says – and those who don't like it can lump it.' I think it will come to it before the end of this fearful business. It would be quite easy to avoid bombing the Vatican City, or any of the historic parts of Rome, because they must all stand out from the air in a remarkable way. It is not like Florence. One bomb in the centre would be sure to hit some Treasure of the Ages – does not bear thinking about.

Apparently a wonking great piece of shrapnel bounced up at my window in Ladbroke Road on that awful Wednesday. The man on the bottom floor insisted on coming up to see if I was alarmed. Mrs Gray informed him I was not there, but he came to make sure. Very kind – as I do not know him at all . . . our only encounters have been in the corridor to and from the bathroom. People can be very thoughtful.

Sunday, 20th News from Greece and Libya is not worse so far as we know; but it seems to me they have drawn a thick curtain down on it – and when they lift it the scene will be very different.

Another raid last night, but not so bad as Wednesday here. Gas at half pressure all day. Returned from Sanctuary and Warning went. Mrs Watkins and I sat and chatted – then at 10.30 p.m. I decided to lie on my bed. I put out the light and was startled to see, penetrating my black-out, a bright light! Jumped out of bed startled, blundered across the room and pulled the curtain. To my astonishment the whole of Notting Hill was as light as Midsummer Noon! My heart gave a great leap. I felt sure a landmine was lowering itself straight upon us, and I prepared for the wretched thing to take the roof from above me – and possibly me with it! The next moment Mrs Watkins came: 'Hold on, I think we are alight somewhere!' I told of the Great Flare. We could see the police on the corner staring down Ladbroke Grove. Mr Watkins suggested a gigantic fire at Kilburn, two miles away, or the Gas Works in Ladbroke Grove. We were glad to know what it was. Gradually the gloom returned – but for a quarter of an hour every target was lighted up.

Two thunderstorms today. Two balloons brought down – just too bad as they cost £500 each. Walked in Park – all lovely and green. The daffodils were lifting their great horns proudly in spite of the storm; a great white magnolia tree was out.

Monday, 21st We slept in peace. No good news! We are getting ready for another masterly evacuation! I wonder when we shall get the measure of those Germans. It is useless to say we had to weaken our arm in N. Africa to help the Greeks. We have known for months we should have to fight in the Balkans. But the Germans are always as the sand on the sea-shore for multitude – always two to spring up where one is mown down.

Just heard that one of our members was badly injured on that Wednesday night – and his wife killed beside him. Their children are fortunately in the country. St. Mildred's Church in the City has gone now.

Letter from Auntie Nell and Mother saying they were glad I was safe! The raids, however, do get more savage in character; but they give us a rest in between – which they did not in the Autumn.

Tuesday, 22nd A quiet day for Germans. News no better. Had an unhappy worried dream about Egypt and Alexandria.

Dr Bell told us a tale of that awful Wednesday. She lives in a flat near Derry and Toms. Fire-watching every night. She could hear chatting above – two girls and a man. Dr Bell could not sleep . . . stuff began to drop. A couple of landmines behind Barkers. Her block of flats swayed like a tree in the wind. Dead silence on the roof. The caretaker went up to see if the firewatchers were all right. They replied cheerfully and began to laugh. This they did for ten minutes – and she wondered when they would stop . . . How brave to stay up there with bombs and landmines dropping all around – and then laugh.

The Nazi parachutist got caught on Derry and Toms . . . a policeman saw him at last. I hear Jermyn St is all wrecked, and a lot of Piccadilly.

Thursday, 24th One is afraid to pick up a newspaper, or listen to wireless. The Greek King has left for Crete. The Greeks are cracking, as I thought they would six months ago when the Italians invaded. After that brilliant stand it does seem hard that they should go under now. One can hardly bear the details of it. I think I shall join that happy band of enthusiasts who read Lyndoe in *The People*, and live in a world of the Future where England wins all the victories – and Hitler is no more!

I am trying to verify a few predictions. April 26th . . . in case the astrologers at Harrogate stumble on truth – but cannot see much hope today.

St Andrew's by the Wardrobe has gone – but that was some time ago. I wonder if they will re-roof them after the war – if there is anything left of the walls and any of us left to do the work! It is amazing, however, how well our nerves keep on the whole. If we are bombed then they go a bit; but if we survive the night, we come up bright and smiling the next morning, very keen to exchange notes on the adventures of the night.

No sign of Jerry tonight. He was at Plymouth for the third time last night. Poor things! Mr Hillyard has been putting up a few shelves. When doing this practical work one seems completely to forget the war. I like to help him. He is of a cheerful disposition – and disapproves of any downheartedness.

Saturday, 26th Not much blitz all the week. We are nightly expecting it to rain down. I dread the news in case it is Brum. How people live in Plymouth, I don't know. With regard to news in general, it is a case of *nil desperandum* three times a day after meals. I may have said this before, but I say it again. Why couldn't we have occupied those Greek islands! It seems so easy when the Germans do it – but for some reason impossible for us. It is beyond me. Anyway it will be good to have a dose of Churchill mixture tomorrow night – it may pull us together.

Most interesting articles in the D.T. about Italy, by an American journalist. When he was there the defeats of the Army, Navy and Air Force had completely humiliated the nation. When the British bombarded Genoa they were almost cracking. Had we gone on, he thinks they would have sued for peace. But, in my opinion, the Germans then would have marched in at once – and the Italians could have done nothing about it. Mussolini, he says, is completely discredited – and the system. Italian naval officers knew they could not fight; because the bore of the guns on their ships had not been renewed in the past ten years – as they had never been fired!

He continues – the Italian Air Force was good some years ago, but it has been allowed to rest on its laurels. It does not know how to recognize its own ships down below! Consequently at Taranto, it bombed its own. All the Services have been sacrificed to Blackshirt corruption.

All this is profoundly interesting to me. I wondered in those far-off days, of 1924–27, how it would work out. I can see Signora Falorsi* now talking of the greatness of Mussolini, of Anna saying he was more wonderful than Napoleon. Now we know what it was all worth. Poor Italians – sold to the barbarians – the same who descended from the Alps centuries ago. This time there was no Savonarola to warn them.

Auntie Nell writes that East Ham Church was badly hit last Saturday. [Have often visited the Rev Morris Hodson and Mrs Mills at the Vicarage.]

Actually got two oranges today! Felt compelled to give one away and shared another. But I did enjoy it.

Sunday, 27th No raid last night. Stayed up reading H. V. Morton's *Women of the Bible*. Loved the chapter on 'Ruth, Martha and Mary'. Always inclined to Martha myself. I like

* Maria Falorsi was married to the famous airman Major de Bernardi, who won the Schneider Trophy for Italy before the war. I knew the family very well.

those practical women who are ready to look after you when you don't feel well.

Bad news. The Germans are in Athens. They are like locusts. Went to Marble Arch to see how the damage was there. Selfridge's have had a nasty fire – several floors burned out. Corner next to them gone. Turned to Park Lane and happened on Green St. Many bombs on it – and beautiful houses gone. Saw the guns in Hyde Park for the first time. Sun came out and the Serpentine looked lovely. The weeping willows are all yellow green, and their graceful light branches trailed down to the water. Many people were boating. Chestnut trees are well on.

Tuesday, 29th Listened with profound attention to the Prime Minister's broadcast. He sounded a little weary. He does love to give us good news – and there was nothing to say, except that there is worse to come! He sketched fearful possibilities of Hitler extending in the Mediterranean . . . and did not seem to think we could do much about it. He did not explain lots of things we should like to know . . . but I suppose we shall some day. If it was inevitable the Yugo-Slavs should be defeated, why was he so elated the other day when he announced they had declared for us! Then how had the Germans got to Libya – and why did we not know they were coming? He did not seem to mind his responsibilities, and faced the future with equanimity; so we must do the same. If he cannot win through – then no one can.

Heard today from a girl in a Government Department that an awful lot of time is wasted. They don't work as we do in this office! She had nothing to do for weeks and weeks, and was paid for overtime – until she made such a fuss they had to look into the matter. Well, if this is going on partout no wonder we are not getting on with the war.

Auntie sent me some dates – very kind. Unobtainable here – what we have in large quantities are Tinned Carrots! We shall probably have to live on them next Winter. We are getting ready for the Anniversary Service on June 14th, at Kingsway Hall – if it is still standing then. An SOS today for clothes for a woman who had been four times bombed. Miss M. found her a billet in Rhyl. Someone called for the clothes, and we sent her a splendid wardrobe, as a supply had just come in.

End of April 1941

MAY 1941

························ ❋ ························

Thursday, 1st No blitz. News is very bad. Cannot help but agree with *Daily Mail* and the Turks, for once. They say we have known for months the Germans would attack Greece. Churchill seems to apologize for sending them help. What we should be apologizing for, they say, is sending so little. It is a year since the defeat in Norway. There we *were* unprepared – but now we have done precisely the same thing again!

Illingworth seems to be a very apt cartoonist. Hope the one about Russia is true. I should love to see them galvanized into life, with their frontiers threatened – and see what really is their policy. And how they would like to be fighting the Germans – with no one to help them.

Last night a ring on the House Bell. Mr Hillyard came tearing down stairs. It was a soldier asking if we had an aspirin, as he felt suddenly faint in the street. He was asked in, of course. I got him a cup of tea. We learned he had been given 48 hours leave, had come on a lorry, which had dropped him at the corner of our road to pick up a bus. The fumes had got inside him, and he felt queer just outside our house. So very sensibly he rang the bell. He just came to the right door! He was most grateful and felt better after the tea and a rest.

Terrible the story of the boys burned in the train. Miss M. thinks the coach was locked, or they could have got along to another part of the train. She has often found this on their Sunday journeys. She has written a strong letter to the Minister of Transport, saying how impossible it is for any passenger to get to the guard. The excuse is that it is impossible to keep the soldiers out of the 1st Class carriages! What an iniquitous excuse! Why should the soldiers with heavy packs have to stand in the corridor with carriages empty?

Just listened to the news. One thing we are good at is retreating! The poor old Navy is always round the corner to pick up the remnants. However difficult it is – they are just as efficient as ever.

Friday, 2nd   We are out of Greece. Another of our masterly retreats. I was much interested in the orders: 'March to the beach, even if bombers bomb you. Casualties will be picked up and taken along. Anyone who shelters will be left behind.'

News from U.S.A. seems more hopeful. They are perhaps moving towards helping us with more than words. I have bought our Cat a Puppy collar. He loses his disk; we dare not ask for a 4th one. He is now on the File with full description, in case he gets lost. This one meal a day is a bad business for him; the solution seems at last to have occurred to him. He just curls up on his own little shelf when his protests go unheeded.

Sunday, 4th   Hitler seems to be befouling the air with a speech today. Listened to Mr Churchill speaking to the Poles. I hope they could hear it, and that it would buck them a bit, poor things.

Went to a lecture at Kensington Town Hall by Mr Arthur Bryant. Sir Gervase Rentoul in the chair. Lecture called: 'The British Tradition'. You would all have enjoyed it. He gave us one of Lord Halifax's favourite stories. Coming, as he said, from such an exalted source he ventured on it. It illustrated the British character. During the General Strike, down at the docks, watching the doors open and close to authorized persons, stood a crowd of strikers. Occasionally out came a lorry load of men, guarded by soldiers, with a notice: By the authority of the Government . . . or T.U.C. There was general animosity in the air. At last the gates opened to allow out a donkey and cart loaded with vegetables. A man in a broken bowler hat was driving it: On the back of his hat, adorned with cabbage leaves, was also a large notice: By the authority of my own bloody self. This was greeted with gusto by the audience. About the war, he said: 'Since every war Britain has waged has always begun with a long series of disasters, due to the fact that we were always prepared for the war that had just passed, he began to be worried, when according to our politicians, this war had gone so well for such a long time. He was really nervous at this unusual occurrence. But he was worried no more. We were now conducting this war just as we had conducted every war in our history.'

We are two hours in advance of ordinary time. So strange.

Monday, 5th Surprise visit from Kit. They are so full at her hospital that some of the patients were in the corridors. She had been given a holiday, and had hitch-hiked down to Devon. She told me the story of Mary Cornish and the children.* Kit had known her personally on the staff of her school: She got her twenty-two children into a lifeboat. Then feeling someone might have been left behind, she made for the cabins. An officer stopped her sternly, and said he would see to that. On her return she saw a lifeboat with Five Little Boys and no adult. Knowing her twenty-two had several in charge, she got in – and this saved her life. It was one of the few lifeboats launched successfully. She was the only woman. She had to watch other boats where all the people were thrown into the sea.

They were afloat eight days. You can imagine what it was like. They were sighted by a Sunderland Flying Boat. It dropped a smokescreen to show the rescue ship where they were. When Mary Cornish got on the Destroyer, she fell in a heap on the deck. She was badly in need of someone to look after her, but the officers with the greatest delicacy left her alone, except for bringing cups of tea – which her mouth was too sore to take. She received the O.B.E. and was personally thanked by the King. She wrote a book about it, and broadcast. [But her memory is still weak, and she never really recovered. The children recovered eventually.]

Wednesday, 7th Walked in the Park with Marie. Trees in fresh green. She had not seen the Elfin Oak – so I did the honours.

* Passengers on *The City of Benares* – 'The Children's Ship' . . . After this no more children were sent.

The News shows no sign of improvement, so I am disregarding it. It is against the law to worry, so I just don't think – and concentrate on procuring food to eat. It is all on rather a low plane, but we talk much about food these days. We have to use all our wiles and ingenuity to get tinned fruit – and such like. Soon, there will be no more. Anyway, I am told tinned carrots are excellent!

Churchill made a splendid speech in the Commons last night. I have read it carefully. The main point to me is his ultimate cheerfulness. We can hold out – he is sure.

A letter to my Red Indian Chief friend, Os-Ke-Non-Ton, was returned by the censor this morning. It does not seem to me to contain anything not published. I don't want to transgress the law. None of my diary has been returned yet.

Sunday, 11th Just trying to recover from last night! We had a terrible time, but mercifully are still intact. The wailers went at 11 p.m. I had not undressed, because I had promised Miss Rowe that in the event of a raid I would return to the Sanctuary. Mrs Watkins and I listened and thought we heard planes. I ran to the front door, and decided they were here in great quantities. I tore down Ladbroke Road, and just reached Lansdowne Road as the guns began cracking loudly. A great bomb came down . . . which made me dive under the desk. I ran upstairs to fetch the Old Lady and Miss Rowe; also to fill the bath and turn off the gas.

These jobs done, we relit the office fire, and settled ourselves down with the Cat. We looked round – and he was nowhere to be seen. I searched the room and found he had tucked himself into his basket under the safe. As a rule he disdains this place. There he remained all night – and what a night!

Bombs came down in dozens. We all dived under the desks, and then laughed uproariously when we got out. The Old Lady looked – with her feet tucked under her – like a little rabbit half-way down a hole. Her heart was bad, and we had to give her brandy. We made tea – and slowly the hours wore on. The caretaker came in from time to time. We heard the fire engines dashing along. Barishnikov came and took me on the roof to see the three enormous fires in the distance. I went up the road at 4 a.m. Could still hear planes, but hoped they might be ours. Was thankful to tuck myself in.

Feel very second-rate today. Did a bit of a tour. The nearest to us was just across Holland Park Avenue. Others fell at N.H. Gate – Station is closed. Behind the Coronet an elderly couple were killed with a direct hit. Several bombs on Campden Hill, but no loss of life. A lot at Knightsbridge. A landmine on Harrods. Big fires in T.C. road, which is closed. Cannot get through to our Shelter at Lambeth. I do hope they are all right. I fear the City got it too – but no details yet.

Anyway 33 bombers brought down is jolly good. One was near the Scrubs. Our caretaker's wife is in Hospital there, and I had been to see her on Friday. She slept through the raid! Have been working late reading proofs, and typing an article for Mr Hillyard.

Went in the Park this afternoon. A time bomb was railed off, and the Gibraltar children were playing, and everyone was enjoying the sunshine. No one looked upset or unnerved, though I don't think many had slept during the night. We walked round Holland House – another bomb there. On to Leighton House with a beautiful garden. I can imagine the Burne-Jones Circle gathering there in those far-off days before the aeroplane was invented. Barishnikov came and discussed last night, and how lucky we had been once more. Children sailing boats on the Round Pond as usual.

Just heard the terrible news that Westminster Hall was hit last night. Also the Abbey and the Houses of Parliament. They saved the roof to a large extent. In the Abbey it was the Lantern. At first they thought Big Ben had crashed! One cannot comment on such things. I feel we must have sinned grievously as a nation to have such sacrifices demanded of us. Indeed future generations will say we have not taken care of what was handed down to us. We should have been more careful to defend it. We must pay the price now; but it is terrible to think of the wasted years, when, sunk in enjoyment, we did not realize that the days of all we looked on as precious were numbered – that our rulers and ourselves had lost their way in a mist of false high thinking, and common sense had gone.

There is bound to be much further destruction, and it is no satisfaction to hear of the treasures of our enemies being laid waste in a similar manner. I don't wish it. But it is grievous that we are not able to protect our own. I shall be careful in future not to follow subtle will o' the wisps. I can see all our ancestors looking down reproachfully, saying: 'We gave it you. You have not guarded it and handed it on as you received it. You have failed your trust – even those who loved it best.'

Monday, 12th Did not sleep well. The Westminster business kept upsetting me all night. I wonder where the House of Commons will meet today. I hear there is a great hole in the roof of Westminster Hall. It is the most damaging raid yet. But we say this every time – and we do the same to them. There is no end to it. Enormous damage in the City, they say. Cheapside, Eastcheap. St Swithun's – the one with London stone inside has gone. Bow Church – but the steeple still stands.

A young woman in Barishnikov's house went to visit her sister on the Harrow Rd, and arrived to find the place down. They were digging out the sister. She was brought up protected by an armchair; but had been 12 hours under the débris. Such stories could be multiplied a thousandfold. But it is wonderful how London recovers from these terrible raids.

Tuesday, 13th Woke to hear the great news of the arrival of Rudolf Hess in Scotland. Cannot take it in – seems too good to be true. When I heard the German announcement that he had disappeared, of course, I believed them, and thought the world was the richer by the loss of one more Nazi!

No further explanations have come to light – only the meeting with the old Scotswoman, and the man who arrested him. Their conversation was largely unintelligible. The other News represents a lull.

Anyway the stars seem to have foretold something against the Nazis for May – a betrayal, or something. In fact Miss M. had a bet on it with a certain Major in Bognor. He told her emphatically it would happen in a fortnight. She replied she would give him three weeks, and would send him a telegram. This was duly sent today! Even the astrologers in Harrogate talked of a mutiny in May . . .

Thursday, 15th All the jokes have been about Hessterday. Is there a hole in it? Why did he leave his family behind if he had turned traitor? Are we still too simple to see through these wretches? Well, I expect Churchill may be able to unravel the mystery.

No water, gas or electricity in the City, poor things. A few more Churches gone – but I have lost count. No one has yet breathed the word that St Bartholomew's has been damaged. The Australians want to help put some wood back into Westminster Hall.

Sunday, 18th Miss M. had a return telegram from her Major to the effect we were to watch the 25th, for news of the house painter! I do not think the astrologers can be right twice so soon. The amazing thing is that the man who prophesied May 11th was killed in the blitz on Saturday night! He never knew his prophecy had come true! You are allowed a glimpse into the future – but you may not survive yourself. However, we shall watch the 25th. All these Nazis seem to be under some psychic influence – if the tales be true. They don't suffer from the ordinary lusts of the flesh, but are under subtler powers . . .

The next raid is to be the worst ever . . . so we know.

The weather is a little better and one can get away from N.H. Gate especially with double Summer Time. All the

Winter one has felt imprisoned – dare not move more than a few yards from one's own habitation. Went to the theatre yesterday. Performance began at a quarter to six, and the play was *Dear Brutus*. The last two seats in the pit. Most enjoyable – felt we had just been let out of prison.

Afterwards walked to Leicester Square, past the ill-fated Café de Paris. It looks all right from the front; then by Trafalgar Square, down Whitehall, past the Horse Guards, which has had a tremendous Biff and looks awful. Reached Westminster . . . two definite holes in the roof of the Hall. Damage to the Abbey is not apparent from the outside. Up Victoria St, Christ Church there is finished. Great crater in front of the Army and Navy Stores – fit to hold a bus. Various biffs and wonks. Station looks battered, but eventually groped our way in to a cup of tea.

Went to the hairdresser on Saturday. The girl is one of the most cold-blooded people possible. On that awful night she was alone at the back of the house. Did not move when the raid began – heard a bomb fall very near. Decided she could do nothing, and as she was warm in bed thought she might as well stay there! Actually two bombs fell. One near the little Church of St Peter, killing two people. The second – a time bomb – fell in the road. So the wardens began evacuating all the people, but no one knew the Hairdresser was there. She heard nothing of the movement in the road, and so was the only person in that row of shops when the bomb went off at 4 a.m. She was tossed like a ball – but even then did not get up. She seems to have awakened cheerfully in the morning to find half the street in ruins!

Coming out found the procession of the Kensington War Weapons Week was forming. Watched for half an hour. An R.A.F. officer led the way, tossing his baton up in the air. This enthralled me.

Much interested in a letter in *D.T.* A conversation with Mr Churchill in 1917 during some of the worst days of the last war. Our fortunes and his political reputation were at a low ebb. He was talking to a friend in the H. of Commons, after everyone else had gone – the place all littered with papers, and looking around remarked: 'You know, it is just this little place that makes the difference between Germany and England. With all their efficiency they will never beat us, because of just this little place, and all it means . . .' He is wise.

Trees heavenly in the Park, heavy with fresh green leaves. Pansies are out in great beds. Found a great portion roped off, but chairs were placed against the rope, and each said on it: U.B. We knew what that meant. People were peacefully sitting on those seats, and some had even penetrated the barrier, and were happily basking on the grass in the sunshine. Shows how indifferent we have got. A year ago they would have closed the entire gardens. Now people lean up against un-exploded bombs! We are an adaptable race!

Tuesday, 20th No blitz on London. Letter from Lucy to say the Rhodesians are being released in Abyssinia. There is great joy, as they were taken prisoner last year. They entered Asmara in triumph. Duca d'Aosta surrendered today. A good job – but it is a side issue compared with the Germans.

Dr Remy seems inclined to view Hess with the deepest suspicion, and thinks Goebbels sent him. Unless there is clear evidence to the contrary he feels it impossible for Hess to have quarrelled with Hitler. All too subtle for us simple English. We must hold on tight, it seems, that Hess is as much a liar and a Nazi as he ever was. We are fools over prodigal sons – there are no such things among Germans. I am definitely laying a stony layer over my heart.

Offered the little cat some black sausage, cut up into most attractive morsels – but it was no good. He gazed at me with the – 'You'd be far better off in a Home' expression. Very common on his face these days.

Other news is not good. This lull bodes something ill. I should not be surprised at a good old blitz on London next Saturday, and I am prepared to see the rest of the Abbey and the Hall go. I don't think anything can save them.

American First Aid ship gone down. Nazis landing in Crete by parashoot. We must be careful others do not follow Hess here!

Wednesday, 21st   Found myself practically sleep-walking in the night. Under the impression a red glow of light was shining into my room through the Black-out, I felt impelled to get out of bed – but knew I must not put the light on. I woke to find myself stumbling over the furniture, trying to get to the window. No red glow – and it must have been a dream. But it shows how this fire-business does work havoc in the subconscious, even in a level-headed person like poor me!

Thursday, 22nd Terrific fighting in Crete. New Zealanders doing their best to cope with the wretches dropping from the clouds. Have had to withdraw our Air Force. Always an excellent reason why we lack the advantage.

A lovely day. Great doings in the City with War Weapons Week. A gigantic bomb in Finsbury Circus – a thousand pounder, which fell and did not go off. Six feet with its fins. The Clock on Liverpool St station is a great attraction, used now as an Enquiry Bureau for selling Certificates. It has been lowered on account of the blitz.

They seem to think the Cheshire Cheese has gone. I was always waiting for some opulent relative to take me there. Now I shall never go – very disheartening. Serjeants Inn has gone.

Sunday, 25th We hold our breath over Crete . . . scarcely dare to breathe regarding it. I feel Churchill is doing the same. He did not seem to mind evacuation of Greece, but he will take the loss of Crete very hard.

Listened to the Free French doing what they can with the situation. Poor things – they sound very sad. Talked of what Vichy is doing with the French Empire. H.M.S. Hood sunk off Greenland. Very bad news. Lord Haw-Haw has promised to lay London flat next time. Don't know which night! But The Tiger is preparing to spring again.

Went to Piccadilly on bus, and walked along Jermyn St and Duke St. Very badly knocked about . . . also the Circus end of Piccadilly. Where the Duke and Duchess of York lived, No. 145, is a ruin. Walked along Rotten Row to see The

Dump. We heard you could buy all sorts of things there, but it is mostly old iron – a quarter of a mile of it. Then a similar amount of wood, then bricks – like Early British Ramparts! Certainly there are baths and radiators, if you could take them away. But I think it is all for making Spitfires. Obviously they are sorting it out. I wonder how many British homes it represents!

Rather a cold wind about. The rhododendrons should be out next week. Have lighted a fire in the office tonight. British Museum damage is at the back, we are told. Battle for Crete trembles in the balance.

Today is the twenty-fifth – and I hope the astrologers are going to justify themselves. We are prepared to give them a few days' grace, but we badly need some good news!

Thursday, 29th We have sunk the Bismarck. What a hunt! Good! It happened on the 26th. Battle for Crete goes on. Nothing bright there, though Mr Hillyard won't let us get gloomy, as we are inclined to do.

Read with deepest sorrow the Temple Church has gone. It was fire and not a bomb. The men left guarding it went to help with fires elsewhere, and in their absence it caught fire. That's no good.

Roosevelt's speech very cheering. Read it all through.

The Maoris are fighting in Crete – hand to hand and seem quite happy about it. Nearly finished the life of Tolstoy – very difficult person. Glad he was no relation of mine. Saints seem as difficult as geniuses . . . Tolstoy was both, and I don't wonder his wife gave way to her feelings in her diary.

Garden looks a picture these days. Laburnum coming out, and the may trees smell exotically as you pass. I have a vase of bluebells on my office table.

End of May 1941

JUNE 1941

Thursday, 5th. After Whitsuntide holiday. Spent most of last Saturday waiting on Paddington Station for my Mother to come from Brum. Could not get near Enquiries. The place was thick with Mothers and Fathers going to see their evacuated children. Decided to stay by Indicator, and meet every train. She arrived after 3 p.m., having been unable to book her ticket, and afraid to board the train without it. My teeth were chattering with cold, but the sun was shining at Hockley. Passed lovely evening with Marie playing a three handed game, called, of all names – Bismark.

Sunday cold and wet, but we walked over stiles and fields to Church. What attracted me was the vicar's son, aged three, who is an acolyte . . . and another aged five who looks after him. They swing the incense. Such darlings. The way five looks after three has to be seen to be believed. Three fell over only once – but he has always got his head looking over his shoulder for his Mother with the baby, at the back of the Church.

Monday we went to Southend. A demand for identity cards. The first time I have been asked for it. Mother had left hers in the bungalow – so when our turn came we put ours well forward, and explained the third was my Mother, who, as usual, with her innocent expression got through. Wandered along the front. Seems all ready against invasion. Lot of ships in the harbour, including a battleship – very impressive. Found a Fish and Chip place in true Bank Holiday style. Excellent – for the day was cold. Went on to Leigh, and found the G.W. Convalescent Home – we had a good welcome.

Had to catch the 8 p.m. train for London. Many people camping out in the Tubes. We wonder how rationing of clothes will affect our Christmas Fair.

We have evacuated Crete. *Daily Mail* not pleased, nor are we. Miss M. says she refuses to be comforted. Had a terrible dream. The sky was black with planes. I knew they were not ours. I could feel it being said over and over again: 'England is bleeding to death . . . England is bleeding to death.'

Dublin has had a raid . . . I wonder how they liked it. The dream is from the subconscious mind, not just weak female fears. I have never recovered from the moment the Announcer said we had evacuated Benghazi – and I thought he must have made a mistake.

Sunday, 8th We have entered Syria. I suppose we have half a division, a few tanks and aeroplanes, and think it is plenty. Garvin expressed what I feel – that the over-optimistic people made everyone slacken down their efforts, which has led to the general feeling that if the War lasts long enough we shall automatically win it. He added that Crete was the last outpost of the Empire to go – the next will be on the Empire itself.

Landmine on Chiswick last night and bombs on Acton. The firemen have condemned our top floor. They laughed at our stirrup pump – and said they doubted if we caught fire whether the Brigade could put it out.

About Tolstoy – it is obvious you cannot have all the pleasure the earth can give, including a wife and family, then renounce them when you decide earthly joys are not in accordance with the Divine Plan. And I do object to men who suddenly decide that women represent Temptation, and that otherwise men would be pure and noble. I consider such views insufferable. But I may be unjust to Tolstoy.

Clothing coupons have paralysed our shopping this week. I have clothes if we are not bombed. May trees are superb in the Park, and the chestnuts. Indeed the world is looking marvellous – if there were no Germans in it.

Government seems satisfied Crete served its purpose. This does not tally with the statement that we should hold it at all costs.

Thursday, 12th Warning last night about 12.15. A surprise. Good deal of gun-fire and much racing across the sky of planes. They say it was the Midlands.

Lovely surprise yesterday. Came in for lunch, longing for some cheese and there waiting for me was a parcel from Rhodesia with half a pound of excellent cheese.

Read Churchill's speech in full, and loved it. He was so amusing at the expense of Lord Winterton, who found it much more invigorating to take a gloomy view of the situation . . . that he woke up in the morning convinced we were going to lose the war in three months, and went about his business with renewed life! This, said Churchill, was typically British.

We are a people who do not in the least mind being told that fearful disasters are about to take place. But nations like the Arabs were quite different. A speech couched in a pessimistic vein made them want to pack up . . . Also such speeches, torn from their context, were repeated in the Spanish Press which stated that a Cabinet Minister was convinced the British would lose the War. Personally, Mr Churchill continued, he preferred to take a gloomy view – it was much safer – but much else had to be taken into consideration.

We are marching into Syria. I do hope the French will join us, and confound the men of Vichy. It is heart-breaking the part France is playing against us. When friends betray . . . there is no bitterness like it.

Kingsway Hall meeting is sold out – if the hall survives until then! It is always raining. The heavens seem to be sobbing over the sorrows of man . . . a non-stop sob, as one of our Printing Staff remarked.

Mother loved Mrs Watkins' cat and dog. I told how they had both been bombed out, and were making do with living in apartments. She earnestly informed the cat that she would take him in if he required another home. He seemed much gratified.

Sunday, 15th The Big meeting passed off well. Better attendance than last year. People came in from the country. I think they resolved to take their lives in their hands venturing to London, and said goodbye to their friends and families first! One lady from Gainsborough expected to see London razed to the ground, and was amazed anything was standing.

Left at a quarter past midnight, almost too tired to sleep. Did not dream of anything whatsoever! Lovely walk in the Park today. Hard to believe about the war, as everyone looked so happy enjoying the flowers and the sun.

Story in *Daily Telegraph* of an African Chief who wanted to help the British. He could not send money, or men, or arms, so he ordered the whole village to black-out once a week!

Wednesday, 18th Two of my old Folkestone pupils turned up. One is a Sister at a Hospital in Chertsey, the other a Billeting Officer in Paddington. Doing such useful work. She had to help find homes for thousands after the last big blitz, when 70 bombs fell on Paddington. All the town was evacuated for a time – and there are few people there now.

Had an R.A.M.C. man in last night. Explained about the *Royal Oak* loss at the beginning of the war in harbour. After the first explosion they could all have got away, he said, but were ordered back to their bunks, and the ship exploded from stem to stern. This man had helped with the survivors. We have never been told the true explanation . . . except that a German submarine penetrated the harbour.

Turkey has signed some sort of a treaty with Germany. Not surprised that they have little faith in our power to protect them. They are not so selfless and heroic as the Greeks.

No raids. It is remarkable. We go there – but they do not come to us, at least for the moment.

Sunday, 22nd Great news at last! Germany has invaded Russia – and we shall see what they can do about it. The

Russians have not been too nice to us in the past, but now we have to be friends and help one another.

Made my tea at 8.30 a.m., ran downstairs for the *Observer*, and was reading Garvin, in which he said that for the first time in all our centuries of war we had not a single fighting ally in Europe! The melancholy truth of this was sinking into my mind, when I discovered it was 9 a.m. Switched on the wireless, and expected to hear we had advanced a few more inches into Syria, and shot down two or three more German planes. This was the most I hoped for – when I was nearly electrified out of bed by hearing that Hitler had made a speech last night, to the effect that his patience was once more exhausted and he found himself unfortunately obliged to attack Russia!

I ran across the landing to tell Mrs Watkins and beg her to come. She leapt out of bed and padded across with bare feet to hear that Goebbels had been talking at 5 a.m. – and the whole thing was under way. In addition the French had left Damascus – and the Free French gone in.

So we have got one fighting ally left in Europe – and I felt my morale rising.

It has been a sweltering day – my room is like an oven. Mrs Fisher came and we made for the Park. Searched everywhere for deckchairs – most were leaning up against trees, broken. Discovered one with only the canvas split dragged it a quarter of a mile, and with a needle and cotton repaired it. We were under a great sycamore tree near the Round Pond – and really if we had taken a bus and a train and then walked three miles we could not have found a pleasanter spot. Barishnikov came and joined us. We ate our sandwiches. Stayed on until nearly 8 p.m. Mrs Horton Smith and little dog found us. She told us all about her Gibraltar refugees. They had visited Windsor and Eton last week. She gets on well with them – but not everyone does. One man helper refused them a second helping of pudding – and they hit him on the head with a tray!

We watched all the sights of the Park. One couple well-known for bringing their Siamese cat for a walk . . . though this time the little creature was draped round the man's neck, quite happy. Then the man who brings the green parrot – he was there.

Tonight have heard Mr Churchill. Says we have just reached the 4th climacteric of the war. One was the defection of France. 2nd: defeat of the Germans by the R.A.F. over England. 3rd: passing of the Lease-Lend Act, and the 4th: entry of Russia into the war. He had already notified the Russians we should support them as much as they wanted us to.

Tuesday, 24th The Germans are advancing into Russia. Of course, the Russians are letting them, and then we shall see what twenty-four years of Soviet Rule has done for the Russian peasant.

Went to see *Goodbye, Mr Chips*. How I enjoyed it. We sat round it twice. Have an idea the boys were from Rugby.

Shopping last Saturday I was behind a dear old lady who had been in her prime under the régime of the late Queen Victoria. She asked for salad oil, and was amazed to be told she could not have any – and moreover would not be likely to have any in the future, as it was unobtainable! 'What are we going to do?' she asked, much puzzled. The shop assistant sweetly replied: 'We shall just have to go without, Madam.' The old lady turned away amazed.

Tomatoes are to be 1/4d a pound on Monday, though I doubt if we shall see any. Sardines are getting scarce. I was charged 10½d for a tin containing four.

Thursday, 26th Managed to buy half a pound of tomatoes. Very exciting. They would not let anyone have more. Miss Mackay got some, so we had quite an orgy.

News is pretty much fifty-fifty with Germans and Russians, but we are basking in a lull of the Luftwaffe. Danzig, and such places, who thought they had been so clever, are now enjoying a few sleepless nights and nervy days. In fact, by the time this war is over, and everybody has had a taste of bombing, and what it means, they will be as sick of war as the men of the 17th century grew sick of religion, and stop quarrelling.

Interview with Miss Moyes is in the *Daily Mirror*. Really very sympathetic and well put. Nothing about Christian Spiritualism, but much about Miss Moyes' philosophy of life.

The hedgehog has gone from the garden. Very disappointing. Marie Idiens has been to the centre of Coventry. She wept as she entered the Cathedral.

Sunday, 29th Not such exciting news as last Sunday morning; but the Russians have been pegging away all the week. The Germans say they have 40,000 prisoners, and have destroyed 2,000 planes. Unlikely, I should think. Garvin thinks if they can hold out for three months, by then the Anglo-American air supremacy will have Hitler taped.

Read Lyndoe in *The People* today with interest. August is to be a month black with fate for us. Invasion is off.

Next week butter ration is to be halved . . . Miaow! Queues for tomatoes in N.H. Gate on Saturday afternoon. I was too tired to join them; but with another week of sunshine there will be plenty for everyone. Auntie Nell has promised to make jam for us all if we collect the sugar.

May get to Sussex next Saturday. Hitler is well occupied, so everyone can snatch a little holiday – we don't know what the Winter will hold. Lovely to hear of those R.A.F. sweeps over Northern France.

Little cat has pestered me for three saucers of milk. He hates Sundays when everyone is away, and he gets no fuss.

End of June 1941

JULY 1941

Wednesday, 2nd   Feel much better this week. Very hot. A jar of honey has been given me. Very pleasant to receive. Able to get one whole pound of tomatoes without queueing for them – so Hitler is not having it all his own way.

Listened last week to the Brains Trust, on Forces Programme. Really very good. Lady Oxford, Professor Joad and Julian Huxley. Some of the questions put to them were: What is a lady? Why is Mona Lisa the most famous picture in the world? I must listen again – it is one of the best things I have heard.

Nice to think King Leopold is vindicated. I hated to believe badly of him – but he is still to blame in not helping with a plan before the war. That, however, is not dishonourable – only silly.

Reading a biography of Churchill – did not know much about his career, but going back into the past one can see how it has all grown and how very far-sighted a man he has been almost from the first. The writer diagnosed his driving power from his American side – just as I did a few months ago when I thought it out. Had he been pure English aristocracy he would not have been able to lead in the way he has. The American side gives him a superiority complex – in a way that

189

Lord Halifax would think is not good taste – but we need more than good taste to save Britain at this particular moment.

I cannot weep for the Russians as I did for the Greeks. They have had plenty of time to prepare for this fight – and if they are not ready, it is no one's fault but their own. They have been so secretive. No vision as to what might happen to them. So one can watch this duel with a kind of detached interest – though we know if the Russians are overcome our day will be on us with a vengeance. Somehow I think Stalin is more a match for Hitler than any of us . . . he looks such an unpleasant kind of individual.

We have some honeysuckle and syringa in the office – it smells so sweet. Got some Kitcat for our animal today and he wolfed it down as if it were a banquet.

Sunday, 13th An agreeable week in Sussex. Went down with some foreboding as to whether I should be allowed into an invasion area. The authorities give neither yes or no – they simply reserve the right to send you back if they think it advisable. Changed at Brighton – much ado about Identity Cards; but I slipped to the left when I heard Hastings train called. Got in, clutching suitcase, handbag, ticket, gas mask and knitting. Auntie Mollie met me, and remarked like all Hodgsons I arrived on the previous train.

Hastings has had pretty well of blitz. It felt very empty. We took the bus. Lovely to be bowling along the country lanes. Much preparation against invasion on every side. Many troops. At the Aunts in Brede had lovely food – had not tasted such nice things for a long time.

Went to Rye one lovely hot day. Glorious Sussex cottages covered with roses. Brought E. F. Benson's book with me. Lamb House, where he lived, had been bombed – but not out of existence. The town is in the hands of the Colonials. They send home unlimited picture postcards. They were, for a time, in the frozen north, and are thankful now for some sunshine. Another day at Winchelsea. Found the Old Mill. Took off our shoes and cooled our feet in the fresh grass. A glorious view across the marshes. Took a long walk to Brede Place and talked with the soldiers, toiling and moiling to get this and that into place. Much barbed wire everywhere.

Attended the Baby Clinic with Aunt Winnie, and helped to weigh them. Much troubled over ounces, pounds and stones . . . not good at this. I ate unlimited lettuce. Saw the boys going over to France, flying low. And saw them coming back.

The great trouble was lack of water in Brede. Everyone wanted to fill their tanks in case of incendiaries on the crops or houses.

Returned to Hastings. They were rather suspicious of me, and I had to prove I came from London. We ran into rain, and I arrived at Victoria in a deluge. Thunder and lightning – and everyone in light summer clothes running for shelter. Such a job to get home. My taxi broke down and had to wait an hour at Hyde Park Corner for a bus. But I thought of Aunt Winnie dancing in the rain with joy!

Tuesday, 15th. St Swithun's Day News full of Russia and our alliance with her – Germans have not rushed on Leningrad yet.

Listened to Mr Churchill. Full of punch as usual. He spoke to the Civil Defence Services of London, and told us to expect a resumption of raids in the autumn. But that we were better prepared. Shelters were being heated and lighted. It has turned cold, but I feel better for my holiday – not that tired feeling.

I forgot to record that I was heavily told off by Kensington Salvage Council for throwing away a crust of bread, which had gone mouldy. It was the heat of my room that had caused it. Seems rather hard that I should be singled out when I have nearly poisoned folk with using up ancient food. I am really one of the most economical of people, but having been far from well I feared to eat it.

Sunday, 20th Very wet all the week. Went to Weybridge to see Mary Bewley. She had planned a picnic – but alas, for human schemes it got blacker and blacker. So we went to a home-made shop for tea. Got into Mary's open car, me with umbrella up. She has a charming bungalow in the grounds of a doctor's house. She shares with his secretary. Visited the Chertsey Emergency Hospital, built as a loony bin, Mary explained. Immense grounds. I much enjoyed visiting her ward. She is Sister, and has 42 soldiers to keep in order . . . she manages very well.

There were two Norwegians, and Free Frenchmen, as well as Dunkirk men still. She was trained at St Thomas' herself, where the spirit was wonderful. Everyone worked for hospital and patients. Here there were rows and bickering. I was proud of her. I feel she is looking after the men very well.

We are all anxiously watching the Russians. They have that mixture of ruthlessness and fatalism which makes them a hard nut to crack. When I read of the peasants calmly burning their homes and setting off on the tramp, leaving everything behind them as a matter of course, I am astonished. The French would not do it! It takes a high degree of courage and resolution. We hear of a Town the Germans entered the other day. Regular soldiers had left. The Townsfolk defended themselves for two days. When the Germans entered the place was empty – except for seven men hiding under the bridge. They blew up the German tanks as they passed over – and themselves as well.

Nothing but the V Symbol these days. Where did it originate? With the unfortunate people who cannot say what they think? Or did Colonel Britton give them the idea? Use of fingers is a good idea – and on the 6 p.m. news they gave us a vivid account of how it is being exploited in thousands of ways . . . Morse code signals can be used on typewriters, trains etc. What an annoyance for the Germans.

Thursday, 24th Studied Lyndoe the other night . . . under Mr Hillyard's tuition. I am inclined to be flippant and disbelieving on the subject of prediction and I get disapproving looks:

Ribbentrop and Goebbels are to go soon.

Japan is to declare war on Russia soon.

Libya – Sea Action in August in Mediterranean.

Italian possessions to have further knocks.

Quick Victory.

Half Kensington Gardens is closed and much is going on. Sunday we lunched at the cafeteria by the Albert Memorial. The sparrows came to my hand to be fed. I feared Lord Woolton would suddenly appear from behind the bushes, but, fortunately, he did not. Who can resist a sparrow on your hand?

With regard to our projected jaunt to the Hockley bungalow, this has been well and truly knocked on the head. Marie came this evening, and said there were two policemen meeting every train, scrutinizing Identity Cards. She asked: 'What should you do if I did not live here?' The reply was stern and official: 'Send you back, of course; that's what I'm here for.' Cath must now stay in Auntie Nell's flat.

Japs seem to be moving in Indo-China, not on Russia.

Sunday, 27th Such a lovely day. Barishnikov took us out to lunch. Tried the Old Vienna part of the Corner House. It is the style of *Bitter Sweet* . . . rep curtains, soft sofas, festooned . . . candelabra and mirrors . . . very attractive and not in the least modern. Having a cast-iron digestion I tried Strasburgers. Also a glass of Medoc, and finished with a mixture of black coffee, rum, sugar and syrup . . . iced. Mrs Fisher and I walked back through the Park, sat under the trees and planned a row on the Serpentine and a day at Maidenhead . . . but cannot say if such plans will ever materialize. Limes heavy with scent – and bees very busy.

Gave Barishnikov Garvin's article on Russia. A lot about all the natural obstacles the Germans were meeting – interminable dusty roads, swamps, forests. If it is not one – it is the other.

Also the amazingly obstinate hostility of the inhabitants. The Russians seem to have guts which the Latins have not. They are fighting for Soviet Russia, as they did not fight for the Tsar. So they must prefer Stalin – though to me he looks sub-human.

Reading *The Last Days of Paris* by Alexander Werth, a journalist who kept a diary of those awful weeks. Apparently the censorship ruined France. No journalist was allowed to say how bad things really were. There was no war effort at all. A group of men of low morals and intelligence allowed France to slide down the slippery slope to her doom. Well, we seem to be wise to stick to our Gutter Press. One can have too much good taste and self-control in not criticizing a Government.

Walked through Portobello Market. Plenty of cherries at 2/- a pound. Could not resist buying half. So great was my longing and greed for them that I ate them all that evening. Queues for tomatoes. Lettuce and beetroot are a reasonable price.

Wonderful postcript by Mr Harry Hopkins. I was nearly in tears by the end, with joy and thankfulness. He is going to send us lots of things. Took my breath away. He said America would not let Britain go hungry. Amongst other delectable articles – like machine tools and tanks – the one that made Miss Mackay and me exchange glances of glee was fruit juice.

I loved the bit where he said: 'Your Prime Minister and the President are 2,000 miles apart. This is nothing. The Germans are 21 miles from Dover – but really they are 2,000 miles away.' Then he finished with glorious words of comfort: 'People of Britain, people of the British Commonwealth of

Nations, you are not fighting alone.' I felt after this the War was won.

It was much more cheering than Lyndoe, though he does his best I must admit, to make us keep smiling. We all feel a bit battered after the Winter bombing. I am sure the munition workers feel that after making all the effort to construct the tanks and endure the bombing, at the same time, it will give them all heart to receive a lot of stuff ready-made.

General de Gaulle had a wonderful welcome in Syria. He seems to me the George Washington of France. I hope he will live to see his dearest dreams realized, and that he will ride in triumph through Paris at the head of the Free French Forces. He ought to be made President; but so often these Liberators are treated with ingratitude. We shall see.

Monday, 28th Last night the Germans sprang an air raid upon us – much to our surprise. I was asleep. Had my window open and only thin curtains drawn when, through the silence of the night Wailing Winny set up. They buzzed over us like bees in a lime tree, for about two hours. Our guns cracked up all round, and as I lay in bed I watched the shells bursting in the sky. Several times put my head out of the window, but the police opposite were chatting away on the step nonchalantly. I could hear no bombs.

Thursday, 31st No more raids, and not much activity. It is all on the Russian side of the fence, and the Germans seem in a rare quagmire – good, gooder and still goodest.

I must record that a lost dog was named Smolensk, because no one knew to whom it belonged.

Mr Harry Hopkins has gone on to Moscow to buck up the Russians. That is good. He is a very invigorating person.

Auntie Nell welcomes Cath to use the flat. The caretaker is a rare person among caretakers – as on the whole they seem a surly race. Dust sheets were off – and he was agitated about tea and sugar for them. But I explained I had brought it and all was well.

Cherries and gooseberries still 3/- per pound. Miss M. has received prunes from Bermudas. They always remind me of boarding school meals, but as they are now a rarity I ate some with profound pleasure.

End of July 1941

AUGUST 1941

··›› ❋ ‹‹··

Tuesday, 5th We have now a whole book of Lyndoe, so now we shall know all that is going to happen for the next ten years! The *Daily Mail* is running Archidamus – so great is the popularity of these prophets.

Cath and Beryl [a schoolgirl] arrived. Saturday we plunged into the City and toured the blitz. Some of the parts I have done before, but not Newgate St and the Old Bailey. Went down to Charterhouse Square and saw the burned-off roof. It is just amazing to see St Paul's rising strong out of the ruins that surround it. How it was saved is a miracle. It gave Cath an idea; but, of course, the child was not interested.

Sunday we went with Barishnikov to the Serpentine. Beryl was delighted by the Cafeteria where the sparrows ate out of her hands – such a glorious feeling when the little claws grip your fingers. A boat for four, and I took a pair of oars. We went right round, skirting the Park and the Gardens. Returned to Auntie's flat for tea, and opened a tin of pineapple we found among Auntie's treasures. Also a tin of prawns to go with our salad.

Monday we did Disney's *Fantasia*. The idea is that every musical sound makes a pattern and a colour . . . these were thrown on the screen. Lovely classical music. One composer wrote *The Creation*, and Disney pictured it all – chaos and earthquakes. Then life appeared with the amoeba, and finally prehistoric beasts who moved in the rhythm of the music. There was a glorious mythological one, where the Flying Horses were among the loveliest creatures I have ever seen. A work of genius.

Wandered along Oxford Circus, surveyed the blitz round the B.B.C. and thought of that awful night when Bruce Belfrage was reading the News, and the bomb fell. Gazed at the remnants of Queen's Hall, and Langham Place Church.

War has gone on, and the Russians still holding their own. Very cheering. V for Victory everywhere. People are wearing them and chalking them up.

Thursday, 7th   Back at the office. Cath and Beryl went to the Zoo and made great friends with the giraffe, whom they fed with lettuce. I should have liked to see it slowly descending that long throat. I am addicted to giraffes, and have always fancied one in the garden.

They did Westminster and the Thames, and joy of joys they got over *Discovery*. Have often wanted to do this, but never found it open. There was the cabin used by Uncle Tom,* with his name on it, and a photo of him. The kitchen was in full working order – a fire going, and a cat sitting in

* My uncle, Thomas Vere Hodgson, b. 1864, d. 1926. He was biologist on *Discovery* during the Expedition of Captain Scott to the Antarctic, 1901–4. His cabin is next to that of Dr Edward Wilson. The ship is near the Temple Stairs, and can be visited.

front. Then on to the Palace where the Royal Standard was flying – they saw where it had been blitzed.

We paid a visit to Mabel Lucy, who says the Lucy Mill at Stratford-on-Avon has been burned down – but not by Germans.

Friday, 8th   Poured with rain all day. They paddled about, but decided that London was no better than anywhere else on such a day. So they came down to the Sanctuary and got busy helping with my Buried Treasure for the Fair. Everybody talked to them and they enjoyed themselves.

Sunday, 10th   This morning I forgot the clocks had gone back, and thought the wireless had gone barmy. Garvin pleased with the Russians. We saved civilization last year with our Battle of Britain – if we had gone under the Russians could not have withstood Nazi Europe alone.

Heard the Queen speak. Very sweet – and quite a few phrases that saved it from banality.

Quentin Reynolds [U.S. journalist] has made a speech. He addressed it to Hitler, whom he called Schicklgruber throughout. This is really Hitler's name. Reynolds sounded like Nemesis himself – or Count Dracula. He had been re-reading *Mein Kampf* and wondered if Mr Schicklgruber still believed that by propaganda you could make people think that heaven was hell, and hell heaven. He mentioned Darlan, who had ordered every newspaper in Occupied and Unoccupied France, to print his picture. And all had put it in the Fifth Column. The picture in every shop had unaccountably fallen face downwards in the window.

He mentioned passages on Bolshevism in the book – and how the Silent Man in the Kremlin had listened, made no comment, but just ordered extra tanks and aeroplanes. He continued: Did he really think that a man called Winston Churchill would ever bow the knee to someone called Schicklgruber? That it was dangerous to wake the dead. That the bombing of Plymouth had roused Drake – and he quoted 'Drake's Drum'. Nelson, he said, was back, and Wellington was not sleeping in his grave. Besides no man minded dying when he was going to join such folk as they.

Friday, 15th Yesterday there was the Declaration by the President and Mr Churchill. When I heard there was to be an important Government announcement at 3 p.m., I thought it might be some sort of union with U.S.A. If Mr Churchill had offered it to France, it would mean much more if the English-speaking countries made one bloc. However, it did not go so far as that. There was a statement of War Aims. All very laudable in themselves – the only difficulty will be in carrying them out. Mr Churchill inclines to making victory the first aim, and all other things to be added unto it.

The Home Guard have caught a German parashot [*sic*], and he has been shut in the Tower. We must not be sentimental about these people.

Sunday, 17th Yesterday was our Garden Party, and all went well. Very tired in the evening, too much so to get myself any food. So have enjoyed my breakfast.

Garvin in the *Observer*: 'Our Russian allies are pouring out their blood in rivers. In eight weeks they have gone through more sacrifice and suffering than all the rest of the anti-Hitlerite world put together has known in two years. Far and wide they are devastating their homes and lands in front of the invader . . . They are killing Germans who were to be our invaders. They are destroying war planes and tanks that would have attacked the lives of our people at home . . .' I think this is very well said, and we must not forget it.

Another writer lamented our susceptibility to Lull Psychology. 'The conviction that Britain cannot be beaten in war is deeply rooted in the hearts of the British people. This unwavering faith in our destiny carried us through the stark days of last Summer, when the logic of events declared our cause was doomed . . . Goebbels would doubtless give millions to be able to create such an unshakeable faith in the German people. It is a priceless possession – but this spirit can also act as an opiate, with a paralysing effect on our war effort.'

He recalled the evidence of this from the beginning of the war. Our rude awakening, and how we toiled like supermen when we stood alone. But complacency soon got at us again. We were just getting roused again with the fall of Crete, when Hitler let loose the blitzkrieg on Russia. 'The effect upon us psychologically was unhealthy. We had found a short cut to victory . . . we settled back to read with satisfaction how our air offensive against Germany was helping our great Soviet ally. With Russia and U.S.A. at our side, now surely all would be well.'

All this strikes me as profoundly true. I understand that we are to adopt the scorched earth policy here in case of invasion, in Kent, Essex or Devon. It made me think when I read that a neutral observer commented that the Germans were manufacturing silk in millions of yards. One parachutist had come – captured by the Home Guard . . . it seems the Invasion Season has begun.

Really the Americans seem to give the best Postscripts. Dorothy Thompson has a sweet womanly voice. Not at all that of a hard-baked journalist used to coping with shouting, gesticulating males – such as we see in American films. Neither has she an aggressive American accent. Among other things, she said: England seemed to her like a gigantic Noah's Ark, riding the flood, with examples of every species inside her for refuge. She had seen everything – and had lived half her life in Germany. She said this Nazi dream was an old one, and must be destroyed. England and America had to do it . . . we had so much in common. There were only little differences and they helped to underline the similarities. This woman is a good friend to both countries – I liked her.

Macaroni seems unobtainable now. A nuisance! Perhaps a shipload will come in. I asked for it the other day, and a man behind me said: 'Can I have three bowls of gold dust, please . . .' However, there are some figs which is an agreeable change. And we can get green apples.

We all have to register for milk this week – but how much we are going to be allowed, I don't know. I take half a pint a day – but it may not be that much.

Heard some sound recordings of events on the warships when the President and Mr Churchill met. It was 'Eternal Father' and 'Rule Britannia'.

I must record that often now we hear aeroplanes going over night and day – but we do not bother any more – we know they are not Germans. This time last year for certain Warnings would have gone every time – as they would have been Germans.

Wednesday, 20th   Very busy week. Barishnikov on holiday. Lots of worry over despatch of paper – plenty of voluntary helpers, but only for unskilled jobs. However, Paddington P.O. have not rung up – so far all is well.

Have lost my key . . . have importuned St Anthony. He seems too busy to listen. I turned back on Sunday to let Scamp in, as it was raining. I have searched the street between the two houses. Very difficult to get new keys cut these days.

Mr Churchill called at Iceland on his way back from the Meeting.

Friday, 22nd   Went to see Mrs South – she is 83 and has been nursing her brother aged 86. When the Black-out had to be adjusted, they called on her, as the youngest in the house, to climb the steps and do it!

She was bombed out early last September. All windows broke and she and her Companion were hustled out into the blitz, owing to a time-bomb. Spent the night in a Public Shelter. Tried to find a cup of tea in the morning, but everything was terribly disorganized in those early days. Ventured back to the flat to gather a few articles, then Mrs South said they must go to an hotel for a night's sleep. Were in the Rembrandt having had a meal, and were going to bed when the Warning went again. Behold they had to trip down to the basement and spend the night on mattresses, with lights on and people talking all the time. The next day she set off for Essex, and just left everything. There an obliging man said if she would return on his lorry to London, they would store her furniture. So this wonderful old lady set off. They managed to pack everything in more or less. The Warning went again . . . Should they risk the drive back to Essex. Yes, she said. And with shrapnel falling around them, and in the rain they took to the road. She said to herself: 'Well, if the old lady can survive this, she can survive anything.'

Wonderful! She informed me that she can see and hear and talk on all subjects with enjoyment – but does not feel quite up to an Evening Theatre now!

Listened to Air Marshal Goddard give his war commentary. He described two cases in which the pilot had stood aside from his body and watched what was happening. In the first, others were trying to release him, and his spirit was struggling to allay their anxiety. In the second, the pilot watched his own body drowning – with the greatest calmness – and then saw it release itself from the cockpit, and shoot up through the sea. Most remarkable to have brought these memories through!

He also said that it was not that our squadrons retired gracefully from Crete to Egypt – but that they were nearly all destroyed. Only a few left. Pretty bad. The Germans are doggedly marching on to Leningrad, and the Russians are doggedly burning everything as they retreat. Marvellous people!

Sunday, 24th Poured with rain yesterday. Went up to the Lord Woolton Restaurant in N.H. Gate. Chalked up on the blackboard was: Londoners' Meals Service. Menu was steamed Fish, or Rabbit with Parsley Sauce, and two vegetables. All this only 11d. Really good. I sat down at an oilcloth-covered table and ate my stew. Not the last time I shall go.

Visited Jean Dowson in her flat for tea. Strange coming home in the darkness with no blitz. I thought of the many times we had all had to hurry home, with the Warning ringing in our ears.

Went to see Kit at Watford. Billeted with very kind husband and wife. Went a cycle ride – have not ridden for years. Found a lovely haystack and picnicked. She explained all her troubles at the Hospital – many auxiliaries leaving. Never get a chance to learn real nursing – solely kept as Chars . . . This is all right for a bit, but not after six or eight months. She says the whole place is run for the doctors; and the patients are the last preoccupation of the Matron.

Had greatest difficulty getting back to London. Awful scramble for bus . . . wanted to hear the Churchill broadcast.

Tuesday, 26th Mr Churchill made a stirring appeal to subject nations not to lose heart. He said how difficult it was to help the Russians, but we were going to do all we could . . . I believe the Great Meeting must have been somewhere near Iceland. He described it in splendid words. Sixty or seventy ships all in great lanes, bringing food and munitions. Round them were British destroyers, and over them the Catalina Flying Boats. Every convoy ship bristling with guns. He reviewed the

Convoy. It sounded like Nelson reviewing his Fleet before Trafalgar – with the ships of the line that they used to speak about in the old days.

Swansea is badly devastated, Miss M. said. They had a terrible time. Place packed to suffocation – no tea after the meeting, and then the long journey home.

Have heard Colonel Britton several times talking to the V Army, and telling them to go slow over everything. It is like an Edgar Wallace novel to hear him talk. Hardly seems real life. They are to walk slowly, be as late as they dare, linger over what they can, say the trains are late, and so on.

I think Thurston, the convict, passed near me the other night in Ladbroke Road. Apparently, he has been disguising himself as an athlete, and dashing about the streets in shorts. A man thus garbed passed me. Was a bit surprised, and thought there might be several more – Army men. But there was only one – hence my suspicions.

Blackberries are to be fixed at 5d per pound – if there are any obtainable, we can make blackberry and apple jam.

Very exciting about Laval. Lyndoe prophesied an important man would be wounded. Tonight he is worse.

Barishnikov described life now in the Isle of Man. Full of internees who are doing themselves well. No rationing. Ample supplies from Ireland. His tales of tinned fruit and oceans of butter are galling to us hard-living folk. He sent us all some kippers. He got through first to the Island by taking his Tin Hat with him, and with his fire-watching badge well to the fore. 'Service men this way,' they shouted to him!

End of August 1941

SEPTEMBER 1941

❈

September 7th Paddington station crowded when I took off. Not many trains, therefore each one is crammed to the roof. Very determined people pushed me on one side, and only by walking the length of the train was I able to find the last seat. Cath and Dr H. met me.

Mother and I went to Open-Air Theatre at Cannon Hill Park. An excellent seat and very cheap. The play, *Yellow Sands*, by Eden Philpotts, I had seen before. Lord Mayor and Lady Mayoress were just in front of us. There was a fleet of buses to take us home. In London theatre-going at night can be a nightmare in these difficult days.

Sunday a thrilling day. The Ginders have bought a caravan a mile off the Evesham Rd. Mother and I went and had tea on the edge of a wheat field, where the reapers and binders were hard at work. Lester and I offered to help, and the farmer let us make stooks. Together we carried sheaves and stacked them – plenty of thistles, but we enjoyed the experience and made 20 stooks.

Tuesday wandered round the town. Building it up wonderfully. Patching up shops – because Brum is bursting with folk, and they do business even if they are blitzed again.

Part of the Arcades open to the sky. Missed the Two Big Bears at the Furriers – perhaps they were burned. I remember them from my earliest childhood – and Father Christmas in the Arcade.

Wednesday went to see Elsie Roberts. Saw their bomb next door. It was as near their doorstep as makes no matter. It was a Czech bomb and only half went off – else their house would have gone too. Elsie was sheltering under the stairs, phoning to Neville – and he had the pleasure of hearing the bomb drop almost on his own house. He seems very tired from want of sleep.

Minnie came over from Coventry – only too glad to do a little shopping at our Woolworths. Coventry is like a city of the dead – as far as shops are concerned. They have run up a few with corrugated iron roofs. But the inhabitants are obliged to shop in Leicester, Northampton or Brum. Minnie has taken two rooms in a village with her father. One night when they started late they drove through bombs, and just drew up in front of a great crater.

We got Mother off to the Cotswolds for a holiday. Then Cath and I went to see the wonderful munitions procession lining up in Hagley Road. It was to attract women to the factories. All firms sent contingents in marvellously coloured overalls – on lorries containing parts of Spitfires etc. with the words: We Made These.

There never was such a talkative procession – they chattered like magpies all the time. One lorry had elderly women. We are all between 60 and 80 . . . we are still working – why aren't you? How happy they all looked. They insisted on a lorry being provided for them, otherwise they said they would walk – but left out they would not be. There were some wonderful Tanks – the fastest in the world. It was a mile long, with a donkey to finish up with!

Sunday I returned to London, and rushed to see Auntie Nell, who has now returned to her flat. Gave me bacon and egg for tea. Very agreeable. We went to her Church, where it was the National Day of Prayer. She had been to the Abbey in the morning.

Wednesday, 10th Exactly a year today that I returned to London to face the blitz. This was the night the anti-aircraft barrage took on a formidable tone, and gave Londoners some satisfaction. They had more to listen to than bombs falling one by one. I shall never forget the next fortnight as long as I live . . . sleepless, terrified nights, and days when you could fall off your chair for weariness, and yet somehow held on . . . the tense look on the faces of all the inhabitants of Notting Hill Gate – for, of course, I ventured nowhere else! At the end of that time I had established myself and my mattress on the Sanctuary floor for the night, and then at last some sleep came . . . and we adjusted ourselves to that extra-ordinary life. Tonight there is not even a Warning, and no Germans are near. I don't feel we can ever go through such a terrible time again – and the one thing that kept us going was Mr Churchill's indomitable courage.

The Russians are going through it now – but they have learned by our mistakes.

Sunday, 14th We have almost forgotten what a siren is! Heard a great explosion the other night – apparently on the out-skirts of London. No Warning. Cannot help feeling they are closing relentlessly in on Leningrad. The Germans pooh-pooh the idea of Napoleon. Mechanized transport, they say, has altered all that, and that they can continue through the Winter.

Grand to have Auntie Nell back in London. Magnificent apples in the shops at 9d per pound. Bought a pound, and felt like wolfing the lot. Auntie is making blackberry and apple jam with the sugar I have saved. Shops are cheering up a bit. Tomatoes are no longer hidden. Lord Woolton says if we are bombed again he will increase our rations to keep us going.

I must record that after Beryl got back from London Dudley had a raid. A small factory near chose to catch fire, a really handsome one, that flared well up to the heavens. Just getting dusk and crowds came to see what it was. Precisely at this moment a couple of Marauding German Bombers, seeing the conflagration from afar, came tearing along to add to the thrill. Cath's headmaster, Mr Greenaway, is the local Head Warden. So far he had had little to do – but at this point he took charge. The first bomb fell well into the flames with a terrific explosion. The Wardens shushed people into Shelters – and the result was that only two or three people were killed, and few made homeless. Mr G. was extremely pleased and Beryl had the fright of her life.

Raids have been keeping to the coast and Hull has had a good deal of attention lately. U.S.A. seems to be nearing war.

Auntie Nell has toured the ruins of the City, and could scarcely believe it. The half was not told her, she said. She was bowed to the ground. We have got used to it. I have been up two or three times, after each bad attack; but it must be a shock to see it for the first time.

Postscript tonight was by Frank Owen, Editor of the *Evening Standard*. He did not think Leningrad would fall. But if the whole of the Luftwaffe is let loose on the city, I don't see how it can survive. The Norwegians seem to be recovering their ancient fire, and are making a great stand against the Germans. Two trade unionists have been shot . . . and this will rouse public opinion against the Nazis quicker than anything.

Listened to the account of the wonderful pilot, Bader. The commentator said that, by rights, he should be an invalid in an armchair. Instead he was a crack pilot. The Germans when they found him with one metal leg broken would conclude you must shoot off an Englishman's arms as well, before you could stop him fighting.

Tuesday, 16th All sorts of rumours about Leningrad – that the suburbs are in flames . . . Dreamt I was on a Free French battleship fighting with them. What a dream for a timid, easily frightened soul like me!

Shah of Persia has abdicated and his son takes his place. He seems to conform to type as Shahs of Persia go.

Thursday, 18th No definite news from Leningrad. When the curtain does go up, I am afraid we shall find the Boa Constrictor has got his coils tighter round the Russian bear.

They have a magnificent view of the bombing of Boulogne Docks down at Fairlight. All last Summer they watched the Invasion of Britain . . . the sky black with fighting planes! One day a Spitfire came gliding towards the roof of Miss Loder. She heard it – the French windows were open – she remembers clinging to a wall, sure that her call had come. But it missed the roof by inches, skimmed the garden and hedge, and burst into flames in the fields. But the pilot had already baled out . . . on to the trees of a Hospital. So no harm was done. But all very unnerving. Who would have thought that a gentle little person like Miss Loder would have come through such alarming experiences so cheerfully. It really makes one feel there is no one like the British.

Sunday, 21st Terribly sorry for those dear people in Leningrad going through what we went through – only worse for them with an invading army at their gates. The Chinese ambassador gave the postscript tonight. He spoke as one who has knowledge of the ages – and to whom five years of war is nothing.

Mrs F. and I determined to go on the river if we could. Took a bus to Hampton Court. Weather dull. Discovered we could take the last steamer of the season towards Windsor at 3 p.m. There were men fishing as in the piping times of peace. If a dog was not beside them there was a cat gazing into the water with rapt attention. Passed Sunbury and Shepperton going through the locks. At Chertsey we got off, and walked about a mile to the town, and returned by Green Line bus.

We never know when the raids will begin and then we shall not venture far afield – but have to run to our little holes as fast as our legs will carry us.

Kiev, the ancient capital of Russia, has gone to the Germans. I don't know if we could help them more. The Italians seem to have sent a mission to U.S.A., preparatory to trying to get themselves out of the mess. But I believe the Germans have said they could crush an Italian Revolution in twenty minutes – and I think they could.

Italian prisoners are doing well on the land here. They like it, and are even making suggestions to the British farmers – who, more amazingly, are adopting some of these. Italians are very sweet people on the whole.

Went to see one of my poor old souls today. She has been getting a bit of chair-mending to do, and was better. She dreads the Winter – as last year she was compelled to beg in the streets; but now we shall help her. The dread of complete destitution is terrible. From Miss Moyes' article we have received quite a bit of money for her.

British bombers arrived at last in Oslo – long expected there, even to being jealous of Bergen and Stavanger! News spread, and instead of taking shelter as the Germans urged, the whole population took to the roofs and began to cheer the boys as they bombed the docks!

After it was over the Norwegians repaired to their houses to have a binge. Out from the backs of their cupboards came treasures of food. Then the news spread that two of our boys were in hospital, and there began a procession of everyone with flowers and fruit. The Germans got more and more embarrassed and moved the boys out. The ambulance had a triumphal journey through the streets of Oslo . . . and then the Gestapo got busy. But it is a fine story.

Splendid to hear of the five French boys who escaped in canoes to England. They came to see Mr and Mrs Churchill and all had a bottle of champagne together.

Wednesday, 24th Dreadful to read about Leningrad. Just as I thought – all gas and electricity gone; they are cooking on braziers in the street. Every day it gets worse, and the only end is The End – with the Germans marching in because we cannot help them.

So glad Mr Churchill has been made Lord Warden of the Cinque Ports. We used to visit Deal long ago when Lord Beauchamp was Lord Warden. There were bazaars and all the Lygon girls in beautiful frocks floated round the grounds. Duke of Wellington's bed is still there – the one he used on his campaigns. Too narrow to turn over in! When it was time to turn over, he said, it was time to turn out.

Thursday, 25th Victor Collins is going to America to learn to be a pilot . . . he loves flying. Thrilling to see him in uniform. When shall we all spend Christmas together again? We are re-starting Fire Practices in our road.

Reading *Insanity Fair* by Douglas Reed. He was all through the last War. Then had a job in Germany and knew that from the moment the Nazis were in we should have to fight them again. He has no use for the school of thought that believes the Germans were badly treated at Versailles. 'Nothing of the sort' he says . . . 'They recovered too soon.' The school of thought to which I am now converted is the – Non-Sympathy with Germans School.

Sunday, 28th   Mrs F. and I set off early. Reading bus full, so went to starting point and found a Thames Valley. I tucked into the back of my mind any misgivings about our return. Sun was shining and a glorious day promised. Had a map, for these days all place names are obliterated, and you don't know where you are. Along the Great West Road, full of factories, then through Slough and Maidenhead. River looked lovely. At Littlewick Green two little figures were waiting – John and David.

Plunged off along a country path – both talking together. Eventually reached the cottage, a primitive little place in a heavenly situation – right on the edge of a wood where the primroses and bluebells were marvels of beauty. Mrs Francis gave us a splendid meal, cooked on an oil stove. Neighbourhood full of evacuees. She is in charge of 45 of them. She has to visit and see they are clothed and medically treated properly. A splendid work. The local gentry are not always too satisfactory. Horlick family have a mansion there. But the poor take them in. A certain Grannie Norris has five! Her photo was in *Picture Post*. It is used for propaganda all over America. She had gone with the children to Sunday School.

A certain royal lady lives in these parts – the one who in her own land rides a bicycle.

In the grounds of a magnificent Park we found large portions of the British Army encamped on Manoeuvres . . .

and jolly tired they looked. Some were asleep under the trees. A group hailed us. I feared they were going to demand Identity Cards. My heart misgave me, for my handbag was at the cottage. But nothing of the sort. 'Do you come from those cottages over there?' the voice said. 'Yes', was the cry in chorus. 'Will you give us a cup of tea – we'll pay for it.' This was a job after our own hearts. 'Give me time to put on the kettle,' shouted back Mrs Francis.

Our excitement and interest were aroused and we ignored the cows of which Mrs F. is very apprehensive, and the bull said also to be there. The soldiers were soon at the door. We invited them in. They had not had a wash for days, and had slept last night under the trees with the rain raining on them. A cup of tea at 7.30 a.m. had been their last – they expected to sleep again in the open. Weren't they glad to have a chat and a rest. One came from East Ham, and the other Lancashire.

The rest of us set off with a large enamel can of tea. Little John decided to accompany us – and we faced the cows again. They are one of the things of which I am not afraid. Bombs yes. Cows no. John pointed out the bull – and the party became depressed with fear. Mrs Fisher declared she would drop the can and run. My idea was to explain to the bull that the British Army needed a cup of tea, and all private and local animosities must be buried for the time being. A village child in a bright red shirt now joined us – and John began to shush the cows! Feeling this might precipitate a crisis I called him sternly to heel. We reached the stile safely with the jug, and hailing C.B. as we had been told, handed it over to a very thankful and weary group of men.

To facilitate the way back I held firmly on to small boy in red shirt, and made John walk behind. Said goodbye to the two soldiers – who seemed brighter for the little chat. They made us a present of their shoulder armlets – a strange gift at the expense of the British Government. But it was all very sweet – and they did not know what else to give us.

We made for the bus – and it began to rain. Bus sailed past us. Gloom descended on us both. We tried passing cars, but they streaked by. Mercifully a relief bus came. We scrambled in and back to London.

End of September 1941

●●●● ❋ ●●●●

Wednesday, 1st Last night our squad had a stirrup pump practice in preparation for the Bomb Rehearsal. We took along our pump and about 20 of our Fire-Watch collected in a front garden. They laid a macintosh on the grass, and put an imaginary bomb and furniture around. Mrs Hoare and I elected to be first in. If you have to look foolish it is best to get it over! She pumped, and I wielded the nozzle on the bomb, lying prone on the grass. But I was not near enough and the pumping not hard enough. This is the drawback to women putting out fires. Mrs Hoare seized the bucket to put it nearer, and what with the pump and so many people watching, she upset it. This was really a success because it gave the experts something to talk about! In the end we got it going and everyone profited by our mistakes.

We are not looking forward to tomorrow night – we have the key of no. 5, and I have a suspicion they will plant a bomb there. It is all blacked out, and we shall need torches.

Buckingham Palace is to lose some of its gates to make tanks. Ours went long ago. No eggs again this week . . . 3rd in succession, rotten!

Thursday, 2nd The day of the Bomb Hunt. I had to search our house, no. 3, before rushing to join the others in the search next door. I tore over all the rooms, and two staircases. Then next door, where it was pitch dark. Mrs Hoare shouted . . . 'Mind the unexploded bomb.' 'What do I report?' I shouted. She, frantically wrestling with her stirrup pump: 'One unexploded, and one active bomb.'

Whereupon I raced downstairs and gave the report to H.Q. at no. 1. I was the second in. Then ran back to the bombed house. By this time Mr Hillyard was carrying the unexploded bomb in a bucket, while others were putting out incendiaries. I thought we had done pretty well, but imagine our surprise when we encountered a gloomy-looking warden who seemed anything but pleased – though had there been a real fire it would have been well out.

He held a meeting, calling all the workers – and proceeded to wipe the floor with us! We were undisciplined – too many people running about. In short we were as bad as bad can be! I was amazed, because I knew it was not so. All the incidents were taken in turn and the gloomy warden went on with his gloomy view about our conduct. Mrs Braddell, I could see, was fuming with indignation. She affirmed The Incident had been reported to her with great promptness. We put up with his remarks for a bit. But Mrs Bryans, prodding her husband, murmured: 'Speak up.'

So he did, as leader of the Squad, and gave an excellent exposition of the affair from the start, and ended up by saying he thought his party had done pretty well. So the warden turned on the G.W. party! I went to do our black-out, and left the others to deal with the rags of our reputation. I was most annoyed; but Miss Moyes can never be got to conform to other people's rules, and with her gammy foot, and Mr Hillyard with only one arm, Mrs Hoare was the only able-bodied member of our party. Miss Moyes had struggled up the stairs with armfuls of shovels and shields and buckets, that made Mrs Hoare laugh so much she could not get on with the bomb!

Next day we received a charming note to the effect that we should take no notice of the officious warden, who was only there to find fault. She suggested we had a practice on our own and criticize ourselves . . .

Sunday, 5th Apples and pears in Portobello market – lovely sight. At a price we can pay. 9d and 1/3d. Visited a house at Sunningdale with Mrs Watkins. Saw Virginia Water which had been drained because it is a landmark. Woods and trees. Took Medoc a walk – a Norwegian elk hound. Very docile creature. Would look grand in the snow. This is three Sundays I have had in the country. So enjoyable but they are coming to an end, for all the buses are being cut.

I have a good mind to take an unfurnished flatlet – if I can get one with a cooker and sink at a reasonable price. I have no furniture – but that is a detail. I possess a mirror and an armchair and an air-raid mattress. I could get other things by degrees. Should love to have my own front-door bell and kitchenette. Then Cath could come and stay with me. I am tired of asking the landlady's permission for this and that. There is always trouble over the milk.

Wednesday, 8th   Auntie Nell has been about an unfurnished flatlet for me today, and it looks as if we have found one. Main difficulty is furniture, but in such things I have faith. It all sounds most promising.

Old Mrs O'Leary came today, and she has bought her Pedlar's licence, as I told her. She is a dear little soul and obeys like a child.

Sunday, 12th   Still pursuing negotiations about my flatlet. Gas people will fit me free a free gas cooker – one of the old black ones; also sell me a gas fire – handsome green one, reduced from £4 10s to 30/-. They are selling off in case the whole stock is blitzed. So far so good.

Lord Beaverbrook just back from Moscow. Gave Postscript. A quick vigorous speaker. I can well believe he is bad-tempered, and fires everyone in a series of wrathful explosions; but at the same time can see through malingerers and grafters. He will get things done. He talks of 30,000 tanks. Only hope he can deliver them to the Russians, because the news is very bad. I thought of them getting to Leningrad – but not to Moscow as well. I suppose in a week or two we start raids here.

Friday, 17th   Germans are at the gates of Moscow – heart-breaking. The place that defeated Napoleon. I hear there is fog over Leningrad and that snow is falling. Mr Hillyard remarked that he wished it were Fire and Brimstone. But no such luck.

I don't see a very nice Christmas for us. The Brutes will then have turned their attention on us – and The Lull will be over. Then – England, pull up your socks, and take it again, for your sins of omission and commission.

Got poisoned this week with some cheap sausage rolls and felt sorry for myself. Had to rush to Gas, Light and Coke Co for my cooker. My feet were wet – rushed into Jolly's for the first thing that came into my head – shop being bunged up with people. Ate them within the hour – and was laid low. Struggled through the day somehow, kept waking during the night with colly wobbles. Auntie Nell came round. My digestion is excellent for any form of wholesome food, but bad sausage rolls it will not accept.

People think I am mad to take a flatlet. Lucy will send me an eiderdown. Mrs South will give me a table. Barishnikov will help me move on Saturday morning. Anyway, I signed the Agreement tonight. It is an adventure. I have always wanted an independent home, and if I wait until the end of the war, it may be years.

Sunday, 19th Managed to get a few things into my flatlet today. Did not like the look of second-hand beds – Barkers may have an air-raid bed that will do. By this time next week hope to be installed.

News from Moscow is always more terrible than the day before. Building barricades in every street. It is said the Germans have lost millions of men in the campaign . . . seems they have called for a million from Italy. Colonel Britton addresses the V Army on Friday night. I believe widespread revolt is fermenting in Europe – one day it will explode, but not yet.

Listened to *Any Questions*. Joad spoke again on astrology. I did not think he could get away with his, 'Bunk!' On enquiry he has discovered that four out of every ten in G.B. read the Astrology Forecasts, and there is an enormous public for them. This shows how clever men can be out of touch. He still denounces it, however. He reasons that the Universe is such a vast organization, and astrology gives to man an importance out of all proportion to his real place. Why should the stars bother about the paltry doings of individual man? Also he considered these cheerful prophecies sapped resistance, and so were bad. This is true. But Joad did not explain The Three Wise Men, and the great belief in stars in the pre-Christian era.

Thursday, 23rd Kit rang up. She cannot stand being an auxiliary nurse any longer. Said a lot to the Matron before leaving! She looks worn out. Is looking for a job, other than teaching if possible.

She set to work on my flatlet like the good pal she is. Took a taxi to her old room, and procured me a bookcase, a bedside table and a stool – also a corner cupboard and deposited them in the room. Glory, Glory, Hallelujah! Mr Dodd, noble soul, employed at Barkers, bought for me a magnificent pre-purchase tax mattress, and has sent it up. Wandered along Church St and found a desirable secondhand shop, there for £1 purchased a camp bed, and a cottage chair for 7/6d. The lady who had vacated the flat offered me a bundle of curtains and a divan cover for £1 [I have it still! later.] No electric light yet, and must sit in the dark over the week-end. But no matter!

Thursday, 30th Here I am in my own flatlet and it is very nice. Saturday was tremendous, and I was all in by the end. Began at 9.30 a.m. carrying small things across the road. Then Barishnikov appeared, and together we moved the big chair and trunks. I was lent blankets and sheets. Repaired to Lord Woolton for lunch.

Purchased a bottle of linseed oil, recommended by all the experts for cleaning furniture. On duty in afternoon, but excellent Mr Meyer was kindness itself. I merely sat by the office fire and dozed, without the energy even to think. Then he helped me with my air raid mattress up the road – I struggled up the stairs and there I was. Mr Hillyard fitted the electric light and black-out. The chaos of my new habitation was so great that it looked as if a bomb had dropped on the room. Then the Bell Rang! My bell! The wonderful Mrs Watkins arrived. Her idea was not to sit on a chair but to clean all the furniture with the linseed oil and vinegar. We then sat down and drank tea, while praising our handiwork. What a difference!

My bed felt a bit hard, but eventually I slept and woke in the morning with the sun shining in. Drank my tea listening to the wireless and looking at the sky. To think that only three weeks ago the whole thing had been the germ of an idea at the back of my mind – and now the reality was before me. I felt as if someone had said to me: 'Take courage. Mount the wave. Don't mind the spray and the buffetings. You will be all right – and it will carry you to a better part of the shore.'

So I hope I don't get blitzed! I can feed the birds on my window-sill. The family can regard it as their Town House. The little sink and gas-cooker make everything so easy.

Last Sunday, after tea with Auntie Nell, I went to Mrs South. Bitter icy wind blowing. She has a beautiful flat. She showed me a table she was going to give to me – a dream of delight. I begged her to think again. We had a grand chat – and then out I went to find a taxi. Not easy on Sunday in war time. I plodded up and down the Fulham Road . . . nothing. But after fifteen minutes in a biting wind I managed to stop a man. 'I'm just going home to my tea,' he announced. 'Well,' I replied, 'if you will take a table over to Notting Hill Gate for me, I will make you a cup of tea.'

So with much ado we got it strapped on, wrapped in a blanket, and set off. He was good, and kept watching it did not slip, plus sheets beneath. In the dusk we arrived at Ladbroke Road – he carried it up the stairs, and I made him the promised cup of tea! I was the third fare, he told me, that had stopped him having his tea!

I am more grateful than I can say to all the kind people who have rallied round and helped me.

Meanwhile the outside world has gone on – with war raging Heavens hard in Russia. The Germans are still outside Leningrad and outside Moscow.

End of October 1941

NOVEMBER 1941

܀܀܀ ❀ ܀܀܀

Sunday, 2nd   Last night we had a siren – first for a long time. The guns lifted up their voice and spoke. Jolly Old Wail set up. Could hear no bombs, and did not think it was to be a big scale affair.

Peaceful week-end, and at last have the hang of my habitation. Went to Portobello Market scouring for a pail, dustpan etc, unobtainable elsewhere. Returned and glad to sit without even a thought passing through my brain. Put some potatoes in the oven, and a rice pudding. The first supper in my own abode. A great event.

Postscript tonight was by an Australian. I got the European Service and heard them calling to the Saboteurs to persevere. The French are deeply impressed with the murder of the hostages.

Pears are 2/- a pound. Bought two oranges. No children under six in N.H. Gate, and the oranges are going bad. A parcel of dried apricots from Lucy. She has not had my diary since April, and specially wants to know about the May 10th raid.

Sunday, 10th Every night in the week working for the Fair. We do not know which way to turn. Have a wonderful shelf over my sink . . . so clever of the Chief Workman to find the right spot in the wall. Have given Mrs Smithers, who has been helping in the office, lunch every day and she enjoyed it. Glad to have her, for the pressure of work was almost unendurable.

Germans are at the gates of Moscow, Leningrad and Sevastopol – all three; but so far they hold.

Heard a recording of Nazi cruelty in a Concentration Camp by a German doctor. Made our blood run cold. He was an Aryan of Frankfort, and had been overheard in a café criticizing the regime. So he was marched off. This after 2000 years of Christian teaching.

Wednesday, 12th Shall be glad when the Fair is over. Eating pears are 1/3d each. Fish very difficult – Notice: No Fish. We are all due to get our Ration Books for tinned things on Monday. This will be better, as we cannot buy sardines or salmon now.

Good show in the Mediterranean the other day. Italians completely outclassed.

No Christmas cards next year, and we have to take all our wrapping paper to the shops. The Old Pole is very worried lest he should be fined. He always thinks they are specially after him.

A madman terrified everyone round here by shooting at random. He was caught after several hours by Flying Squad, on Kingston by-pass.

Sunday, 16th Yesterday managed to buy a bucket in Portobello Rd for 4/3d. Ridiculous price – but I was thankful to get it. Mr Hillyard managed to buy me a dustpan in the City, so I shall manage now.

The *Ark Royal* has gone at last; only one man lost. But all the Christmas presents the men were bringing home for their families went down with it. We have lost *The Cossack*, too, in the same week.

Two pints of milk per week for each adult. Difficult at the Sanctuary, as we do so much hospitality.

Friday, 28th Too busy for last fortnight to write up Diary. What a time we have had. We made £500 – and that in war time. Found it impossible to sleep for more than four hours any night – so I looked a wreck during the day. My Venetian-style dress was good – I felt like Bianca Capella . . . Mrs Hoare dressed as an Indian Squaw. She was lent one of the costumes used for Hiawatha at the Albert Hall. A few other helpers dressed up, and we looked quite festive.

The days before, putting the decorations up and moving the office furniture were hectic. One night I worked until 1 a.m. and most until midnight. Mr Hillyard helped me with the Buried Treasure Map. It was reckoned a success – and I have written the article about it for G.W.

Sorry the family could not come up, but I should have been utterly unable to look after them. On the Thursday a swarm of folk came up from Portsmouth, and you could not move on my Caledonian Market. My helpers were in great form selling the junk.

Had my first all-night visitor just before the Fair. Mary Bewley came. I cooked roasted potatoes, with beetroot and celery – finished up with oranges. She slept well on my air-raid mattress. Talked to me a lot about her Hospital, and why all the auxiliaries were leaving.

Germans are still held up . . . weather bad. But nothing to what it will be. A thousand pities if they get into snug houses for the winter – let them remain out in the snow like the Emperor Henry IV.

To return to Food. My one egg during a fortnight was bad – and they refused to give me another! Then milk rationing came in and this has driven me nearly demented all the week. But, at last, I have got a Doctor's certificate for Miss Moyes, and she is allowed a pint a day. The rest of us spread our miserable two pints over the week as best we can. The Cat is being initiated into a water and milk diet. He thinks we have gone feeble-minded. But he must live on the fat of his earlier days for the time being.

We are invading Libya – and seem to be marching on.

End of November 1941

DECEMBER 1941

Thursday, 4th Auntie Nell is back and coming to see the new domestic scene, with Mabel Lucy on Sunday. Gave Ivy curried lentils for supper, but difficulty over milk for tea. Also we are to economize with fuel – so there is hot water every other day. Felt it was too good to last.

A lot of points for one tin of salmon. Sardines are 7, and baked beans 4. Pears have been seen at 3/- each. Apples are practically unobtainable. Powdered milk has now appeared in the shops, and I bought nine pennyworth. It does not sound very nourishing, but you can mix a few spoonfuls, and put back the lid. Tins are a nuisance, as you must use them up rapidly. Shall be glad when the cows are doing full time again – I am more than ever in favour of cows.

Auntie Nell told me about Aldershot Hospital in the last War, where she had done a year. She left because she could not stand the low standard of military nursing. They thought more of losing an egg-cup than looking after the patients! It gave her horrors. She lost charge of her ward because she attended first to the men's wounds, and made the beds straight afterwards. Also because a V.I.P. came round, and the men's wounds had to wait till he had gone! She – a crack

surgical nurse from The London Hospital. So she sympathized with Kit's complaints. All my friends seem imbued with
the reforming instinct and I take off my hat to their courage in
bearding authority.

Very anxious to get home for Christmas. They say I must
come even if I come on a bicycle.

Sunday, 7th Nice bright day. Should like to get rid of trunks, but
something will come. Glad to return in evening to my dear
little room, listen to wireless and pack my Christmas presents,
picked up at the Fair. In spite of Government prohibition I
intend to go home for Christmas.

The Russians are doing marvels and have the Germans on
the run in the snow. Cannot help but wish it covers them.

Very sad about the *Sydney* being sunk with nearly everyone
on board. Seems incredible that no one got away.

Tried the powdered milk tonight. Not bad. You take some
warm water, sprinkle the powder on and whisk it in. Then it
begins to look something like milk, and is all right for cocoa,
puddings or an emergency. But it is amazing how we are
getting used to spinning out our ration. In the country they
don't feel the shortage – Auntie Nell had as much as she
wanted while she was away. But there is no playing about with
the United Dairies. Everyone strictly to the ration.

Tuesday, 9th We are now at war with Japan – and the Whole
World is in it. Air-raid warnings in San Francisco, and though
I do not wish anyone to be bombed, a little wholesome shaking-
up is good for people who contemplate the sufferings of

others with equanimity. Like we did the Czechs – and only woke up when we came within the orbit of the enemy ourselves.

Listened to the Midnight News on Sunday, after they told us at 9 p.m. that American bases in the Pacific had been bombed. Studied the map of the area, found Hawaii, and it looked so far from Japan – but we had forgotten Aircraft Carriers.

Poor dear people in those islands of bliss, sunshine and fruit drinks. They must have had an unpleasant Sunday afternoon. Lots dead, they say. Honolulu had a few bombs. The Americans seem to have leaped to their feet like one man. I should think Colonel Lindberg has retired to a room with dark blinds – not to be heard of for many a long day.

Listened to Roosevelt at 6.30 p.m. and heard all the applause. They sounded happy as sand-boys. Then Churchill at 9 p.m. Apparently he looked very serious in the House with a heavy scowl. He just told us we must work, and work and work. Well, if I must go, I must. The Calling-Up Date gets nearer to me; but it will not be until after Christmas. I shall let things take their course, and shall be guided, I feel sure, to take the right course. I wish I had a private income – then it would hold no qualms for me. I could pay my life insurance, keep on this room and not worry. But it may work out all right.

Still more excitement over the Pacific, today. Australia is waking up, and I hope the Socialists do a bit of thinking. Hitherto they have been so safe. It does everyone good to have a taste of danger. Then we learn to value the things we have.

As I came down the road saw a queue of aliens before the Police Station. There were a few Japs looking very ashamed of their yellow faces.

Wednesday, 10th Went up for lunch and was stopped by Miss Lambart on the stairs, asking if I had heard the news . . . The *Prince of Wales* and *Repulse* both sunk off Singapore by the Japs. I was horrified. This after hearing that the Hawaiian Islands had probably been lost to U.S.A. Poor Mr Churchill felt it dreadfully to announce such terrible news.

All so confused in the Pacific. There seem to be half a dozen battles going on in various parts. Roy Davies is out in Singapore. One of Cath's staff killed on Friday night in the black-out, by a Red Bus. Such a shock for the school.

Our Works Manager, who was exempt on health grounds, has to go to a War Factory within a month. A great blow. It seems only food and munitions are left to work at. Our machines, however, are only adapted for printing.

Everyone in Notting Hill looked very blue with the Battleship News. Just like after a big blitz. The Russians, bless them, are still pushing the Germans back in the snow.

Friday, 12th Events move fast and furiously, and we listen to all the News we have time for. Mercifully they have saved more than 2,000 men from the Ships; but what a time they had – and how sick they must have felt with all those aerial torpedoes falling around . . . dodging them, until they could dodge no more. The Commander-in-Chief is missing, and it is a resounding smack for us. Churchill did not try to minimize it. I like that about him. The news is bad – and he admits it.

But the Americans have come round with a swing. Also the Australians. Even a Warning at Port Darwin. The war reaches their gates, when it seemed so far away. Have heard all my life of danger to Australia from the Japs – and it seemed so vague. Now it is upon us – and what the British public does not know about geography will soon go on a 3d Bit. We have to wrestle with Japanese names now.

Sunday, 14th   Poured with rain all day. *Observer* quite cheerful. The Giant Awakes is the theme . . . There appears to be nothing in living memory like the awakening of America this week. Last Sunday they were still arguing in a torpid sort of way about this and that. In a flash it was all swept away by the news that Japan was on their doorstep, and if they did not move it would be too late.

According to Dr Remy the War will last another two years . . . but things are going well. According to Barishnikov it will end sooner. We shall see. Have been sleeping better – I was sick of lying awake night after night until 2.30 a.m.

Just read the life of *Grand Duke Cyril*. He was in the flagship at Port Arthur sunk by the Japs years ago. He seems to have lived well until the Revolution. But no one can have sunshine all the time. It has been good for the Russian aristocracy to do their own charring for a bit. I often think of the luxurious people of earlier days – the beauty and the dignity of the figures who have played such a regal part on the stage of this wonderfully safe little island. Well, we all look the same now in an Air-raid Shelter in the middle of the night! We have come down to fundamentals.

I am to go home on Tuesday, December 23rd, by the last

train – unless they push me off the running board. I don't mind discomfort if I can get through. In fact, am rather partial to the Guard's Van.

Wednesday, 17th Japs have landed in Sarawak. I wonder how the Raja and his family are getting on. It is a place that has always fascinated me. Of course our Navy, after the disaster, is conspicuous by its absence in those waters. A bad lookout . . . I don't think things are going well for us. But much is robed in silence.

But the Russians cheer us every day. They have recovered Tolstoy's estate – and found his grave desecrated. Village after village they are recovering . . . but now spotted typhus is breaking out in the German retreat.

In Libya we seem to be advancing and taking lots of German prisoners, even a German General . . . the first. Italians come in with greatest alacrity . . . there does not seem to be a nation in Europe who likes fighting less than the Italians.

Friday, 19th We seem to be losing Hongkong. Did not like the sound of it yesterday when the Japs asked them to surrender. I wonder if the Navy – if it exists at all out there any more, will take the people off. All those fine words about being ready for any eventuality in the Far East, are again just words. Marvellous capacity we have for under-rating everyone else, and over-rating ourselves.

What joy in Moscow and Leningrad and what mortification in the secret rooms of the German command. I am sorry for the Finns – I fear they backed the wrong horse.

Managed to get a pound of apples out of the Old Pole. Also some prunes. He is quite kind to me. Burning question is – shall we who are braving the Ban on Travel get home for Christmas! News from stations is conflicting. Some say all people are getting on – others that hundreds are left behind. I feel my journey on Tuesday will not be without adventure.

Sunday, 28th A journey almost without adventure! I was giving out toys and clothes etc. money up to the last. Mercifully the Morris family turned up – and I managed to leave the office at 4.30 p.m. Miss Moyes departed early – so dark had been the picture painted concerning the fate of travellers over Xmas. We just hoped that everyone else would be frightened – and leave the trains for us. Barishnikov amused himself with tales of broken ribs and barricaded platforms . . .

The truth was far otherwise. Paddington at 5 p.m. resembled a deserted village Platform – a few folk wandering about – a mild queue here and there. I consulted a porter. He told me confidentially that if I wanted to avoid the crush I should proceed to the end of this platform, and approach No. 2 from the other side. I thanked him, and padded along. Crossed the bridge, and was faced with a stern portress who demanded my ticket, and seemed amazed I wanted to go on so early.

The Cardiff train they said, had to load and depart before train for Brum could come in. I watched the travellers. In came Cardiff and one for Swansea. People all snug and warm were settled, when an important person strode on to the Platform and seeing the Swansea train with only about one person in every compartment, gave orders that only one train was to run! So all the Cardiff people were tipped out into the one for Swansea.

Still there seemed no particular crowds streaming in for the Birmingham train. We were just a thin line. In short, I have never travelled so comfortably! Had a corner seat. There was a nice little girl and her Mother who got out at Banbury. Snow Hill is all mended from the bomb, and looks tidy.

Christmas Eve, I toured the town. They have cleared the top end of New St . . . it is just waste land. Midland Arcade has ceased to exist. Mother went and booked seats for the Rep. *The Cricket on the Hearth*.

Christmas Day. Put all my little gifts round the table. We were seven altogether. Cath, Annie and I cooked the dinner – a goose, purchased by Cath and Paul. We felt ourselves lucky. We sent Mother to Church.

Visitors from next door arrived for the King's Speech, plus two airmen billeted on them. Cath and Beryl went along to the Ward Post to cheer up the person on duty there. One airman was from Edinburgh, the other from Galashiels . . . both young and homesick. Cyril Franklin arrived as usual. Then Neville called for me. Elsie, he and I had an excellent chiaccherone. From the back of Elsie's cupboard came plums and whipped cream. Then Neville poured some exciting looking liquid into glasses, and we did some Toasts. Not until we were half-way through it did I discover that it was champagne . . . brought out specially. So kind.

Then he had to return to the Ward Post. It was a glorious clear night. The paid staff were given the day off, but volunteers did one hour each – except Neville, who slept there as usual, as he is in charge. I returned home – later other friends came, and we were nine for supper. Very pleasant.

Went over early to Sutton Coldfield to see Ariel and Cecilia. I cooked the dinner. Later in the afternoon, Mother, Dr Hillier, Cath and Beryl arrived. We listened to Churchill's Speech from the Senate, and were thrilled! When he reached the part about America and Britain working together after the war, how our prayers went out to back him. It lasted half an hour – but it might have been only five minutes so fascinated were we.

We played table tennis and Cecilia put on her Titania frock, and looked more like a wild rose than ever. Dr Hillier left early, as he was on fire-watching duty at the General Hospital.

Cricket on the Hearth was excellent. But News has not been good. Manila has been heavily bombed. I hope the Americans have learned a lesson – they still think they can fight with kid gloves. When I heard they were leaving the town without defence, my heart dropped. It seemed an act of lunacy.

Sunday we returned – Cath has come with me. She likes my flatlet. Lot of people on the train – no heating, and we were three hours late reaching London. Our feet were frozen – but we thought of the Russians and the Germans and were silent.

It had been a happy time. We thought of all the people who were not with us. Dr and Mrs Remy, Victor. Roy Davies in Singapore. We managed well with regard to food. Dr H. had had a tin of butter from S. Africa, and Lucy has sent dried apricots.

End of December 1941

THE YEAR
1942

'From utmost east to utmost west'

THE MAIN EVENTS
OF THE WAR IN
1942

1942

January	2	Fall of Manila
	21	Japanese invade Burma; Rommel opens Libyan offensive
	24	Macassar Straits naval engagement
February	15	Fall of Singapore
	27	Java Sea Naval Battle
March	8	Japanese occupy Rangoon
	9	Conquest of Java completed
April	9	Fall of Bataan
	30	Japanese close Burma Road at Lashio
May	5	British land in Madagascar
	6	Fall of Corregidor
	7	Coral Sea Naval Battle
	27	Rommel's Second Libyan offensive opens Japanese complete conquest of Burma
June	4	Midway Island Naval Battle
	21	Fall of Tobruk
	30	Rommel held at El Alamein
July	2	Germans take Sebastopol

August	7	United States landing in the Solomons
	9	Germans take Maikop
	19	Dieppe Raid
	22	Stalingrad offensive opens
	31	First Battle of El Alamein
October	23	Montgomery attacks at El Alamein
November	3	Rommel begins retreat from Egypt
	8	Allied landings in French North Africa
	11	Germans occupy Vichy France
	12	Solomon Islands Naval Battle
	27	French warships at Toulon scuttled

JANUARY 1942

※

Thursday, 1st The first day of the new year. We all feel better than we did this time last year, and by the Last Day of this year we may see the end in sight.

Cath has gone back. We had a happy time. After the first night she found my air-raid mattress not so bad. I got quite attached to it in the end. She trotted round the town with Auntie Nell, and surveyed the blitz in the City.

We listened to Churchill's marvellous speech from Ottawa. It was superb once he got going . . . a new note crept into his voice, and one could feel the inspiration pouring down on him and loosening all the organ stops. I loved the 'narrzi – the Japanese frenzy and . . . the Mussolini flop.' His contempt for the latter knows no bounds. His lip curls every time he mentions him. It is true enough . . . he is a boaster who has been found out. Hitler is a boaster who has done big though horrible things . . . Mussolini has done nothing at all . . . just words.

How he lashed the men of Vichy. What had they gained by licking the hands of their conquerors, instead of standing up to them? He told us what the French had predicted for us . . . our necks to be wrung in three weeks . . . 'some chicken and some neck.' This brought down the house.

I am glad he emphasized the fact that Britain and her Commonwealth had carried on the war alone for a whole year, and walked the darkest part of the valley without anyone to help. He is cautious in his predictions, which is so wise . . . he thinks such and such may happen in the inscrutable future – but who knows? One can only echo Mr Mackenzie King's wish from the bottom of our hearts – that Mr Churchill may be spared to us at the day of victory, for which he has done so much to prepare.

[With regard to the above I have a note at the side: I cannot think it is anyone else but Fougasse . . . 'Alone . . . fifty blooming millions of us.']

Russians are still advancing. Doing spectacular things in the Crimea now, and relieving the pressure on Moscow and Leningrad. They had even begun to move food out . . . it seemed so hopeless. Yet the miracle happened, as in the case of Napoleon – only he did get inside the city. I find he reached Moscow early in September, and stayed five weeks. Began to go back in October.

The Philippines seem to be doomed. Japs advancing on Manila, which by the sound of it has been bombed out of recognition.

Managed to spend my points. Got some stewed steak. Next month they are going to release tinned fruit on points. Barishnikov went to Fortnum and Mason to spend his points, and got lobster and salmon. He saw grapes at 35/- per pound, and caviar at £5. So there is still some money in England . . . I should never have dared to go to such a shop.

Sunday, 4th Just listened to Anthony Eden making his speech about Russia. He seems to have got on well there. He is better at the arts of peace. He drew an awful picture of the Russian Winter, and the German soldiers he had met.

They say there are no quislings in Russia or Poland. There is a rumour that the King of Denmark may abdicate because he will not follow the anti-Jewish propaganda.

Nice parcel from Lucy. Cannot send butter, as they have no tins.

Feel I must record Cath's bomb, though some time ago, for the benefit of the family. I knew she had tackled an incident, but this is the full story. It was last Autumn – she was standing at the entrance of the Ward Post, Five Ways – the blitz was on. A bomb fell very near . . . they knew it was Broad St. Immediately the Warden Squad hurried to the scene – clouds of dust rising.

On their way they met crowds of panic-stricken people hurrying up from town. They had been caught in cinemas and theatres. It was about 10 p.m. By this time an oil bomb had fallen on Marshall and Snelgrove in New St, and kindled such a fire that it was like mid-day all over the town. The Wardens directed the people into the nearest Shelters. Then one man told them the bomb was just the other side of the road.

Cath was the messenger. She hastened back to the Post with the report that probably people were underneath. This was phoned to Control, and Rescue Squads and Ambulances were told to come. Meanwhile Cath had returned to the incident. Crowds had gathered, and another bomb fell! They all flattened themselves on the pavement. It was in Grosvenor Rd West – very near. Cath did not hear it fall. [My theory is that when you are as near as that you go temporarily unconscious.]

They picked themselves up. Some drunken youths were walking over the debris – this was very worrying because if people were underneath, it was making things worse. But as she had only just become a warden, she left it to Seniors to order them off. Instead she did her best to direct the Fire Engines, which by this time were hurling themselves along Broad St going to town. She stood in the middle of the road and yelled: 'Well over. Well over . . .' meaning thereby over to the other side of the road, owing to bricks and rubbish.

By this time the Wardens had established that, fortunately, there was no one in the shops, but there were people in the next house. They came out – shaking with shock – the old man carrying the dog, and the old woman crying for the cat and kittens which she had left in the kitchen. The Wardens said she could not have all the animals in the Shelter. Cath told her not to worry as they would go and find the Cat and kittens. With this the old soul went into the Shelter, where she was well looked after. The Cat and kittens were fetched.

Several times Cath had to run back to Five Ways with a progress report. All at home were in the Anderson Shelter, and I can imagine how Mother felt with Cath out in it. This is just a typical experience of hundreds of simple people, who never thought they would have to face anything like it. So I record it. I think she did pretty well.

Tuesday, 6th Listened to European News where they gave the story of a Russian prisoner held by Germans. They asked him where he came from. He replied: 'This is my country. Where do you come from?' They proceeded to maltreat him. Then again: 'Now, will you tell us how many are in your regiment?' The Russian answered: 'One hundred and ninety millions of us.' He died soon after he was rescued.

Bought rhubarb today. Very good. Bought also a little shell basket chair from the lady below . . . only 15/-. Promised to pay her in a few weeks, as this Rent in advance does me in for the time being.

Reading an old book – Lord Riddell's diary. Mentions Churchill a lot, and one can see his ideas have been maintained over the years. Also Lloyd George. An astrologer before the First War told him he was reserved for a purpose, and after would go into the desert. He has. Why has not Churchill given him a post? They were great friends in the past.

Sunday, 11th Gone very cold. I have my fire on in the morning – and before I go to bed. Do not work so late, and am sleeping better. Even had the energy to go to the Pictures. Managed to get a packet of soap powder. Clutching this began to wait in the queue. My feet as cold as ice; but after waiting half an hour, felt I must wait the other half. Lovely and warm inside. Saw Mr Churchill giving part of his speech. Looked old though, and I am afraid that when the need is over, the string will break suddenly. Charles Laughton with Deanna Durbin – very good show. Also *Bombay Clipper*. But these

American films go too fast. In the end I did not know how the villains were defeated, nor on which side they were.

They say the Japs have invaded Dutch Borneo . . . Very interested in Colonel Britton giving the names of the different Quislings, often addresses, too. Danes, Norwegians, Czechs . . . it sounded like Edgar Wallace . . . 'Be careful. We may come across the North Sea for you one day.'

Lux seems unobtainable now. Have a strong feeling soap is going to be difficult to get. All rations have gone down – fat, sugar and soon cheese.

Tuesday, 13th Wonderful postscript by Emlyn Williams. He gave a heartrending account of the actor, Esmond Knight, who was blinded on the *Prince of Wales*, just as it was going to sink the *Bismarck*. He is now in St Dunstan's.

Japs creep on in Malaya. Australia getting restive. One of the Dutch islands has fallen.

Managed to get a pound of apples from the Old Pole. Auntie Nell in with a savage cold. It is snowing hard.

Sunday, 18th Very cold, and sky full of snow. Set off to see Mrs Boyd. Have not contacted her for years. All very blitzed along Cromwell Rd. Now they are removing all the railings it looks more untidy than ever. Had tea with her. She is not cheerful – has received a few parcels from S. Africa, but living in an hotel you do not get much food. Must try and find her a jar of marmalade.

Walked back through Kensington Gardens. Snow covered everything. Neat piles of railing waiting to be collected. All very bare. A few people exercising their dogs – all very happy. The seagulls have come to N.H. Gate. A great shadow kept falling across my room, and on looking out it was a seagull circling round – perhaps he had come to wolf up the bread I had put for the sparrows.

Still retreating in Malaya. But the Russians are doing all the work. Mr Churchill is back safe, thank goodness. Our copy of Magna Carta with the Declaration of Independence have been put away somewhere in America in a bombproof place. Those two historical documents cuddling each other . . .

Went to do Auntie Nell's marketing for her in the Edgware Road. Found a mob of women waiting outside the Home and Colonial. One woman said she did not know if it was the Meat Queue, nor why we were not allowed inside. At last got in and offered ration books at Meat Counter. No meat until 2.30 p.m. Very cold in Edgware Rd, and decided to return. Watched the assistant bringing in great joints and tins of corned beef. At 2.30 again offered books. Heard an unpleasant voice behind me. ''Ere, this is meat queue. We've been waiting since ten to two. What are you servin' them folks for?' I could see I was wrong – I must have got into the wrong queue – so hastily grabbed the beef given me, and paying at the door, gained the exit. I could hear the controversy going on with the man . . . I fled the place. Auntie laughed very much – she could see where I had gone wrong. There may have been a riot after I left, I don't know.

Wednesday, 21st Have been looking after the sick, and padding through the snow with eatables. Snow deep – a minor blizzard. Miss Jones, a part-time worker, was sent home with bronchitis, and as she lives alone in a flat I went along. Found her very seedy. Made her some tea, and promised to return. At 8 p.m. went again, and found a friend rubbing her with wintergreen. However, the friend could only come occasionally. So I have been lighting her fire, and heaving scuttles of coal from the basement, and generally putting the patient in order. Mercifully I was brought up practical and can put my hand to this sort of job.

But it has gone on – rushing four times to the invalid, then back to the office to do some work. Auntie Nell better, and she gave me a meal. Arrived back at my flat to find I had forgotten to close the window, and a snowdrift half filled the room. But a lot of people are ill. Managed to get a pound of russet apples. But we have to divide up these treasures – and we only get a sniff of them . . . but just to look is good.

Important speeches from the H. of C. are not to be broadcast, or recorded. Mr Churchill, though disappointed, is not pressing the matter. He speaks as a man very sure of himself. He invited criticism, a true democrat.

Sunday, 25th Very tiring week battling with snow, and dodging in and out after invalids – doing their shopping, and trying to keep the office work going. Everywhere I was, I felt I ought to be elsewhere! Snow has gone now, thank goodness. Jean arrived, and also was tired. Her flat had been flooded with melting snow. Gave her a nice tea.

Sun shining this morning. Listened to *Any Questions*, and also to Dorothy Sayers' much discussed *Life of Christ*. Found it vital throughout. I suppose there will be a scream from the Lord's Day Observance Society. I hope no attention is paid to them, for it is so difficult to get religion presented to children in a way they will listen.

General news is pretty bad – and one does not rush to switch it on. Japanese menace has come with a rush to Australia. Dreaded so long, and yet never thought to be practicable. We always said: The Navy will stop it. But the poor Navy has too much to do, and must have air support now. Japs are descending on all the little islands like a swarm of locusts.

Russians are still pushing on; and quite calmly, one day, they will enter Berlin. Their delegates here are a lively crowd, touring our factories, and have not spared us, I gather.

In Music Hall last night a woman talked about the difference in attitude of butchers now: She said: 'In the old days he used to beg and pray of you to come into his shop. Nowadays you have to walk in bare-headed, and walk out backwards.' This sums up the position with every shop!

Tuesday, 27th The latest is that Mr De Valera is annoyed because he did not know the American soldiers were coming to N. Ireland, and he had not been consulted. Who does he think he is? Not lifting a finger to help in the fight for freedom, and thinks he should be consulted about defence! If the Germans come here, does he imagine the R.C. Church would continue to wield the power it has done for centuries.

The Australians are saying things they do not mean. Instead of regretting the sending of their men to fight, they ought to be kicking themselves that they have not a second army ready. The Russians have been training second and third lines of defence all the time – but the English expect to win wars from armchairs.

Mr Churchill spoke in the H. of C. this afternoon, and we were not allowed to hear it! Why don't they pass a law for a few months, and then repeal it as they liked. But I do feel his speeches are of an order of oratory we do not often get – and they should be recorded. We hear of Burke and Sheridan, but have no idea what they were like. We have had it on the radio in short paragraphs, and some of the power and might came through – but not the emotional appeal of the vibrant pungent phrases.

It seems we were not sure that Japan would attack. Personally, I think the people of Malaya could have done more. They have everything to lose. If they had got together an efficient Home Guard, they might have given the Japs a little more trouble. Hong Kong fell sooner than expected. We have had bad luck over the loss of the Battleships, and it looks as if we shall lose Singapore, and many of the islands. But Mr Churchill doubted if they would attack Australia. Equipment is being sent there, and the boys can go back and fight for their homes.

So the Speech went on – he took full responsibility for everything. He said that when he became P.M. there were not many candidates for the job! Now the market had improved. Then he had offered us nothing but blood and sweat – now he could see a light on the horizon gradually illumining our path. But the war was to go on through 1943 . . . and then our strength would be at its full height.

Another blizzard today. Got caught in it. Had to do shopping, spend my points, buy sprats for the cat, and so on – getting more and more snow covered. Mighty glad to get in.

End of January 1942

FEBRUARY 1942

❀

Sunday, 1st Blown a blizzard all night. A white world once more. Snowed all day. Went to Auntie Nell for dinner, and we got so excited over the state of Singapore that I pushed my chair nearer and nearer to the fire, and the tea cloth Auntie was drying on her famous stick caught – and it was all ablaze. She rushed to pick it up while I flew to open the window, and seizing the burning stick held it out in the snow. Room full of smoke, but mercifully nothing was damaged . . . it was all Hitler's fault. We resumed our repast, feeling as if we had successfully disposed of an incendiary bomb.

Woke just after nine, and listened to Tommy Handley. Also to a bit of Pepys – always a joy. This was done by Joseph Macleod, the announcer, who Miss Moyes always says reads out the Worst Possible News as if he were offering chocolates and biscuits all round. A better description of him could not be found, I think.

The News is awful. We seem to be at bay on all sides . . . ten years out of date in everything. Singapore will fall in a fortnight – or less. As one M.P. said, it cost 20 million to build, and it won't last 20 weeks.

I hate the word Benghazi. Wretched place. We take it and rejoice – and lose it the next minute.

They seem to have millions of tons of snow in Brum. No wonder neither Mother nor Annie could get out. I asked the price of unpainted tallboys in Barkers. The most miserable specimen is £3, and those that were 25/- are now £5. Bought a spare hot water bottle. They say there will be no more for years; so I am keeping one in reserve until we get Malaya back – and the trees being to grow again.

Wednesday, 4th News not much good except the indefatigable Russians. We are retreating in Libya, and the poor folk in Singapore seem to be having a thin time . . . No balloon barrage and no fighter defence – I don't see what they can do.

Lord Beaverbrook is to be Minister of Production. Seems to be a favourite of Churchill. He went with him on that awful journey to Tours, when the French were breaking and asking to be released from their agreement with Britain not to make a separate armistice. Am reading a book called: *Truth on the Tragedy of France*, by Elie J. Bois. He is a Frenchman and truly ashamed of all that happened . . . My word, how they had the jitters! What a collection in their Government! One cannot attempt to imagine Churchill's feelings during those awful days. No wonder he keeps on saying how much better off we are now.

Auntie Nell went to an Exhibition of Modern Art – friends urged her to go. They ought to have known better, she said, snorting with indignation. She would not disgrace her back kitchen with such pictures . . . To cheer her soul she went to the National Gallery to look at the Rembrandt of *Marguerite Tripp*.

Sir Kenneth Clark spoke on *Any Questions* about the greatest picture in the world. Mentioned the Rembrandt – but said it was impossible to name any one picture. There were the windows of Chartres – the Rubens' landscapes. Mona Lisa was entirely different in appeal from Rembrandt, having an atmosphere of mystery as opposed to representation of character. He also spoke of the Sistine Chapel.

Going home last night had to hang on to the railings, the pavements were so slippery. Thankful for my snow boots, in which I slop about very happily.

Sunday, 8th Just heard soap is to be rationed. One by one it comes. Don't know how much it will amount to, but there are to be four coupons a month for soap flakes and toilet soap. I expect things will adjust themselves, and we shall be able to help one another.

We had a heart-broken woman in on Friday. We often help her, because she is looking after a neighbour's children as well as her own. Thursday she joined the Rabbit Queue, and got so cold that she put her hands up her sleeves and her handbag under her arm. It was soon whisked away. In it were her own few shillings, and £2 separation allowance for the neighbour, who was coming out of hospital. Poor Mrs Cameron did not know what to do. She was to pay the rent and buy the food – and now all the money had gone. She tried to borrow it, but the sister-in-law was ill, and had no money. She came to Miss Moyes, who told her she had had the lesson of a lifetime! We gave her the money. Such things easily happen when you have a lot on your mind.

We can get no coal. Fortunately the coke did come, and we are burning that. Tonight no fire in the office – and I am enjoying (?) the discipline of sitting without any fire, like the people of Berlin.

News is still consistently bad. Libya is a wash-out as far as we are concerned. Singapore is waiting for the onslaught – and no one knows what the outcome will be. I am inclined to be optimistic. But that is a bad sign as I am usually wrong about places falling. Like Moscow and Leningrad – they don't. So probably Singapore will. The Japs are swarming like monkeys all over the island, and it is difficult to stop them.

Amazing to see the patience of the women in the Cat Food Queue. It was snowing. They were loaded with heavy shopping bags, and then came a long wait for food for the cat! But they seemed amazingly cheerful. They waited for Pussy's dinner with the same good humour they had waited for their own.

Mice are said to be in my house up the road. Hope they don't reach my flat.

Tuesday, 10th News from Singapore steadily worse. Japs landing on the island. A few notes from an American journalist expelled from Berlin and Rome. He was in Berlin during some of the R.A.F. raids. Bombs on Unter den Linden just missed all the Ministries by a fraction. But once we destroyed the largest grain warehouse in Germany. Berliners rarely smile. Goebbels gave him 24 hours to clear out. Took a plane to Rome, where the people were smiling. Then little by little Germans appeared on the streets – and the Italians became busy elsewhere. He said since the Russians came in the Germans were more united . . . felt they must fight to the death now.

Singapore holding by a thread. Poor thing! Could not sleep last night for thinking about them. Then this morning we hear of Those Wretched Battleships steaming up the Channel! Though we attacked them with all the bombers and aircraft we could rush to the spot, we cannot sink them. We have bombed them a hundred times in dock – and yet they can wander up and down the Channel, and take their way to Heligoland. It really is enough to make one scream! We lost two battleships to the Japs – yet we cannot sink one in our own waters. They can put up smoke screens – we don't seem able to. We need a spot of good news from somewhere very badly!

Apparently the announcer is doing his best at Singapore, while women and children stream to the ships. Reinforcements are on the way. The wonderful defences of Singapore have never been used . . . the guns are embedded in concrete facing the sea! An attack from shore was never contemplated.

Sunday, 15th Singapore has fallen to the Japanese! It has been a mighty pleasant week for the British Empire! The German Fleet passing our doorstep; and apparently it being impossible to stop them. We do seem to be biting the dust – and no mistake. Everyone is uneasy, and no one knows exactly what to do. Mr Churchill is to speak tonight at 9 p.m., and perhaps he will give us back a little confidence, because at the moment we seem as near Zero as when France betrayed us.

The *Observer* somewhere makes allusion to the Dutch sailing up the Medway, in the reign of Charles II, as some parallel to our humiliation of this week. Our poor boys did their best. It is heart-breaking to read of the *Swordship* men – not one of whom came back.

Yesterday was lovely. Snow had cleared and I set forth into the Great Wide World. Nothing at our little cinema, so took a bus to Marble Arch. Walked along Baker St. Found Druce's with a few hastily put-up shanties, and further up a space like a hockey field. Don't know what had been there. Pushed on to Marylebone Rd. Madame Tussaud's still extant, but Cinema a ruin. Walked along T.C. Road. In the Crescents facing Gt Portland St they had had big bombs. Maples only a façade. The rest is Non-Est. Enjoyed Heal's – lovely fabrics still. I do love satin curtains – but never expect to own any. Kept thinking of the night Miss M. and the others walked along, ankle deep in broken glass, with the blitz overhead.

All cinemas had queues. On to Oxford Circus – was very tired. Gave up and took bus home, but had enjoyed the sunshine and change of scene.

Listened to Brains Trust. Malcolm Sargent excellent on swing music. Commander Campbell was sure Shakespeare had sailed before the mast, as all the remarks of the sailors in *The Tempest* were exactly right. Women do not do themselves justice – always seem self-conscious. On the relative merits of Plato and Confucius Joad said there was no doubt that Plato was the greater man. Every problem which still worries man was known to Plato, and discussed by him.

Am saving all points for tinned fruit, which should come

on 23rd. But we do not know – indeed, one feels that nothing is worth while at the moment. Time is getting on . . . what will Mr Churchill say?

Tuesday, 17th Listened to Mr Churchill and hung on every word. He announced the Fall of Singapore as a great English and Imperial defeat. It seems that things have been far worse than the most pessimistic of us ever thought! At no time have we been in a position to defend the Far East against Japanese attack. That is why we had to put up with their sauciness. Yet the public was soothed by hearing of all those reinforcements to Malaya! The poor men have availed nothing and vast numbers are now prisoners! Apparently some of the pilots got away – fighting their way to their machines, as the Japs pressed into the aerodrome . . . and the ground staffs remained to be taken prisoner.

Reading behind the speech, one can see what a burden he has carried. Though I still feel the people there could have done more – as the Australians will have to do to save themselves. No use depending on us – our poor Navy is a very thin line. The difficulties of supplying the Libyan army at all, is shown by the fact that ships with tanks and ammunition have to go round the Cape! The Mediterranean is closed.

He showed us the perils we have come through – that America has come in for us at last. He never thought the Japs would be so mad as to attack them. Now we must wait for America to mobilize her full strength before we can take the offensive!

It all sounds very plausible, and I suppose we could have

done no better. He contemplates further disasters, and we must be prepared for other losses. The Japs are very quick, and we must be the same. But when you are accustomed to the feeling of security given by the Navy, it is difficult to adapt yourself to the fact that you are naked to the world!

Mr Hillyard is as optimistic as ever and will allow no gloom. He says it will all come right in the end, and we shall be listening to a long procession of victories! How lovely!

There seems to be a murderer about killing women in lonely flats – hope he does not settle on me as a likely subject. I walk up the middle of the road, and swing my torch around. Dying for one's country is one thing – but being murdered by a maniac for your handbag is a very poor ending to life!

Jean and Mary came to a cosy supper and felt the state of the world was awful. Jean goes to a new job. I am sorry for we were co-operating over some of the poor folk in Paddington.

Miss M. went shopping and was shocked at the prices. She looked for cups, found some yellow ones chipped round the edges, and was asked 21/6 for half a dozen! Then saw a complete and pleasing set – price £7. Soon we shall be drinking out of basins.

Port Darwin badly damaged. If it has only 3,000 inhabitants who live in small bungalows, there cannot be much left of the place. I should hate to retire to a Mangrove Swamp! The day of reckoning is here.

Sunday, 22nd Sir Stafford Cripps has taken a big position in the Government. We shall see how he shapes. He is not the mildest of men. Much is expected of him.

Miss M. stopped a riot in Woolworths on Saturday! She found two Canadians trying to buy some soap. One proffered a pound note. But the girl could not sell without coupons. The men argued they had come to London for a week, and could not do without soap! Miss M. hastily gave them some of her ration. The soldier declined – and things began to look lively – so Miss M. explained she had visited Canada, and she would be deeply offended if he did not take it. Obviously a remedy needed for this state of things, for the men were angry.

Tuesday, 24th Listened to account of debate. Mr Churchill sounded very depressed. The whole prospect seems one of unrelieved gloom. I suppose in twenty years time some of us will be reading books of reminiscence on Singapore, and much will be revealed. The Service chiefs thought the place could be defended – and sent an army of men without aircraft. In reality, it was not possible . . . the men were lost, and all was too late.

Princess Elizabeth is to be Colonel of the Grenadier Guards – that is the only cheerful piece of news.

End of February 1942

MARCH 1942

❀

Sunday, 1st Thank goodness February is over! A real black month for weather and news. Very busy the last few days. The Pig-breeder arrived with a few hundred weight of coal for us to distribute – better than money. He is one of the many excellent but eccentric people interested in Miss Moyes' philanthropic work. He often sends us money, but the other day he came in person – in yellow corduroys and gum boots – and looked to me seven feet high. Would give no name or address. The two Morris* children, Florrie aged ten and Jimmie thirteen, came along with a wonderful barrow. Wheeled it back to Chalk Farm. Thousands have no coal in this bitter weather – and all London houses are restricted. We have none, but our coke is due on Monday.

A bit of news has trickled through about Singapore from refugees arriving here. Lady Popham went there, fresh from the London blitz, and tried to teach some A.R.P. No one interested. Tennis, bridge and dancing seemed to continue to the last. A man on radio said how terribly he felt the loss of the

* One of the families the Association helped in whom we had a special interest.

place, as he had lived there for many years. He could see in his mind's eye the British flag, that had waved there for 100 years, being taken down and the Rising Sun taking its place. He could see those Indian and Australian regiments piling up their weapons – and the Japs grinning – as only Japs can grin. A nice picture!

Tuesday, 3rd Auntie Nell not too well. She has been over-doing it looking after other invalids.

Japs are well into Java. Wavell sent to India. The Dutch felt that, as the place will probably be lost, they may as well lose it themselves as let someone else do it for them! They are sore. They have been slow – but we have been slower. Glad to see Australia is about to conscript everyone.

Wednesday, 4th Garvin has left the *Observer*. Indeed a bombshell. I have read him every Sunday for 25 years. He has quarrelled with Lord Astor over policy. Garvin is all for Churchill. Does that mean the Astors are not?

Rumours that the *Exeter* has been sunk. This from the Japs – our people do not say it – but I daresay it is true. Bad news usually is.

Sunday, 8th Auntie Nell is ill with cardiac asthma. It has shocked us all. With rest she may pull round. She has been warned not to gad about and do everything she would like to do. I got her away to Mrs South's flat. She seemed very happy there.

I have to register on June 13th. How much longer after that I shall be able to remain at the Sanctuary is all according to how fast they can absorb the women – and how the war goes. I do dread being taken off my job where I am fully occupied, and whisked off to some place where I only stand about.

News awful – Java practically gone. All communication ceased, and the defenders have said goodbye to us.

Shall go after tinned fruit in the morning. This will be the last before the War ends. It is to save shipping. Rations are to be cut. But the Food Minister has shared things around and no one can grumble really – only the Food Fads are suffering.

Wednesday, 11th Awful news from Hong Kong. I dreamed I was there – that the Japs were after us, and we had to ride on horseback 400 miles to escape! Mr Eden read a statement, and it was all he could do to read it. British officers and men were bound hand and foot and bayoneted to death. The sick not attended to – the dying were left – the dead not buried. No sanitation in the Camp. If I had anyone left in Hong Kong I should go crackers. Same may be going on in Malaya and Java. The Japs are drunk with victory, and are behaving like the mercenaries in the Thirty Years War at the sack of Magdeburg.

A wave of horror has passed over England, and the H. of C. could hardly bear to listen. But various people have escaped and told the tale – so there is no doubt about it.

Miss M. wrote to the Canadian military authorities about the incident in Woolworths. Their H.Q. sent back a charming letter – and three cakes of soap! They thanked her for her part in the affair.

Wonderful story the other night of four men who came down in their aircraft on a snowy mountain in the North of England. Each man found himself propped up outside the plane, which had descended in flames. By rights they should all have been burned – no human hand had lifted them out. It reads like a genuine miracle.

Russian women are really formidable. Nurses jump by parachute on to the battlefield. Hospitals are so far away, and the men need skilled attention immediately as in the intense cold they may die if wounded.

Sunday, 15th Auntie Nell is better. Hectic day Saturday. Worked in morning, ate lunch standing up, went for her rations, and set off with many things from her flat for Mrs South's. Lovely Spring day.

Battle of Java Seas is out. Very bad. We lost *Exeter* – and other ships. Pathetic to hear that *Exeter* had radioed about the two Jap cruisers closing in on her, crippled as she was. Then no more was heard and she must have fought to the last, poor thing, and then blown up.

More disclosures about Hong Kong. All terrible. Miss Harrop, who escaped in some miraculous manner, has been telling all the horrors she has seen. Do not bear thinking about – the poor women, the nurses . . . and so on . . . what a fate!

Food has come in from America. Glorious day. Snowdrops on sale in shops.

Monday, 16th Air raid warning this morning. Great surprise. It was a lone reconnaissance German plane – within 30 miles of London. It got in under the clouds.

Terrible shock today when I had an urgent call to go home as Mother has incipient appendicitis, and must lie up for several weeks. Difficult to drop everything. Rang up and shall go home at week-end, and see what can be done. All most upsetting, as I had had such a happy letter – and she was coming up for Easter.

Lots of people ill. Our caretaker in hospital. Mr Resti off sick. Mrs Hoare's mother – the Little Old Lady – is just pulling round.

Wednesday, 18th Miss Ashton said she had passed soldiers at Tube Station. I ran to the gate. They were English lads breaking ranks for 10 minutes after a 17 mile route march! One of them laughed and said: 'Got a chair, Miss?' Whereupon I invited those near the house to come in. I sat them in the Library where they lighted cigarettes. No time to make them tea – but I brought glasses of water, and handed round a tin of sweets. Then someone called from the road, and they all had to tear off to join the column. They seemed very pleased with the interlude.

Went for an osteopathic treatment tonight. Felt as if in the hands of the Gestapo. They pummelled my spine and neck until I was unable to move. The more he hurt me the better he seemed pleased – because it showed there was trouble. Lasted for half an hour. It is a Poor Man's Clinic, but you go by appointment, and conditions are nice. Shall give it a three months' trial.

Sunday, 29th Too busy to write Diary. Went home, Cath met me. She had had a terrible week, dreading to leave Mother all day with only Annie, and not able to stop away from school herself . . . and struggling to find someone to come. I propounded my plan to have Mrs Idiens for a month. She wired to say she would come on Monday.

Very strenuous weekend at home. Mother goes up and down. Everything difficult. I have to register on June 13th. Seems an idea to return home, and do part-time work in Brum.

Terrible week in office to make up for my defection. Went to see Auntie Nell. She looks white, and is very weak.

Dr Prosser, who is attending Mother, asked me to go and see two elderly friends of hers in Elsham Road. Found the place. They had been bombed, and were in financial difficulties. Two Poor Old Dears . . . had had incendiaries and had had to leave their house in flames in the middle of the night. Returned to find it deluged with water and soot. A bomb had gone through the Water Tank! They have never got the house right – walls are growing fungus. Clothes thick with mould. They have neither strength nor money to put things right. The remains of nice Parsonage furniture were in the room. I was sorry for them. Anyway, I can let Dr Prosser know.

News much as usual – deplorably bad. But we seem to have raided St Nazaire, and closed some dock gates – so the *Tirpitz* cannot get in or out – I don't know which . . . Sounds good piece of work – but some of the raiding party were left behind.

Dr Hillier is off on holiday . . . he looked as if he needed it. Has been at the Hospital every day for a year, and three nights a week fire-watching.

Colonel Britton seems pleased with the V Army – says they are slowing things up in Europe.

Crocuses are out – with the sunshine. Coal and coke arrived . . . great windfall.

End of March 1942

APRIL 1942

✴✴✴✴ ❋ ✦✦✦✦

Wednesday, 1st My Birthday ! Almost too busy to notice it. Had a treatment tonight. My osteopath is very interesting – we talked about Red Indians.

Sunday, 12th Home for Easter. Had a holiday time spring-cleaning ! Tried to cope with the mice. Spoke my mind to the cat. It is disgraceful that all the Cats have joined some sort of Pacifist Organization. To keep a cat in these awful days of food scarcity – and then have to catch the mice yourself . . . is a bit thick. I explained this to our animal.

Mother seems to be making progress, and even came down to tea. The trouble is to keep her from crashing again. She and Auntie Nell are both so ambitious about what they are going to do. She even thought it would be nice to have Auntie Nell to stay with her for a month as soon as they both got better – and she would look after her! You see, there is no holding these active people back . . .

Got back to London rather worn out, but soon settled down into my own routine. Went to my osteopath, who nearly killed me. Mr Hillyard is also going for his arm.

Seagulls have gone now, and only sparrows come for my crumbs.

Monday, 13th Decided to go to Wimbledon and see Mrs Grace. She had survived the blitz, though bombs had fallen all round. In the next road they had had all the ills possible . . . no water, no electricity, no roof, and the bombed-out all cuddling into one house. Almond trees were all in blossom. I met a young man carrying a tennis racket. Amazing sight! I stared at him.

Got to Lambton Road. Ellis family thought I had been killed on the night of May 10th, and had been relieved to hear from me. Toured the bomb damage in Worple Rd, and can well imagine what it looked like after the event.

The war goes on its unhappy course. The moment our ships show their noses in the East, they seem to be found and sunk. We never have enough aircraft. So the tale goes on. The only cheerful thing is that we raided Italy last night, and the Italians having tired of the Blackout, were all alight, and could be seen very well. How typical! Like children they do not like the dark. I expect Mussolini has given them a good hiding.

Wednesday, 15th Aunt Winnie brought me the world's most Magnificent Saucepan. Have never seen its equal. Apparently there is a famous shop called Staines in Victoria St. She went on Monday morning, and was allowed one. They will be pleased in Brum. Am now trying to run a kettle to earth, and then we may survey the war in peace on the Kitchen Front. Japs and Germans seem much more trying if you have no kettle.

It is amazing the number of people who think we shall win back the Empire with the greatest of ease. Personally I think we shall lose a good deal, and receive a good drubbing – as we did in the American War of Independence.

APRIL 1942

Daffodils are out in all their glory. Invalids are better. Lucy sent me a most scrumptious parcel, including: butter, cheese, sausages and very enticing little tins – also sugar. Am more glad of the butter than anything else.

Sunday, 19th Such a lovely day – almost like Summer. Friday Miss Moyes went away, so did general things. Cleared out much of the bombed furniture which has been given us. Got really dirty. Put some things for the Morris family who are glad of anything. Renewed egg and milk special for Miss M. Walked back along Holland Walk. All the little Maltese children were playing there. Most of them about two or three years old. There was a Siamese cat sitting on the garden wall, and they were shrieking with delight at this animal – and babbling in Maltese to one another. Holland House is now visible. Walls are standing – but close to I suppose it looks awful.

Went to Auntie Nell, and helped her hang her new Black-out. She feels well, but is breathless with the slightest exertion. Mabel Lucy was there. She came back to my flat. Unfortunately, I introduced the subject of *Men Must Weep* by Beverley Nichols. I always forget Mabel is an unrepentant Pacifist. Even now she will not admit that their Propaganda has largely led us into this mess. He writes of the idea launched some years ago, that a body of non-belligerents should march between the battling armies and stop them. He says how ludicrous it all sounds now. When the Test came it did not come off, as people thought it would not.

Listened to the item *Strange To Relate*. It appears that the other day a man was sketching the ruins of St Clement Danes, and while talking to a workman, he saw on the floor a farthing! Looked again – found five in all. They were covered with white dust from the fire. They thought of the old Rhyme: 'Oranges and lemons say the bells of St Clements. You owe me five farthings, sang the bells of St Martins . . .' They were both so excited over the discovery that the finder took the five blitzed farthings to the Trustee of the Church, who is having them framed. Certainly rather curious.

Took a book on Father Damien into the Park. Trees all have a mantle of green and look so fresh. The lovely yellow flaming bush is out everywhere, and a wonderful white tree just at the ornamental end of the Serpentine. Sat down by the water. Crowds of people had boats out. One full of sailors, who did not bother to feather their oars – I suppose on the Atlantic you have no time for such elegancies.

Back in time for *Brains Trust*. Lay on my divan, drank tea and enjoyed it thoroughly. Malcolm Sargent a delightful speaker. Hope Lucy heard it, for it was broadcast to the Empire for the first time. Miss M. and Auntie Nell are aroused to frenzy by this programme. But surely it is an education to the British public to listen to entirely opposite views expressed with politeness and good humour.

We have flown to Augsburg in broad daylight. A mighty feat. Tokyo has been bombed – and we all feel better for that news. There is nothing like dosing out the medicine all round. But the little yellow men are still advancing in Burma – and we do not seem able to stop them.

Sparrows and pigeons cannot understand my open

casement. They congregate and listen to the wireless – seemed to enjoy the Brains Trust.

Sunday, 26th All is not well on the home front. I thought Mother was going away yesterday to have a fortnight in the country. But she has had a relapse. Specialist fetched, and he thought an operation advisable, as otherwise she would always be much of an invalid. So Cath took her to Hospital. Auntie Nell seems to think Mother will stand it well, and come out hale and hearty. All very worrying.

Had a scrumptious repast with Auntie Nell – the first since her illness. She is all excitement because the Secretary of the Art Collections Fund has invited her to Manchester to see the Drake Globe given him by Queen Elizabeth; it is being bought for Plymouth. She will be allowed to hold it in her hand. We were very jubilant about this, and Auntie seemed to have some idea I could get the morning off to come with her!

Have bought a piece of bombed furniture – perhaps madness, as I may have to return to Brum.

Went to see dear Mrs South. Often have I planned the day when I could take Mother with me – now it seems further off than ever. A Mrs Sutherland was there to tea, a young widow, who had lived in Hong Kong all her life. Her whole heart and soul was there. She had returned home owing to her Mother's illness. Now they have lost all their money – is penniless, and is working in London in the Bank of Hong Kong. Her brother is a prisoner, and she is terribly worried about him.

She is obsessed with the idea of going out on a Hospital Ship to the East, getting somewhere near the island and swimming ashore. She knows the Chinese would help her and she would search for him. It is all so tragic. She spoke well of the faithfulness and loyalty of the Chinese, who have affinity with the English.

She spoke of the Salt Gabelle and she knew the Tweedie family – as I did, for both the girls were at Poggio Imperiale. Muriel and Pat, both married now. Joyce Turner, daughter of Mary Borden, was there at the same time. All most interesting and unexpected.

Walked back along Holland Walk – trees of freshest green. We are all heartened by the terrible raids on Lübeck and Rostock. It is dreadful to be so glad – but we cannot be anything else. They raided Bath badly yesterday, and Exeter. We brought down five.

Our raid on Tokyo had repercussions in Japan. They seem to be chopping off the heads of all their A.R.P. people. There cannot be much shelter in wooden houses with paper walls.

Malta people highly delighted about the raid on Augsburg. I love the story of the old woman sitting in a Shelter, muttering to herself, during a raid on Malta: 'Please God, send the Italians . . .' over and over again. They certainly don't seem to be terrifying enemies. A story from Libya runs that Italian soldiers advance with one hand up in surrender – the other carries a suitcase.

Quite a lot of magnificent soldiers in N.H. Gate clad in Khaki cloaks of vast dimensions. I wonder who they are?

Wednesday, 29th Germans have bombed Bath, Norwich and York this week. Minster not touched, but before this war is over it and many other places may be. Damage in Bath considerable. Many teachers killed. Roman Bath not hurt. Japs are creeping on in Burma, though we are taking the offensive on the Continent.

No news of operation to my Mother yet. Lots of people engaged for fuel rationing. They may want me on the same hop.

End of April 1942

MAY 1942

❉

Sunday, 3rd Mother satisfactory – had a wire – went sick inside and felt ill for an hour. At the same time relieved. She is quite contented in Hospital, and so is forcibly prevented from doing odd jobs. Shall go home for my week's holiday and see how things are.

Auntie Nell also better. Was allowed to handle the Globe for half an hour. Helped her hang her curtains, and did some hoovering.

Sir Kenneth Clark spoke on light – he thought the Russians had produced no great artists because it is so dark there. Someone else said that material things were so excellently organized in Sweden that he began to wonder whether the spirit did not suffer in consequence.

Mary Bewley has left her hospital because she considers the occupational therapy man is a lunatic at large. She is going to live six miles from Haworth Parsonage, and help her brother with sixteen impossible children. She is matron. He is warden.

Went to Kew with Mrs Fisher. Sun shining – no wind. We took a bite to eat – sat under the trees, and felt glad to be in the fresh air after the Winter. The flowering trees and shrubs are all in blossom, many from China and Japan. The Wilderness with the empty thatched house always intrigues me . . . always makes me think of Marie Antoinette. No bluebells yet, but some aristocratic ducks were on the lake – rust colour. Also a swan with a white body and black neck. Queues to enter the Gardens as we left at 3 p.m.

Mock invasion of London last night. Saw many Polish and Canadian soldiers about. Bath is badly devastated. As to York – it kept Auntie Nell awake most of the night.

On the whole war news is a bit better, though Mandalay has fallen and the Burma Road is closed. Sir Stafford Cripps gave postscript – sounds a nice person. Points are going up for lots of things, and we have only 24 a month.

Wednesday, 6th Cath's birthday. Hope she received my card. All the week there have been raids on our Cathedral and small towns . . . Eastbourne, Exeter, Cowes. A lot of damage; they call them Baedeker Raids, because they are starred in the Guide Books.

More has come to light about Commando raid on St Nazaire. French joined with us. Two British officers were captured, and asked if the *Campbelltown* carried explosives. They denied it – and invited German V.I.Ps. to come on board. They collected a lot, and it blew up with all on board. What a glorious death! They deserve the V.C.

Corregidor, as well as Mandalay has fallen. Now the Americans can see how difficult it is to move troops and planes to distant places. But I so fear for all the poor people being prisoners of the Japs.

In spite of these bad happenings in the East, there is a feeling that we are on the attack over here. Our raids over Germany are powerful – and get more so. Stalin does not have one idle moment. He is moving two-thirds of the population of Leningrad to the interior of Russia. What a job! We are trying to take Madagascar from the Vichy French.

Sunday, 10th Anniversary of the Last and Biggest Raid on London. Rained today for the first time for weeks. All gardens will be glad. Tea with Mrs South – such a congenial personality. All ears for the *Brains Trust*. One question – which is the nicest word in the English language? Someone said – Felicity. Another – oblivion. Joad said – Over the hills and far away. Commander Campbell said some words sounded nicer when broadcast e.g. paraffin! The Question Master summed up: He supposed the Brains Trust wanted to go over the hills and far away to find felicity and oblivion with the aid of paraffin . . . Rather neat on the spur of the moment, with eight million people listening!

On Monday night we are all going to *The Immortal Garden*. Miss M. went and gave it such a good write-up in the paper that the author rang up, thanked her, was very agreeable, and sent along half a dozen tickets. So a bunch of us are going – including Auntie Nell.

Ivy Croucher back from Hereford where she has been playing in *The Passing of the Third Floor Back*. But she had a row with the producer and left. It was not finding a place to live that did her in. The town is bunged up with military, and rich evacuees, so there is no room, and little food for travellers.

She got a room in the end, but it was too late. Having played with Esmé Percy and Seymour Hicks, she could not allow an upstart producer to bully her.

There has been a big battle near Australia – and the Americans have sunk a few Jap ships. It is to save Australia from invasion, and is of the greatest importance. Otherwise we have not been bombed here much this week – though I hear planes were over Northern Ireland. Assembly Rooms at Bath are said to have gone. Exeter Cathedral hit – High St ruined. Such a pretty little town.

A poor old lady wrote us from Norwich for some shoes. Her little place had lost doors and windows and ceilings. She had been billeted in five different places all the week. I made up a good Clothing Parcel, and sent 10/- to help her.

Auntie Nell has given me the piece of Venetian Glass called in the family The Holy Grail. Brought back by Aunt Roscoe on her Wedding Tour. Now the old trunks have gone, my room looks quite presentable for a modest person like myself.

Wednesday, 13th Phone call from Cath was not so good. Auntie Nell thought she had better go down to Brum and see for herself. I jumped at the offer, though she gets easily tired and is not too well. But I know Beryl and Cath would take care of her – and Mother would love to see her.

In spite of being worried, we went to *The Immortal Garden*, and so much did we enjoy it. It is a play of the Next World. A General, who has a lovely country house, discovers that his Garden has been chosen as a Crossing Place from this world to the next. He can see them pass into it through a french window; but only he can see them. He bids them welcome. At the end of their lives, it seems, many people who had visited it in life think of his garden. He guides them to the path when they hear the call, and takes those back to Earth who are not ready to pass over. A little story is worked into it. The light and beauty of the Garden were most attractive, and I would cheerfully have passed over then and there!

War news is not worse, except for Burma. Over Malta they bring down planes like tame pigeons. But all the beautiful buildings of the Knights of St John seem to have been wrecked. Have taken Madagascar and the Americans are setting about Martinique. Gone colder.

Sunday, 17th Mrs Ellis and Margaret from Wimbledon came to tea. Opened a precious tin of blackberries, and of ideal milk. So it was a celebration. Margaret had done a walking tour. Youth Hostel one shilling per night. You buy bread and cook your food. You have a bunk with blankets, and after a seventeen mile walk you sleep comfortably.

Auntie Nell returned. Mother's operation not yet over. But all was well, otherwise. Beryl had looked after Auntie.

The Admiralty need all old photos of the Continent to help them with Commando raids. Shall send mine of the Gulf of Spezia.

Just read Lord Elton's book *St George and the Dragon*. He represents a new planet in the sky for me. He analyses the thought of the last 20 years and the movements that have influenced us, and why our supreme unpreparedness for this conflict has nearly cost us our freedom. So much that we thought was dogma unanswerable has turned out to be the flimsiest puff of smoke. He speaks of the virtues of Loyalty, Endurance and Discipline to which we must return, if we are to survive. 'I believe that change should have its roots in the past. I am a Christian . . . We thus embarked upon a new war handicapped by twenty years of propaganda against the virtues needed to win it.'

Japs are massing an invasion fleet for Australia. One story says that a woman, hearing clothes were to be rationed, bought 37 pairs of shoes . . . at least we manage things better here.

A vase of bluebells in the office this week. Lilac is out and smells heavenly. So often I see the flutter of wings on my window sill.

Wednesday, 20th Going home to Brum for Whitsuntide. Exchequer getting low with all these trips. Can take the grand new saucepan and kettle.

Our exhausted army is back in India. Japs are in full possession of Burma. Dr Evatt spoke for Australia on Postscript. He implied we were not worrying sufficiently about their danger. He said they had worried terribly about us after the Fall of France. But we have lived for so long now with the Germans within twenty-one miles of us that we cannot quite see it from the Australian point of view. They have not been tried by fire, nor lived under the shadow of terrible danger – gone to bed with it, got up with it, for months and months and months. They are young in adversity. It is no use telling you and me – we can do nothing.

Managed to get apple rings today. My flat neighbour was making marmalade for all she was worth . . . oranges were up the road, and more at 3 p.m. Thought sadly of Mother and how much she loved them. So went to the Old Pole, bought potatoes, saying disconsolately: 'I suppose you have no oranges?' They are really for children, but when over-ripe can be sold for adults. But his were all sold. I explained about Mother. He agreed to keep some of the next lot, and gave me five half-bad ones to get the juice. Then I looked in at the apple ring shop. Could hardly believe my eyes – a whole pile on the counter! Out came my Points Book – could I have a pound? Came out with two pounds! But am dividing them among people who never find any – so it was not so greedy. What a triumph!

[Diary lapses for a week]

Wednesday, 27th A mob at Paddington last Thursday. Watched the Thirds being stormed, but made for a First. It was quite full – but comfortable. Found that dear Mother had had the operation – not so serious as anticipated, being appendix with adhesions. So our Lady Doctor was right in her original diagnosis. Saw Mother in Hospital and she looked bad, but cheered up when she heard of the oranges I had brought. I fed her with them every time I went. We hope now she will be better than she has been for years.

Sunday did a short walk with Dr Hillier. Fine but windy. I just gulped down the fresh air. Hospital again with Cath. Neville picked us up, being able to combine it with A.R.P.

duties. Glad to see him, as it was pouring in torrents. Picked up a large and imposing Inspector on the way.

Elsie gave me a marvellous supper – some real lettuce, some radishes – the very things I craved for – cheese and coffee. While eating this sumptuous repast, and with her bright face opposite, I forgot for a moment there was a war on. We are both devotees of the *Brains Trust*. She thinks Jenny Lee is the best woman so far. Neville and Inspector returned from Divisional Office, and we had another half hour when we forgot the war. I was made to drink something which is 'not now obtainable'. The Inspector told us about the Italian prisoners who had escaped. They had quite a good name round here and got on well with the farmers. Cath said the police stopped every bus on the Wolverhampton road – looked under all seats and asked if anyone did not speak English. The conductor replied that so far no one had spoken at all! They caught them. A few at first, and these obligingly gave a description of the others. They were airmen, so it was necessary to prevent them getting into an aerodrome.

I had to tear myself away, and piloted by the indefatigable Neville, I was spirited back to Edgbaston . . . past an Identity Card check at the Oratory. But Neville announced in a lordly manner that a Police Inspector was in the back of the car. So we sailed past Authority with great dignity.

Whit Monday dawned cold, wet and windy. Never have I met such a day! We started for a country walk – Cath, Dr H. and I. We were blown across a few fields. My umbrella inside out half the time. I felt I was about to be parachuted up into the sky. After a bit the others said: 'What about it?' I replied: 'If there is a bus in sight, I go on it.' At this moment a beautiful blue and yellow one raced along – and with great joy I threw myself on it, leaving the two stalwarts to battle with wind and rain.

Hospital again, and felt very sad to be leaving Mother. Drenched as I came out. Poor folk waiting for the cinema were drowned as they stood. Dr H. took me to station, and I travelled comfortably to London.

Sunday, 31st Such a lovely day. Ariel and Cecilia arrived on Saturday as arranged. Went up to Lord Woolton's restaurant on Campden Hill – Lord Phillimore's house. A filling sort of meal. They are delighted with my tiny flat. Later they came to the Sanctuary and talked to everybody. Then over to Mabel Lucy's. She was just back from Stratford-on-Avon, which is full and noisy, and she found Bayswater quite a treat. Back to Auntie Nell.

It was fun all bedding down for the night – three of us. Cecilia heard innumerable planes going over. We had breakfast, prepared lunch, and set off at 10.30 for Kew Gardens. The sun shone – and it was not too hot. The Gardens were a picture. Cecilia caught her breath at their beauty. She had expected nothing like it. Wonderful variety of trees – azaleas, rhododendrons, bluebells and the lake . . . vistas and glades on all sides were ravishing. Thrushes and blackbirds came up to our feet and followed us everywhere. We found the Queen's Cottage. Ariel had some knitting, but did not do it. I took the *Observer*, but did not read it. Wherever we turned it seemed the loveliest thing we had seen.

From the News we learned that 1,000 bombers went over to Cologne last night. No wonder Cecilia heard some activity in the sky. What a terrible raid! The largest so far on any side in the war. They said there were over 500 last May 10th against Westminster, so I can imagine how the people of Cologne felt. However, the Germans will certainly take revenge, and probably flatten our York Minster or Canterbury Cathedral.

A big battle going on in Libya, but we cannot tell the outcome yet.

Just read *Atlantic Ordeal*, the account of Mary Cornish's eight days in the Atlantic with the little boys from the *City of Benares*, in the lifeboat. Gets no better on reading it. Those kind people in Glasgow not realizing they were really ill – and putting on a round of festivities! She describes how she upset some water all over her bed in the hotel, and the first night had to sleep on the springs! My heart bled for her. I believe she has not recovered yet. I should have been thrown overboard, as my endurance would have given out.

Ariel is taking home some tomatoes for Mother, and two oranges. Am sending cornflour for Beryl to make blancmanges. She is only on butter. Lucy sent some, and all the household gives her their ration. That tin from Rhodesia was worth its weight in gold . . .

End of May 1942

JUNE 1942

Monday, 1st They say Canterbury has been bombed – but there is terrible silence about the damage, on the News. I am afraid many mediaeval buildings were destroyed in Cologne – but not the Cathedral. I hope not. It seems as in *The Shape of Things To Come* by H. G. Wells. But I am glad the Germans know at last what devil they have let loose on the world. They are much given to whining, and now they have something to be sorry about. Cologne fires were seen from the Dutch frontier – it must have been hell outhelled that night.

Wednesday, 3rd We had the old Familiar Wail ourselves last night . . . about 3 a.m. I put on light, and was at the ready; but the All Clear went in twenty minutes.

It is Summer today, and I have put on a light frock. We can now start on our new Clothing books – if we have any money to buy clothes. I let other people have my coupons. Men seem to be the greatest difficulty, as the laundry wears out their collars at a phenomenal rate.

Lucy has received most of my diary. She talks of more parcels. I fear she will be desolated at what has befallen our Cathedral cities.

Sunday, 7th Anniversary over for another year. Did some cooking for those staying the night. Bought gigantic cauli-flowers, and with a piece of cheese sent from S. Africa and a tin of milk, made four dishes of cauliflower au gratin. It was a very hot day. Lots of people. We set up the bookstall at the Kingsway Hall and began sales. After the meeting an avalanche descended on us – it was like the storming of the Bastille. Nearly cleared the stall. We took £15 – last year £5. Flew back to Sanctuary, and when the folk arrived some sort of a meal was ready. At a quarter to midnight we all had a cup of tea. Went up the road – but did not sleep well.

Sunday, 14th Yesterday I went to register. Letters D to H had to go between 1 p.m. and 2 p.m. It was near Olympia. I said I did social and secretarial work. She entered me as a Welfare Worker. Was I full time? My reply – Very much so! She did not think I should be called before Christmas. Met another of my age group coming out. She said pathetically: 'They have put me down as unemployed – and I am looking after my aged Mother and have other responsibilities, and have done so for years. I don't know what she would do without me.' I told her not to worry – they would only take her for part-time work.

Letter from Cath. Mother is ready to come out of Hospital. Her nice room is ready for her – fresh air, and a beautiful tree to look at. It faces south, and she will get sunshine. Beryl will run up and down stairs for her. She wants oranges, but the Old Pole has none. However, there are tomatoes – and the cherries will be here soon.

I do not like the sound of things in Libya. It would be awful to lose Tobruk after we have had it so long. I realize the Dominion troops have been sent back to Australia, so we must be weak in Egypt. But it does seem hard.

Sir William Beveridge and Professor Bodkin of Barber Institute on Brains Trust. He has a delightful Irish accent. His opinion of the Surrealist Movement was heartily endorsed by Auntie Nell.

Read *I, Too, Have Lived in Arcadia*, by Mrs Belloc Lowndes. All about her parents. Her mother was Bessie Parkes, descended from Joseph Priestley, and connected with Birmingham. Her father, Louis Belloc, a Frenchman. A very happy marriage. Belloc family most agreeable. Letters from Paris during siege in 1870. Hilaire Belloc is her brother.

Last week worked through *Lawrence of Arabia* – tributes to him by his friends. The Ms. of *Seven Pillars of Wisdom* was stolen or lost, and he had to write it all again. It nearly unbalanced his mind. It sold for £30 per copy, and people offered £5 per week for the loan of it. Churchill wrote of him: 'He was out of harmony with the normal. His pride and many of his virtues were superhuman. He moved upon a plane apart from and above our common lot.' He was not a happy man.

Also read a lovely book called *Snow Goose* by a man called Gallico. It is a story of Dunkirk. Men on the beaches saw a beautiful white bird flying above a boat. Perhaps it is founded on fact, like the Angel of Mons.

Friday, 19th We back-pedal in Libya – a brilliant withdrawal. The only thing we are good at. Mr Churchill is in U.S.A. He won't be pleased. It seems strange to talk of a Second Front – when we cannot even keep one going.

A Grand March-Past Buckingham Palace last Sunday, but no one knew it was going to be except the Civil Defence Workers. The King and Queen, the Princesses; General de Gaulle and a few exiled kings were there, all in a row, and were loudly cheered. Should love to have seen it, but was not in the know.

The King failed to win the Derby. The crowd so stunned by the failure that they forgot to cheer Watling Street, the winner. He was fractious and behaved badly at the start, but evidently made up his mind half way that it was his race. He came in from the back, like Brown Billy, passed everyone else, and finished first at the post. Big Game, the King's horse, was sixth. The King took it very well, as he does everything about himself.

Sunday, 21st Letter from Mother in her own handwriting – two pages. So she must be going on well. Auntie Nell says the new idea about operations is not to think about yourself at all, but to buck up and do things. This she considers madness, and prescribes that you should always do less than you think you can.

Just heard on the News that Tobruk has probably fallen with 20,000 prisoners, to the Germans. It really is humiliating. So discouraging to the Russians who are still holding out in Sebastopol. Last time we rolled back in Libya we did not lose Tobruk and we thought things were going better now. Disgusting. All those poor men who fought so well to end as prisoners! They must be furious. I wonder what broke down. We shall read the real story about thirty years hence in someone's reminiscences. It is just over a year tonight that the Russians were attacked, and just over two years since the Fall of France. How time flies! Ever since the war began, it has just seemed one year only.

Mabel Lucy and I thoroughly enjoyed *How Green Was My Valley*. Cheapest seat was 2/6d. Enormous price for a film, but is result of Government tax. But it was worth it – all about a Welsh mining valley – feel much more interested in the Welsh now.

Had a day out – a great adventure, for except Kew I have been nowhere this year. Mrs Gabriel met me – house a dream of convenience. Garden lovely – and all round sweeps of country. I took my meat ration, but she would have none of it. Sat all afternoon in the summer arbour, and listened over a cup of tea to the first Trans-Atlantic Brains Trust. Brilliant.

Tuesday, 23rd Still stunned by the fall of Tobruk with 28,000 good men and true. Mr Attlee made a statement from General Auchinleck today which seemed to consist entirely of the word – unfortunately. The enemy did not seem to understand what was expected of them, and failed to fall in with our plans. Grrrrr! As Miss Moyes says it makes you see green, pink and heliotrope. I woke up in the middle of Sunday night, and thought of that convoy delivered with so much blood, sweat and losses to Tobruk on Saturday – to fall like ripe fruit into German mouths. I squirmed beneath the bedclothes and ground my teeth with rage.

Thursday, 25th I believe that Rommel is well into Egypt. I dare say the constant change of command is something to do with the loss. But I will return to the activities of Lansdowne Road, where we had a Street Fire Practice. Siren supposed to signal at 8.25 p.m. By 8.30 gunfire, by 8.35, all dressed in helmets and gas-masks we were to repair to Lansdowne House for detailed orders. This we did. I was in the 4th party with Mrs Starmer and Sadie, and two men. These latter were duds, and preserve me from being on a real job with them.

There was a bomb at 72 Ladbroke Road. I knew just the house. Mrs Beck had to find the bomb – which was said to be at the back. A very large house – eventually it was found in basement. We got the pump going quickly, the Warden said. I was first on the nozzle, then went to fill buckets. I had seen a notice on a door: 'Baths full on first floor'. So I rushed there, but a pond had been found in the garden. Bomb extinguished and we reported back to Lansdowne House.

A further fire was reported at 181 Ladbroke Road. We had no water, so I offered to fill buckets. They had a job to find the basement through the blitzed part of the house. The firemen had arranged a real fire. Two stirrup pumps were on it. I took a nozzle, while someone worked the pump. We got choked with smoke. We asked one of the men to take a turn, but the creature put his head inside and said dolefully: 'Oh, I can't stand that – I must put on my mask.' He calmly stood there for ten minutes trying to do this. Words failed us. . . . When the fire was nearly out Mrs Beck called for a shovel. I left the nozzle and rushed to no. 1 to get one. With this we turned the fire over. The fireman gave us a good mark over the shovel.

We heard the report. The firemen were quite compliment-ary, and said we were adequate to deal with a small fire. Anyway it was a good practice, and though we had dreaded it, in the end we enjoyed it.

Sunday, 28th Tea with Dr Bell in her high-up flat. Lovely when you get there. From the roof one can see the Surrey hills, and Westminster, and W. Kensington clearly. She is entirely without fear, and when the raids were at their worst she and her daughter were on the roof watching the bombs fall. They could see masses of planes in the sky, darting to and fro. I should never have ventured. When the landmine fell behind Kensington Square, their whole building quivered like an aspen tree. She has tiny birds flying about her flat – the cage door is never shut.

Lamented with Auntie Nell over the British Empire in general. At East Ham vicarage the opinion was the Germans would never reach Suez – plenty might happen before then. News is full of a new gun just invented – and how brilliant we are. Surely the height of folly. Why not wait until the thing has done some service in battle, and proved that it is remarkable! We are sworn to secrecy over trivial things – and a new gun is shrieked from the housetops. It has me beat.

Went to Ken Wood with Mabel Lucy. House closed – all pictures stored away. Went to Highgate village – such secluded property. Mostly empty. We passed ponds, sheep and lovely trees – not like London at all. Could see St Paul's in the distance.

I quote from *Lawrence and the Arabs* because it shows the

Germans are the Germans still: 'The only detachments that held together were the Germans. Lawrence for the first time felt proud of the enemy who had killed his two younger brothers. They went firmly ahead, proud and silent, steering like armoured ships through the rack of Turks and Arabs. When attacked they halted, took position, fired at the word of command. It was glorious. They were two thousand miles from home, without hope and without guides, footsore, starving, sleepless; yet on they went, their numbers slowly lessening.'

These are the people we have to defeat now. The Battle for Egypt has begun.

End of June 1942

JULY 1942

Wednesday, 1st News goes from bad to worse. Germans well on way to Alexandria, and I don't see how it can stand. Mr Churchill back from U.S.A. Debate on Libya today. Apparently he looked in a very grim mood. I am glad. Rommel is making straight for the Suez Canal, and we look as if we shall be driven out of the Mediterranean.

It has been revealed how Canterbury Cathedral was saved. The Dean, Dr Hewlett Johnson, had arranged intersecting ladders all over the roof, and the firemen were able to run over it, and sweep the incendiaries off in dozens. Hope other Cathedrals will copy this excellent idea. Dr Johnson is a live wire – a Socialist and always in favour of the Russians. If he is a pacifist, he is one of the best I ever heard of.

Sunday, 5th A controversial book by H. V. Morton, called: *I, James Blunt*, is dedicated to Wishful Thinkers who believe Britain is still an island, and that Russia will win the war for us. He imagines 1944, when England has been in Nazi occupation for five months. It makes you feel quite sick. But there are many who are sure the British Empire will never end. It would be a pity – but it did for the Romans.

297

Kit came. She told me lots about Bath, and how scarce water is still. But the city pulled itself together marvellously after its terrible blitz. The school was hit – but none of the children. There is not a Crescent without damage. Kit is billeted with some rich people who think the world was made for them.

Mr Churchill's Speech did not contain much comfort. He dominated us as he always does, and we surrender to his overpowering personality; but he knows no more than any of us why Tobruk fell – that he expected it to hold! This does not cheer us. Auchinleck expected it to hold. We lost the Battle of the Turks and no one knows why. We started the day with 300 and by nightfall they had mostly disappeared! Most disconcerting. The men may not understand Desert Warfare – and I am sure it is not learned in five minutes . . . by men who have spent their lives in Surbiton or Wigan. I believe in letting people try again. So long as Mr Churchill is confident we can all remain so. But the road to Victory is going to be a long one, as he told us at the beginning. It seems it will take another two or three years.

Sunday, 12th On Thursday, Dr Remy came and we had a few nice hours together. A sumptuous meal at the Ninety-Eight, a restaurant far beyond my modest purse. But Dr Remy insisted in his generous way that we do ourselves well, as it was a celebration. As I ate the excellent sole I forgot for a moment that we were in the midst of the greatest war in history. We called on Auntie Nell and over a cup of tea discussed the News. Auntie's brain, when she is talking of England, is as keen as ever and she has lost none of her wonted fire. Then he visited my tiny flat, and I hope he was impressed. We talked of Carola's visit in 1939. He goes to Harlech for the Summer.

Tea with Mrs South, and a delightful expedition to Chelsea Old Church. The Rectory is an immense old house, covered with creeper; it looked very desolate. Lovely trees in the garden. Little houses with shutters in that street – full of atmosphere. We reached the River and the ruins of the Church. Had I not been told I should never have known what had been there! We consulted a clergyman about Sir Thomas More's tomb. He said the More Chapel was beneath the new brickwork, covered to save it.

We walked along Cheyne Row. Many houses empty and looking miserable, windows gone and all badly shaken. Carlyle's house still upstanding. All houses have little steps to the front door. There is an air of dignity, leisure, horses and carriages about the whole street – crinolines seemed to be touching the pavements as we walked along them.

Germans seem to be breaking through on the Russians; but as they are so competent, I don't propose to tell them how to push the Germans back. The Russians are disputing every step. Rommel is up to schedule, but we are counter-attacking. But we have had so many disappointments. It is something, however, that the Germans are not camping out in Cairo.

Mussolini is in Egypt, preparing to march in triumph through Alexandria. How we shall squirm if he ever does – cannot you see him! The conceit of the man.

There are cherries about at 1/6d per pound. To show how the British public is enjoying a little fruit, I was told by a lady that yesterday you could not walk down Oxford St for cherry stones!

The little cat tormented me and would not let me listen to the Postscript. He galloped in front of me down the stairs, looping the loop all the way, and made me fetch the fish from the shelf and give him some.

Sunday, 19th An Alert early in the week – just after tea. Sky was heavy with rain, and it felt like November. We were all rather despondent – when there broke in upon us that Awful Wail. The cat looked up so astonished and indignant that we all laughed. A roving Hun had crept in with the rain clouds, and dropped bombs on Greater London – but exactly where we don't know. He was soon chased off.

Mrs Gabriel turned up with a basket of blackcurrants. I phoned Auntie Nell. She fell for it like a bomb. Mrs Watkins helped me prepare them, and Auntie was soon deep in them – seven pounds of jam.

Miss J. searching for a flatlet like mine – but they are unobtainable. People are returning to London. Six months ago she could have had a choice. I am very lucky – I only lack a carpet.

Jean Dowson and I set off for Hampton Court. Wonder of wonders, the sun came out. She talked much about Nigel Tuckwell, her fiancé, a lieutenant in the army. He is very lucky, and I should say is a very nice man. He will get only 48 hours leave, and they will be married in September at St Mary Magdalene, Harrow Road.

We wandered through the old gateways and out into the

garden. Fountains were playing, and the water lilies were in flower. The Big Gates being open we walked by the side of Long Water. A few men were fishing – with water boots on. Few people about. We ate our lunch – the sun shining sweetly. Then wandered into the Home Park – saw an immense herd of deer and lots of baby ones. We sat down, Jean knitted and I scanned the news. The outlook was reckoned obscure! The phrase of an inebriated gentleman about the night was recalled; he described it as 'hellish dark and smells of cheese'. He was, unfortunately, looking into a cupboard and not out of the window . . . Our outlook was reckoned to be of a similar nature . . . even to the cheese, for our ration is now doubled.

The trees in this part are superb. A gentle warm breeze was about. After being in all the week a day like this is a godsend. I feel a different being. Wandered slowly back to the Tilt Yard. I could go no longer without a cup of tea . . . such a lovely pot we had. People were enjoying themselves. Along the herbaceous border the heliotrope was in flower. I love its heavy scent. Looked on the Knott Garden and Henry VIII's Pond. I can always see the Old King, clad in silks and satins, walking these paths.

Wednesday, 22nd We were all sick to read of the death of Paddy Finucane. To go down like a stone – what a blow to the men circling round trying to find him. One must suppose his time had come and his work done. He seemed to think it was. He was one of The Few in the Battle of Britain.

I see the Earl of Lytton has lost his only remaining son – the elder one was killed in an Air Pageant, and the father wrote such a beautiful book about him from his childhood. They are such a nice family. It is tragic.

Not much news. Germans have begun to receive rubber from the Far East. It ought to be coming to us. We hold on to Egypt for the moment, though we understand Mussolini has been trying on the suit in which he will march through Alexandria . . .

Listened to a programme on Socrates. He was, it seems, the first European thinker to announce that we possess a soul. His death was dramatized, and very moving. Joad said how happy he would have been to be a disciple of Socrates, and to have questioned him about the soul. Joad is unconvinced that we have one which survives physical death.

On Sunday Sweet Rationing begins, we are told. Two ounces per week. I go on my holiday on Friday. Not to Stratford-on-Avon – it will be too crowded. We go to Ariel and Cecilia. Mother must be taken away for a change. We are much looking forward to it.

Sales of cherries are fabulous. Queues at every shop. British Public cannot believe they have got some fruit at last – we eat them like people starving.

End of July 1942

AUGUST 1942

❧❧❧❧ ✿ ❧❧❧❧

Tuesday, 4th   Left London on Friday. Barishnikov helped me as I had food, including the precious pound of butter from Africa – and a saucepan. Dr Hillier met me. Mother looked not too bad. Cath arrived from Camp. She had had practically no sleep all the week, with 60 children on her own. The housekeeper was nearly crackers when they arrived – worn out with a succession of young toughs. Most of the beds were broken. One day they did pea-picking and the farmer was pleased – the money they earned was given to the Malta Relief Fund. But Cath had an altercation with the local vicar, as her little wretches had taken some of his plums from a bough overhanging the road. She was handicapped by having no older girls to help with discipline.

Went to a meeting of the Free League of German Culture. The M.P. for West Bromwich was chairman, and various Germans spoke. Dr Liebert had been nearly imprisoned, but came to England in 1933, and was doing munition work. Lord Vansittart came in for much criticism. But the Germans should prove him wrong – not shout. He needs some refuting. These people wanted to raise a Free German Battalion like the Free French. Somehow I hated hearing German spoken . . .

We took a taxi to Sutton, where Ariel and Cecilia greeted us with rapture. We knew we should be happy – and we were.

But about 6.30 a.m. Monday, a Warning went. This is a rarity for Brum. All Clear soon. At 9 a.m. another Warning. A bomb dropped in Solihull on small houses where people were breakfasting. Took Mother out in the Push Chair. But at 2 a.m. Warning again, and I could hear the well-known thrum – things began to get hot – guns going, and much activity. Got Mother downstairs, and we all sat under the stairs. We felt ourselves shake all over, the reason being that a thousand pound Bomb dropped within half a mile of us – just at the entrance to Sutton Park. We got through the hours somehow. Ernest was upstairs watching the attack on Brum. We knew Cath would be in the thick of it, and we did not like it. Ariel and I laughed and talked so that Mother and Cecilia should not hear the bombs dropping. Firewatchers up and down the road were a great comfort to us. All Clear at 5 a.m.

Rather low all of us in the morning. Ariel and I biked along to see the damage. No one was killed – it had dropped in a garden – but the houses . . . the blast went up to Sutton Parade, and all windows smashed for half a mile. Houses looked as if they were drunk.

I rang Cath. Five Ways seemed for a few minutes the centre of the raid. She and another Warden several times had to flatten themselves against a wall and get full length on the ground while something nasty fell. It is no joke. A bomb fell straight on a Surface Shelter in her sector; but the people who had been in it had decided to move to the next one as it was damp – just three minutes before. The bombed shelter piled on top of them – but they were safely dug out.

Periodically Cath returned to 73, Francis Road to see if it was still standing. While on patrol she found a tram cable had fallen – her colleague guarded it, while she reported to the police station. They knew – and were sending barricades. Streets were covered with broken glass – ambulance could hardly get through. So Cath and her pal got brooms and began sweeping it up. They were still guarding this lamp standard. Fortunately a man came along and wrapped the cable round. Cath was amazed he remained alive – but he explained that so long as part of it was earthed all was well. The All Clear sounded. People poured out of the Shelters to return to their battered flats. Cath only too thankful to get to bed – but at 7.30 a.m. was roused by a wrong number! Person quite distraught. She had feared it was from us to say something was wrong. She then went to School – not feeling too frisky.

Wednesday night we were roused again. Such a thrumming of planes – it sounded to me like the whole of the Luftwaffe from all fronts. But much of it was ourselves. It was a Fire Attack on Brum. Ernest was at the Midland Bank, fire-watching – at Erdington, and we were on our own. We gathered as before – I hopping upstairs now and again to watch, and keeping an eye on our bucket and spade. Quite a number of incendiaries fell in Boldmere Drive. One down a manhole, and it bubbled and frothed in an alarming manner.

Dr Hillier came over at mid-day to our surprise. He said they had evacuated all the patients from the General Hospital, as they thought there was a delayed-action bomb in the courtyard. He had had a busy night putting out incendiaries by the dozen on the roof. They could not save it entirely, but the Hospital was not burned. The firemen enjoyed themselves sluicing water everywhere. All the ambulances made a sensation arriving at the other Hospitals with the patients.

He brought news of Cath. An exciting night in Ladywood. One of her colleagues found his Works nearby on fire. She went with him to see what could be done. Queen's Gravy Salt had caught fire. It is an unlucky place. A new phosphorous bomb fell into a cauldron of fat, and the whole works shot up in flames. However, with the canal near by the firemen were able to put it out.

The Salvation Army Canteen arrived promptly, and doled out tea and coffee. Cath helped to collect bits of the bombs and put out several small incendiaries. With the All Clear she retired to bed. School again in the morning at Dudley.

At Sutton after lunch we all fell asleep. The next night it was Wolverhampton and Walsall. I returned home, leaving Mother behind. Went to Elsie and Neville for supper. I suggested helping in the A.R.P. office. Neville promised me some cream cakes . . . very curious as such things seem something one only dreams about at night. Did an easy copying job – a police sergeant was phoning all round about the new incendiaries. I was allowed to be taken home by car, as I had worked at the Post. The cream cakes were super.

Sunday, 9th   News is just as bad. Gandhi handing India over to the Japs. He has let subtlety run away with him. The poor Russians are retreating. It is said Churchill may be in Moscow. He would go and buck them up if he could.

Sun rose bright and shining this morning. Mrs Turner said she heard that the Americans play baseball in the Park on Sunday afternoon. We took two chairs and sat down to watch them. It is a sort of glorified Rounders, though I expect they would not like us to call it that. The Fielders and Players wear strong rubber gloves. The ball comes a wonk against the gloves. Splendid catchers. Bat is the funniest thing. Long and rounded. Only occasionally did someone hit the ball. Players shouted at one another terms of encouragement. Referee behind the wicket-keeper wore a mask. I could not understand the game at all – but it was interesting to watch.

Thursday, 13th Several Alerts lately. Tuesday was our fire-watch, so I lay in bed with one eye open, but could hear no gunfire, so did nothing. Bombs fell in N. London and some people killed, I understand.

Reading a book by Oliver Baldwin. A lot of it is the sentimentalism of a few years back, which fell to pieces when the Hun was at our Back and Front Door. He seems attracted to Spiritualism and communication, in which he firmly believes.

Had some plums tonight – raw. What a treat! I asked the Old Pole humbly for a pound from a green-looking lot. But he slipped to the back and produced a superior sort of basket and said: 'Two Pounds.' I demurred. At this he regarded me severely and remarked: 'When I tell you to have two pounds, you'd better have two pounds.' Wonderful – five pence a pound. Have been eating them tonight.

Sunday, 16th Garden Party over and all was well. About 200 people came. Rain held off. I tripped round with cups of tea and buns along with other helpers. Mrs T. and I had arranged a little stall with any odds and ends of material we could get hold of, and people were invited to take some and make things for the Fair. They arrived in a mob.

Thursday, 20th So Mr Churchill has been to Russia as we thought he might. But I did not think of his calling at Cairo, seeing all the Army, and Smuts. It must have made many things plain. I expect he explained to Stalin why a Second Front is not possible now. However, we have had a Commando Raid during the last 24 hours. Most of them back now. The Free French went with them. How their hearts must have swelled – and how excited the Unfree French must have been.

Had a queer experience: I was lying in my bed in my little top room. Could hear voices outside my window – and then outside my door. Then a light under my door . . . A powerful force seemed to enter the room. I seemed to sit up and tried to put on the light – but no light came. I struggled with the switch on the skirting board – no result. Then to my wireless set – but no comforting music came. At the same time I could see the two small rugs on my floor undulating; and walking towards me were two kittens and a mouse. They seemed to say they had come for a frolic and I must not put on the light. One kitten jumped on my bed and began to play. I was not at all happy all this time. Had something the feeling of Prospero's Island with Puck in charge. Then it seemed a strong force wrapped itself round my body – and I could not move. I heard a querulous voice at the door – and passed into nothing-ness. Finally I awoke and all was normal. I felt as if something had departed from the room, and with trepidation tried the switch. It worked – and I slept again.

All very vivid. I cannot remember ever before feeling in the grip of an occult force. Interesting – but I do not want it again.

Friday, 21st Still getting news of the big Commando Raid on Dieppe. It is no joke to steal across in the dead of night, to hear the boat grounding on the beach, seize your rifle and start scaling the cliffs. It reads something like the taking of Quebec; but no one read the famous poem. Great credit is reflected on us at last. We now seem to be aware we are not fighting the Crimean War. Lord Louis Mountbatten appears to be the head of it all. I wonder what the Duke of Windsor thinks. He is far away – and his cousin is leading the troops. Lord Lovat, too, is holding the honour of Scotland.

Sunday, 23rd Bad news yesterday was the loss of the submarine *Upholder* with Elspeth Kinloch's husband, Commander Wanklyn, V.C. in command. I knew such a brilliant man would soon go. It was like Paddy Finucane – a lot of publicity – they try to live up to their reputation, and now the whole ship is lost. It was about our best submarine, and the Admiralty is very sad at losing it. He leaves one son – so that is something to remember him by . . . I used to teach his wife years ago.

Excitement over the mulberry tree in the next garden – house unoccupied. Along with various others our caretaker raided the fruit. A policeman came to know if we were allowing our Printing Works boys over the wall. The Manager swept him off the premises. We suspected he wanted a mulberry pie for himself. Our lady gardener, also, is a formidable person, and would rout Scotland Yard, if they interfered with her. The net result was a Mulberry Pie for all. Excellent – something between a raspberry and blackberry, only sharper. The moral side appealed to me. If I had been caught I should have appealed to Lord Woolton himself, saying it was against the national interest to let fruit rot on the trees. Our conscience is clear, for we have tried to get in touch with the owner.

Wednesday, 26th   We have been stunned today by the loss of the Duke of Kent. I could not believe it when I heard the 8 a.m. News. A man so full of life, and so seemingly joyous, to be cut off in a moment in such a tragic way. Poor Duchess and poor Queen Mary. He had such a pleasant personality – and all his elderly aunts liked him, so I am sure he took trouble to please them. No one is allowed too much happiness in life. At one time the Duchess and her two sisters seemed to have everything. Now the sun is behind the clouds for them all.

The Flying Boat cannoned into the hillside. It burst into flames – horrible. One man was thrown clear, and he wandered about for some time before he found a crofter's cottage. He is badly injured. He will give details – their cries must have been terrible. I cannot understand why they crash into mountains – wonderful instruments do not seem to help over simple obstacles like mountains.

Sunday, 30th   Mary journeyed from Yorkshire to go with me to Jean's wedding. Very tired – as you can get nothing to eat on trains. I tossed her up a meal, and she felt better.

Her job is terribly strenuous. Ten problem children – sent by the Committee of Mental Health. When she went first the place was bedlam for some months. These young rips broke all the cups, so now they are drinking out of jam jars, as cups are impossible to buy. They flooded the house as well as nearly setting it on fire. They raided the larder, so had to starve for a week, almost. The staff had to starve too. They got on the roof. They packed their bags and prepared to depart. They broke all the locks, and stole whatever they wanted . . .

One child was the ring-leader of all this. He blames the others, who at first all thought he was wonderful – until they found him out. His power is on the decline. They are beginning to find obedience a novelty! The staff, however, never ceases to marvel when an order is obeyed! One set off for Brighton – he was given half a crown. They never get very far – he met a member of staff who took him a long walk, and he was glad to go to bed. Mary is growing fond of them in spite of all their wickedness!

End of August   I listened to the account of the Duke of Kent's funeral. How they all sobbed. I understand the Duke of Windsor has offered to come back and help, but I doubt if they will have him.

A broiling hot day. Mary and I got ourselves buttonholes. A photographer snapped us going into the Church. The bridegroom looked happy but serious. Jean was given away by her uncle. Lovely dress – veil over her face. She looked radiant as she walked down the aisle, smiling at everyone. He then seemed wildly happy. I had a word with her at the door.

The uniforms looked so nice. Lots of her nursing friends there.

Rushed back to the flat where Mary brought a friend for tea. Rested and then went with Mrs T. to *The Man With a Load of Mischief*, by Ashley Dukes, at the Mercury Theatre, which resides just opposite me. Costume play – good.

Got locked in the bathroom, and they had to fetch a fireman to get me out. He was so afraid I should get panic-stricken.

End of August 1942

SEPTEMBER 1942

❊

Thursday, 3rd We enter upon the fourth year of war today. How well we remember the beginning . . . the Germans invading Poland, and we preparing the Black-out. We expected to be bombed – and we have been!

We all bought union jacks in the street today, and assembled at 11 a.m. in Miss Moyes' office for the broadcast Service – Printing Works staff as well. Hymns were: *Holy, Holy, Lord God Almighty*. Then: *Lord of our life and God of our salvation*, and *Lift up your hearts, we lift them Lord to Thee*. Auntie Nell went to the Abbey.

She has been making crab-apple jelly all the week, as someone brought piles of rosy little crabs from a garden in Ealing. With grandma's straining bag stretched across a pole she produced many pounds. The British Public is nearly swooning with the amount of plums on the market. After being starved all Winter and Spring, this raining down of purple plums is almost too much for us. I expect we shall all be taken ill – until the flood vanishes and we are reduced to prunes again.

Sunday, 6th Kit rang me Friday evening saying she had a flat in Ealing lent her, and would I come. Felt it would be nice and quiet, so I went. Most comfortable. We hoped to see *Mrs Miniver* at the cinema, but no luck. Kit misses her home in Guernsey. We listened to the News, and were relieved that Rommel, instead of walking in triumph into Alexandria, was back-pedalling across the desert. Long may it continue. But we have counted our chickens before, and Rommel is a resourceful General.

Went for a walk in the sunshine and had conversation with four horses in a field. They looked thankful to be resting under the trees. I like Ealing – it used to be a village outside London.

Listened to the Western Brothers. Is your journey really necessary? was a good skit. One verse concerned the feelings of a traveller who found himself one of 20 in a carriage, with 40 in the corridor – when the door opened to admit the British Army, plus Geraldo and his Band!

Tuesday, 8th Last night we had a Warning. It was our Fire Watch, so we donned tin hats and began patrol, letting ourselves be seen in the road. A bit of gunfire and flares – but not a big raid. All Clear before midnight. Kit was sleeping in my room.

Mr Churchill has just made a statement. Many things were wrong in the desert to lose 80,000 men, and war material, which the Germans promptly turned against us.

Plenty of blackberries – so we wallow in fruit.

Thursday, 10th Raced about too much on Tuesday, and consequently had a severe gastric turn. Kit gave me first aid in a most efficient manner. Felt green all Wednesday, and crawled around. Auntie Nell gave me Bovril and made me lie down. At 8.30 p.m. went to bed, slept and woke restored. I knew we should be laid low with all the Fruit!

An eclipse of the sun today, but we did not seem to notice much.

Tomatoes are plentiful at 1/3d per pound. Pears are 1/- or 1/3d. The Japs have scaled unscaleable mountains. They would . . . Pétain is conscripting all Frenchmen and women to work for Germany . . . Can you beat it!

Sunday, 13th Went round to see the Bride. Saw her wedding dress and presents, which were mostly money. She is putting it all by for after the war, when her man is home again. Spent her honeymoon in London. They did a restaurant every night for dinner and dance . . . the Hungaria, the Trocadero, etc. Went to two Shows, and had taxis everywhere. Nobody dresses in London these days, even at the smartest places. She hates being alone now, and having to go back to work.

She and I went to a Whist Drive at the house of Nigel's aunts in Streatham. A large old-fashioned place. Immense rooms of Victorian furniture. A dear old aunt of 80 was sitting by the fire knitting, and two maiden aunts received us. So nice they were. A few old dears came in – the idea being to cheer everyone up. We had four tables. Jean has married into a very nice family, and she loves them all. There were two old servants who had been there for 50 years.

Took Kit to tea with Auntie Nell. Of course they talked nursing. When Auntie trained you could not begin until you were 25. She worked 84 hours per week! Later she had to do a period in the East End, and once nursed a wonderful old lady, the widow of a Bargee. She refused utterly to have an operation, and the surgeon went away. So Auntie nursed her with such skill and patience that the abscess came away – and she recovered. 'No nonsense of any kind about hours of work in those days,' commented my Aunt. 'If you nursed a patient you nursed! '

Wakened on Friday night by squeaking at my window. Got up and lifted the Black-out. There, positively screaming with annoyance, was a handsome black and white Persian cat. He leaped with a thud into my room, and wandered round lamenting loudly about everything, and why did not someone immediately take him home. I lifted him up, and it was like picking up a battleship – Lord Woolton would have been horrified. I feared to waken the house, but gradually got downstairs. The caretaker called out that he lived next door, so I thrust him into the street. He really was looking for a Best Eiderdown on which to repose himself.

Thursday, 17th Such a struggle to get an onion. Tried the Old Pole. None. Went to Mr Bybest – he had a few, but they were all booked. I took his refusal humbly, and bought a pound of carrots and a stick of celery, thinking sadly of the onion. I could see an idea was germinating in the man's mind, so lingered on. Finally I won without saying any more – a voice murmured: 'If you only want it for flavouring, I will let you have one.' Pouring thanks and blessings on his head I walked away triumphant. A victory indeed!

Germans are in the outskirts of Stalingrad. Losses in the Dieppe Raid were very high.

Sunday, 27th Just back from a week at home. Have mastered the art of boarding the Birmingham train at Paddington, and getting a seat. Travelled with the Army, Navy and Air Force. A sailor sat beside me. There was a Home Guard in the compartment who had been nourished in the school of thought that the Germans were badly treated after the last war, and let Hitler in. He was allowed to talk a bit – then the sailor gave his opinion of the Germans. The Home Guard dried up. The sailor divulged that he had been convoying in the Mediterranean for two and a half years. It was Hell, he said, to take a Convoy to Alexandria and Malta. He had had two ships sunk under him. Had witnessed too many men drown, and allowed to drown by the Germans, to have any feelings but of horror for the whole business.

The sailor concluded by saying he had been invalided out, and never wished to go forward again. He mentioned the *Upholder*, and said he had been on the sister ship. Commander Wanklyn was due to go home on leave and then take a new command; but he volunteered for another patrol – and none of them returned.

Cath and I purchased at an enormous price some fresh black-out for the bathroom. She had been fined one pound. She was recovering from a wasp sting on her foot, and forgot the window when she switched on the light. The beam had hit an officer of the law full in the face. We decided this must not happen again.

I also wanted the bath re-enamelled, if possible. Various firms gazed at me as if I were an imbecile. I stared hard at them and said a hard experience of life had taught me that by perseverance things can be done – even in the midst of the greatest war in history. So I toiled on. Finally Dr H. bethought himself of his Lab. assistant. This excellent individual has come and done the bath – and though it is out of action it looks snowy white. He descended on us like an angel from heaven – I am all for laboratory assistants.

Went to see Mrs Styles, formerly Miss Sutcliffe, my history lecturer at the University. She said the Beazleys had been persecuted out of Birmingham, but agreed that the dear Professor was innocent and deluded, thinking the Germans were as much gentlemen as himself. I hope he is a sadder and a wiser man. They are in the West Country.

Mother and I went to see Paula and heard all about her incendiary of the last blitz. She, the children, and Elizabeth with a neighbour were in their Shelter. Whole house shook from head to foot when a large H.E. fell on a house in Selwyn Rd. The people were killed. Paula heard showers of incendiaries falling round her house and St Augustine's Church. She went to look, but there was so much activity overhead that she decided to let the house burn. After a pause she and Elizabeth ventured to the house – filled with smoke. They knew nothing of the new kind, so went after this incendiary with enthusiasm. It had fallen through two floors into the nursery, and a bed was on fire. She rushed to the front where dozens of folk were filling the road, and shouted for the Fire Brigade. Then raced back to help Elizabeth who was getting buckets of water from the bath. They hurled water on furniture and beds – and the firemen put the finishing touches. The house was in an awful mess. Her husband who is helping in the Fire Service, was in Harborne putting out a fire, while his own place was burning.

We went to a lecture by Admiral Larsen of the Norwegian Navy. He was in Copenhagen with his wife when he heard that German ships had sailed for Norway. Summoned home immediately, and witnessed the Invasion. For 120 years the Norwegians had had no war, and it was difficult for them to start killing. However, the *Blücher* was sunk, with 300 Germans on board. He gets a constant flow of information from Norway. They have wireless sets in their forests, which they move every night. They ask that, though they will be glad to have law and order re-established in the world, they want 48 hours to themselves – to settle some accounts, before the United Nations get busy. The Quislings are ours, they say. After the war Norway would enter under the protection of the two great English-speaking powers.

Dr H. came to see me off – and I had an uneventful journey back to London.

End of September 1942

OCTOBER 1942

※

Sunday, 4th Picking up the threads again. It is said that the advert for Sylvan Soap Flakes showing a Dieppe Beach Coat was a cryptogram advising the Germans. I remember seeing the advert and wondering – why Dieppe? Scotland Yard are said to be investigating it. No wonder we lost half our forces. Auntie Nell was probably right, and it was a doubtful success. The Government won't say straight out – they want us to think these are victories. The only event I shall believe in future is that we are actually in Berlin.

A bomb fell on a Boys' School the other afternoon in Sussex. Terrible. The place completely wrecked. A delayed-action one, and it rolled down the chimney. All the boys told to run – but it went off and is said to have killed twenty of them. Others sheltered under desks when the roof fell in. There was frantic searching by distracted parents. Nowhere is safe.

Still the siege of Stalingrad goes on. Behind all the trivialities of this diary we are all thinking of that wonderful city, and the heroic stand it is making. We have sent a Convoy of stuff, and only hope some of it will arrive and help the people. I cannot imagine how they can defend the place. Is it an industrial town like Brum? I don't feel we should do anything so well – even with Neville to defend Selly Oak, and Cath at the Five Ways . . .

Friday I worked until 11 p.m. and have broken the back of the accumulation of work that met me after my holiday. Trees are just turning, and the leaves beginning to fall. I am afraid we are going to feel the cold very much. Mother must just stay in bed.

Have booked for *Hedda Gabler* at the Mercury. Always wanted to see it. During my holiday read again *Wuthering Heights* . . . but one can never quite recapture the first horror of contacting Heathcliff – and the voice at the window. Also going through *Vanity Fair* again. It seems another world.

Listened to *Water Babies* on the Children's Hour, adapted by Barbara Sleigh, daughter of our artist friend at Chipping Campden. Cannot get on with typing his book yet. No time for myself at the moment. Have to obtain a kettle and colander for home somehow – they are unprocurable. They seem well up in saucepans mercifully.

Wednesday, 7th Disturbed about news from the Channel Islands. Kit and her sister will be worried. Their father is there, and many relations.

Horses are to have Ration Books! I wonder when they will issue them for cats. And what about donkeys?

Terrible goings-on in Norway. They are being so brave, poor things. Miss M. and Auntie Nell are much enjoying the book by Blackie, the nurse of King George V.

Developed a bad cold like everyone else. We feel it morally impossible to have a fire – so we must get used to it. We start our Clothing Coupons again, but are urged to Make Do and Mend as much as possible. Towels will be on coupons.

The village where the Boys' School was hit was Petworth, near Chichester.

Sunday, 11th   Have to sit with a rug round me in the office – but one is always leaping up to do things, so it is awkward. But so far October has been kind.

Stalingrad still holds out – though three quarters of the city is in ruins. The Germans may, however, be having another Think. I like the sound of that relief army getting nearer.

A Warden turned up on Friday asking us what we could do in the event of paratroops landing in Hyde Park . . . and Notting Hill Gate being isolated? He took all our names and qualifications. This house being so well equipped could look after the infirm and children – and this we said. On the other hand the men at the Sanctuary are convinced that the Battle of Notting Hill Gate will never take place. The English, however, are waking up from the dream that nothing can ever touch them. They now seem to visualize Germans racing down every High St – while we put up the barricades. Well, like the women of Stalingrad we may have to carry ammunition yet – but I hope not. Nor do I really think we shall.

Had the great pleasure of a speech by Mr Churchill last night. He was made a freeman of Edinburgh. He bucks us up no end. Harry Lauder led the singing and the speech ended with: 'Keep right on to the end of the road.' There is much of Christian in Mr Churchill – with the same cautious optimism and determination . . .

As the Germans seem to have put some of our men in irons, we have done the same. Letters in the *D.T.* say it is foolish to try and compete with the Germans in this kind of thing. On the other hand Mr Churchill says it is madness to show weakness to such a man – and I think he knows best. I have left the sentimental school now, and am all for hard knocks.

Hedda Gabler splendidly acted by Sonia Dresdel. The play is highly emotional, and gripped the attention. But really in the end I was rather at a loss to know what all the emotion meant. Have a vague idea that Ibsen showed the New Woman, and that his plays were considered very advanced. If she had had a job of work she would not have had time to analyse her emotions so much. But I enjoyed it.

Sunday, 18th How brave the Belgians were to put flowers on Nurse Cavell's statue in Brussels, in spite of German occupation. The Belgian Minister in the European News gave a glowing tribute to her. She was trained at the London, like Auntie Nell – but was a year or two ahead.

The great chestnut tree outside my window is now red. Went to see the Ellis family in Wimbledon. Margaret is full of enthusiasm about World Citizenship and internationalism – just as we all were 25 years ago. I suppose all young people think they will succeed where their elders have failed. That means another war . . . because these lessons are not passed on to the Race. It is all disheartening. These youngsters are just as opinionated as I was at their age.

Everyone jubilant that Smuts is here. We all hope he will

stay – he is considered the only one who is Churchill's size. I believe he invented the phrase – The British Commonwealth of Nations. I missed most of his Speech, but read it the next day, and was so grateful for all that he said about England. Miss Megan pointed out how historic was the occasion. Forty years ago Smuts was a Boer fighting for his people. Lloyd George, who took the chair, was having a hectic time as a pro-Boer. Mr Churchill was a prisoner of the Boers. Yet in the British Commonwealth they were all three on the same side now, respecting one another, and fighting evil things, as represented in the Germans.

Sunday, 25th Mrs Roosevelt is here. The King and Queen went to Paddington to meet her, and took her to see the blitz. People soon gathered to welcome her.

Mr Evans who gives me treatment tells his patients a great deal about Hermetic philosophy. Most interesting. He thinks theological Christianity is dying, and that the ancient teaching of know thyself makes for strength and real men. He was in the wilderness himself for twenty years as regards what to believe and what not. Then he met a man of powerful intellect and great gifts who put his followers through stern discipline.

Several Alerts last Monday. No gunfire. Thames Estuary towns had bombing – Southend High St.

Got four oranges out of the Old Pole for marmalade. He dived to the back of the shop and gave me also two half-gone ones. So I am to present him with a pot of marmalade.

Frightfully busy preparing for the Fair. Never get home

until 11.30 p.m. My cold still a frightful nuisance. Trying to make myself a Russian hat to wear . . . and intend to pass myself off as Catherine the Great or Lady Macbeth. Both sinister women . . .

The cat has just been in. There being nothing for him to eat he has shown off at me. Gave him a Curtain Lecture, told him to tighten his belt and be thankful he was not in Stalingrad. This has given him food for thought, and he has settled down. He has still a well-covered little body, so I am not terribly sorry for him.

Jean, my bride, came to dinner and tea. We listened to the Trans-Atlantic Brains Trust. Dorothy Thompson was splendid. She said Hitler's magnetic power did not grip her – but she is not a German. It certainly is difficult to see why 'a shabby little man with an unpleasant voice' can have dominated the German people as he did. Dr Summerskill was the woman this end. Very good indeed. Donald McCulloch was as witty and deft as usual.

We visited Auntie Nell, who was drying almonds before the fire. I was glad to see the fire, for Old People must look after themselves a bit – else we shall have to nurse them. Jean is modern about nursing. She loved her training, but thought many of the restrictions were nonsensical. She never returned to the Nurses' Home with any sense of pleasure. Five Years she was there. No wonder the girls will not go. Auntie Nell was of a generation who would put up with anything. Jean liked the Home at Queen Charlotte's much better. She snatches a week-end now and again with her young husband.

End of October 1942

NOVEMBER 1942

❊

Sunday, 1st Very rainy week. So cold we decided to lift the ban on our office fire. Everyone felt better. Then we heard it had been lifted all over the country . . . and our consciences were at rest. Even this Sunday evening, though I was prepared to sit and freeze as I wrote my diary and some letters, I found the fire on and am enjoying it.

Presented Auntie Nell's pot of marmalade to the Old Pole, together with a card from her – salute to Poland. He looked surprised and pleased. He came from Warsaw thirty years ago. Had been back once, and his brother was still there. His father is with him and his wife.

Mrs Roosevelt is dashing all over the country. Hope she broadcasts. The one on Sunday was from an engineer about the building of the Simplon Tunnel. They never would have started it had they thought how colossal would be the job. Then about the Suspension Bridges at New York and San Francisco, and how plastic was taking the place of iron and steel.

Kit is teaching at the Royal Commercial Travellers' School at Hatch End. She met me and we toured the shops. To my amazement I saw a bunch of kettles. Could not believe my eyes, and hastily purchased one. They are 2/11d . . . before the war would have been 11d. But was I glad to get one. I enquired for a colander – but the woman shook her head like everyone else.

Kit has the dearest little sitting-room with an electric fire, and a bedroom with cupboards. The lady cannot do too much for her. After the hospital experience this is heaven. Did a lovely walk up Pinner Hill . . . oaks and elms turning colour. From time to time we passed a beautiful house in a clearing, as if the people had said: 'We will cut down some trees and build our house here.' Trees all around were left. Saw a long white house where Bulwer Lytton lived and wrote his novels.

She teaches the ten-year-olds. Their little desks all untidy and full of oddments. School is self-contained – large grounds and a swimming bath. The Head is away on service. Saw the boys come out of tea – it seemed like a Mr Chips' place. No communication with the Girls' School, but possibly a few surreptitious assignations under the oak or elm tree! Kit shops for the boys. They can come at six years old. I spoke to two young shavers, who said they loved school, so they must be happy.

We had a sumptuous tea round the fire of lettuce, tomatoes and prem [a preserved tinned meat]. Pastry and blancmange. I had brought margarine and cooking fat for the owner of the house. Then a warning went. I am a reserve Fire Watcher, and if the others are away I reckon to go down to the Sanctuary. And here I was miles away in Middlesex! Mercifully the All Clear went. Made tracks for Paddington at 9.30 p.m.

Have had tea with Auntie Nell. Beverley Robinson was

there in magnificent naval uniform. He will soon be a full lieutenant, and is to take up an appointment ashore as Amenities officer for the Ratings. He has had a splendid time at Greenwich Naval College, dining well, fruit at every meal – even grapes! Nice little W.R.N.S. to wait on them. The officer W.R.N.S. dine with them . . . all in the Painted Chamber. It is the finest Naval Mess in the world. Wonderful candelabra down the tables. He has got through a stiff course. He is a trained lawyer by profession. All interesting.

Sunday, 8th   The Desert army is sweeping Rommel along the coast like dust before the broom. They want to catch him well and truly this time. He has wisely dropped all the Italians to be scooped up by our troops. They don't mind, I expect. The Germans will stand a better chance without them. But Rommel is a clever man, and we dare not rejoice too soon. Twice before we have grown wondrous cheerful over Libya – only to find it was too easy. Now, however, they are better equipped to consolidate their gains. Always a help to learn from previous mistakes.

Montgomery sounds a hard nut to crack – so perhaps at last we have got the right man. An American broadcast today says the General Grant tanks and Flying Fortresses from U.S.A. were not successful – and possibly that is why we had to retreat. They only moved on a small part of a circle – whereas the Germans moved their guns a complete circuit. He castigated his own people, reminding them that after Pearl Harbour, the British, out of their small store, sent anti-aircraft guns to Panama because the Americans had none.

Much interested to learn that the Volga is two miles wide near Stalingrad . . . some river!

A song I like on the wireless goes: She's coming round the mountain when she comes. You can put any words to it. The soldiers love it. 'She'll be eating eggs and bacon when she comes . . .' is one of the pleasing varieties of wording used!

The postman told me how he went to deliver a parcel in the road, but as he went up the path he realized the telegraph boy had been before him. A poor woman was sobbing and calling out – 'He can't be dead . . . my Harry.' It was just another of those painful tragedies that are going on all over the country. You realize what war means. The postman thought the parcel was from Harry, so he decided to deliver it the next day.

I had a letter from Betty Wanklyn, widow of the *Upholder* Commander. She said she had had hundreds of letters saying no commander past or present had ever achieved such successes. Poor girl! They had three years of happiness.

The question of character is the crux of the whole business of life I think. Lord Elton makes a great point of it as does my osteopath. I quoted Father Damien to him as being one of the bravest of men, and he drew all his inspiration from Christianity. But Mr Evans said it was the man's inner being, and his religion was pure accident. However, I got him to admit that other religions had people nothing to boast of. You meet excellent people in all faiths – as well as those far from excellent. Religion does seem something extraneous. Sir Richard and Lady Burton had totally different religious opinions, yet their devotion was complete. Even though one was a Roman Catholic and the other was a Mohammedan. It is a question of vibration.

Sunday, 15th Still the victories go on apace! It is quite time we had a Set-Back of some kind. Winning battles like this is unlike us . . . Mr Churchill spoke . . . 'It is the end of the beginning,' he said. I gather from the *Observer* that had Alexandria fallen, Mr Churchill would have fallen too. Now M.P.s are cordial to him. He had to keep silent all the time, though he had been preparing this stunt. Even Stalin did not know.

Mother is very sorry for the Italians abandoned in the Desert. I wonder how Mussolini feels. He has had a good run of his own way; but though a militarist himself he has not been able to make the affectionate good-humoured Italians into a fighting force. Their engaging smiles as they are taken prisoner must be delightful to see.

My thoughts turn to Corsica and my colleague at Poggio from there. The Italians seem to be there. The *Observer* comments that Italy kept agitating for the return of Corsica, Nice, etc. But Hitler would not give it them. Now it is tossed to them in unfortunate circumstances . . . 'Well may Mussolini, who has an eye for the classical as well as the Imperial pose, remember the saying of the ancients that the gods fulfil our wishes in their wrath.'

Mr Morrison has just given the Postscript, reminding us that in London we had 57 nights on end of big bombing – death overhead for hours and hours – every moment expecting to be blown up. Yet we slept, and worked through the day. I am not surprised it has taken us two years to get over it. We have had heaps of raids since, but they gave us a day or two in between to recover – and that meant a lot.

Heard the voice of General de Gaulle calling on French North Africa to join the allies. A clarion call. I don't feel people generally appreciate him at his true value.

Miss Moyes has just reminded me that on the opening day of the war she ran into the road to tell the special policeman standing there that any people could come into the Sanctuary if they wished. This man was pale cream in colour and kept peering into the sky, as if he expected swarms of German planes – which we did! He just said: 'Thank you, madam, but I cannot move from this spot. I have been put here and here I remain.' What he could do just standing in the middle of the road Miss Moyes could not imagine . . . but it was all in the Spirit of Britain! We were all untrained, but determined to stick to our posts though bombs rained down on us that instant minute.

Sunday, 29th Been so busy with the Fair that I could not write my diary – but the News has gone on. We are winning Victories! It is difficult to get used to this state of things. Defeats we don't mind – we have all developed a stoical calm over such things in England. But actually to be advancing! To be taking places! One has an uneasy sense of enjoying a forbidden luxury.

We wander back in Africa over all those places that have given us so much disappointment in the past – Sidi Barrani, Derna, Benghazi. How well we know them all. Our Army is at present sitting down in front of Rommel near the bend in

Tripolitania. We are gathering fresh strength. He is struggling to organize what is left to him.

The Americans have invaded N. Africa, and so far all is well. The crux is to be Tunis. Germans are being flown to this place as fast as they can. We are advancing towards it. A battle is due to begin.

The Russians are taking our breath away once more. Stalingrad is relieved. Germans are retreating. It is heavenly news that another Winter will be on them – and they cannot tuck themselves in anywhere. Their treatment of the Russians seems to have been blood-curdlingly inhuman, and if the Russians go berserk when it is all over, one cannot be surprised. An English journalist gave a few horrors on the wireless today.

Found a note in some paper that if any of our airmen come down in Belgium, sooner or later they get back to England. Also that in many a Belgian home an empty chair is set at all meals. A neutral brought back this story. He asked who this chair was for . . . and the reply was: For the absent English-man who is coming to deliver us.

Tonight Mr Churchill broadcasts. With what joy and relish he will address us now things are getting better.

General de Gaulle likes not Darlan – and it is a regular pasticcio. The Free French consider him a traitor. De Gaulle had lunch with our P.M. yesterday, and I hope they under-stood one another. The French Fleet has committed suicide. A strange business. Why could they not have got out and made a run for Gibraltar? Better to have fought their way out than go down as they did. All those ships would have helped our hard-pressed Fleet in the Mediterranean. We shall know all about it some day, I suppose. The episode has a little redeemed the honour of France – they have died sooner than give themselves to the Germans. Hitler must be wild. The French Admiral last night asked for homage to them – and was very moving.

Now for the Fair. We made £800 – and that, in the midst of a war, and against masses of regulations, was good. But it was a terrible strain – Thursday, Friday and Saturday. The people came pouring in before I had distributed money bags to my helpers. At 2 p.m. some of us crawled upstairs for a cup of tea, and a sandwich. Those serving there had no time to drink one themselves. My Caledonian Market did very well. I sold all the white elephants that people had challenged me to get rid of . . . the old clock, the lantern, the watnot, the brass school bell, the broken cupboard. All went in one mad rush.

Then we had to clear up. Somehow I had to produce some food for the Office Staff. Nearly midnight before I left, and could only just walk up the road. Had been on my feet for sixteen hours each day for three days and I am not used to it. A moonlight night – so beautiful. Did not bestir myself early and had only strength to make a cup of tea. Later managed to go down where Mr Hillyard was nobly carrying away stalls and getting the place in order. A Tea Party for 25 in the afternoon – but that is a mere bagatelle. Left at 11 p.m. I felt as if I was at the bottom of a very deep well. . . .

Only a month to Christmas. Have just shared a piece of cake with the little cat. He is used to the typewriter and likes to sit beside it.

End of November 1942

DECEMBER 1942

⊷⊷⊰ ❀ ⊱⊷⊷

Sunday, 6th News from North Africa is rather that of two tigers waiting for the spring. But the Germans will not easily be hurled into the sea. Darlan business still in obscurity. Questions in Parliament, and Eden obviously not happy about the replies. Our Government very cool about Darlan being in power, and the U.S.A. does not seem to know what its soldiers have engaged themselves into, with that very doubtful patriot. But the *Observer* seems to like de Gaulle as little as it likes Darlan.

Have been reading a book in the modern manner about Moses. Cannot help but see a parallel between Churchill and Moses – and between us and the Children of Israel. In our worst moments we do resemble that very tiresome people. They nearly drove Moses dotty – and certain of Mr Churchill's critics resemble those in the Sinai Desert.

We have been enjoying a pumpkin this week – a most attractive-looking fruit, and its connection with Cinderella made it most romantic eating.

Our Gates have gone. The workmen never even knocked on the door to tell us – but just began to hack them down.

The Beveridge Report has set everybody talking this week. It is apparently a very sensible document, and has been hailed

by all Parties as a workable Plan. I do not attempt to understand it yet, but gather only that we can be buried free of
charge – which is a comfort. It seems to imply Pensions for all
– which is also a cheering thought. I have visions of Cath and
me – two old ladies in a Country Cottage – helping at Church
Bazaars. I, having some experience of Bazaars, might be
useful on the Committee. [The country cottage has come true
. . . V.H.]

The *Front Line* book has just been issued, and we are all
reading it. Managed to snaffle Mr Hillyard's copy before he
had seen it himself, and have wept many tears this week-end
over all the sufferings and heroism. It gives a true and vivid
picture of all we went through during those nine awful
months. Lots of it one did not know; but we just dimly realized
all the work of the Rescue Men and Firemen out there, with
that Hell going on above. Every time I heard a bomb fall my
imagination gave me a good idea of what it meant. How we
lived through it I do not know – I never expected to.

I like the story of the little Welsh boy who was dug out. He
was found because he could be heard singing 'God Save The
King', over and over again beneath the wreckage. He was only
six – and it took six hours to release him. He sang all the time,
because his father being a collier had told him that the men
always sang when trapped underground, and he thought he
had better do the same . . .

The writer of the book has wonderful understanding. We
were very frightened – at least I was, and I know many were
even if they would not admit it: 'There was never a trace of
public panic; but the blitz was not a picnic, and no fine

slogans about taking it should obscure the realities of human fear and heartache.'

Read side by side with my diary written at the time, this book will give Lucy a good idea of what it was like. I just wrote down what we felt as the Screamers were coming down. The Book does justice to every place. Birmingham is well up on the List, as one of the Arms Towns – but being a large place it does not show as in some of the smaller ones. It seems some 20,000 bombs were dropped on London during September, October and November; but no Londoner heard anything like that number because it is so vast. Whereas in Coventry every citizen heard each bomb that dropped.

Sunday, 13th Another *Front Line* story was of a shepherd out on the moors, looking after the ewes and lambs. He had a private blitz to himself – but he carried all the ewes and lambs from the pens which were in danger of fire from incendiaries raining down on them all. His dog vanished – the situation being too much for him.

Miss M. has received two lemons from British Columbia, and if I can extract an orange from the Old Pole Auntie Nell will make them up.

Near Christmas and am sending an advance parcel with food, and beyond anything – a colander, which has taken some getting. But Mr Hillyard achieved one from Selfridges at 6/6d for me.

We were electrified by General Catroux, the Free French leader in Syria, stating that were he commander in N. Africa he would not like to have Admiral Darlan in his rear. *Observer* thinks General Eisenhower badly advised to make any arrangement with him. De Gaulle party very upset – but the Americans say the influence of de Gaulle is negligible! Cannot understand this.

Bombing Italy all this week. If it is not Turin, it is Naples. Can well understand the Italians rushing off to the Lakes or the mountains. Feel very sorry for them. Evidently Mussolini had the arrogance to think we should go under, and Italy would never be bombed. How little he knows us!

Thought I was going to be clever and get some Chinese figs for Xmas. Waited in shop for ten minutes only to be told: A sweet ration and a half! Ruefully left the shop. Don't know what they will manage to get at home. As long as we have Bread Sauce with an onion, I don't mind.

Dr Remy rang me up with the glad news that he has been appointed to one of the biggest legal firms in England. His perseverance has won the day. He will be back in London in the New Year.

Unnaturally warm for a week or two – hope January won't bring the snow.

Sunday, 20th   News continues to be good, though we have not romped into Tunis. Rommel is scampering back to join his pal there. Then a nasty brew will be prepared for us. However, we have not been thrown out of anywhere for quite a month or two, and it is a welcome change. Russians are pounding away. The massacre of the Jews is awful to read of, and I don't propose to bear anything but animosity to Germans as long as I live.

A queer business about Darlan – the Fighting French won't stomach him. Seems to be the first difference of opinion among the Allies.

Letter from Auntie Mollie saying they get nasty daylight raids down Brede way. A Nazi got in and machine-gunned a woman pegging out the clothes – and a baby in a pram may be killed. Bomb fell on a shop full of people on the South Coast the other afternoon. Horrible.

Terribly busy with the Christmas charity lists. Saturday was one continuous stream of Mothers and children from 9.30 a.m. They came for clothes, and the few toys we had – also some money. I get tired of going up and down three flights of stairs. The children seemed to want religious pictures.

Went to Carol Concert at the Albert Hall, as I had been given two tickets. Felt very elegant in Lady Palmer's box. Malcolm Sargent was the Conductor. Megan Foster and Norman Allin the soloists. Not a vacant seat. All the Choir ladies were in white dresses, so nice. Pouring with rain.

End of December 1942

THE YEAR
1943

'And so through all the length of days'
'Come labour on. Away with gloomy doubts and faithless fear'

MAIN EVENTS
OF THE YEAR
1943

1943

January	3	Russians relieve Leningrad
		Casablanca Conference
	23	British enter Tripoli
February	2	German surrender at Stalingrad
February – March		Russian Winter offensive: Rostov: Rzhev: Vyazma.
March	4	Bismarck Naval battle
	20	Montgomery attacks Mareth position
May	12	Axis forces in North Africa surrender
July	10	Allies invade Sicily
	25	Fall of Mussolini
July – October		United States – Australian advance in New Guinea
August	18	Allied conquest of Sicily complete
	23	Russians retake Kharkov
September	2	Italian surrender signed
	9	Allies land in South Italy . . . Salerno
	12	Italian fleet surrenders at Malta
	25	Russians retake Smolensk

October 13 Portugal opens Azores base to Britain
November 6 Russians retake Kiev
December 2–7 Teheran Conference

JANUARY 1943

→→→→ ❊ ←←←←

Sunday, 3rd Must go back a long way with my diary as Christmas has intervened and I have been home. The week before I was terribly busy with the Poor of the Parish. They all came for their extra bits. Also we sent a lot of money by post. Had to go and find one family who had not turned up . . . walked miles along little streets – I had the wrong address, but finally found them.

Great effort to get a cake at Fullers in Queensway. After three separate visits cakes were visible, took my turn and obtained a Slab. Heard talk of rabbits at the butcher's . . . yes, if I would call again at 2 p.m. Phoned Mr Hillyard, who was thrilled.

Barishnikov helped me to Paddington – busy, but not too much. Is your journey really necessary? was ringing in my ears. Yes, definitely! Sat down thankfully. Beryl met me. Mother is getting on amazingly well. Bernard Sleigh arrived for Christmas – so we began picking up old links. Began to embroider a tablecloth for his cottage. He is very deaf, but read us one of his own stories on Christmas Eve.

All very jolly on Christmas day. Presents laid out at breakfast. Dr H. thought the Liberty handkerchiefs very handsome, though he did not reckon to use colours. However, as they were linen, and we were in the midst of a great war he thought the principles of a lifetime might be waived.

Mother and I went to Cardinal Newman's Oratory for part of the Mass. Packed with people. Most interesting-looking Crib. Then on to St Chad's Hospital to see Florrie [a Sister, and once our Nurse]. She was giving a tea party to the nurses, and an operation had just come in, so she was busy. We discussed the last blitz with her. They heard the first bomb fall – but nothing else, not even a gun, as they were too busy with casualties. Two wardens died before they could do anything – also a Burmese medical student. One casualty, a woman, had been sheltering in her pantry, and all the glass and china was sticking into her in thousands of little pieces. They got a lot out – then the surgeon had to do something. Poor thing! The bomb which dropped in Waterworks Rd just behind the Hospital, nearly shot the ambulance men down the stairs with the stretcher and the casualty. It was a terrible night.

Beryl, aged fifteen, prepared the dinner. No turkey, no fowl, no rabbit – only the usual joint. The child had been time and time again to the shop – but the man would not let her have a fowl. I had brought a Plum Pudding from London, which I cut with trepidation, as it only cost 1/9d. It was one of the best we ever tasted, and a vote of thanks was passed to Peek Freans for their brilliant effort. The London butcher had let Mr H. have the rabbit, and let Auntie Nell have a hare, which required a special licence. She was delighted and gave him a pot of damson cheese as a reward. She made jugged hare, and served it all round her flats.

Listened to the King's Speech, and loved the story – 'It's not a burden, sir, it's my brother.' Someone with a delicate touch is behind the King's Speeches. Had music in the evening. Beryl sang, and Cyril Franklin came to tea as usual. Boxing Day Mother and I went over to see Ariel and Cecilia. The others came in the afternoon. Dr H. produced a tin of butter from Johannesburg, and so we all had bread and butter. Magnificent. Sunday, Beryl went home, so I cooked the dinner with Annie's help [She was a little old soul, bombed out, whom Mother took in. She was not much use – but just another pair of hands.] We also sent a meal into our neighbours, laid low with flu.

Cath and Dr H. saw me to the station. I got a seat and chuffed back to London. Two years ago I had gone back into an enormous blitz!

The great outside news of Christmas Eve was the assassination of Darlan. I have no use for the man, dead or alive, but I wonder if the murder will help matters. Most people think it has cut the Gordian knot neatly. Giraud has been put in his place! It does not seem to be realized that de Gaulle is not just one of many French Generals, but the only one who refused to give in to the Germans, and who has kept the French standard flying from the first second of the French Government's betrayal. He came here with a half-filled suitcase and not a penny piece, burning with fight against the enemy. Giraud probably does not know what de Gaulle has been doing the past two years.

There is an article in the *Observer* by M. André Philip. I am not well up in who he is – seems to have escaped recently.

I agree with him when he says: 'The unifying governing body can consist only of men whose past is irreproachable, whose word once given has always been kept, who like de Gaulle took an unequivocal attitude towards the enemy, when such a decision involved a risk . . . the man who by uttering the call for resistance, when all others were plunged in despair, has in the eyes of our people become the symbol of the Mother Country.'

The United Nations' Red Cross Rally at the Albert Hall was, it seems, most thrilling, according to one of our part-time workers who was there. The place rang with cheers as General Dobbie stepped down from his box to join the Malta Contingent. Also the Red Army brought the audience to its feet.

When we heard that Abyssinia had declared war on Germany, Italy and Japan, Miss M. flashed out: 'It's like a fly putting its tongue out.' Rather neat I thought.

Sunday, 10th Busy week finishing with a Show for the Christmas Fair helpers. Raced down to Richmond to get scones for the tea. All well, but glad to reach the peace and quiet of Auntie Nell's flat. Later did some washing – but am not a washerwoman by instinct.

Gremlins discussed on the Brains Trust – the airmen say they inhabit aeroplanes. Another point was about being married to an artistic man . . . Donald McCulloch deduced from the various answers that it was rather a strain being married to anyone at all!

Have just had 50 tickets for the Zoo given to us. Must be

used before the end of January. So I am to take lots of Mothers and children. I wonder if the Zoo will prepare us Tea . . .

Dr Remy is now installed in London, and I hope to have him next Sunday at the flat to exchange news. We are frightfully short of fish – in fact have been for weeks. Same in Brum.

My osteopath told me the story of a young owl from a wood, caught by a naturalist. The bird broke its leg, and the naturalist noticed a spot appear in the iris of the bird's eye. He nursed the bird, and as it gradually recovered he noted the spot disappear little by little. The bird flew away. It seems Mr Evans once had a patient whose eye showed that he had mercury in his system from medicine of years previously. Minerals, he said, that have not passed through the vegetable kingdom are dangerous for human beings, and against natural law.

Sunday, 17th   Fairly mild weather. Different from this time last year when we were under snow. Evenings are drawing out.

Went to explore the Zoo before my expedition on January 30th with the Mothers and children. Officials most helpful and the cashier especially over Tea. Visited the Parrot House – all friendly, and let me touch them. Finally I put my arm out, and one came from his perch and sat there. The Brown Bears on the Mappin Terrace were charming – they sat up and begged for buns. The Grecian ibex looked most picturesque on his rocky promontory. But the joy of the show was the chimpanzee. A small boy was feeding him with a carrot on the end of a stick. He was made first to clap his hands, and then received a reward. Three of them came out and laughed at us showing all their teeth. A grey parrot was screaming happily up in the trees.

News is pretty good. We raided Berlin last night. I wonder if that means they will raid London. As I am fire-watching I must be at the ready. Rommel is on the run in Tripolitania, and the Germans in Russia. Heard Hitler's voice on News today, promising that Stalingrad would be taken. The place is in ruins! But it is still Russian – salute to them!

Wendell Wilkie ought to be ashamed – the idea of coming here, making himself so agreeable, and then returning to belittle everybody. Never heard such nonsense talked. That anyone in a University called Duke was equal to Stalin, Roosevelt or Churchill, and could do what they have done . . . France is an object lesson in what can happen to a country where no man of principle and courage is in charge.

Bad raids on Dawlish and Teignmouth during the week. The aunts, when they go into Hastings, never know if there will be a diabolical raid.

Victor Collins sent two wonderful letters to his mother from Canada. Having the time of his life training to be an observer. Says he is seeing in a few months what he might never have seen in a lifetime. He is so grateful, and assures his mother that should anything befall him he has enjoyed life to the full.

Miss M. and party went to Coventry last Sunday; mis-directed in the Black-out on their return, got the wrong train, and reached London at 4 a.m. Phoned me in a melancholy frame of mind. They reached Euston, no taxi, no tube. Waited various half hours here and there . . . of course the authorities would ask if their journey was really necessary. I was sorry for them. They had had to stand in the corridor for the journey. Nevertheless they worked heroically all day on the paper, and did not get to bed until 11 p.m.

More tinned fruit is coming. Good . . . 8.30 p.m. We have not had shell eggs for I know not how long. Then one came. It was so unusual I forgot it! A few days later I remembered it – cooked it, and it looked nice. But as I lifted the plate to go and sit by the fire I caught tray and all on the edge of the table! Exit egg all over the mat. Rescued a bit, and ate it in a very sober frame of mind!

Lavender Yates, my former pupil, with her parents is a prisoner in hands of the Japs. She is 22, very fair and very English. Does not bear thinking of.

Air Raid Alarm just gone!

Sunday, 24th Had just finished my diary last Sunday, when, behold, the old Wailers set up as they used to do so regularly. I jumped up, looked hastily round for the tin hats. They were up on a high shelf, where they had lain since the Fair. Climbed up and after a hasty dust clamped one on my head. Got with speed into rubber boots and ran to the front door.

A mighty barrage had set up. Seemed as if it was going to be the greatest of all air raids. Miss M. and party not returned from Ipswich. Filled the bath. Met Miss Mackay on her way to fetch The Old Lady. After gravely watching me fill the bath she proffered the advice that it was unwise to take a bath now! Ran round all stirrup pumps, buckets of sand, spades, water etc. Found I had forgotten how to deal with phosphorous bombs, so began to turn over my notes hastily!

Mercifully at this point the party returned. They had had a shock. All as usual at Liverpool St, but in the Tube stations they noticed people all talking together, but thought it was just a big rain storm. Imagine their amazement coming out of Holland Park when they walked straight into a noise like all the guns of Europe barking at once. I was glad to see them, as it is no joke in this great house with three old ladies. Mrs Hoare soon got into her war paint, and Miss M. too. Things got so hot, we could not get the 9 o'clock News. Raid lasted two hours.

Went back to my flat. Sirens again at 5 a.m. Me not ready – no shoes or torch handy, as I thought they would not be necessary. But they were. Barrage became terrific. From my skylight I had visions of incendiaries descending and barring my way to the door. So descended to next floor. Stood and talked with Miss Lambart, who is a British Israelite. She returns to the subject like Mr Dick and King Charles. As her theme got hotter and hotter so the barrage grew louder and louder. I escaped down to the front door, where in Ladbroke Road was the ping ping of shrapnel.

Some time before I could sleep. We discussed in the office where the damage was. Not Kensington, but Peckham, East Dulwich, East Ham and Golders Green. Apparently there is a bomb sitting outside the Vicarage at East Ham, Auntie informed me. Bob's two little girls were there and frightened into fits. So Mrs Hodson has taken them to Worcestershire. Not evacuating the vicarage as the house, they think, will stand the shock. But people round have been moved – the experts hope to draw its teeth.

Wednesday, we had a daylight raid. Loud round here, but we did not realize the devils had done such awful damage until later in the day, when rumours trickled through that a school had been hit, with great loss of life. A bad business. Six raiders snooped into London. Not realized where they were making for, so no alarm given. Thus the School had no chance to get the children to the Shelters. Seems to have been at Grove Park, where 150 little girls were assembled for lunch – and the centre of the building caved in. Other bombs outside killing people. A dreadful scene. Every kind of help raced to the spot – great cranes to lift masonry. They say 40 little girls were killed outright, and six of the staff. All to be buried together on Monday. Rescuers worked all through the night, though Warning went – frantic parents joined in the search. The school was a tall building, and the bomb went straight through. For those who died they never knew what struck them . . . It is difficult to see the reason for these things.

Many people killed last Sunday by shrapnel. Wardens begged them to go inside. At the Marble Arch they pushed them into the Shelter at Marks and Spencers, as the Hyde Park guns were in full cry. In Kensington Gardens the Wardens were re-opening the trench Shelters. Mrs Yirrell, one of our people, was there airing her dog, and talking with an old lady who refused to budge. Noise devastating. Mrs Y. did not like to leave the old lady alone. This was near Queen Victoria's statue. Poor old Queen! I wonder what she would have said had she been alive.

Much talk of Shelters being locked. But we were all taken by surprise.

News is good in Russia and Africa. Tripoli taken – and I permit myself to rejoice over this. Mussolini must be looking green. No more wonderful speeches from Palazzo Venezia – calling on the Italian people to march towards their destiny!

The Russians are also permitting themselves to rejoice over the relief of Leningrad. They go on fighting somehow and extricate themselves to fight another day. Must be the result of 25 years of hard work and self-denial – not years of the good life. Professor Joad, please note. Real name of Stalingrad was Tzaritzin, Barishnikov says.

Nothing settled in N. Africa with de Gaulle. Cannot imagine why the Americans could not follow our lead – wherever we have entered French territory and captured it, we have handed over to the Fighting French. This has worked admirably . . . Madagascar, Syria etc. The Americans begin a new stunt – and no one is pleased.

Friday, 29th Have made all preparations for the Zoo visit. Mr H. still away ill, so bedded down on Sanctuary settee for Fire Watch. Curled up – when I heard a thrum. Came from the office. A bomber overhead? Then a flood of inspiration – the telephone! Groped my way in the dark. A young, entreating and apologetic voice explained that he was Miss Mackay's nephew, a merchant sailor, and could he come for the night . . .

I galloped upstairs – Miss Mackay asleep. Sleepily she responded Yes. Bed was ready, but he ought to have let her know sooner. Down I went with this good news. But in still more apologetic tones the voice said there was a friend . . . could he come, too? Up the stairs again. Miss Mackay was far from pleased, but I pleaded for sailors on leave – something must be done. So a much relieved voice explained they were at The Monument, and would be along in half-an-hour. So we spent the intervening time airing sheets, getting hot-water bottles, making cocoa and I thoroughly enjoyed myself.

Two nice youngsters arrived at 12.45 – very smart in uniform, full of apologies. They had been to their ship, but it was sealed for decontamination, and they were not allowed on board. Had just had an awful Atlantic crossing, waves like mountains. Thought the ship would never survive. Several in the convoy had been sunk. Not an atom of comfort – ship infested with rats. So that lovely room with gas fire burning, the hot cocoa and our nice welcome, seemed like a bit of heaven.

They had to leave at 7 a.m. Dear Miss Mackay made them breakfast and fell in love with the friend on the spot. I returned to my fire-watching and at last fell asleep. Wandered up the road at 7.45 a.m. and made a cup of tea.

Churchill's visit to N. Africa astounded us all. Roosevelt is a trump to come so far. It will be sad when these two fine men cease to work together. Stands to reason we cannot always have them. Roosevelt will not be President again – and Churchill is getting tired. Besides, I do not think the Conservative Party likes him.

A gale blowing. Wind and rain against my window. Great tree uprooted near here. Must have raged in the Channel.

JANUARY 1943

Not surprised the Germans did not come . . . though we bombed Berlin, just as Goering was beginning his speech.

Sunday, 31st Yesterday looked anxiously at the sky. Black clouds scudding across, but occasional gleams of blue. Not too promising. Barishnikov greeted me cheerfully. Did odd jobs, carrots for the chimps, biscuits and buns for the bears. . . . The escorts arrived in good time. Sent these off with their respective families. Perhaps some would not come as their clothes would not stand a drenching. Left Mr Symonds to bring the stragglers. This was a mercy, as a family of six turned up an hour late! He carried a child of two on his shoulder for the rest of the day.

At the Zoo I pinned little rosettes on the children to recognize our party. Found the Morris family waiting an hour at the wrong place! We all loved watching the sea lions walloping out of the water, and shuffling over the rocks to get their fish. Crowds of scouts there. Then down came the rain. It poured. All turned helter-skelter for the Monkey House. Weather improved, so off to the Bears on Mappin Terraces and buns distributed. Down again came the rain. Imagine my feelings with all those little children. I sheltered some under my mack, and gave others my umbrella. But they declared they loved it! We splashed our way to the Tea Room.

Here our luck turned. We fell headlong through the door and settled down to a glorious tea. Nice and warm and dry. The Manageress took us under her wing. I had stipulated for cream buns – not real, of course, but a jolly good imitation. Our two-year-old dived into his, and emerged with cheeks covered with the stuff. I wandered round them all and they were quite happy. Then I phoned Miss Moyes, who was most relieved. She had watched the rain come down and heard the thunder! I assured her none of us had been washed into the Regent's Park Canal.

We made for the bus. A huge queue. The conductor looked at us and remarked: 'Oh, Zoo chuck-out!' Gradually escorts and children got on. It did not rain again, and eventually all were safely back at the Sanctuary. I admit I was tired. There is a good deal of mental strain attached to taking forty mothers and children to the Zoo on a wet day in the midst of the Greatest War in History!

Kit was in my flat. Come for the night to attend the Service at St Martin in the Fields for the Channel Islanders, at 9.30 a.m. today. Her family, the Sauvarys, are born and bred Islanders, since the 15th Century.

Did not sleep well. Rain beat on the skylight, and rattled the dormer window. Kept imagining myself back at the Zoo with the children. The Alarm Clock was set for Kit at 7 a.m., but as it is not quite right in the head there is no certainty about it. Mercifully all was well, and Kit left for her service. I tuned in later and followed it. The Archbishop of York took it. He used to be Bishop of Winchester, and the Islands were in his diocese. He took as his text: Comfort ye, comfort ye my people. He spoke feelingly to the huge congregation. They sang the last hymn all kneeling: 'O heavenly Father, in Thy mercy Hear our anxious prayer.'

When our Commandos raided Guernsey they snatched some newspapers. Many of Kit's friends are among the names of those sent to Germany. But she is sure her father has not been taken. There is much about bartering shoes for bread . . .

A Music Hall item: It concerned the position of shop-keeper and customer in England today. The latter must be cajoling and polite; the shopkeeper must be wooed into parting with his precious commodities. In bygone times the Great Lady would ring her fishmonger; 'Five lobsters – mind they are fresh, or my custom will go elsewhere . . .' Nowadays the Great Lady takes her basket to the Fishmonger, and in her most ingratiating voice implores him to send her what he can. As she departs, she looks sweetly at him, 'Shall see you at my Cocktail Party tonight – and bring the kippers with you.'

End of January 1943

FEBRUARY 1943

Friday, 5th We seem to be in the midst of tremendous events. Russians are rolling on in all directions. German Generals captured while shaving . . . No wonder Goebbels was speechless with rage, and Hitler must be throwing fits in a back room somewhere. The Russians let us down in the last war, but they have come back with a vengeance. Barishnikov can hardly contain his spirits. Stalingrad will be found written on Hitler's heart. It is a treat to pick up a newspaper. Find myself getting far too pleased. But de Gaulle warns us the Germans are not beaten yet. But the fact that someone can make them retreat is a bit of a change. It has been surrenders and retreats with us for so long – and there seemed no end to it.

Miss M. and I used to get depressed at times, but Mr Hillyard never did – he said always that the tide would turn – while I reached a point when I could almost see the Nazis marching up Notting Hill Gate.

Tuesday visited a little girl in University College Hospital. She ought to have come to the Zoo – but had appendicitis. They make no trouble about visiting hours. I walked in and saw her. She was in a bomb-proof basement and looked blooming and happy, reading Angela Brazil.

Coming out I took a look at the British Museum. Dome seemed rather a mess – but it may be only the glass that has gone. Firemen were practising outside with long extending ladders – they went right up into the sky. Could not but notice the quiet of Tottenham Court Road. It was like a country town – an occasional bus, a taxi here and there, but almost nothing on the streets. I believe Cairo has all the traffic nowadays. Our roads are all peace and quiet.

The Old Pole has taken to selling mushrooms, and he is amazed the British public is prepared to spend so much money on them. More tinned fruit on Monday. So I opened a handsome tin of blackberries from our Invasion Reserve.

Invasion not imminent, so I took the risk. Biscuits and cake much more difficult. No marmalade – but I am not surprised as I learn the American soldiers are having all ours.

Dr Joad gave a good Postscript on the Advantages of Science. But stated that our wisdom in making the best use of our blessings was well behind our mastery of the forces of nature. We could rush through the air, dive under the sea – but we could not spare green fields in the centre of London where children could play. In fact we did not know the Good Life any better than the Ancients – though we had twice their advantages.

Sunday, 7th Saw Kit again. She says the Channel Islands Service was wonderful and warmed their hearts. The Bishop is a saint . . . said exactly the right thing to comfort them all. Afterwards outside the Church the scenes were indescribable. One thousand six hundred people – everyone knowing hundreds of others, and some not having met since the evacuation. They talked and talked in the rain . . .

The Queen went to see the injured children from the bombed school. They are in hospital. She took some bananas Lord Louis Mountbatten had brought back from Casablanca for the two Princesses.

Count Ciano has been dismissed. What part is Edda* playing – does her deep attachment to her father still persist, or does she take her husband's side? Her days of glory are over – receptions in Rome – Ascot wearing marvellous toilettes. I wonder if I shall get to Corsica after the war and see Loulou Ferrandi.

Mr Churchill is safe back. What a relief. I hope it is not our destiny or punishment to lose him in the moment of triumph – the wise hand that has guided us through the valleys of humiliation. His statue should go up in pure gold in Trafalgar Square . . .

Thursday, 11th Great commotion about fish in London. Hunted about in the rain, but was confronted with large notices – NO FISH – or by closed doors. The only place to buy it is on the beach when the fishermen come in. Heavy meals are easy to come by – but light food for invalids like Mother, are impossible.

Walked to Robinson and Cleaver last Saturday. A multitude of uniforms in the streets. All types and nationalities. Hoped to buy some coloured sheets. No coloured ones – in

* Edda Mussolini was a pupil of mine at the Poggio Imperiale.

fact no sheets at all, except linen ones at £9 per pair! Nearly fainted in the shop. Took a bus from St James' Church Piccadilly – what a mess, just a wreck – got to Barkers and asked humbly for sheets. Over £2 per pair – so just faded out of the place.

Such mild days. Spring seems nearly upon us. No snow – what a joy to the Fuel Controller. Snowdrops are out.

Some daylight Alerts. When the sky is dark with rain they sneak through in small numbers, and bomb some isolated school or Church. Coast towns have a terrific time – life and property in danger every day. You go out shopping one afternoon – and never return. In the obituary the other day three sisters were killed simultaneously in Eastbourne. A bomb straight on the house. But people still carry on and take danger as a matter of course.

Heard much of Smuts. He had a brilliant academic brain as well as being a man of action. A pronouncement he made about Russia during the last war struck me. To the effect that she was like Samson, blind, turning the wheel in the House of Gaza – but the time would come when she would recover and be greater than the Germans – pretty good for twenty-five years ago!

Just heard some of Churchill's speech. Moses talking to the Children of Israel, warning them not to criticize before they have tried our suggestion. As one of the aforesaid naughty children of Israel I thought – well, I hope General Eisenhower is all they say he is. Let Moses have his way. We won't grumble yet. Churchill is one of the most generous men in spirit – always ready to take second place for the General

Good. So I shall trust him over it all. He hints that the Russians are doing such colossal things that if we do not hurry up and assert ourselves by doing similar deeds of derring-do, we shall find ourselves out of the picture!

Hope to go with Marie to *She Stoops to Conquer* at the Mercury. Mrs Churchill went while her husband was in N. Africa. Heard all Marie's adventures in her peach of a job. Sort of Agatha Christie setting. I feel some mystery should develop. Perhaps there is a skeleton in the cupboard of this noble family . . .

Terrible fire in Norland Square. Our organist was there on the first floor. A burning coal fell out in a room below her. Retreat was cut off. Mr Bruce, an old actor, picked up his dog and made for the stairs to warn a father, mother and baby at the top of the house. He was 72 – and never got there. Overcome by fumes he and the dog were found dead on the landing afterwards. Meanwhile the little family were on the balcony. The father holding the three weeks' old baby under his coat – the mother in a faint at his feet. Some soldiers climbed on the roof of the next house, broke a partition, and all were rescued. But the old actor has been much praised for the way he took his last call. The fire brigade arrived and put out the flames – but what an experience.

Sunday, 14th Another lovely day. It is after 6 p.m. and still light. Russians are near Kharkov and Rostov. Dr Remy thinks the Germans will re-form and drive the Russians back. I hope he is wrong. He says the German war machine is very strong still – although they have lost the war. But he feels it is too much to hope that the war in Europe will be over this year, and that he will see his beloved wife and children again.

Listened to the Tripoli Review – marvellous to hear the pipes playing, the drums beating and Mr Churchill speaking to them. How did they manage to transport all their Party Frocks so far! They hoped to take Tunisia at a run, but could not. Plenty of ingenuity still left in the Germans. Not easily caught napping. However, it is all marvellous compared with the days of the Sinking of the Great Battleships and the Surrender of Singapore.

Damage to home counties last week pretty nasty. British Restaurant at Reading was hit . . . also at Manor Park there was damage.

Pathetic letter from Dr Remy saying he had been ill with flu, and being alone in a boarding house he had never felt so desolate in his life. Finally he had called out and the district nurse was summoned. She was beyond all expectations kind, and so all was well. But I reprimanded him severely for not getting someone to ring me – and Auntie Nell would have gone round. I do not usually sit still with folded hands when my friends are in trouble.

Visit from Mrs George King and Gretel. After 15 years to track them down at last. How I wish Mother had been there! We remembered all the happy times when they had come to Brum and given us tickets for the Operas. Mr King died in sad circumstances . . . he had to give up his post as producer at Covent Garden, and that seemed to him like the end. Gretel is a good harpist, but it is all very precarious. The show may come off at any time. She has broadcast a bit, and done T.V.

when it was on. But their nerves are shattered by Mr King's long illness, and spending every penny on him. Then the blitz. The last opera he produced at Covent Garden, Mrs King said, was *The Tales of Hoffman*. Sir Thomas made him take a call with him. It was also the first opera he had produced years before for Sir Thomas, and had taken a call then. He was such a fine, handsome, stalwart man – full of kindness, so merry and full of vitality. Most pathetic!

Thursday, 18th Americans retreat a bit. Rommel's panzers being worsted by our Desert Boys, have turned on a less experienced target. We had to bite the dust, and learn to measure our enemy at his true strength. A few American tanks with a lot of shouting will not finish the war. I liked Eisenhower when, after being appointed Generalissimo, he was heard to remark: 'Holy smoke.' The exclamation of a young spirit.

Bad raid on Chichester this week. Cathedral undamaged. It was afternoon and many people about. Miss Mackay's friend was due in the cinema that was hit, but her pony caused her a small accident – so she went to the doctor instead.

Poor Mrs Cameron went up to Yorkshire to see her boy in hospital. He is just alive, but opened his eyes at seeing her – could not believe it. 'Mum, where did you get the money to come?' She replied: 'Never mind. I have good friends who gave it me.' 'God bless them . . .' murmured the boy. Deeply moving, I thought. It was out of our Shelter Fund. They are moving him to a brain hospital. I do hope he recovers. He will never fly again.

Monday, 22nd Cups without handles are now appearing. A queue in Brompton Rd for saucepans – the first for three years! But I cannot imagine why handles on teacups are so difficult.

Listened to Red Army celebrations in the Albert Hall. Very impressive. Sybil Thorndike's voice rang out. Mr Eden spoke and he managed a few vivid phrases. Mr Churchill is ill. We don't like it. They give him M and B . . . a new drug. Hope the after effects are not dangerous. It would be awful if mental decay was caused.

Really everyone is ill – it must be the diet. We are all overtired with these years of Black-out and war and Anxiety and Domestic difficulty. Mr Hillyard looked spent this evening. Mother is not too well. They say Slippery Elm is good. Two large country apples given us today, beyond my wildest dreams. I baked them – they were good.

We are still discussing the Beveridge Report. A woman spoke on it. A good song on the wireless: 'If you're up to your neck in hot water, be like the kettle and sing.'

Discussion about changing human nature! It was said the Russians have altered their people by their system of government. This may be so. Systems can bring out the best and the worst. But what do the Russians do with the malingerers and the lazy? They have always existed. This is a free country and the difficulty is to help the deserving while discouraging the unworthy. Utopias here seem to break down.

Sunday, 28th War News picked up a little. Germans making no further progress in Tunisia, and the Desert Army still stepping forward – Bless them! Mr Churchill has been more ill than the general public knew.

Wonderful story of heroism in Plymouth during the blitz. Fires were everywhere, and a naval man heard a woman screaming in a house. Bystanders urged him not to attempt a rescue, as it was an inferno. But putting a wet muffler round his face he plunged in, found the room where a man and woman were pinned by a beam. He released the man, and together they carried the fainting woman – ceiling half down. Stairs were well alight. The naval man hewed down a door with some fire irons, put the man on it with the woman in his arms, and launched it through the flames jumping on it himself. It went clear down. They discovered a window at the back. They lowered the woman out and then followed. As they did so the roof of the house fell in. He would not give his name, nor did he try to find out the people he had rescued. If that does not show courage and resource, I don't know what does!

Elsie, like many people is having trouble. Her mother is lying ill in a Nursing Home at Parkstone. She has to dash to and fro from Brum to Dorset in between her job at the University, and looking after her home with all its wartime miseries. In addition, her husband, who is a Divisional Warden, has chosen this identical moment to break three ribs!

Went round to Auntie Nell, and bought a few articles from the Rummage sale in one of the flats. Some dirty linen curtains were £6 – could not afford these. They were soon snapped up. Returned to my flat and slept. Feeling hungry put some nut meat brawn to boil, as instructed on tin. Punctured the hole – alas the liquid squirted out in volumes, and I had a dose of vegetarian brawn in my eye.

End of February 1943

MARCH 1943

❧❧❧ ❀ ❦❦❦❦

Saturday, 6th A raid on Wednesday night. I was having a treatment, and wondered if Mr Evans wished to dash home; but he continued on with such interesting conversation that I forgot about the guns. There was a lull, and as his assistant was going my way I walked with him. We were lucky – guns began just as I reached the Sanctuary doorstep. The raid was not on Kensington, but on Putney, and the Tube between Mansion House and Charing Cross was closed for a time.

The terrific Shelter disaster at Bethnal Green was announced on the News. Looking at the plan one can see that an accident could easily occur. The stairs down had only rough walls with nothing to hold on to . . . it was wide and dark and the guns were going. I could understand a few people getting smothered, but 178 seems incredible. Also that no one was able to shout. The poor Wardens down below must have been distraught when they discovered what was happening. Mercifully they phoned the police at once. Why so many were knocked over before he or she could move must remain a mystery.

Have been reading a series of unpublished letters from Army Nurses. Miss Katharine Jones, Matron-in-chief of Army

Nurses, has a sister who works part-time with us. What hair-raising escapes some had – others were drowned or taken prisoner. What they went through in Crete and Singapore can be imagined. In France during the retreat two Nurses tried to stop our Army Lorries for a lift before the Dunkirk rescue – when finally they boarded one every soldier was dead asleep, and the driver almost . . . no one had slept for days. That explained why the nurses had not been seen when hailing from the ditch in the road.

Seem to have been bombs at Exmouth. Also they say the Harwich express found itself in a bomb crater. Elspeth Wanklyn was at the Palace the other day, with her husband's mother, to receive his V.C. and other decorations. She looks just as sweet as she did at school.

Went to Liberty's for curtain material. A very superior gentleman showed me some at 30/- per yard. Was rather dashed, but kept calm and began to look round. At last we happened on something just suitable for 5/6d per yard. It was pre-war price and without purchase tax. Well-pleased, my pal and I wandered round the gorgeous Chinese embroideries and Italian cushions at nine guineas each.

Wedding at Sanctuary of daughter of one of our helpers. Difficult to arrange a Reception, but the ninety-eight at Notting Hill Gate did their best. Invited some of the guests back to my tiny apartment. One was a Red Cross helper from the Cambridge Hospital at Aldershot. There are still men, she said, from Dunkirk. Others from Dieppe and Madagascar. One Dunkirk man has no arms and only one leg. Incredibly he shows no bitterness, and is prepared to face life and make something of it. It is difficult to entertain – biscuits are scarce, and cake – if you can get it – is of poor quality. So I made toast. Two of them could not eat margarine. Mercifully I had not felt impelled to give my butter ration this week to an invalid. And I had some cigarettes left over from a Christmas present.

One day made myself a salad with some soused herrings I had seen in a shop. No fish for months. They were 8d each. Bought water-cress and beetroot from the Old Pole. Very good.

Sunday, 14th Took the bus to Oxford Circus. Walked to Trafalgar Square. Such crowds of people – men selling flags and gew-gaws. Soldiers going round the Square in a jeep. Edged my way in and saw the big bomber . . . O for orange. A Lancaster. Slid into the centre, and found firemen selling stamps to stick on the bomber. Bought one and with great satisfaction stuck it on.

Some Air Force cadets were enjoying themselves in the fountain. They were trying to raise one million pennies to buy a Typhoon for Westminster. They paddled about in a rubber dinghy – such as wrecked airmen use. You threw pennies to them – other cadets were splashing around in waders for pennies fallen in the pool. A bag came round also, so I put mine in that. All great fun – and people seemed in a Coronation mood. Found a man displaying two lemons, and shouting through a microphone that they had just come in the Gibraltar convoy, and were to be auctioned that evening in a theatre.

Then went on to see the St Paul's Bomber. There it was

sitting in all that desolation. One can only think that a miracle took place to save St Paul's. All buildings around it have been pulled down – except for one wall of a little Church. This bomber was H for Harry. A shabby-looking giant. It had been on 62 bombing raids, including Berlin. We walked beneath its wings, and could see the guns sticking out. Lots of little boys were gloating over it. Airmen were discussing technical details. I bought another stamp – this for Lucy and stuck it on.

Feeling tired took a bus to Marble Arch, and walked back through the Park. Early daffodils were out and the masses of crocuses beneath the trees were a sight. The tree barks were black and their branches had no buds – yet the temperature might have been June. No such Winter in London for thirty years.

Dr Remy came to tea. Cooked some of Lucy's peaches, Barishnikov had wangled me a cake. With anchovy toast it was quite a show. My visitor pronounced it delicious, and said we were not starving in England. Lively discussion on the House of Lords, which he is in favour of abolishing. My point was that the English political system had stood the test of time, and that neither France nor Germany were examples to follow. I assured him he would get used to our traditions in time. He thought the English very kind. In his Guest House each one strives to help the other obtain what they need. No one in Germany would do that, he assures me. He brought me a lovely green vase and bowl. I like them immensely. I have bought his wife a Tea Caddy spoon with the arms of London on it. I must try and find something for the Two Little Girls, Ilsa and Helga. But Dr Remy does not think the war will end before 1944. He was full of information on British law, and where German law differs.

News is So So. Germans are picking up against the Russians a bit. N. Africa is a slow process. War will not be over in another five minutes. Those optimists who thought we should not have another Winter of it are mistaken. So we must darn and patch for a long time. We are not allowed to spend money or buy clothes, as they wish to spin out the goods. We shall all be threadbare if the war continues for years.

Many people are far from well. My osteopath says it is calcium in the bread – it gives skin troubles, he says.

We have adopted a pig. He has a special bin, and we can put anything in but rhubarb leaves. We don't know yet about tea leaves. His food is collected every Friday. Shipping situation bad; but bread is not rationed yet.

Sunday, 21st Went over to see Mrs George King and Gretel at Golders Green. Modern house, very nice, but was blitzed. I don't know how it held together . . . it ought to have sat down in the garden and given up the ghost. I consider it showed great presence of mind in standing upright. The bomb fell a few houses along, demolishing six at one fell swoop. The blast missed the next ones, and descended full and strong on Mrs King's little place. Mercifully they had gone to Devon. But her sister arriving in the morning was amazed to see the road full of people, and furniture vans going off in all directions.

Gretel is tall and thin with digestive trouble. Practically all the food she ought to have is unobtainable. She dreads the food news in case one of her few remaining items is to be cut off

. . . in which case she fears she will not survive the war, through lack of suitable things to eat. It made me thankful for my tough digestion! Gretel finds it difficult to take her harp about. Anyway I am sure she is clever and has her father's backbone.

Had no biscuits or cake for Marie who is coming in to tell me all about the aristocratic lady to whom she is temporary secretary. I tossed together some flour, powdered eggs and powdered milk, and put the mixture in the oven. Quite good. Really the biscuits one buys look as if they have been left over from the diet of Holloway Gaol.

Hastings had a bad raid last week. Auntie Mollie nearly went in, but was helping with a pneumonia case. But a neighbour from Brede had a thorough fright – all windows and doors of a house in Hastings she visited were blown in. Newcastle too had their worst raid. Marie was there, but after being in the London Blitz she said it was not too bad.

The Postscript on Monday was by an Australian journalist. I liked him – he had punch and vigour. Some years before the war, he said, the Grenadier Guards played in Sydney. Everyone was much impressed, and they invited one of the guardsmen on retirement to come out and teach them. He was Bandmaster Cobb.

The French Partisans are holding out in Savoy. British officers are there too. Much enjoyed *Workers' Playtime*. Jack Train took off the Brains Trust again. Joad is a gift.

Sunday, 28th Another peaceful Sunday. The sunshine woke me through the side of my black-out, and having slept well, I hastened to draw the curtains and let it flood into my room. The daffodils have come to town. What a joy on Friday to see the shops loaded with them – great yellow masses. A week or two ago they were one shilling a bloom. Now a bunch is l/3d. In the newspapers it says sixpence . . . but there is always a difference between theory and practice.

A big raid on Berlin last night. The biggest ever. But they say this every time. I am expecting, therefore, a raid here. Tomorrow is our Fire Watch, so I shall make my bed on the couch at the Sanctuary, as Mr H. is away, and Miss M. and party are in Portsmouth.

Went to see Auntie Nell with collected jam pots. Was dressed in my handsome long warm Rebecca gown. I wanted her to see how well the grand sash she had given me went with it. She was in good spirits. I have long read about eating raw cabbage, but hitherto had not tried it. Auntie shredded some, and with beetroot and her home-made salad cream we had tea in great state and discussed the affairs of the day. I made myself one at home – not so good as Auntie's, but enjoyed it.

My pupil, Margaret Ellis, has obtained a vacancy at Girton. The schools hastily sent in their best students, as Mr Bevin would have called them up. She sat for Entrance at a moment's notice, was selected for an interview, and knowing the English don Gwynneth Lloyd-Thomas, I wrote a line on Margaret's behalf. I should be happy to think it helped.

An indoor wireless day for me. *Workers' Playtime* was good. Jeanne de Casilis ringing up the Enquiry Office at the station was delicious. I like the song: 'You are the cream in my coffee. You are the salt in my stew. You are my necessity. I cannot live without you. You are the starch in my collar . . . etc.' Also 'The Little Brown Bird'. It is 200 years since Handel composed *The Messiah*. Magnificent. Also listened to Mr Middleton. Not that I have any intention of growing the things he talks about; but I like his personality and the way he says pertaters.

Last Sunday Miss Moyes surpassed herself. Nothing is allowed to prevent her from getting to a meeting. She was down beyond Southampton seeing her sister. But she had to reach Bournemouth. Yes, there were buses to the station – but no bus of any sort arrived. She returned to her sister's, borrowed a bicycle, and rode all through the New Forest, her long dress for the Meeting flying all around her. Her brother-in-law pounded behind carrying her suitcase. The forest ponies scattered like Catherine Wheels at this phenomenon . . . she caught the train.

Russians not doing so well this week, but we cannot expect it all the time. An R.A.F. plane flew over Rome. It came from Malta, circled the Holy City, and attacked some trains a little way out. Then made for Naples. They say Florence is full of rich refugees from Milan and Turin – sleeping in bathrooms. The Germans think the English would never attack Florence. Of course, one of our Special Bombs – and the Renaissance would perish at a blow, for the place is so small and the treasures close together. But I cannot think it possible.

Churchill's speech packed with interest. He disposed of people who believe the war will end this year or next. Rommel is a bulldog in Tunisia – and they are sinking our ships at a terrific rate.

It seems Aneurin Bevan had been more than usually personal over Randolph Churchill in attacking the Prime Minister. Miss Rathbone, surging with wrathful indignation, caught the Speaker's eye, and in a few short sentences disposed of Mr Bevan once for all on the subject. The House rang with cheers for the seventy-one-year-old Independent Member for the Northern Universities. Mr Churchill seemed as if he did not know whether to get up and thank her; but finally decided that, as a woman had taken charge, a mere man had better sit back and do nothing. The honours were all with Miss Rathbone!

End of March 1943

APRIL 1943

※※※ ❋ ❦❦❦

Sunday, 4th Full of Birthday celebrations. Two tin boxes full of woodland flowers – primroses and violets in moss, from Cath. Arranged some in my new glass bowl, and took rest to the office. All gathered in Chipping Campden. A cake from Bernard Sleigh himself. Auntie Nell made me one with marzipan icing and soya bean flour – this for the Office Party. Every member of staff throws a Tea Party on a birthday. The Aunts from Brede also sent me primroses, and my tiny flat took on the appearance of a bower. Very touched I was by all these remembrances.

My Swiss colleague came to tea on Saturday. He wishes that such flats were obtainable for men . . . Gave him Rhodesian apricots; and used the muffin dish bought from the Rummage sale for toast. You pour hot water in the under container – a priceless possession.

Went to Wimbledon to hear about Margaret and Girton. There were 100 Candidates and only 12 vacancies. Studied the exam papers with her, and was relieved I had not to do them. She is overcome with the beauty of Girton and its wonderful grounds. Mrs Ellis produced a wonderful meal in spite of rations. Mr Ellis and I had our usual argument – then he went off fire-watching.

Saturday took a turn in Kensington Gardens to see the daffodils, and find out if the Palace were open. It wasn't. But the daffs were in full bloom. I do enjoy the Mrs Buggins' broadcasts on the Kitchen Front. First-class fun.

Sunday, 11th A real Florentine Spring. Went with Mrs T. to find 'Dirty Dick's'. Have long wished to do this. It is a Pub in the City with an ancient legend attached. In the 18th C. the story goes, a bride was to be married from this place. The Wedding Feast was laid. Some disaster happened to the bride, and the feast was never touched. Great was the sorrow of all – and the Feast was left until everything went mouldy, and rats and mice played about among the viands. Tradition says it was shown to visitors until all parties were dead.

We found it opposite Liverpool St Station. Dirty signboard outside. We descended to an underground vault, filled with men of all nations having a drink. No women there. Mrs T. bravely approached and we had two glasses of port. We drank to her son in *H.M.S. Sussex*, and her husband serving in India. We looked around. Innumerable sailors had scratched their names and ships on the walls. American soldiers were interested: Old leather bottles, heavy with dirt, hung from ceilings. One old scallywag seated on a barrel, gazed at us much amused. In spite of the dirt and cobwebs somehow the place was pleasing to the eye.

Upstairs was another bar done in the old style with notices inviting people to go below and see the Old Vaults. But no available history to buy during the war.

I suggested 'The Cheshire Cheese' for lunch, not bombed. We poked our way up an alley. No lunches on Saturday. We opened a sliding door and saw the sanded floor and wooden settles. It looked expensive and no place for me. But we found 'Ye Old Cock Tavern' in the Strand. Sort of 16th C. Inn. Old prints round the walls, a painting of Dickens, glass cupboards of old china and an ancient fireplace. Built in 1549. We had fish and potatoes and Xmas pudding. Not much of anything, but we enjoyed ourselves. 3/ – each.

Walked through the devastated Temple. The most serious scene of ruin concentrated on one set of historical buildings. Just appalling! Went to the river and saw *Discovery*. The sea scouts were playing about in rowing boats.

Expecting Mrs Idiens. She had been to *Love for Love* with John Gielgud. A brilliant company. Years ago Lucy took me to *The Way of the World* with Edith Evans. They say this is just as good as that was.

Dr Remy and I had tea with Auntie Nell. He considered I was in an optimistic mood. I felt we ought to count our blessings. Sir Alfred Baker, head of his legal firm, has died. He was Chairman of the L.C.C. and had done much for the refugees. A whole family, friends of Auntie Nell, the Smallwoods of Birmingham, had just been drowned at sea. She was very upset.

Actually a little cod fish this week – not much taste, but we have enjoyed it. Cheese ration to be lowered.

A Warning last week. But the All Clear led to two Anglo-American horses running amok. They were just passing Ladbroke Rd Police Station when it boomed out. The horses started at a gallop. The brake broke and the unhappy driver could not hold them. They charged straight for the main road, crossed it and crashed into a tree at the corner of Holland Walk. When Miss Ashton passed the ambulance was taking away the driver. Other people were coping with the horses. When I arrived both poor creatures were up Holland Walk, shaking with fright. One had a piece out of his shoulder and a damaged eye. The other was all of a tremble. A little boy had jumped clear, and he was holding them while a woman was covering the uninjured one with a rug. No bones broken. The Vet was putting stuff on the wounds of the other.

Worthing has had bad raids. Miss Jones was going there to stay with two sisters. She wrote and no reply. Their brother sent word that they had both gone out to tea to a house with two ladies – it had a direct hit, and all were killed.

As to the war, we seem fast turning Rommel out of Tunisia. In about two months we shall attack Sicily. Perhaps this is too optimistic. Fatal for me to get cheerful – some awful disaster always follows rapidly.

Sunday, 18th They say no Spring like it for fifty years. With a bound we have gone into Summer frocks . . . 80 degrees in the Straits of Dover! This is the only part of the country that is allowed to advertise its temperature. Windows wide open – make me think of Poggio Imperiale garden with the lemon trees all out. Have thought often of those Italian girls – some of them came from Trapani and places in Sicily we are now bombing.

Saturday night Marie and I went to *Petrified Forest*. Setting in Arizona. All very exciting. Came out in daylight. Piccadilly is a thrilling place these days. All the uniforms of all the nations jostle you on the pavement, and since there is hardly any traffic you can walk right round the Circus in the road. Some of the soldiers label themselves – Poland or Canada! But there are lots with just emblems. Such varied faces and manners. Girls, too, in their trim Service uniforms, by the hundred. Few fashionables – because all the pretty girls are in battle dress. I wanted to go on walking round and looking at the people, but Marie wished to go home. Tossed her up a rice dish. Her aristocrat may return to Newcastle – a creature of moods.

Today walked in the Gardens. Fresh green grass was like fairyland. Very hot. Went along the Flowery Walk. Prunus in blossom. Found Prince of Wales' Gate, and Holy Trinity, Brompton. There was a Passion Play on. Lovely Church – found a seat and sat down.

We all sang a hymn, then off went the lights and the play began. All in front of the altar. The Virgin sweetly portrayed. Face and manner just right. Judas, with a red beard, played the best of the men. Red beard is traditional from the Mystery Plays, I believe. Mary ends with speaking of the Risen Christ and – There is no death. Came out into the sunshine. Went into the Palace – saw the bombed room. It was incendiaries, and mercifully only part of the roof went. That was October 4th, 1940. I like best the Nursery and bedroom of Princess Victoria – arranged by Queen Mary.

An Alert today. Several brief visits lately. Thursday night was bad at Chelmsford. Gaol had a direct hit . . . masses of incendiaries which the prisoners helped to put out. Searchlights are marvellous these nights. Our planes are up and the lights try to catch them – silver specks in the sky.

A confession about a bottle of Lemon Cordial! Brought me by Kit some time ago – rare, so I determined to save it for my visitors. In this I failed utterly. Each night arriving back have felt cruelly thirsty, and this glorious bottle reposing on my shelf was too much. Little by little I have drunk the lot. The craving for lemon juice by the British Public is almost an obsession – we feel we could drink it neat by the gallon.

End of April 1943

MAY 1943

Sunday, 2nd Been home for Easter. Many people travelling. Found a seat and others piled in behind me. A foreign male voice asked if there was room for a Mother and baby. There was – opposite to me. This little family made the interest of the journey. The baby definitely did not think the journey necessary, and announced her opinion. Fortunately the man beside me had a way with him – he made funny noises which intrigued the baby, who subsided and decided to make the best of the situation. The young father was a Dane or a Czech. The mother English. He joined them after putting the pram on the train. Then the baby must be fed. We all watched intently as the gear was brought from the rack. But, alas, the most important item had been left behind on the kitchen table by the father! He looked most upset – as did the baby. But the young mother let him off lightly, and proceeded to make a liquid which she stirred with a villainous looking knife out of father's pocket. Quite a drama.

We all got out at Leamington. In the corridor a girl of about fifteen asked me to let her know when we were at Bicester! Poor child! Directed her to the station master for the next train back. Stations are all pitch black . . .

All well at home. Beryl had made an excellent meal. Breakfast in bed. So different from last year when Mother was ill, and I had to set to work on spring cleaning. Lovely run out to Bidford to meet Bernard Sleigh. Old bridge and red-roofed village, like a painting of Delft. No meal. Inns too full of fishermen. However finally we found cold ham, tea, bread, margarine and rhubarb tart. Ages since we have tasted cold ham. Then out to Cleeve Prior along Buckle St – Roman road. Met Dr H. Mill dismantled. The dam over the Avon burst in 1938, and they have not mended it, so we could not ford across to Salford Prior. Pathway all blocked with fallen trees and barbed wire, in case of invasion. Thrilled to find dozens of bees coming in and out of a tree – legs laden with pollen. One would have to cut the tree to get the honey. Gilly flowers growing out of Cotswold stone . . . Cath and I were offered synthetic grape fruit drink, and were instructed to drink from the bottle, as the man had neither glasses nor any cloth with which to wipe them. We struggled through!

Sunday, 9th Weather changed – beautiful warm air has become cold and blustery wind. So we are let off central heating ban until weather is kinder. But the red and white may trees fill us with joy. The laburnum begins to hang in golden bunches. My colleague hopes to return half time next week, which is something. Worked late to help Mr H. catch up. Hope he will not be ill again. Have to scold all the men in turn – for their own good.

We are all cheerful over the news. To have Tunis and Bizerta on one day – after all our miseries and retreats and general disasters. Mussolini's hair must be greying rapidly.

Took a bus to Hyde Park Corner, and walked Piccadilly. Town house of the Duke and Duchess of York looked awful. Important looking officers were getting in and out of taxis at various hotels. Turned in to Studio One at Oxford Circus. Very comfortable. Saw the Desert Army, and General Montgomery – looks a thoroughly nice person.

Helped Auntie with spring cleaning. She cannot put up curtains and pictures herself. Found Marie in my flat. She seems to have fallen on a bed of roses with the job at her Earl's.

Dr Remy came to tea, and as cakes and scones are un-eatable if bought from shops – unless you are starving, which we are not – I made some. Tossed together something or other. He and I discussed the excellent news, but cannot believe the war will be over this year. However, we visualized a Tea Party one day in my flat with Carola and the children.

Mr H. has lent me the book on minesweepers. In the *Observer* review it speaks of words which 'glow and shine and ring'. This is a good description of all these war books.

Saw Giraud on the newsreel – tall and orthodox looking. Then tuned in to the French news. They were full of jubilation – much martial music. Some celebration for Joan of Arc. An impassioned address about all that the women of France were doing moved me to tears.

Sunday, 16th Wonderful week of news. Mr Churchill reminded us that it is like the Seven Years' War in Chatham's time – each morning one had to get up early to enquire for victories in case of missing one. Every day German prisoners have mounted . . . with guns, food and equipment. Total collapse. We hear that General von Arnim is in England – a prisoner. He surrendered with great ceremony and saluted all his officers. It seems an Indian regiment finally took him. What a time for our boys out there. They will tell it to their grandchildren with pride and joy.

The Bey of Tunis has been hoofed out by Giraud. Poor General de Gaulle – he should have been the one to enter Tunis in triumph. It seems if he appeared in Algiers the people would go mad with joy. So Giraud won't have him. Anyway he ought to be the first to enter Paris.

Our boys are walking over the land of ancient Carthage, though not a trace remains of that civilization . . . *Cartago Delenda Est*. I really feel this Tunis business has avenged not only Dunkirk, but Singapore as well. Articles in the *Daily Mail* reveal the secrets of Wavell and Auchinleck. How they gambled on nothing to hide their weakness. At first they brought it off. We could not be told on how little it was founded – or the Germans would have known too.

The Paris radio calls the Desert – the Promenade des Anglais. Now we are on a firm foundation. In the Newsreel the Italians looked depressed and miserable. Our boys, whether maimed or on stretchers, were wreathed in smiles.

I shall never forget our disappointments of last year – and my little faith. Those days are over, let us hope, and we can take heart once more. But it has been a near thing. In another 25 years I don't think we shall have a second chance. We shall sink at once, if we are not ready. It seems we must go on to the end of time armed to the teeth. The Italians are in a state of panic, I expect, and Barishnikov says Mussolini will die by internal explosion. It is reported that the King of Italy may abdicate. Perhaps Mussolini and Edda will hop off to S. America. What a fall was there!

Have been to the Review of the Home Guard in Hyde Park. Stood at the Marble Arch, and watched it start. A glorious afternoon. All the units were assembling. A distinguished officer, marked Home Guard, was riding a magnificent white charger, with gorgeous swishy tail. Then four police officers on dappled greys came up and led the Procession. Men of all shapes and sizes – some with glasses, some fat, some thin. But all ready to do or die – and we are most grateful to them. The King was in the Park! But I did not see him.

Mr Churchill reminded us that three years ago the Home Guard had scarcely anything but their own fists to fight with. A few had old guns, and a little ammunition. Yet in 1940 all were prepared to do what they could. I remember it so well. The authorities expected a few thousand men; instead innumerable thousands lined up at all the police stations to register.

I was with the Clives at Eardisland the week before the entry of Italy into the war, when we expected German parachutists any moment to drop from the sky. I talked with a hedger and ditcher – we both kept looking upward. He only had his scythe, and wished ardently for a rifle, as he said he would have more confidence. How little we knew the poor defence we had! We thought things were bad, but had no idea the whole country was defenceless from end to end. No wonder Mr Churchill looked unapproachable within 50 yards that day. Auntie Nell saw him in the Abbey.

Sunday, 23rd A week of Warnings – just nuisance raids, but since we had rather got out of the habit of them, we have slept rather ill. Monday was our fire-watching, so I camped out on the settee. The sirens screamed out. I was up with tin hat, torch, whistle etc. in no time, and appeared in the Drive. Miss M. came pelting downstairs – also the others, and made it known that their Fire-Squad was on duty. All Clear. But in another hour we had to leap up again. Did not hear the Third until the gunfire. At 8 a.m. drifted up the road to make myself a cup of tea. So it has gone on all the week. There are many empty houses around, and various fire stations have been closed.

We heard Chelmsford Cathedral was saved by two firewatchers digging out incendiaries with an axe. Have I recorded the Navy's admiration for the Home Guard? They say it is the only one of the Services they have not had to rescue! They have constantly rescued the Army. This was in the old days, however – the British Army is on the map once more. Glory Be!

Mabel Lucy is very good at visiting our poor people in hospital: one poor old soul fancied biscuits. With great difficulty I obtained a few, and Mabel took them. She may return to Stratford-on-Avon soon. A friend of Aunt Winnie's was walking in the country near Brede, when she heard a great whirring of wings, and thought it was a gigantic bird. To her horror it was a wounded German plane hopping over the fields. She did not see it crash. Fancy buckling to and arresting a few German airmen when you were out for an afternoon walk!

Sunday, 30th Went to *Love for Love* at the Phoenix. Angela Baddeley was in it – Leon Quartermaine, Ernest Banks and so on. Lovely Queen Anne furniture, setting and costumes. Definitely Rabelaisian in humour. Everyone enjoyed it – represents a world far away from war, where the most important thing in life was an intrigue or the latest fashion. Not a virtuous person in the whole bunch! But how elegant they all looked. It ended with a Dance where they all flopped on chairs like Alice in Wonderland. John Gielgud was as fascinating as ever – did a ridiculous scene so well.

Busy week with Anniversary. Bad raids at Hastings and Bournemouth – many killed. Also Torquay. Death of Professor Ernest de Selincourt. Brings back memories. I can recall the thrill of his lecture on Shylock when he read us Schiller's appreciation. We gave him rounds of applause.

De Gaulle has gone to Algiers. I want to see him riding into Paris with Joan of Arc's banner floating above his head. That is what he deserves. But there is much jealousy among the French, and much dirt to be cleared out.

Magnificent parcels from Lucy. A summer frock – dried peaches, apricots and sugar. None of her gifts seem to have been sunk.

Have begun a Case Book of all the people we help. Have long wanted to do this. Problem of shoes is funny. Each shop can only sell a quota a day. When this has gone they shut the door. You must go first thing in the morning and find a pair – if you are lucky.

Wonderful rush on tinned fruit this morning. Plums, damsons and rhubarb of English make came off points. I suppose they were badly tinned and would not keep. I called in at various shops and collected four tins. Ten minutes later there was nothing!

Everyone short of clothing coupons, especially men. Must hang on to my few for stockings.

End of May 1943

JUNE 1943

Sunday, 6th Mr Churchill is back and we are relieved. We began to be anxious when the Air Liner was attacked. Definitely the Germans thought he might be on it. They have never attacked these planes before. But to lose Leslie Howard is grievous. I heard him on the Brains Trust, as well as seeing him in *Pygmalion, Romeo and Juliet*, and surely he was Ashley in *Gone with the Wind*? I am sure he cheered the others up in those awful moments before they fell into the sea – or at least comforted them. They must all have been killed instantly.

Invasion of Italy sounds imminent. They say two Desert Generals are in London – were seen at the Ritz – but nothing is said in the papers. De Gaulle and Giraud are very funny. Affairs in Africa read like an episode from *The Gondoliers*. They do everything in twos. They have to breathe simultaneously – and who goes first through a door I do not know. But it is something that they have met at all.

Monday night, our fire watch, we were all roused at 2 a.m. Pouring with rain. Went to front door where Old Chips was delighted to be let in. He thought the Warning was for his benefit. Could not see an inch. Miss M. came down – eyes sewn up with fatigue. As soon as gunfire died down I bravely walked down the drive. Mr Bendall was at his porch, and we talked to let the road know we were on duty. Had a word with the porter at Lansdowne House, and padded back in streaming rain. Soon All Clear. Bombs at Dulwich and Thornton Heath. Several killed – so you never know.

Went to the Zoo to book tea for my next party of Mothers and children on June 19th. The Old Pole is open on Sunday, so explained my plan of action. He found me some aged radishes and lettuce and with his compliments to the animals he gave me extra. As we queued for the bus we watched the uniforms. We seem to be a stronghold of American soldiers. The yak snorted at me with seeming disgust, but I discovered he was trying to tell me to throw the radishes into his open mouth. Once I understood the rules of the game all was well. I had rows of admiring youngsters. The panda was there, but rolled up like a sack of potatoes in the back of the cage. I booked the Tea.

Sunday, 20th Relieved to see the Lecture Party return from Hastings last Sunday, as a raid on a south-east town was announced at 6 p.m. It was Eastbourne. They had the benefit of it – for just as they reached that station the Alarm went. Passengers alighted – the train moved on for Hastings. The fun began. Seven German raiders were over the train! Pit-a-pat – ping – could be heard on the roof – probably machine-gun bullets. Everyone was leaning out of the windows! The man at the adjacent one was wild with excitement – he was hoping to be in a Raid!

All over in four minutes, but they could see the smoke and

dust and débris arising from Eastbourne as the bombs fell. All exciting if you survive, and are not too disturbed about the people beneath – but raids are no picnic. Fourteen bombers, of which two were brought down – then the rest streaked off like lightning. A nasty raid – and one does not know what the Germans think there is in Eastbourne.

At Hastings, Mr Bendall announced the Service would go on even in the event of a Warning. There was – but not a raid.

I read that in Malta tremendous raids have destroyed houses, but not people in the same proportion. The deep tunnels have saved no end of lives. Jean's husband is wounded in N. Africa, but not dangerously. Her baby is expected in November. She continues her job until the time to go to the London. I am sure the baby will not dare to come at other than the appointed time!

Went home for Whitsuntide. We are paying for our mild Winter and glorious Spring. Went down in Summer coat, but regretted it – cold wind blowing. Went to Cannon Hill Park Open Theatre with Mother to see *Bird in Hand* by John Drinkwater. Then Cath and I saw the film *In Which We Serve*. Splendid – we sat through it twice. Saw Dunkirk, and several sea battles. Blitz on Plymouth was exact – wailing of the sirens and the fall of one bomb after another. We have heard them so often, but have been luckier than the family in the film, for so far we have not been buried under the débris.

Heard Eric Linklater's play *Cornerstones*. It is a discussion between Abraham Lincoln, Lenin and Confucius with a soldier from Tobruk. One could hear it again with profit.

They say the English and Chinese are much alike – the same insufferable self-satisfaction and complacency . . .

No sirens in Brum, and I slept well. Took a few photos of Cath in her Warden's uniform outside the post. Films are almost non-existent, but someone managed it for me. Cath has three stripes and a star in Civil Defence, and even takes the chair at committee meetings. It involves quite a lot of work.

Dr H. saw me off to London. Went to see Auntie Nell, who is worried that their nice caretaker is going. He was so good during the blitz. All their flats were looked after – nothing taken, and many residents were away for over a year. Uncle Morris [vicar of East Ham] is to have an operation. As Miss M. had given me an orange for Auntie, she was able to take it to him in hospital. More jam made. Cath is to have a pound, as she seems to live on dry bread for her lunch at school.

A Warning as I got back. A stray bomb on Hammersmith – under a mile from us. I could hear the raider race across the sky. But on Friday it was worse. Nothing short of an oil drum straight on Mt Pleasant. Mr Hillyard found his office down to the ground. All the Parcels section of ingoing and outgoing foreign mail was débris and burned. All his records gone again!

Teamed with rain all Friday, which made me very cheerful! We can circumvent showers, but not pouring rain with 50 Mothers and children. However, midday on Saturday, there was a gleam of light in the sky, the clouds rolled away. Miracle of miracles. I badged all the children and sent them off with escorts. Blazing hot at the Zoo! Great success. Had tea in a sort of Loggia on the Pavilion roof. Ran round the Zoo like a great sheepdog. There were donkeys, camels and llamas to ride. The caretaker of our flats came with a three-year-old . . . the joy of the party he was, chatting all the time. Could not understand half he said, but one could take him to Buckingham Palace and he would do the right thing.

The last of us was back at 7.30 p.m. Returned to my room and dropped on my divan. Marie spoke from time to time – but I heard her not. Just lay in thankful bliss that it was all safely over, and that I had a bed to lie on.

The King is having a splendid time in N. Africa. Postscript tonight was by three men who love their country . . . a Scots farmer, a Welsh trade unionist and a London costermonger. All excellent. When the costermonger gets to heaven the first thing he is going to ask St Peter is to give him a barrow . . .

End of June 1943

JULY 1943

·

Thursday, 8th Sent on lots of food for the three of us to the cottage before I left London. Journey to Brum interesting with an amusing soldier. He came from Sutton Coldfield, and was a physical instructor. He had many songs, but the only one I remember went: 'It's been a wonderful day . . . I've lost the missus, I've lost the train, and someone's stolen my watch and chain – oh, it's been a wonderful day.'

Also a young Air Force girl going to Stafford. She said it was the worst camp she had ever been in. She had joined up for the Barrage Balloon and liked that; but they had taken the girls off them. Now she was on clerical work. The Squadron Leader would have done no work while she was away, and it would be hard work to catch up. She had to travel back all night, and go straight on duty. The camp had blackbeetles which got in everything. And if you wanted a bath you had to go at 5.30 a.m. or queue for an hour. However, she found it a grand life, and would not have missed it for anything! Nice type. Just managed on the money.

Reached Brum at 11.30 p.m. Dr H. met me. Sutton Coldfield soldier proposed to get there by walking five minutes and running for ten – in which case he would arrive in

395

one hour. Had a cup of tea and tumbled into bed. Dr H. had to return to the Hospital for fire-watching.

Mother and I went by train, very slow, but the country got better and better. There was a small bus. I got Mother in somehow – others were hanging on to the back. A dear little Shetland pony and trap met someone. Mother nearly took possession of it all. With difficulty I got her away, and it pounded up the hill behind the bus, with a big load of children and luggage. I wish I could have hired it to take us about.

Bernard Sleigh's cottage, the Old Forge, Chipping Campden, was a dream of beauty on a June afternoon, with thatched roof and roses growing up the front. The lovely Church Tower was hard by, playing airs in the chimes. And we were there a whole week. We could get fruit! Campden is full of cherry orchards. As we came along we gazed anxiously at the trees, hoping there were cherries left for us. There was no holding us back, so fruit-starved are we. After tea we went and bought some from an old chap straight off the tree. One and sixpence a pound – but he gave us good weight. In any case there is nothing else to buy here, not even picture postcards. Bernard said I should be ill, but far from it – my system just absorbed redcurrants, strawberries and plums . . . what a feast!

I soon mastered the little gas stove. We had new potatoes, peas and beans, some from Bernard's garden. He has an extra Dig for Victory garden alongside a ruined cottage. We had onions and lettuce. He took me delightful cycle rides. Once through Weston Woods, where we gathered wild strawberries.

Then along near a great Manor House with thousands of red poppies. Weather perfect . . . we sat on the grass near an ancient earthwork, looking over the country for miles, glorious in the evening light.

All the Cotswold villages for 20 miles around are all lovely and all different . . . Cotswold stone and thatched roofs. Roses grow up the chimneys, hollyhocks border the ground – centaury in profusion. Sun shone on us and I rested in the heat of the day on a hammock strung up in the walled garden. One day we cycled to Broadway, and this led to a story. The place is rather self-consciously beautiful. Very hot. We parked our bikes on a heap of gravel, climbed a stile and settled down under a tree to picnic. Soon joined by a Mother, Father and small daughter, all in shorts. We gave them some of our cherries. Then we began the climb of Broadway Hill. Who has not done this hill on foot in the heat of Summer does not know what it involves! But the countryside unfolds as you go up, until you feel you see half England. Finally we reached the Fish Inn . . . To our relief we were able to get glasses of cider. The Tower is a landmark for miles. Some eccentric person built it. It is inhabited by a family. One has the impression of being on the roof of the world.

Run back to Campden was easy. I owed Bernard some money for the cider – but where was my purse which had been in the bag with the lunch? It contained my two return tickets, my wireless licence, and the key of Auntie's flat. It dawned on me that it had fallen out between Campden and Broadway. Bernard had it in his basket holder. I passed a bad night! I called on St Anthony! After dinner next day I determined to go

– rain or no rain – on my bike to look for that purse, in case the fairies were taking care of it. Slowly I pedalled through Broadway. Neared the lunch spot – men were mending telegraph wires. Towards that heap of gravel did I push my bike, and there, sure enough, under the same green leaf where it had fallen was Vere's purse – intact!

I rushed across to the men with my joyful story. To fine myself for my carelessness, I gave them two shillings for a drink. On my journey back I saw a Gypsy Encampment on the roadside, having tea. Caravans, horses tethered, children, old women and men all out on the grass round a Camp Fire. Thrilling! We visited Evesham one day. Explored Abbey and Gateway. It must have been a hive of activity in the Middle Ages. Sat by the River for lunch. The fruit baskets in Evesham are unbelievable to us who never see anything but tins of peas and carrots, or a few expensive lettuces.

Ariel and Cecilia came one day. Mother had saved a tin of Grade 1 Salmon from a long time ago. It takes lots of points. I made a great trifle with redcurrants, sponge cake and custard. This for war-time England is sumptuous, and it is amazing that on occasion we can manage it. They cycled from Honeybourne. All very happy. Bernard put on records for us in the evening. We piled in somehow for the night. Next day, very loth, we all returned to Brum. And I to London.

A letter from Miss M., marked urgent, awaited me, saying the pig-breeder wanted me to go and gather fruit on Monday! I went and picked gooseberries, but the stooping and the smell of 400 pigs made me feel very ill. He and his son were kindness itself, but I was very tired. I felt I should faint while in the bus, and drop all the eggs he had given me.

Jean rang me to say Miss Hollingworth must have been torpedoed when she went out East in 1942. So the Old Girl's Party was the last time we should see her. She was not among the saved. I did not like her, but I am sure she met her death with courage. All honour to her.

Sunday, 18th   A good story is that during a broadcast function in Copenhagen the Danes began singing the Norwegian National Anthem. At first the Germans did not twig and went on. Then it was hastily switched off. But the Danes had got it in well. Captain Hansen, our nice Norwegian sea captain, called to see us in the office. He had just heard, via Sweden, that his wife had died in Stavanger during his absence. She was quite well when he left Norway. He was very sad.

It is worth noting that twice we should have been starved – once in the 1940 Spring, and again in 1941 – if the Americans had not come to our rescue. This was announced in Parliament. And still people grumble at the food – though only a few. Most of us are thankful that we have had enough, difficult as it is to obtain. No bread queues. All due to the Merchant Seamen who bring it here.

Still worried about General de Gaulle. The Americans seem to have made a pact with Giraud, who has stipulated that he should command a European expedition – the very idea! It is obvious to all in N. Africa that the great dynamic character is de Gaulle. It will require a strong man to clean up France. But de Gaulle does not make friends easily, it seems.

We wait every hour for news from Sicily. Wonderful how well the men have got on. Commander Kimmins' account of the landing was rich in the details we want to know. There seems to be some fighting, though the Sicilians crowd round and are as pleased as punch to have their photos taken. One story is that two American parachutists were taken prisoner. Then the Sicilians decided to reverse the situation, and gave themselves up to the two paratroops! But Sicily is not Italy. Naples is having a terrible pounding. Poor things! It is their own fault. Churchill and Roosevelt have called on them to give up fighting for Mussolini. I wonder what his feelings in the Palazzo Venezia are now . . . and Edda's! Game is up.

Have just been talking with a merchant seaman who was on a Hospital Ship which did seven journeys to Dunkirk. It nearly finished him. He had been on one of the Jersey Channel steamers before the war.

Auntie made a jorum of jam with my gatherings. Altogether I picked 26 pounds of gooseberries, and 3 pounds of red currants, and the Pig Breeder gave us a large proportion of my work. We have all benefited. Hard going – but I felt very patriotic.

Monday night a Warning. We all hopped up. A glorious night, and our lime trees smelt beautifully. London buses have no red paint, so they are appearing in maroon colour.

Bad incident at East Grinstead cinema – direct hit. Many people and children killed – worst we have had for some time.

Sunday, 25th The announcer's voice became very solemn on the 1 p.m. news on Monday, when he said that Rome had been bombed. Much for and against this has been discussed. The *Observer* says that since it is crammed with war materials it had to be . . . send the bill in to Mussolini. The Pope tried to get it declared an open city. The pilots were specially trained not to hit the Churches – but San Lorenzo fuori le mura is badly damaged. It is one of the four great basilicas. A terrible warning to the Italians – though such a basilica is not so valuable to me, architecturally, as Canterbury or Milan Cathedral. But it is a terrible step to take to bomb this ancient City, which has been the head of civilization for so many centuries.

All the week good news from Sicily has continued. Delicious stories of the friendliness of the Sicilians. They are the strangest enemies . . . do nothing but offer oranges and melons to the troops. Palermo has fallen. One correspondent writes that he had dreamed of receiving such a welcome in Oslo or Athens, but not Palermo! It was like the entry of Charles II into London after the Restoration . . . the ladies in their best frocks at the windows throwing flowers to the soldiers who bowed and received kisses galore . . .

End of July 1943

AUGUST 1943

Monday, 2nd, August Bank Holiday A most exciting week, for it has seen the Fall of Mussolini. After all these years of power when he seemed invincible, and it was all so imposing – it has crashed in a heap. The end has been more sudden and complete than anyone expected. What is behind it all we shall not know for many a long day. That Ciano voted against his father-in-law seems one of the features of the situation. News has been trickling through all the week. Rumour has it that Donna Rachele, the younger children, Edda Ciano, Bruno and his wife are all enclosed in a villa. The only one I am sorry for is Donna Rachele.

Badoglio has been in charge all week, but he has disappointed everyone by not making overtures for peace. We can see his difficult position, but waiting won't make it easier. The Italians cannot slip gracefully out – with no stain on their characters, as they seem to think. It is going to be hard – they have to pay up.

To think of all the laughing about democracy I used to hear when I was in Italy . . . how that eldest Falorsi son would have scrapped the house of Savoy and the Pope – all for Mussolini. How must he feel now! Democracy has won again – and we are not proved an effete plutocracy! It's great.

Barishnikov thinks the King of Italy will abdicate, and Badoglio will not last a week. I am sure Mr Churchill hopes a stable government will emerge – we do not want to take on the civil government of Italy, feed all the people and fight the Germans too.

Damage to Hamburg this week is colossal – almost wiped off the map, even as Hitler promised to do to our cities. The Berliners are frantically digging trenches, just as we did in 1938 and 1940. They expect to be the next target. It is a terrible thing – but we must give them a taste of their own medicine. They began this bombing.

One of the families we help has lost their father. He was a stoker on the aircraft carrier *Indomitable*. It must have been a torpedo through the engine room as they covered the Sicilian landings. Henry, his eldest, came to show me the telegram ... Missing Presumed Killed. Went to see the wife. She had neither eaten nor slept since the news. He leaves four children. There is no hope. She has the pension papers. Married 13 years and they so happy. She has struggled to keep the home going, and pay off the furniture they had bought. He was in a good job. What could I say? I gave her money, and have written the case up in our paper. The Admiralty has given her a free pass for Portsmouth to find any news of him.

I have not been away this Bank Holiday. Had several invitations, but the crowds have been colossal, and the bother of taking food and struggling with trains is not worth it. Am thankful to remain in my little flat. People have been away in hundreds of thousands. They didn't mind sleeping out all night. The Government should have helped them more. The munition workers were frantic for a change of scene – making bombs for months and months is deadly. The gentlemen who tell the workers to stay put, do not do so themselves. Nor do they live in streets all on top of one another. They get away for surreptitious week-ends and enjoy some leisure. The weather has held for the most part – that is to say in the Straits of Dover!

Last Monday at our firewatch we were roused and had to parade the Drive for an hour. Miss M. and I sat on the step.

Mr Hillyard and I went to the empty garden to gather some mulberries. We are supposed to guard the place in case of fire. The house has changed hands, and I don't suppose they know about the mulberry tree. However, someone phoned the police, and an inspector said they were trying to prevent people going into enclosed premises. Mr Bendall mismanaged the whole interview. It is absurd when the country is short of fruit to allow it to rot on the trees. If I had my way I would gather them, and face the police. But I am not allowed.

Cath is going cycling in Wales with Bernard Sleigh. Auntie Mollie has sent Mother some sheets. No present could be more welcome. She is in ecstasies. Mine are patched, and this morning I had to patch a patch!

Marie took me to see Lady So-and-So's flat in Piccadilly, above Fortnum and Mason. Two lovely rooms, one opening out of the other. Lady Blank has had it decorated in off-white with a silver gilt mirror and a good picture. The settee and chairs come from the Castle – covered in red. Glorious material . . . £3 per yard. It gave a warm glow to the room.

Parquet floor. Bedroom in pale blue and silver. Chairs were Hepplewhite. Door knobs of solid crystal. So there is still some money in England. Marie's job with them is finished now.

There is a book called *Guilty Women* – Edda Mussolini is said to be one. Mrs South and I want to read it.

Did a bit of walking – felt tired so tumbled into a Tea place. They brought me what they called Cottage Pie and salad. It is not often I leave food, but that Pie was beyond me. I ate a few lettuce leaves and drank the tea, which was sweetened. Two waitresses presented me with bills, one for 1/4d – the other 1/8d. I paid the former. The food was not worth 4d. Turned into a News Theatre. Saw the Sicilian Landings – airborne troops coming down, and the people handing out oranges to the Boys in exchange for flour. Saw Mr and Mrs Churchill visiting the Zoo. Also sundry pictures of Mussolini.

Sunday, 8th Italy not having surrendered we have begun bombing again – Milan, Turin, Naples and Genoa. Sicily nearly conquered. The voice of Hitler is not heard on the air. He was full of speeches when the Germans had thousands more tanks, guns and planes than anyone else. What a contrast with Mr Churchill who did so much to hearten us in those dark days of 1940 – he, the bravest of us all – and the only one who knew the worst about our position. It makes one shudder to think of it.

General de Gaulle has at last taken the premier place. Case of the dominating personality winning. General Spears, Mary Borden's husband, believes in him. I do by instinct, but I am not, of course, in possession of all the facts. Apparently the intensity of his personality has taken many by surprise . . . but not me. When I heard him speak during the week of the Fall of France, it was like dynamite across the air.

Should like to attend Ascot in these days – the medley of vehicles is like the old days – many an old moke is there, and thousands of bicycles.

My old school-friend, Helen Neatby, arrived. Just the same. A little greyer, but as full of vitality as ever. We went to Hampton Court. I learned from her that the north of England is not so short of food. At her school they use their own eggs and produce. She has a cottage on the Yorkshire moors. Talked of our visit many years ago to Haworth Parsonage. Also the time when she rowed me on the Lake of Lugano – a glorious day that was – and we walked down a mountain covered with primroses. She is full of plans for the future, feeling like me that no one wants to stay in teaching all their lives. But she wants to be sure of a pension and not end in the workhouse. Helen had never seen Hampton Court before. She does not feel the cold. We went into the Maze, but the middle eluded me this time. Ate lunch under a yew tree. The scent of heliotrope in the garden enchanted me. We saw the vine – lovely dark grapes hanging so regularly they looked a tapestry pattern.

I showed her a few bombed places in Notting Hill, because these Yorkshire Moor people don't really understand the blitz. She is up for the Annual Meeting of the Society of Friends.

Sunday, 15th Generally speaking the tide is still running in favour of the United Nations. At last! To open the paper and find constant good news . . . well, we are just not accustomed to it.

As I lay in bed the other night I heard the Deep Purr of our bombers winging their way to Hamburg . . . This is a comfortable feeling. I turned lazily in bed and glowed at the thought, going back in my mind to those awful months when to hear that noise overhead was to know the Germans were going to pour death and destruction on us. It meant in those days a readjustment of the mind to the fact that this might be one's last night on earth – or that by the morning one might be homeless and possessionless. One cannot help feeling it is good for the Germans to know what it feels like. Perhaps they won't put the machine in motion again so light-heartedly. Several nights this week an Armada of the Sky has passed over us.

I have recorded that we were forbidden to gather the mulberries in the garden next door. Our caretaker is an Irishman. There is now an Irish policeman on duty round here. These two have met, and discovered they come from adjoining villages in Tipperary. They talked for hours in the drive – both losing account of time. The upshot of this was that our caretaker took a ladder and gathered masses of mulberries! His wife does not like them, so they were all brought to me. Auntie Nell made them into jam with my sugar. Each of us had a pot including caretaker and policeman!

Have read *Guilty Women* by Richard Baxter. He calls Edda Mussolini the most dangerous woman in Europe. Describes Poggio Imperiale as a Finishing School – it was not this in the English sense. It was devoted to serious study. The book says her father intended her to marry Prince Umberto! I can hardly credit this. She had very peasant contours when I knew her. Neither did she walk out of the school. She remained until the end of term, and never returned. She disliked the English because we did not make a fuss of her. But she dined with the Prince of Wales and went to Ascot. In Berlin arrangements were more to her liking. She became enamoured of the Nazis, and began to push her father along the pro-German pathway. In my day the English were all that is good. But our character deteriorated. It may have been Edda's ambition that has led her father, and Italy to this pass. Interesting.

It is wonderful to walk about at the Marble Arch. Very little traffic at any time, and less on Sunday. So we see each other plainly. Everyone strolling in and out of the Park. I wish I knew one quarter of the uniforms. Fascinating to see all these men who have come from every part of the world to help us. One evening saw an armada of bombers going forth on the night's work. They go so bravely forth, but one knows they will not all come back. It is a fine sight, and gives us a feeling of strength.

Sunday, 22nd Saw the searchlights playing about our fighters. They catch one and follow it all over the sky. It blazes like quicksilver in the blinding light of perhaps a dozen lights criss-crossing. It is a favourite game.

Auntie Winnie goes to Church in a pony and trap. How lovely! Nothing like it for the country. Plenty of plums, apples and tomatoes in the shops. Went with Mrs T. to *The Moon is Down* by Steinbeck, about Norway under the Germans.

Cedric Hardwick is the German officer, occupying a mining village. We saw the stunned demeanour of the inhabitants, and the terrible awakening to what had befallen them – and the gradual rise of opposition.

All people inclined to be pacifist should see this film, and they would realize what we have been saved from. The Navy and Air Force saved us by a hair's breadth. What we owe to those few gallant souls who prepared in time! Just a few people of exceptional intelligence and perspicacity knew long ago and got ready, while the rest of us were stupidly repeating: 'There can be no war . . .' In so many cases these Few lost their lives saving those too blind to see the danger.

A Norwegian pastor gave his experiences this evening. He had escaped and told about the tortures of the people. They will eventually be rescued, but in this generation they will never be the same. To think that a blameless little country should suffer so. One can understand the Germans being jealous of us and our possessions, and wanting to lower our pride – but not a country like Norway. It is marvellous how they are standing up to it.

The French now are being exceptionally polite to the Germans, and smiling at them, and taking walks in the country. They have been urged to learn about their own countryside in preparation for the day.

The Abyssinian campaign official account is out. While Baldwin and Chamberlain were complacently assuring us that we had plenty of defences and need not worry, in reality there were only a few hundred men to defend the Middle East, and a few guns – not of the latest pattern! These few had to pretend to be thousands when the war with Italy began. Poor Mr Churchill, with all that burden on his back! He knew – and told us so. Yet people can get up and suggest a vote of no-confidence in him. Anyway the worst was staved off. In June, 1940 when invasion of these islands was imminent, Mr Churchill spared some divisions for the Middle East – and that saved it from slipping away completely. Some were Indian troops who did marvellously. Heroic retreat in British Somaliland. The Somalis like us – which is a comfort, and many evacuated with the troops. They fought every inch of the way . . . men firing guns for days and nights without rest. One soldier, after two days and nights of this, paused to fetch some food from his haversack – and found a picnic ham. He looked at it and remarked: 'What! Do they call this a ruddy Picnic.'

On the News we saw the Royal Family at Sandringham. Two nice little girls on their bikes with their father. The Queen with a pony and trap. Elizabeth is a fine-looking girl – beautiful teeth and such an unself-conscious air, without too much self-possession. She will make a splendid Queen.

Went to the Pig Breeder's to gather blackberries – thousands of them. I picked for two hours and seemed to make no impression. Got very scratched. He and his son invited me to join them for tea . . . spread out on a handsome piece of newspaper. Bread and butter, jam, biscuits and cake. Food tastes good after working in the open. The Pig Breeder gave me all his experiences in the last war, making munitions.

Sunday, 29th   Wickham Steed on the Postscript about Italy, which he knows well. He is an individualist, and lives just opposite here at Lansdowne House. Most interesting.

My osteopath just back from the Castle of Kilrorke in Nairn, where he has a patient. Seems to be 12th C. but every modern convenience inside. As for food they do not know up there that there is a war on. He had cream on his porridge every morning – and pints of it seemed to be wandering round the house.

Saturday went to see *Citizen Kane* – one of those old classic films. It was about a blustering unlovely American business-man. His last word on earth was Rosebud, so the film digs back into his life to see what it meant. Never discovered. Most unsatisfactory!

I enjoy listening to the gospel singer on the radio.

End of August 1943

SEPTEMBER 1943

Sunday, 5th Still mystery surrounding the death of Boris of Bulgaria. Did he poison himself because he is in such a mess? Poor Queen Giovanna! I remember well when she and her Mother, Queen Elena, came to Poggio one afternoon, and we were all gathered in the Grand Salone, and curtseyed to them. They were in mourning for Queen Margherita and black did not suit them.

Great excitement over a light at no. I. Everyone there away or out. But a light was showing, and a passer-by rang every bell in the house to let them know. Caretaker and others ran to the door half-dressed. Another tenant said she could hear footsteps in the empty flat, so rang the police to say burglars were there. Meantime the caretaker went for his master key to put out the light! He returned to find the house surrounded by police! Just as if a murder had been committed! All sorted out by midnight.

Warden of Toynbee Hall gave the Postscript. Just been a lecture tour in U.S.A. Very much appreciated there – American girls most friendly and adored his English accent. One story he told them about the blitz. A woman bus conductor said to a passenger, who did not seem sure whether to stay on or get off the bus . . . 'Make up your mind, mister . . . it's the only thing a woman can't do for you . . .'

Visited an East End Youth Club in Old Ford Road. The boys and Mr Callow had painted it, and hung a sign swinging away – Tyburn Mission. It was being dedicated by a Bishop of the Liberal Catholic Church in regalia. Sang a few hymns and he spoke. Went upstairs to a microscopic canteen for tea. Mr Callow, at first, did not seem a likely person to appeal to East End boys, but he had been doing it for ten years. The boys were clean and well-behaved. They have a football club and play on Hackney Marshes.

Walked back with a lady and daughter. The mother was a Florentine! Daughter on industrial welfare work but began the canteen at Holland Park Tube station during the blitz. Was there every night, and well remembers the occasion in October, 1940, when the bomb skimmed our roof and nearly fell on the hundreds in the Tube station. Lots rushed into the street. She is now looking after 1,000 women doing railway work.

Mary Bewley spent night in my flat. She has abandoned the Problem children up in Yorkshire. Now has a job with Mental Health.

Sunday, 12th The Italians are in a jam – and no mistake. Sorry for them, but they have brought it on themselves. Last week we landed in Southern Italy. Unconditional surrender of Italy – just as Mr Churchill said it would be. Really he ranks among the major prophets. Italy once more a battleground. Germans have taken over, and it will be the dickens to get them out.

Danger to Italian art treasures is not over. I suppose the Germans are occupying Florence. Wonder how Poggio Imperiale school will be affected. Mercifully it is out of the town. According to accounts Badoglio kept the Armistice secret as long as possible to save what he could from the Germans. Marie José, the Crown Princess, and her children went to Switzerland, and the Government has moved to Sicily. Rome is German occupied. At last the Italians are fighting on the right side, and we have their Fleet. Cunningham seems pleased about that.

The lighted bombers, as they were going over in droves, gave the V sign. They looked fine, and we felt safe beneath them – but many will not return, and it is all so senseless. Hitler has screamed into the microphone some kind of speech. He gabbled for all he was worth. Goebbels made him say something. Defection of Italy has hit him hard.

Badoglio started negotiations the moment Mussolini fell, but he was in a predicament with Germans at his back and front door. He sent agents in secret to Lisbon – but it took so long, so he sent another, accompanied by one of our captured Generals, General Carton de Wiart. Mrs Grossi, my former landlady often spoke of him. He had lived in her hotel during the First World War. She said how nice he was to her.

Had dinner with Dr Remy at his hotel. We talked for three hours without ceasing. He is annoyed that Hess is treated as an invalid. The English are incurably silly, and will not believe that these people are hardened criminals. He is optimistic over the war ending in Spring. Germans, he affirms, are not sentimental like the English – they will only pity themselves.

Berliners will pity Berliners, and Hamburgers – Hamburgers, but they won't bother if it is not themselves.

Walked back in the moonlight along Bayswater Road. Trees in Kensington Gardens lovely. A perfect night. Auntie Nell came Sunday morning – she was off to Church for a Thanksgiving Service – the Surrender of Italy. She put on her Alfred Jewel and a Rose for England. Looked magnificent.

Had promised to take Clive, aged 3½ and Anne, to the Pig Breeder's. Buses were full and it was a struggle. However, Clive adored the pigs in the sties, and had to count them. Anne gathered blackberries. The Pig Breeder wanted to adopt them both. But he was too busy to provide tea, so we got back to my flat as soon as a bus could take us . . . both children starving hungry. Fried Anne an omelette, and little Clive jammed himself well and truly – also my tablecloth. Tidied him up and took him home supremely happy.

Apparently the Gestapo murdered Boris of Bulgaria. He never had an interview with Hitler as was stated. Hitler discovered that Boris had been toying with the Russians, so put him out of the way.

Have just found moth in one of my suitcases, packed since the blitz in the event of being bombed. Just discovered it in time. Lots of moths about. Horrors!

Sunday, 19th Week filled with even more stirring events than usual. Paratroops have rescued Mussolini from the top of an inaccessible mountain in the Abruzzi! One must lift one's hat to the Germans in the way they did it. It is like one of the Saint thrillers I used to read – he would drop from a plane on top of a moving train, and kill the spy in a first-class compartment . . . The only approach to Mussolini's prison was by funicular. So the Germans dropped from the skies, overpowered the Italian guards, and flew off with him. It was his week-end hotel where he used to meet a certain lady. We did not believe the rescue story at first; but Hitler has produced him on the microphone, where he made a speech tearing the House of Savoy to pieces.

The European commentator remarked that Tojo could come and rescue both Hitler and Mussolini, and take them off to Japan – but the United Nations would get them in the end. This is the best way of looking at it, though we should all be gladder if Mussolini were safely stowed away in an Allied dungeon. It is creating chaos in N. Italy, where some of his discredited followers have reared their heads again, and proclaimed a Fascist Republic.

Mussolini always liked to ape Napoleon – and this is his hundred days.

A terrible week on the Salerno Beaches, only now are we safely ashore. The Germans tried to panic the men by radioing that ships had come to take them off, and shouting to them in English to leave the guns and make for the beaches. It was rumbled in the end – but they must have had some terrible days. Thrilling to read Christopher Buckley's account of his journey from the Eighth Army with a few officers, to join the Fifth to tell them help was coming. Best of all it was coming without opposition. They have joined up, and the Germans are being pushed back. Also they are being thrown out of Sardinia.

A real honest to goodness raid on Wednesday . . . at 10.30 p.m. Could hear Germans racing over our heads. Guns were popping, and the big one on Wormwood Scrubs bellowed forth into the sky. Thought we heard something drop at Shepherd's Bush. As all the houses are down there already it did no damage – a time bomb which went off at 3 a.m.

End of September 1943

OCTOBER 1943

Sunday, 3rd Have been following the fight in Corsica with intense interest. Germans are still in Bastia, and we are bombing it. What is Loulou Ferrandi and her family doing? [She was my beloved colleague at Poggio Imperiale.] Shall I be able to get in touch with her after the war? I hope so. I fear the little port and town are suffering severely.

We have rescued Benedetto Croce from Naples. He is 77, and a consistent friend of freedom all his life. Opposed Fascism from the beginning, but was too important even for Mussolini to silence. They burnt his Library in the early days. However, we have staged a Commando raid and brought the old man out.

I hear Modane is practically flat – entrance to tunnel destroyed. How well I remember Modane and Chiasso where we showed passports. Germans are all over Italy, and the plight of Tuscany and the North is hard. My Directress has left Florence, but Adèle is in Milan with her husband. We are fighting all the way to Rome. Italy is trying to work her passage back. Badoglio is to declare war on Germany as soon as he dare. Where is Ciano?

Managed corner seat in the train. Was just about to heave

up my suitcase when a tall man put his there. In tones of disgust I explained. He smiled pleasantly – 'We are not going to fall out over that. Let me lift yours up and put it on mine.' I liked his face and decided to make myself agreeable as I had been so cross. An interesting person – with wanderlust. He was born at sea and had travelled ever since. Gassed in the last war, and during the years 1919 to 1921 had practically begged his bread in Birmingham. I was horrified – but I remember it all so well and the tragic expression on the faces of the men. All he struggled to get was one shilling a day in order to stay at Rowton House. He is now a mechanical engineer, and was taken on by the Midland Red. All the men who went through that terrible time would never forget it. 'Nothing that can happen to me now can be worse,' he said. Owing to the gas he lives in the open air as much as possible and is happy. He got out at Leamington.

A soldier saw me reading the Abyssinian book, and asked me if the Transvaal Scottish were mentioned, as he had served with them. He was just back from N. Africa, invalided home, after two and a half years in the Desert. 'They'll have to be pretty hard pushed to send for me,' was his remark. He admired the Indian troops. Gave him the book to look at. Such a nice man – and glad to be home.

Found Mother had made amazing strides. Beryl and Annie looked after me very well. Did my bit by cleaning the furniture with linseed oil and vinegar – an excellent mixture which feeds the wood and removes the dirt. I was still running round with an oily rag five minutes before I was due to catch my return train. Went to see *Life and Death of Colonel Blimp*. Low created this character in the years before the war as a figure of fun, but when trouble came we had to depend on him and his like, for there was no one else. When the new men got going Colonel Blimp was put in the Home Guard. He was a gentleman, and attributed to his enemies his own high motives. Anton Walbrook, as the German of old-fashioned honour, would have pleased Dr Remy. There is a decent German in the film – something rare. However, they do exist.

One morning we had coffee at Kunzle's, and an ersatz cream-bun. They tell us that the last genuine Cream Bun in the world was eaten last weekend *in Portugal*! Now all is finished until the war is over.

Rang up my former History Lecturer. Her husband is writing a history of Stratford-on-Avon, and is interested in the Lucy Mill. As my grandmother was a product of this Mill I can perhaps add a little – how her grandfather came up from Sussex as a Claimant to the Charlecote estate. One of his sons came to Brum as a corn merchant and was Mayor more than once.

Showed them *Guilty Women*, and Philip Styles became absorbed in it. We talked of Sir Raymond and Lady Beazley, who are in Dawlish. He would not discuss the war. I do not like this much. But I feel Lady B. must be unhappy, and I should like to link up again with them.

Went to *Blithe Spirit* by Noël Coward at the Alexandra. Excellent seats for 1/3d. It is a skit on Spiritualism – medium not a fraud. Spiritualism can afford to laugh at itself so long as it is accepted as genuine. This woman was like no medium in heaven or earth . . . a hearty lady, who rode a bicycle, and would have captained a Hockey Team with success. All extremely funny, and the wraith in grey chiffon floating round quite frightened me at first.

Mother and I had a Children's Party. Ariel and Cecilia biked over from Sutton. Paula brought her boys, Arthur and Roy. Very well-behaved. Arthur is bookish. Roy has no desire to learn at all, and remarked that he had not had a sandwich with his tea . . . I was sorry about this.

Dr H. met me in town – he and Mother saw me off. I wondered what the coming week would hold. After a holiday it is usually steep.

Sunday, 10th Jolly old Wailer set up on Thursday night. This time it was the goods. Gunfire loud and frequent. Searchlights filled the sky and planes caught in them. Lots of people watching. Ladbroke Square gun cracking out. Donned my tin hat – courage returned and I joined the sightseers. All London was doing the same. Shells bursting and amazing fireworks filled the air above us. Went in for the News – then came another wave of bombers. Our bombers were on the way out as the Germans came in – sometimes the searchlights caught one of ours, and sometimes the enemy.

Heard next morning that 30 tons of bombs had dropped. Woodford, Ilford, Grays, Battersea, Hampstead . . . some say Red Lion Square and Vauxhall Bridge. Windows of Woolworths in Kensington High St blown out by one of our shells. It might just as well have dropped in Lansdowne Rd and put us out of action. Felt our conduct in being out in the road was most reprehensible, but I did enjoy it. Had seen a bit of the

Battle of Britain. Anyway, then Mr H. and I settled down to work, and it was 11.30 p.m. before I went up the road.

Armies are plodding diligently up the Italian stocking, but it is heavy going. Duke of Wellington has been killed. That makes three Dukes lost so far, which is a good quota, considering there are not many of them. Heavy raid on Frankfurt and I thought of the Remy family there. Naples is having a rotten time.

The Germans are using the word elastic as the phrase of the moment. This has amused the European News broadcaster. It is to explain their retreats . . . the situation is elastic . . . So he suggested that they would soon get tied up in their own elastic, and be unable to get it undone.

Sunday, 17th We are obliged to gnaw our way up Italy like gnawing a bone. Count Sforza now appears on the scene. Said to have been a consistent opponent of Fascism, and lived many years in U.S.A. He is openly in favour of a Republic in Italy after the war, as the House of Savoy has identified itself very much with Fascism. He goes back to the City States idea, and a republic would not be alien to the Italian character.

Barishnikov has had bad news. Tidings have just reached him that both his parents died in the siege of Leningrad over a year ago. His sister-in-law has got the letter through; but whether a bomb killed them, or they died of starvation, he does not know. She, her husband and family, moved to North Russia, where it is terribly cold. The brother, though only forty-two, has gone completely white.

Little Nurse controversy goes on. I did not think so hardly of her broadcast as many people did.

Kit has found a flat and is furnishing it. Rang up to fetch her camp bed, and also may need bedside table. People are lending her things, and she even has a carpet, which is more than I have.

Mrs O. came for the week-end. Went to see the *Battle of Britain* produced by the Americans. Idea is to present to the American people exactly what we did for the world in 1940–41. Splendid. Mr Churchill gives the introduction. All very vivid – pictures of Hitler and Goering planning this and that against us. Bombing depicted. The women buckling to – men rushing to catch the paratroops or join the Home Guard.

Dr Remy and the others in Canada read about the Battle of Britain, and thought it was only a matter of days before England was finished. All glorious for us – Mr Churchill remarks that the generous Americans say things about us we could not say ourselves. It telescopes events – seems to imply that the House of Commons, Westminster, St Paul's etc. were all hit in the first 28 days. Never mind. It was wonderful on the bombed people and the big funeral at Coventry. Wept copiously throughout.

Walked round the Marble Arch, only waiting ten minutes for lunch. Mrs O. loved the uniforms. In Hyde Park a Canadian was feeding birds. They were flying on to his hands and all round his feet. We watched from a distance. He was obviously fascinated. We found Rima and enjoyed the lovely trees. I returned to entertain Dr Remy. He submitted in great good humour to my aggressively English attitude. We decided to consider that Carola and the children were safe in Frankfurt.

Sunday, 24th A week of raids – every night, and bigger ones than for a long time. Mrs O. had my bed, and I spread my mattress on the floor. The Alarm went and guns banged out. I was beneath the skylight and saw no fun in being beneath a shower of broken glass. So we got up and descended the stairs . . . twice. Road well-sprinkled with fire-watchers, talking and laughing in between bursts of gunfire. Nearly 6 a.m. before I slept, and at 8 a.m. had to prepare for the day. Felt all in at night. But it was our Fire-Watch.

Alert went at 11 p.m. Donned our helmets. Miss Moyes and I took up our stations at the front door. Mrs Hoare was with her Mother, and Mr Bendall with his sisters. Surmised Mr Hillyard was on the roof as all good firewatchers should be. Miss M. feared he was without his helmet. She returned to say that far from being on the roof, he was blandly combing his hair in his room! On being reprimanded he said he could see no fires to put out, and why worry? Gunfire heavy. Bedded down on settee and slept.

Bombs had dropped at King's Cross. Other nights at Earls Court – on a block of flats called Coleherne Court . . . a phosphorous bomb, one killed and many injured. Every shop window in Brompton Rd for some distance had gone. Mother Superior of a Convent had only just got up when a huge piece of plate glass landed straight on the bed.

Listened to the speech of Smuts at Guildhall. He said that the Nazi domination of the continent was 'unilluminated by the mercy of Christ.' He characterized Mr Churchill as the greatest leader we have ever produced. I agree.

Russians are constantly firing salvoes to commemorate

their victories. Apple rings in again, and we like them. Mr Lloyd George has married again at the age of nearly 81. Seems against the laws of nature to me, but I suppose Miss Stevenson wanted him. Megan does not appear to have been there.

Sunday, 31st Russians getting back the Crimea, but in Italy we are not moving very fast. Fighting in the Abruzzi – terrible country. Italians are suffering – they have fought well, one hears, in the streets of Milan, but are now an Occupied Country. Any German soldier shot means that revenge is taken on a dozen civilians, who are put up against a wall and shot. Awful for a civilian population to withstand the cumulative effect of such treatment. So sad our Prisoners could not get out . . .

Mr Churchill made a wonderful speech on restoring the House of Commons. He wants it copied, more or less. These great amphitheatres, though excellent, do not work in practice, he says. 'We shape buildings, and they shape us. The House has shown itself able to face the possibility of national destruction with classical composure . . . the most powerful Assembly in the whole world.' Long debate on it – just as there was 100 years ago when the Duke of Wellington dominated the proceedings, and had his way. Mr Churchill ended up, looking round the House of Lords . . . 'Mid pleasures and palaces though we may roam, be it never so humble there is no place like home . . .'

Mrs Kirkland Wilson, who lives in a flat next door, has a distinguished son. He is attached to Lord Louis Mountbatten, because he is one of the few English officers who can speak Chinese.

Auntie Nell went to the funeral of Sir Dudley Pound. Mr Churchill with a bulldog expression walked behind the coffin. All the Navy there. She heard Chopin's funeral march coming through the doorways of the Abbey.

Leaves are falling swiftly, and the Winter approaching. Milk is to be cut again next week to two pints per week for everyone. Fire in the office tonight – great luxury. Caretaker lighted it this afternoon, else I should not have done so.

End of October 1943

NOVEMBER 1943

Sunday, 7th Have been so busy scarcely time to notice how the war is going. Must record that the Russians have taken Kiev – one of the ancient capitals of Russia, which means much to them. They feared the Huns would destroy it before they could drive them out. We are pushing slowly towards Rome. Not so easy. Germans say we have bombed the Vatican City. Ridiculous – the bomb fell on the station.

Good many Alerts during the week. Bombs for the most part on Outer London. Nothing in Kensington all the week.

Good Postscript last week by a French woman who had sampled Occupation at first hand. She described Nazi methods. First the most handsome Germans possible, with exquisite manners, are sent. Very nice to the inhabitants. Give up their seats to the ladies in the buses. Simple people are taken in. Then more Nazis arrive – not quite so polished and polite. They begin by confiscating Jewish property. They explain that this does not matter. Imperceptibly they go on to other people's property. Then the mask is off. In Algiers they systematically did it – all the linen in one street one day – all the pianos the next.

A comedian was imitating Haw-Haw the other night as

follows: 'Gairmany calling – Gairmany calling' . . . the good old nasal voice, describing a British raid on Germany . . . 'Three hundred British planes brought down for two of ours. One town is missing.'

Lord Dowding turned up at one of Miss Moyes' meetings. Very nice of him. He has been addressing a number of Spiritualist gatherings in London lately.

Kit came and camped out on my floor the other night, but she has done this on the Canadian prairie and knows the tricks of making herself comfortable. She was collecting for the Channel Islanders at the Marble Arch Pavilion.

Fair looms nearer. All Saturday we were clearing one of the rooms and setting up the stalls. We are flooded with apple rings – possibly from Canada, for our apples do not keep so well. Auntie Nell flourishing.

Sunday, 14th Last Sunday night a few stray raiders over us, and gunfire, but we did not think it was much. On Monday morning news began to trickle through. Miss Ashton, of our staff, brought the terrible account of two large bombs, probably aimed at [Putney] Bridge, which had fallen on a Milk Bar and Dance Hall full of people. Killed and injured extensive. Putney had been up all night. Hospitals called on day staffs to help the night ones, doctors mobilized from miles around – everyone who could help was roped in to do something. Local cinemas were turned into First-Aid stations or as mortuaries for the dead. Putney High St was feet thick in broken glass, and looked as if a typhoon had blown through it. It was a High Explosive that fell on these unfortunate people – all young, many were Boys on leave, nearly 300 killed, it seems.

Miss A. herself thought the Raid was over and was expecting the All Clear, when a roar filled the air, which they thought was to be on them. She could see the path of the bomb through the Black-out, just as I did the one that crossed our roof. This was one of those unlucky hits where many people were crowded together. We heard of a son and his mother visiting friends. She took a long time to say goodbye, and this saved them. They reached Putney Bridge and heard it coming. The son said: 'We're for it, Mother!' But it dropped the far side of the bridge from them!

Another woman, coming from Windsor, with her husband arrived at Putney Bridge station, and had a premonition of danger. Her husband had mislaid one of the tickets. She urged him not to bother, but to pay again. 'Hurry, hurry,' she continued to say to him. So they walked the streets very fast, and just as their own door closed behind them, the bomb fell. It seems half Putney is bandaged up.

Postscript last week was by a returned Prisoner of war. Three and a half years of it – before Dunkirk he was taken. He described how they kept their spirits up in front of the Germans, and never let them think they were down-hearted. Even when an exchange was a disappointment, and they were marched back to Camp, they returned singing. The worst moment was in 1940 when the German doctor came hurriedly in one morning, and said he could do little for the wounded as he had to report in London the following day! A grim moment. He said how wonderful the parcels were. They liked serious reading – soon got tired of cards and detective tales. The Camp became a University where lectures were given on every conceivable subject . . . even Hebrew, as soon as they began to receive books from England. It was a hard time, but they came out spiritually richer, as they had time to think.

Russians will soon have the Germans out of their country. Mr Eden seems to have made a hit with Stalin. Hope the Conference is as good as they think. Lebanon is seething with revolt, and the French seem to have tripped up badly. *Observer* openly against de Gaulle. Working for power, they say, and will not be a friend to England. Time will show.

Sunday, 21st Christmas Fair over for another year – and thank goodness for that. A great success. We have made £1,200 – wonderful. It knocked me out for the time being. I wanted to die every moment of the day last week – or just retire to a country cottage, away from the turmoil of life – and never do a stroke of work more. That is still my ideal! Then I could read about other people keeping the struggle going. However, feel better now. Miss Moyes and Mrs Hoare are superhuman. I admit I am not. Aunt Nell took me in hand, and trotted round with food and good advice. It was working every hour on my feet up to midnight, and staggering up the road almost too tired to go to bed.

To go back a little. Thursday was thronged with people. Friday a little quieter, and Saturday was foggy. But my Caledonian Market was most popular – made £87 – all in threepences and sixpences, mostly. Buried Treasure, which

Mr Hillyard and I had worked out, was also a success. No sooner had everyone gone than we had to clear our office, and get straight for Monday. On my way home I found three American soldiers lost – I put them on the way to Lancaster Gate – just as I reached my door my torch failed.

To return to news of the great wide world. We do not know what the flare-up in the Lebanon is about – nor where is the fault. Brigadier Spears and his wife, Mary Borden, are there. They know de Gaulle as a friend.

Bombing of Berlin is the great news. It must be rocking to its foundations. Mr H. does not want Hitler to die in an air-raid – it would be too easy.

Jean Tuckwell's baby was born on Nov. 12th, a daughter. Jane. Margaret Ellis enjoying herself at Girton. She won a Surrey major scholarship. She is tall and sylph-like, and a joy to look at.

End of November 1943

DECEMBER 1943

»»»» ❋ ««««

Sunday, 5th Just back from week-end in Kit's new flat. Such a joy to be out of London and take in some mouthfuls of fresh air. I, knowing what it means to get one room together in these times, realized what an effort it meant to do ceilings, walls and clean the paint by herself. We gloated over every article of furniture – what had been given, what lent, and what bought. Lunch was ready and after a cup of tea we set off for Harrow School.

Walked up a steep hill where there was a Church and spire to be seen for miles. The School is clustered round it. Immediately we saw some of the boys with those amazing hats, put on with elastic I am told. We found the elm tree where Byron wrote the famous lines, marked by a stone. He seems to have reclined in the shade and gazed on fields and trees in his day. Inside the Church was a large and friendly tabby cat walking round the pews.

Kit had written the custodian – so all was organized. We scanned the Notice Board with interest – their Prep, signed by different masters. There was the Library. One of the boys said the public could go in. It is a modern building. All the boys had their heads buried in books – no one looked up.

Next we found a chapel-like building and heard the organ playing. No, we were not trespassing the player affirmed pleasantly. He was a Malvern School boy, having come from Blenheim Palace, which they did not like. He was most polite, but quite clearly was just going to his tea. Off he bolted, but indicated the War Memorial on the other side of the road. It was a Museum. The custodian took us round. Great luck. The Old Boys' Room has magnificent carpets in blue and buff. Tables and chairs inscribed with names of donors. I sat on the Churchill one. This is where they all foregather on Speech Day, and sing the Harrow songs. Portraits all round.

There was the Fitch Memorial Room – a Harrow boy of 19½ killed in the last war. His portrait was over the mantelpiece. All panelled, with a glorious Refectory Table, old chairs and chests. Much of the furniture came from the boy's own home. Tea parties and Receptions are held here. Books contained the names and photos of all the old boys killed in World War I. Over 200 so far have been killed in this one. A room where films were shown produced two small boys already waiting. The moment they saw us they leapt to their feet and clutched off their hats. It seems they are taught to be polite. We saw Honours Boards of Harrow Boys who have become Prime Ministers. Also the flags of those who have won the V.C. The custodian was interested that I knew something of Clive Ponsonby Fane, whom he remembered.

In Old School no one bothered about us. We went into classrooms – just the same textbooks that I had used e.g. Ritchie and Moore! Spiers French drill. Then we knocked on a locked and padlocked door. It opened. We were told we were late, but Kit's letter softened the porter, and he let us in to the original Harrow School built in Queen Elizabeth's time by John Lyon of Preston. Black oak benches are there – seats for various masters, the Headmaster at the top – and the Birching Seat, where boys were spanked up to 15 years ago. Now abolished! The panelled walls are covered with names – Byron, Sheridan, Anthony Trollope to Mr Churchill. Nowadays the boys get someone to carve their names. New boys are still received by the Headmaster here.

Kit had news from the Channel Islands brought by those who had escaped in August. Germans are polite to the Islanders, but they have brought unfortunate Russians, Poles and Dutch there, whom they treat abominably. Many die and no one bothers. Bread there is awful. Her father has been moved from his house. She hears via the Red Cross. Awful to think of them in the coming Winter. There is a hope that in six months the Germans will have collapsed. I hope there may be truth in it for the sake of Europe – so many will not survive if we do not rescue them.

A lovely walk in the afternoon along the Hemel Hempstead road, found the towing path, and saw several barges – but not with horses as in my youth. Lovely bridges and locks. On our return there was Joyce, Kit's friend, with whom we had a meal – Vere making some pastry, her one accomplishment in the cooking line . . . I was sorry to take the train back to London.

Now to general news, and not so much about myself. General Smuts has made an impressive speech. In his view France is finished as a Great Power. If she rises again it will be a steep climb. Italy is finished, too. Germany, in the crash that will follow the end of the war, is also finished. We are left with Russia – the new colossus of history. Her rise during the last twenty-five years has no parallel in history. She will have no check in the East after the defeat of Japan. What she will make of it we cannot say. Great Britain will emerge with an honour and prestige that no country has ever enjoyed in the history of the world – but she will be poor. She has put her all into the war. There is nothing left.

This speech has reverberated round the world. I am much impressed with it.

Is Mussolini dead? He has spoken once on the wireless. It may or may not have been he. He may be an ill and broken man. A wonderful Conference in N. Africa with Churchill, Roosevelt and Chiang Kai-Chek with his remarkable wife. Now they have gone to Teheran to meet Stalin. We shall all be glad when Mr Churchill is back in this country. It makes our blood run cold at the thought of the risks he runs.

Sunday, 12th Just back from a week-end with Miss Aird at Radlett. Travelled with some Navy boys from the High-lands of Scotland. Their accent made me think they were foreigners, at first! An A.T.S. girl was there. She was billeted in an empty house, and walked three miles for all her meals, including breakfast. She collected all our old newspapers to light a fire when she got in! Many people in Radlett use a horse to get about. I saw and envied them.

President Roosevelt has called on Malta. We are expecting him here in London, but there is nothing official yet. All the world is down with flu. Mercifully we are well – our office has a coal fire, and is well ventilated. Neither do I have to struggle with tubes and buses like so many people.

Sunday, 19th We are pretty well on our beam ends as far as Christmas Fare is concerned, though we all have enough to eat. It is the Fifth Christmas of the war. No chance of turkey, chicken or goose – not even the despised rabbit. If we can get a little mutton that is the best we can hope for. A few Christmas Puddings are about. Have managed one. Barishnikov has obtained one each for Mr Hillyard and Mrs Hoare. He deserves the highest praise. There are shops with Three Puddings and 800 registered customers!

Mr Churchill has been taken again with pneumonia. Most worrying. He went out with a temperature, worked night and day, flew here and there, and, of course, was laid low. They are using M and B. If they can prolong a life so valuable for a few years that will be something, though the Nature Cure people dislike this treatment.

The Romans were hoping to welcome us for Christmas, but it seems doubtful. Our poor soldiers would have liked to be in a civilized town instead of God-forsaken mountain villages. They must be having such an uncomfortable time.

The American soldiers have done much for the children. They have given them somewhere a great Dinner, a Christmas Tree and Father Christmas arrived in a Flying Fortress. The culmination of the wish of every childish heart!

I was invited to Brede for Christmas, but I always go home. But I will go for Easter if the Invasion danger is completely over. I am hoping by that time Hitler will be up for trial!

Won't it be lovely if this time next year there is no Blackout. Coal is a worry now. It may be a hard Winter. A lot of deaths from flu this week, and thousands down with it. Epidemic all over Europe.

A Happy Christmas to all my readers. Also a New Year without the shadow of air raids on our beloved little island.

End of 1943

THE YEAR
1944

'The golden evening brightens in the west'

'Watchman. What of the night?'

THE MAIN EVENTS
OF THE WAR IN
1944

1944

January	22	Allies landing at Anzio
February		Americans invade Marshall Islands
February – March		Russians recover Ukraine
April	7	Japanese attack Kohima and Imphal
May	9	Russians retake Sebastopol
	18	Allies capture Cassino
June	4	Allies enter Rome
	6	Allied landings in Normandy
	7	Japanese retreat from Imphal-Kohima front
	13	*Flying bomb bombardment begins. V.1s*
	16	Americans invade Marinas
	27	Cherbourg taken
July	9	Caen taken. Allies break out of Normandy beach-head
	20	Attempted assassination of Hitler
August	1	Polish Home Army Rising in Warsaw
	4	Myitkyina recovered

	11	Guam recovered
	12	Allies enter Florence
	15	Allies invade Southern France
	24	Rumania capitulates to Russians
	25	Allies enter Paris
September	3	Allies enter Brussels
	4	Allies enter Antwerp
	5	Russia declares war on Bulgaria
	8	Bulgaria capitulates to Russians
		Rocket bombardment begins. V.2s
	17	Airborne assault on Arnhem
October	2	End of Warsaw Rising
	13	British occupy Athens
	19	Americans invade Philippines
	20	Russians enter Belgrade
	21–22	Leyte Gulf Naval Battle
	22	Allies take Metz
December	16	Last German offensive opens in Ardennes

JANUARY 1944

❧❧❧❧❧ ✿ ❧❧❧❧❧

Sunday, 2nd Christmas has come and gone. Busy week before. Large numbers of deserving folk came for money, clothing and the few toys we had. All most grateful. Marvellous Christmas dinner at the London G.W. Shelter. Tea, and presents. Same at Leeds.

Went home on the Thursday. Paddington not unduly full. Dr H. met me. Bernard Sleigh had already arrived with his cat. Cath brought her on her bike and by bus from Campden. She is so good – name Doodles. She found three other cats in our house. One day when I entered the dining-room I discovered three cats on three chairs and one on the hearthrug. We all sat round the fire most evenings, nursing aforesaid animals. One is ours – Jack. It is thought that his earthly life is nearing its end; so a stray by name of Dusky has been adopted and given to Annie, who dotes on cats. Then Cath had to take pity on a poor Mother cat from school, who has eaten all the mice there – and no one is left to feed her. She is a humble little thing.

Beryl was sorting letters for dear life at the P.O. Full of earnings, Cath and I prowled round the town trying to buy Dr H. a pair of socks – an almost impossible feat these days.

You can only obtain amazing things in bright red, green and purple – all squares. If he turned up at the Hospital in these the patients would never recover from the shock – and Matron would swoon outright. So reluctantly we had to give it up.

Christmas breakfast was as usual, with little parcels by each plate. Mine were mostly from my Caledonian Market – but decent of their kind. I cooked the Xmas Dinner – they had even found a chicken. Listened to the King's Speech. He finished with a curious quotation from John Buchan. Cannot say I really understood it, but perhaps someone will explain it to me.

Cyril Franklin came as usual, with a copy of his presidential address to the Metallurgical Society for Cath. Discussion on H. G. Wells. Don't care for him too much. He foresaw the catastrophe which would fall on Europe – but thought we should go down. He did not see a Churchill, combined with the genius of the British race, rising up to surmount the disaster. This is to me the difference between the logic of the scientist and the faith of the humanist.

On Sunday all of us went over to Ariel's. A grand tea – all the ladies in pretty frocks. I took a tin of long saved-up cherries. We played table-tennis, and arrived home 8 p.m. Monday had the great joy of a meal with Elsie and Neville, who mercifully had a few bits left over from Xmas. Like us they had been able to get poultry. Neville made a great show with wine and liqueurs. He has become a pessimist . . . thinks we shall have another wartime Christmas.

But we did have the marvellous news of the sinking of *Scharnhorst*. It ventured out, because the men were tired of doing nothing in that Arctic twilight, which is guaranteed to depress people with better consciences than the Germans. The British Navy sank it.

Sunday, 9th Saw Dr Remy for tea. He had spent a slow and depressed Xmas. Tried to cheer him up making him think of his blessings. But the bombing of Frankfurt is worrying. We can do nothing about it and must have faith. Carola must be only too happy he is safe in England, and she has only the children to worry about. Some good talk. He quoted a German friend as saying that the Germans have no 'civic courage'. Sound statement, I feel.

Have had a few Alerts. Bombs on East Putney, Wimbledon, Feltham.

Sunday, 16th We are nearing Rome and the Russians are close to the Polish frontier. Great joy over Mr Churchill's recovery. I feared all the remedies would kill him. Barishnikov, being a Russian, does not love the Poles. He is not satisfied with the Polish Government in London. Thinks Stalin had the problem out with Churchill at Teheran. Nothing very clear to me. Anyway, he considers the Poles in Poland will welcome the Russians as liberators from the Germans.

Oxford Group not allowed to send religious books to our prisoners of war. I rang the N.Z. Government office about a young soldier whom we knew. Miss M. could send him psychic books.

Went over to Wimbledon – my chop in my bag and some cooking fat. They made me bring it back. Margaret invited me to Girton later on. She says Quiller-Couch is still as rude as ever to the women students. One day there were no men present for his lecture – he walked out.

Have been to Auntie Nell's. A fearful fog. A lady asked me to take her to Ladbroke Gardens, but I was in a maze, not knowing if I were in Kensington Park Gardens . . . or Ladbroke Grove. Handed her over to someone else. Auntie not too good – a boil on her head, which keeps her awake at night. We agreed she had every luxury – warmth, wireless and kind neighbours in the flats.

Question of Italian art treasures is exercising the minds of the authorities. They must be saved if possible. So experts in battledress are with our armies to do the necessary when possible.

First seagulls circling round my roof this week, and driving away the pigeons. Must be dozens at the Round Pond.

Execution of Count Ciano – said to be by the Germans, but neither Edda nor Mussolini tried to save him. He has had row after row with Mussolini. We are plodding on to Rome, but not yet in sight of the Seven Hills.

Cinema hit in London by a lone raider. Dropped right on the stalls, killing six people and wounding others. I was in a Cinema the other evening, when Alert went, but most of us stayed on.

Sunday, 23rd Mr Churchill suddenly appeared in the House of Commons. Members shouted and cheered with excitement. We are very annoyed about the bombs in our oranges. The Spaniards are searching them – we have been waiting for weeks – and they may go bad.

Terrific barrage on Friday night. Went to front door, but it was a bit too hot – sky lit up and shrapnel fell. Again in the middle of the night. Stuck it for a time, then went downstairs. Found Miss Lambart there; but as she always starts on the Pope, I did not stop, but descended to see how the fire-watchers were getting on. Heard one great swish – seemed as if near St Mary Abbots Church.

It seems Edda Mussolini is in Switzerland with three children. What an end of Ciano!

Cannot cope with Russo-Polish situation. Too difficult. I have no background knowledge as I have of Italy.

Sunday, 30th   Terrific display of gunfire on Saturday night. I had a visitor when the Warning went. Noise deafening, so retired to landing, and heard ping ping on the roof, but no shrapnel through my skylight, I am glad to say. Three times we did this. Three planes brought down.

End of January 1944

FEBRUARY 1944

»»»❋ ❝❝❝

Sunday, 6th They talk of our being 17 miles from Rome. Sounds very close. I can imagine the excitement in Rome – but the Germans are clever. About the King it seems more feasible to wait until we reach Rome before hoofing him out. But others think differently.

Have bought a little Canterbury to hold my wireless. It was £2 12s. and a decent piece of furniture. They say real walnut . . . really it is a music stand, which no one needs particularly at the moment.

The authorities have chosen to place a Pig Bin outside our house in Brum . . . to Mother's great annoyance. The milk horse comes along, lifts the lid and noses about to see if there is bread inside. He eats it and rolls the lid on to the road. He moves on. Then the local cats stroll up and leap into the Bin to see what they can find. Scatter the contents in a large circle and retire. You can imagine the charming scene round our front gate . . . It never occurs to the authorities to bring two or three Bins for the overflowing contents of one, and the lids would remain securely on. Mother is on the warpath and is going to write to the Corporation about the conduct of the Horse and the Cats and the Bins!

Noisy air-raid last Thursday and Friday. Had a good view of the star flares. Most were gold – some blue – like glorious fireworks. Barishnikov says they are not ours. Our guns kicked up an awful din – deafening. Sat up and watched, hoping nothing would drop on me. Seems there was a bomb on Harrow Road – comparatively near here. Line of shops done in. Also Southend had it badly, they say, and all the Thames Estuary towns. Dymchurch police station was hit.

Two more raids on Frankfurt. Berlin will soon be like Carthage, I should think, and we shall end by ploughing it up.

Oranges in N. Hill Gate, but so far have not achieved any. Long queues at the Old Pole's. He never knows when they are coming.

Just reading a book called *Us and the Americans* . . . what they do not understand, and what they like. Our gardens impress everyone. Nothing like them anywhere else. It is our appalling climate which produces this fresh luxuriant growth . . . they love our green lawns, and flowers growing up the houses. Slower tempo of life here. In America the air is so invigorating that you can rush about from morning to night with never a pause. They never leave their guests alone for an hour to amuse themselves, as we do.

Went to the Pig Breeder's. Lovely day and good air out at Hounslow. They had made a brazier of fire to dry one of the pigsties. Saw some Saddlebacks, with white shoulders. Cost £20 each. The pigs were curled up to keep themselves warm, all in a circle – noses to the middle and snoring in unison. Cats stalking about. Seagulls and planes overhead. The son knows all the Liberators, Lightnings, Spitfires, Fortresses etc. They were returning from a big raid. Lovely to see them come back – bless them.

The Pig Breeder and his son are unusual and individual – they made me a pot of tea. For themselves it is cold tea out of a bottle! The old man loves to tell me about his life – has worked in several of the Royal Palaces. In what capacity I don't know, probably a carpenter. He is 70 – tall, upright and magnificent, with great strength. Interested in psychic experiences and in helping poor people – he is most generous to our funds. I told him about some of our cases.

Lovely moon all week. Very frosty. Our cat low in spirits and difficult in temper. We surmise he has had Flu. Winnie, the Zoo lioness has succumbed to pneumonia, in spite of M and B. Should not care to nurse a lioness ill with pneumonia . . .

Sunday, 13th Not too well myself, but must go round and see Auntie Nell. She is trying a homeopathic doctor now, with different treatment. Have made her some scones and home-made ginger wine.

Postscript by Sir Lawrence Bragg – very good. He has the same urbane and pleasing way as his father. Not one of your dogmatic, inhuman scientists convinced he knows the last word on the world, the flesh and the devil. Before the war I went with Elsie to some grand reception at which Sir William spoke.

An Antarctic blizzard all the week. We need rain. If only we could exchange weather with the poor Fifth Army. They have all the Pioggia, and don't want it. We do and have none. Things not too happy on Anzio beachhead, but Mr Churchill has told us to comfort ourselves, and I hope he is right. They are all squashed like sardines in mud – not oil.

The King will not let Princess Elizabeth be Princess of Wales. A pity, for we should all like it. He is very diffident about his family.

Dinner with Dr Remy, who was in better spirits. He attacked me as usual; but I think it is on purpose to see what I shall say. I never yield one inch – re coal fires, etc. We kept ourselves warm in coats. He lent me his, lined with mink, and I felt all Russian. How Carola will laugh when we tell her. Very dark returning along Bayswater Road. Some sailor boys asked me the way to the Y.M.C.A. or a Services Club; but I only know the Canadian one.

Heard a splendid programme about Sir Ernest Shackleton and his men on Elephant Isle – how he took a boat and rowed 800 miles to get help . . . got it, and rescued them.

Sunday, 20th Had a busy week. Awakened by the guns on Friday night. Had not heard the Warning. Stuck it for a bit, but as it was so noisy I hopped out of bed and into dressing gown. The whole sky was light as day, festooned with three magnificent red star flares which threw amazing colours all over Campden Hill. Shots going for the flares – occasionally little bits of them fell off and dropped like falling stars.

Old Dears all assembled on the landing below. Racket increased. My British Israelite, who is a thoroughly nice person, invited me to her window. A great red glow filled the sky as from a fire. For an hour we hopped to and fro. Once a roar filled the air, and she called: 'Come away – that's a bomb.' I did not seem to be frightened, and I can honestly say I saw it flash down – it seemed to be on N. Hill Gate. Heard some glass go, and thought it was my skylight – but still I did not worry.

Finally we decided to go up on the roof. Very cold as we climbed by the fire escape. Firewatchers were like ants below. White frost on all the roofs, and in the direction of Portobello Road there was the sound of a crackling fire. We knew it was near. Other fires round about. We well deserved pneumonia, but could not resist such an amazing sight from the roof. We then had a cup of tea, refilled our hot water bottles and returned to bed, but it was long before I slept. Heard the fire-engines clanging through the streets. Finally dropped off, thinking – Well, saved again.

All felt second-rate next day. News came of a bomb on the College at Campden Hill, where the Gibraltar refugees live. Also of a bad business in Portobello Road. Told Miss M. that I had better go and see how was the Morris family, whom we have helped a lot. Donned my snow boots. The stalls were just going up for the Portobello Saturday Market. Morris house was intact, but poor Mrs Morris was sitting on the stairs more dead than alive. She and Ann and the other children had dragged themselves round to the Shelter. Her husband and Jimmy had stayed to watch the house. Asked her if they were cold in the Shelter. 'Well, really Miss, I was so bad I did not know if I was hot or cold . . .'

For them all it had been an awful night. Great fires in a timber yard next door to a garage. Petrol had to be drawn off before they could pour water on the fire – for two hours firemen had to watch the place burn before they dare do anything. At 3 a.m. a great cheer went up as the hose began to play. Further down an H.E. had fallen and many were killed. I penetrated further. Firemen were looking tired and grimy. Hoses lying around and fires smouldering. It was Tavistock Crescent. Saw dozens of children bombarding a burnt-out shop. It was the local Sweet shop and the youngsters were trying to salvage what they could from the mess!

Their school was burnt out. A bonny little girl spoke sadly of the shop. An invalid woman had kept it for years. Now she had lost her home and business at one swoop. Certainly it had been Portobello's bad night.

Ealing, Acton and Chiswick all had damage. The Old Dears of my flats had been out exploring. Part of Kensington High St cordoned off – a bomb either side of Barkers or Pontings. Auntie Nell tells me that someone on her roof saw a parachutist bale out.

Midday went to St Albans; but made a mistake and took train from King's Cross instead of St Pancras. Travelled with a weary-looking fireman. Had been working all night in Wimbledon, where a Convent had received a direct hit – and rescue men were still digging out the nuns. Such a nice man – had been in the 1940 blitz on the Dock Fires. On one night 300 firemen were killed. He was just going to see his little boy, who was evacuated.

Train stopped at Hatfield and I raced for a bus. Miss Aird wondered what had happened. Went round the Abbey. Back to Radlett for tea. Had to teach Handicrafts mistress my

Italian stitch . . . Returned next day to St Pancras. West Hampstead station almost burnt out on Friday night. Wedding Party killed near here.

Monday, 21st Wireless went off last night in middle of Post-script. Warning came. Joined the Old Dears. Through the bathroom window could see searchlights probing the sky. One seemed to pin something down and move overhead. I shouted to the others that he was above us. Then the whole house shook from head to foot – window and doors rattled, and the noise was deafening. Heard a whistle, rushed to the front door where the fire-watchers were running round. Incendiaries had fallen all around. I galloped to the top of the house, but all seemed intact. We breathed again.

Huge fires reddened the sky in all directions – Shepherd's Bush and Bayswater. Then all went quiet and we ventured into the street. Pembridge Square seemed to be on fire – and as we all had friends there we tore upstairs, flung on coats and big boots, and made for the area. One end of the Square was a blazing inferno. They said it was the United Dairies. Lady Montague's house also on fire – and spreading rapidly. We circled round Palace Court – lots of people now out of the Shelters. We could do nothing and returned to our beds. I have never seen such a horrifying fire. Another Warning at 3.30 a.m. We cursed it by Bell, Book and Candle – but no guns, and I slept again.

Sunday, 27th It has been hell's delight most of the week. Back to my investigations on what happened. Had to go down

Church St for Miss M.'s extra milk note. Found the R.C. Church at the curve of the street burnt out, only the front wall standing. Duke St with the little Queen Anne houses is all right, and the monastery only damaged in the roof. One of the Fathers was outside talking to friends. He seemed relieved it was no worse, and his own room was all right. Top floor of the Gas, Light and Coke Co. showroom had gone.

Made for Palace Court to see my fire of Sunday night. In the cold light of day the place was a blackened mass. Spoke to a weary-looking fireman who lamented they could not get all the help they needed. No fire-watchers could have put it out – incendiaries cascaded down in hundreds, attacking many buildings, and so it was a Conflagration.

Asked about the United Dairies' horses whose stables were there. Mercifully they had got them out at once – two incendiaries fell straight through the stables, and set fire to the straw – one of the horses was busily stamping out the fire with his hooves! This the milkman told me, for he was on duty. They were led into Moscow Road and tied to the railings. All their records had gone.

Every London district seems to have caught it. We have been helping people all the week, especially in Shepherd's Bush where we know many families. Coal very short as the wharf there was hit, and some of the horses injured. So I rang the Pig Breeder and he sent some, which I helped him deliver to the right houses. Clothes were needed for a baby of a month old. The mother had snatched the child up and evacuated the house, as there was a time-bomb outside.

The week has gone on – Tuesday, Wednesday and

Thursday, short but horrifying raids while they lasted. St James' Palace was hit – the clock. Damage in Whitehall, incendiaries in Downing St. Fulham Palace had a terrible hit. At Wimbledon the curate and his wife of St Andrew's Church were killed together. Fortunately these raids were before 11 p.m., and so I was at the Sanctuary. It is warm and comfortable in the office, the house is solidly built and full of people. If you have to die it is better not to be by yourself. Mr Bendall says we are all to carry whistles, and if we are buried it will be useful to whistle rescuers. A useful idea – and if necessary shall whistle with all my might.

Our Fire-Watch Party has been reorganized. Not to be out in heavy gunfire, but to take shelter from shrapnel. At my flat have been talking seriously to the Old Dears, and we had stirrup pump practice to see if we could pump easily upstairs. I found the best way to unroll it – for it can twist like an eel.

No sooner was the Fire-Watch meeting over than the barrage set up in a horrific manner; chandelier flares, rocket guns and star flares filled the sky back and front. Seemed to be drifting from Paddington to N.H. Gate. Mr Hillyard kept dashing to the top of the house. I watched at the front door, on to which I hung, and shut it instantly I thought a bomb was about to drop in the drive. It seems just like that at times. Office is full of people, for they come in and take refuge – all trying to forget the Hullaballoo outside. I left near midnight and stepped into the clear air, all peace and calm. Does not seem possible it is the same world.

Queues for the Tubes start at 4 p.m. . . . children, prams, old people. At Holland Park there are bunks for 500. They have had 1,500 people there this week. They sleep on the platforms with trains passing. One night they had to send the train on as the passengers could not alight among the sleepers.

Lemons on sale this week. I have had four and made pancakes three nights running.

Monday, 28th Phone call from Auntie Nell to say Auntie Mollie has broken her thigh and was brought to the London Hospital.

Incendiaries fell on Harrow School the other night – straight on the boys' beds. They all got up and put out those on the roof. Punch drawing this week with three worried looking Directors interviewing a lady secretary. They offered her a partnership if she would Brush and Clean . . .

Went to see film of *San Demetrio* about the Jervis Bay Convoy. We follow the fortunes of one lifeboat. After three miserable days they sight the *San Demetrio* again, their own ship, which ought to have blown up. They reboard her, though in flames and with petrol – she is a Tanker, and after amazing hardships bring her safely to the Clyde.

End of February 1994

MARCH 1944

***** ❁ ❦❦❦❦

Sunday, 5th Quiet week-end for raids. Some think it is the moon. Americans and ourselves pounding Germany all week, and I cannot believe they have planes free to come here. Anyway, whatever the reason – God be praised.

My first oranges. Lady in next flat queueing up, so kindly took my ration book and got me three lovely ones. She waited threequarters of an hour. We have seen orange peel in the street – most refreshing even to look at it.

Saw *The First of the Few* with dear Leslie Howard. Went with one of my former Wimbledon pupils. It is the story of R. J. Mitchell who invented the Spitfire. He died before the war, but did as much as anyone to win the Battle of Britain, and save us all. I was specially interested in the Schneider Trophy. One year the Italians won it – it was Major de Bernardi with great rejoicings. A nice modest hero he was – I knew the family well in Florence. When we won the Trophy outright I watched from the Solent. Did not realize Lady Houston gave the money for us to enter, and that we learned no end from it. In my short-sighted fashion I deplored it all at the time – not being able to see any use in tearing through the sky at such speeds. But it was a glorious sight – sky a perfect blue.

I believe Lawrence of Arabia had much to do with the Race. Many great minds were working to save England even then. But most of us little realized it at the time.

Gratifying letter from John Fossett: 'Very many thanks for two instalments of diary. Joan and I derived hours of pleasure from reading it aloud to each other. How we laughed about the Mulberry Tree. We passed it over to the R.A.F. and how they enjoyed it. It seemed like being at home again as we lived through your experiences.' He was in South Africa.

Saw also a Picture of the burning of Kiev – how deeply the Russians must feel as they re-enter their ruined cities – seething with the desire for revenge. It was heart-rending – mercifully a silent film, as we could hardly have borne to hear the agonizing cries of the women as they found relatives dead by the burning houses. Some turned their faces to the camera. My blood ran cold, thinking how easily it might have happened in London or Birmingham.

They have bombed Florence railway station – the first time. The Tower of Giotto was not built to withstand an earthquake – my heart misgives me for this jewel among cities.

Sunday, 19th We are all upset that the miners are on strike. I gather the Porter award is a muddle. Many experienced miners are not getting much more than the Bevin boys. Most annoying to them. *Observer* says miners have a strong case. I know myself that the people who experience the conditions are not consulted; and rules are made by those who do not know what they are talking about. Very exasperating. I cannot help feeling that the miners are decent Englishmen and only want fair play.

Have received gift of a nice Sheraton style armchair from Helen Neatby, who has accepted a post in Uganda.

Tuesday night the band began to play. Mr H. and I had just finished the letters. Paid no attention at first, but when the guns began I hastily donned rubber boots, in which I feel – for some reason – powerful and competent. Yirrells came tearing round. We took action stations . . . Hullaballoo terrific. Great blaze by the water-tower on Campden Hill – also near the Albert Hall. Later at my flat I discovered some of the Old Dears had been round to see – they said it was Kensington Parish Church and one in Vicarage Gate. Next day Resti told us he was out and had seen the spire of St Paul's, Vicarage Gate fall in.

Auntie Nell not well. Aunt Winnie has come from Brede to visit the Hospital, and wants me to go to them for Easter. My relations seem to need me; but I am loth to leave G.W. as the work interests me.

Visited bombed Church. Poor thing – it looked nearly too tired to stand upright. The Carmelite church is a complete ruin.

Have had a new complaint myself . . . beneath my right shoulder blade. Auntie Nell says it is intercostal rheumatism. Operates on a large scale when I type or sit long in one position. Very annoying. In bed feel nothing. Glorious parcel from Lucy with a tin of butter. Shall keep it until Mother and I go on holiday in June.

Frankfurt bombed twice this week. I do not care tuppence about Berlin, but am sad for Frankfurt and only hope Mrs Remy and the children have left the town.

Sunday, 26th Still striving to take that wretched town of Cassino. Really it has ceased to exist; but there are tunnels beneath and the Germans use them. They are not recent, but possibly were made when Italians were searching for Roman treasures. What happens is this – we bomb the place to bits, then the Germans saunter out in hundreds thoroughly alive and kicking, from the holes. So sorry for our boys. And the Americans who like to move quickly must be aggravated in the extreme. Not a question, it seems, of fighting house by house, but room by room.

Russians are pushing on happily into Rumania, and mopping up batches of Germans on the way. Some air raids for us this week. We all got to bed with a little evacuation bag by the door to pick up easily and get out, if necessary. Paddington station took a biff – some luggage trolleys were heaved on to the roof by a bomb. Had to run down the road from my treatment one night. My torch was giving out. Cannoned into many folk making for the Tube. Just reached the Sanctuary. Bombers were turned back. Same on Thursday. Friday a long and noisy raid. We stood at the door. What a sight are the rocket guns! We seem to have a lot. They fill the sky with showers of flame – then a bang. Very cold and the Racket was enormous. All Clear at 1 a.m.

Jean Dowson is at Tunbridge Wells with Baby Jane. Obviously they could not remain in that top flat with fire bombs dropping. Her husband is a prisoner. Great relief – as he was reported missing.

Week-end away with Kit at Watford. Lovely to be off the chain. Took a lemon to make pancakes. Good lunch. Train for St Albans. Just meandered round Abbey and Gatehouse, now part of the school. Must have been an enormous monastic house. Alban was a Roman soldier who sheltered a British priest ten years before Constantine made Christian the Roman Empire. He was beheaded outside Verulamium, and a tiny Church built on the spot. Down the centuries it grew in glory and magnificence in the golden days before Henry VIII. Roman material was embodied in it. We wandered round the town – pretty houses – all different and weathered by time.

Kit had hypnotized the butcher into giving her some suet, so I made a pudding. Heard about her clever cousin in the Secret Service. She has no idea what he does, naturally. Slept well – heavenly not to worry over raids. Visited a Canadian soldier in hospital. Corporal Harvey Stevenson, who has lost a leg. Thanked him on behalf of England for what he had done. Told him the only Canadian I knew was a Red Indian! He was tired. Having a leg off is no joke, but he is very good about his loss. Easy-going hospital. Visitors at any time. Even given a cup of coffee. All Canadian run. Best of food.

Loth to return to London . . . shall curse the Germans if they spoil our hearing of Mr Churchill's broadcast.

End of March 1944

APRIL 1944

April, 2nd Listened to the Brains Trust. Much enjoyed it. Joad very good – the Doctor very poor. Not the Radio doctor, whom I like, but another one who had not much to say, and even that was not worth saying. He had a discussion with Joad about the difference between mind and brain. Joad maintained they were not one and the same. The Doctor obviously had not thought about the matter at all.

It has been 'Salute the Soldier' week. Have not seen much of the Festivities. We have had a Target in the office. Doubled it by Friday . . . that is £40. On Saturday found Barishnikov dancing round the office with glee. The Association had invested money, and our Full Amount was £200.

A big how d'you do in Parliament this week over Equal Pay for Equal Work in teaching. Cath says the men do less work than the women. But Mr Churchill took exception to some amendment, and everyone had to retract what had been said. Mrs Cazalet Keir said it was not common sense; but to show Mr Churchill that everyone loved him and thought no one but he could win the war, they would vote as he wished.

Auntie Nell is pleased with my chair and we discussed re-covering it. We had a party for my birthday. I opened a tin of damsons and one of Carnation milk. We had ginger wine and coffee. The Misses Coombes came and Dr Remy. The former have lived in Russia – so we talked Russia and Germany without pausing for an instant. He thinks the Russians will be in Berlin by June. This is optimism with a vengeance. Perhaps the Second Front will not be necessary.

Easter Monday, 10th Back after a visit to Brum. Cath with me. Good journey, but lots sitting in corridors, especially from Leamington and Banbury. She went to see Dr Remy, I to Auntie Nell, who lent me an egg, which Cath will repay tomorrow. Would not dream of taking it otherwise, as Auntie is prone to give away what she should eat herself.

Last week listened to a young New Zealander on radio. He said out there they always think of England as home. He criticized various things about us, but about the aristocracy he gave me an agreeable surprise. It seems a few Dukes and Marquesses had done him well at their 'little places'. One of them said to him: 'I suppose in one hundred years time such people as I will be an extinct species. We are an anachronism in modern life.' The New Zealander replied: 'I for one hope not – the English aristocracy is ours, and we look upon it as such.' Dr Remy says I am a champion of the aristocracy – this I knew not.

Russians have captured Odessa. All our A.R.P. Posts are betting on the Second Front. We've all got to stay put for three days wherever we are. All main line trains to be used for war only. Neville and Elsie bet on May as the month.

To return to Brum. Very busy before. One young Mother

arrived with baby girl of five months, wearing a magnificent robe the father had sent from the Azores. But one thing worried me. Like all soldiers' wives she has difficulty in managing on the money. The pram made a hole in her allowance. We paid any money she owed; but she said how thankful she was to be able to feed her baby herself – and a look of fear crossed her face – as to buy food for it would be so expensive. It seems wrong to me that a mother should be worried like that. She had kept her boy from school while his shoes were mended.

At home was looked after very well by Beryl. Began to stain the surrounds – needed doing. But could not buy enough. Neville and Elsie came. Great argument with Cath over the miners. She was all for instant nationalization. Neville said the Dudley miners might have to come out in sympathy – but what it was all about they did not know, as those in Dudley are model pits. I should hate to go down a mine myself, and I think the miners should be well paid. But I don't think they should sabotage the Second Front. We are all short of coal – in Ladbroke Road house we have no coke and no hot water.

Monday, 17th Russians nearing Sebastopol. Cath in Cambridge is enjoying her Course. Auntie Nell lent her an umbrella. Umbrellas have all changed hands in recent years . . . steadily lost by one section of the community and acquired by another. But our own lost one is difficult to trace; they are impossible to buy, so we lend around as aforesaid.

World is looking fresh and green. Almond and cherry trees in full bloom. No coke in the house. Listened to Priestley's play *Desert Highway*. It is a conversation of a bunch of our boys lost in the Syrian desert, owing to a broken-down tank. The Second Act is a similar group of travellers lost in the same spot more than a thousand years ago.

An Old Dear in my house comes tapping on all our doors from time to time: 'Oranges in Notting Hill Gate – Oranges, Oranges!' Thereupon everyone clutches their ration books and pounds up to the shops. One of them gets mine. Lucy sent me a parcel with a jelly inside. Unheard of luxury! As I was going to a little party with children present I sent it along. Barishnikov gave the party for David and John – with true Russian hospitality!

Sunday, 23rd, St George's Day   We get nearer the ancient City of Rome – though we have been running on the spot for some time, and that's not much fun. The Americans call it the second-hand front.

Spring is here in all its glory. Trees have raced ahead in covering themselves with fresh and glorious green. Sun has shone and the air is warm and balmy.

There has been a bus strike, which affected many people – but not me. Soldiers were put on the buses, not to take fares, but just to shepherd the public. Soldier drivers often lost their way, and were directed by the passengers. These often had a whip round, so the men went home with pounds in their pockets. Strictly against regulations – but to stop it would be asking too much. Trouble is over the Summer Schedule – evidently made without any concern for the workers, or any consultation. People do these things without realizing it is all the height of inconvenience. British workpeople do not mind putting up with anything that is necessary; but if it is just due to lack of thought by the authorities they object. No one grumbled about driving through the Bombs!

Raid last Thursday night. Infiltrated myself into a few clothes, and joined the Old Dears on the stairs. Rocket Guns go off with showers of sparks, and then the Boom of the Recoil fills the air. House shook tremendously, but we could see no fires. At the office we heard it had been a bad business. West Middlesex Hospital at Edmonton was hit. Being at home at Easter was lovely, with the feeling of not being disturbed, except by the cat demanding entrance . . .

Helped Auntie Nell with her spring-cleaning. She ought not to be on steps at all. She hoped she would not live to do another spring-cleaning. [Note: She did not. V.H.] Uncle Roscoe has cabled from Durban. He is very worried about us all.

A Queue Story: Approach to shop door blocked with people waiting for 9 a.m., and oranges on sale. Suddenly a little man began to push his way to the front. Much fuss! Then he shouted: '*Let* me get to the door. Do you want oranges or not! I own the shop.'

Went over to Barkers and then into the Park. Elderly folk enjoying the sunshine on the seats. Met a nice woman of about 70 near Round Pond. She informed me she had worked in a factory making the smaller parts of Mosquitoes. Whenever she saw one in the sky she wondered if she had had any part in it. She was pleased with herself, for she was 70 years of age, and thought she could do nothing to help, but being clever with her hands had joined a factory, half-time. Paid 8d per hour, and worked with an erection of lights on her head. She became an overseer. The aristocracy helped . . . Lord and Lady Grosvenor, aged 82, put in several afternoons. All very happy together. After a time they moved the aged to a special room for simple jobs. Affectionately known as the Village Idiots – or simply the V.I. Room! My informant had to resign as the lights affected her sight; but she was at the Town Hall on Identity Cards. Her daughter and grand-daughter were doing this and that, and she was thankful to be doing a little herself. We said Good-bye cheerfully.

No daffodils in the Park – all stolen the minute they came out. Very mean. Cath called in. The burning question of the hour in Schools is the Teaching of Sex. Hence the Cambridge Course. Cath is a Biology specialist. Sir Eric Drummond was one of the speakers. Venereal disease is lowest among miners and agricultural workers!

Sunday, 30th Some coke in our house now, and we can get a bath. Five weeks with no hot water! A small inconvenience, but I record it.

Second Front not launched yet. Letter from Canada from our Red Indian Chief, Os-ke-non-ton. Hope he receives my reply with our news.

Must remark on the beauty of the Spring – after five years of war one notices the prunus trees. The wild cherry on the opposite side of the road seems like being present at a Wedding every time I pass. Thrushes are tame. Heard a great Hullaballoo in the tree one morning. It was like Geraldo and his band. Behold it was a thrush in the fork of the tree answering another one in the lilac bush.

Have managed to buy a double saucepan for five shillings. Ordinarily unobtainable, but I begged the lady to let me have the first refusal if one came in. She did. But no sheets yet . . .

Went to Redhill to see Auntie Mollie at the Convalescent Home. Lots of uniforms at Victoria Station – anyone in civvies in England now looks all wrong. Brighton train sparsely filled, as it is a banned area – only the Services and really important people can go there. Home a bit difficult to find – it was outside Reigate. Auntie has a bed right across the window with a lovely garden to look at, and wide stretches of country. She is out of pain now. Matron very nice – is doing the cooking, as there is no cook at the moment. Left about 4 p.m. and went on to see Mrs Boyd at The Lodge. She is very deaf. One old man in the room was sure I was starving – so went and procured me another jam tart with my tea!

On the way back saw an officer in a Khaki coat and Beetroot-Coloured trousers. No identification marks. He was English and carried the Academy catalogue in his hand.

Should love to know what he was – something special I realize.

End of April 1944

MAY 1944

» ❀ «

Sunday, 7th No Second Front yet. We await news every day –
big raids on the Continent. Quiet nights here. Much colder in
the 'Straits of Dover' this week. We have had a fire in the office
as everyone is sneezing. This week they have had to relax the
ban in the North. One judge in Manchester sent all the jury
for their overcoats, as he said they could not concentrate,
shivering with cold.

Went to *Daily Telegraph* Exhibition of Prisoner of War
Camp, in the grounds of Clarence House. Said to be an exact
replica. On my way saw the Thatched House in Trafalgar
Square built to attract recruits for the Harvest. Windows of
Carlton House Terrace have gone. Plane trees towards the
Palace are this peculiar golden green of early Spring. Saw a
queue and joined it. After an hour was inside. Some of our
boys, rigged up in German grey uniforms, were patrolling the
grounds – an ugly little machine gun at the ready. Sentry had
too nice a face for a German – he kept giving us a roguish
smile.

First hut is the living quarters – bunks, with a table they
made themselves, also knives and forks from tins, with wire
handles. Photos and snaps all round bunks. In Handicraft

Hut were paintings, needlework, boats, trains and a weaving machine. Another hut was a chapel; another a theatre; also the barbed wire university. Also saw one of Monty's Caravans . . . fitted comfortably. The parcels were wonderful, and with one a week they will not starve.

Been economizing, as paying my life insurance, the rent and the electricity bill has knocked my Bank Balance sideways. So presented my sweet coupons to Barishnikov, who does not economize much. Made porridge in my double-saucepan – great joy with milk and sugar.

To give friends in foreign parts some idea of our meals: Meat ration lasts only for three evening meals. Cannot be made to go further, that is, Saturday, Sunday and Monday. O.K. Tuesday and Wednesday I cook a handful of rice, dodged up in some way with curry or cheese. But the cheese ration is so small there is little left. Thursday I have an order with the Dairy for a pound of sausage. These make-do for Thursday, Friday and part Saturday. No taste much of sausage, but are of soya bean flour. We just pretend they are the real thing. A little fish would help, but there are queues for it. All rather monotonous, but we are not hungry, and the authorities have done well for us, we consider.

The book *Grey and Scarlet* is wonderful. Letters of Army Nurses from all over the world. Thousands of people can rise to the greatest heights of heroism. Not only the march to Dunkirk, but during the gradual approach of the Japs. Everyone did their valiant duty in whatever situation they found themselves. One nurse and her fiancé felt the lifeboat sinking beneath them. At a word from him the nurse slipped off her coat, and they both took to the water, swimming about for an hour in a shark-infested sea! Finally they were taken aboard another lifeboat, which floated for fourteen days. They got through and were married.

There is a programme called Home News for soldiers. Very homely. They did not say in neutral way: There was no enemy aircraft over Britain last night. Instead, it is: 'We all had a quiet night last night.'

Wonderful to hear the recording of the Nightingale on the Anzio beachhead. I was thrilled. Have discovered the Officer in the Beetroot-coloured trousers is a parachutist . . .

Sunday, 14th Seems movement in Italy at last. As I came from St Pancras tonight they were shouting 'Big Eighth Army Advance'. Second Front not opened yet, but they say for miles inland across the Channel from the coast no life stirs, and the R.A.F. roam over it unchecked.

Must go back to last Sunday night. Left Sanctuary about 9.15 p.m. Met party returning from Portsmouth. All was serene. By 10.30 p.m. the house was on fire! Mrs Hoare had done the Black-out, checked the top floor for lights. At 10.30 p.m. Mr Hillyard returned from Parkstone, climbed stairs to his room, smelt something suspicious, opened a door, and was greeted with volumes of smoke and flames from floor to ceiling. He yelled to the entire community: 'Bring the pump. House on fire.' He seized the Stirrup pump kept on the top landing. Mrs Hoare brought water. Miss Mackay rushed next door for Mr Bendall. Miss Moyes dashed to the phone and dialled 999. No response. Rushed next door for her god-daughter. No response. Found a policeman who went and phoned at the Tube.

Meanwhile, the two heroes were still pegging away. Mrs Hoare took over, as Mr Hillyard has only one arm. By the time the Fire Brigade arrived they had really got it under. Much credit due to them all and the Stirrup Pump! One fireman touched Mrs Hoare in a fatherly way, saying 'You leave it to us, lady'. She was right glad to follow this comforting advice. Terrible fright for everyone. Another quarter of an hour and the roof would have caught. Cause was a defective flue in Miss Moyes' chimney.

At Radlett over the week-end. Read some of Maurois' *The Fall of France*. I remember poor Maurois making his way to England and giving that last despairing broadcast. He asked us to send our last plane and last gun to France. A nice mess we should have been in if we had. We saved ourselves and gained time. He describes the whole tragedy as he watched it. But saw nothing in advance, as Churchill did. In 1935 Churchill took him on one side, saying: 'I want you to put aside novels and biographies and write one article every day, telling the French people that they have no Air Force.' He attributes the Fall of France to the divorce of her best men from public life. All she had were talkers and lawyers who hated each other more than they hated the Germans.

He gives an excellent description of Mr Chamberlain going to see Hitler for the first time . . . 'that amiable gentleman had not the slightest idea of the Fuhrer's character. He regarded him, not certainly as another member of the Birmingham Corporation, but at least as a member of the

Manchester Corporation . . . shock of his life when he was left to have what passed with Hitler for conversation. Hitler roared at him for twenty minutes without ceasing, and Mr Chamberlain had to leave the room.'

Sunday, 21st We have taken that wretched Cassino. We had been bogged there for so long that the British Public had given up all hope. Now the town is taken and the Poles have the monastery. Indeed we are a few miles on the road to Rome, when for weeks we have not taken an inch a day. Preparations are enormous for the sailing of our Armada. But when it will set off we do not know. In Cassino there is no civil administration appointed because there is nothing left to administer. The inhabitants have nothing to return to . . . it is just . . . waste, as they said in Domesday Book.

Poor Ivor Novello. But it is no excuse to say you do not know you are breaking the law. He feels the disgrace keenly. But there is good news about Ralph Richardson and Lawrence Olivier – both released from war service to run a theatre. John Gielgud is also organizing a repertory company. Martin Harvey died this week. Shall never forget the thrill when, as a schoolgirl, I saw him first. Mother used to take us to *The Breed of the Treshams* and *The Only Way*. Beauty of voice and dignity of manner were indescribable.

Walked across the Park on Saturday – what a sight was the red may and yellow laburnum. Had been to the Royal School of Needlework – have done nothing for years, but my interest is now coming back. Popped into V. and A., but little is open. Had a look at Round Pond and sat there for a while. A nice young soldier in a Tam was also there, so we opened conversation. He came from Elgin; had been in Palestine and fighting since the beginning. I told him about the blitz – and how it was due to Churchill that there was an England and Scotland to come back to. He seemed very fond of a Mother and Sister in Elgin. Was due to go on the Second Front. James Morrison was his name.

Took the Pig Breeder's son to Auntie's flats to collect the Pig Food there on his rounds . . . the old ladies cannot carry it any more. Auntie came down to interview him. He seems tired of Pigs and all the hard work. Not a happy man, I feel, but I told him it was no use quarrelling with life – we none of us get all we want. Don't know if this general philosophy cheered him.

Whit Monday, 29th   Did not go home. Trains cut all the week. Soldiers to be first – and they mentioned Paddington particularly. It was not only going, but the coming back . . . though the Second Front may not be until middle of June. I read of one thousand people for each train, and queueing for three hours . . . could not have faced it.

Wonderful speech from Mr Churchill, all about our friends, half-friends and enemies. He spoke approvingly of Spain, because they had turned a blind eye to our Convoys landing in N. Africa. They were waiting under the Spanish naval guns, and no one drove them away. He is so grateful that he handed out numerous bouquets to the Spaniards. But there were wry faces in many quarters. He spoke of Italy, and how sorry he was, and hoped Rome would be spared. I worry more about Florence – if anything goes there I should think the Florentines would commit suicide. Anyway we are only fifteen miles from Rome – too wonderful. We are trying to cut the Germans off – but we have tried before, and, drat them, they seem to get away!

Stars on Army Vehicles mean they are destined for Europe. Lots of these about. Weather very hot in the Straits of Dover – hundreds of degrees in the shade! We have plunged into summer frocks and no stockings. Though at the moment there is a thunderstorm.

Did some exploring – three days in succession, quite free and no hurry. I revelled in it. Have had four eggs given me from a Nameless Source. Sh! Sh! So with one, hard-boiled, with some writing paper and a book, I set forth into the Park. Tramped on and on in the heat. Lupins glorious! Reached the Bird Sanctuary, found a chair and sank down. Opened my little packets, but was thirsty – and thought of the men in the Desert and how awful that must be. Wrote some letters. Rolled myself on the turf and felt the touch of the earth beneath me. Someone has a theory that power comes from actually touching it – which does not come through asphalt pavements. I think often of this, and bless the Good Earth when I lie on her.

Eventually found a Cafeteria, lined up and drank a fragrant draught of the best of all Beverages. On to Speakers' Corner where lots of American soldiers were listening with amused smiles. Took bus to Holborn. Staple Inn there as of old, though Holborn itself is badly hit. I looked into the courtyard – usual plane trees and cobbles. So pretty. On to St

Bartholomew's, Smithfield. Lucy will be relieved to hear it is still intact . . . Rahere's tomb has been encased in bricks. A lady, dusting the pews, said an incendiary had come through, but most fell on a school which had been burned out.

Looked in at the courtyard of the Hospital, which Rahere founded. Plane trees and a fountain – dappled with shadows. Looked round the Square, all very ordinary and peaceful, though possibly haunted by the ghosts of the martyrs, not to mention Richard II and Wat Tyler. Went along to St Sepulchre's – which escaped the blitz and has been lent to Leslie Weatherhead, as the City Temple is a ruin. This borders on the awful square mile of desolation that once was London.

Entertained my Swiss colleague on bits and pieces carefully saved to make a feast. A hoarded tin of plums – a piece of fish miraculously obtained and so on. One can only do it once in a way.

Just heard the awful news that the Sanctuary Puss is dead: he was found under the bushes in the front garden – only eight years old and in the best of spirits. Blood on the side of his face, though he looked asleep. His little presence will charm us no more. A great loss to the office.

Miss Moyes fainted at her Meeting. Very unusual. We have no coke and no hot water. Auntie Nell also is very seedy . . .

End of May 1944

JUNE 1944

»»»» ❋ ««««

Sunday, 11th Well, what a week this has been! The Fall of Rome – and the Second Front! For both of which we have waited so long.

I believe we marched into Rome last Sunday, but I cannot remember when I first heard the news. All came with a rush. We were dreading this and that and then – then, in the end, the Germans just rushed out one end as we drove in the other. The Romans pelted the boys with flowers, kissed and hugged them, and life was sweet to everyone. The Pope blessed one and all. Poor old thing! He is always there to do the Blessing – on whoever it is. However, the city is untouched and the world breathes again.

One American soldier had promised his mother he would address the crowd from the balcony of Palazzo Venezia in Italian, just as Mussolini used to do. Behold he has done it – the radio announced.

The Romans had a holiday. Our boys went pounding on after the Germans, but they are running so fast it is difficult to catch up with them. We hear they are seventy miles north of Rome. Great!

Just to go back to Tuesday. I pricked up my ears at the

8 a.m. News when the voice, in suppressed excitement, stated that paratroopers were said to be landing on the Seine estuary, and that German ships were fighting invasion barges in the Channel. Could it really be? At the office people came in later to say Eisenhower had spoken and invasion was on. At 1 o'clock I was amazed to hear correspondents' reports, and even the sound of gliders. Someone spoke from a bomber over the French coast with the boys landing below. Thrilling!

The King spoke at 9 p.m. So sincere, like himself. He brought the Queen in, and told us all to pray. We learned the event had been put off from Sunday because of the weather: Eisenhower had had to give the word. The boys went in at low tide, with horrible mines sticking out of the water as they waded ashore.

Herbert Marshall was in one of the barges and you could feel the swing of it – they were all thrown into five feet of water. Another B.B.C. man had dropped with the paratroopers, and would report later.

But what organization! How different from four years ago, when we were reeling from the Fall of France, and the entry of Italy against us. The *Observer* rightly observes:

'Today we are most happy to salute great Marlborough's great heir, who never, amid catastrophes more awful than those which beat about the heads of a Job or a Lear, lost nerve or faith or grip. Last week's thunderstroke is the result of a design of grand strategy which Mr Churchill adopted four years ago; to which he clung with stubborn faith when it seemed little more than a visionary dream; and which he pressed through with single-minded energy and persistence, regardless of peril, defeat, pressure abroad, and clamour at home. The 4,000 ships and 11,000 planes which carried a gigantic Anglo-American-Canadian army to France last week were four years ago one man's vision . . . it would never have become reality but for that man's undaunted faith and creative energy.'

Let not Future Ages forget it!

We have taken Bayeux. No one knows where the Tapestry is. Perhaps the townspeople buried it. Could not help thinking, when I heard the Sabine Hills mentioned so constantly, of my struggles with Virgil – of Romulus and Remus. So much history has rolled around these hills, always with Rome at the centre.

To return to lesser matters. Lucy's butter is excellent. We are almost afraid to eat it. Auntie Nell puts hers out on a special plate. She urged me on – but we both gaze at it with awe, and dig in our knives gingerly in case it turns out to be a mirage on the table.

The general opinion about our little Scamp is that he was hit by an Army lorry careering along at night – and he just lay down in the bushes and died. He had no intention of dying that Friday night. He intended to live on to the piping times of peace, and have a good tuck-in. He had the best home ever, and it is lamentable that he should have been an Invasion casualty. So good he was when the bombs were dropping on us, and made us laugh through many a bad hour.

Last Saturday it was the Anniversary at the Kingsway Hall. Miss M. was ill all the week. Place full of visitors. I kept trotting upstairs to tell her who had arrived – this quietened her. She carried through the Meeting, but it was painful to watch anyone so ill. There was a big Supper Party. Mrs Yirrell and I did the tea, Nurse Roberts served out wonderful pies. Got home a quarter to midnight.

Postscript excellent! A surgeon on a ship described his diagnosis of appendicitis on a seaman, and how the ship had to be stopped for him to do the operation. He was far from sure he was right, and what a fool he would feel if wrong. He could remember little of how to do the operation. Had seen it performed. But, after the first cut with the knife, he felt his hands taken over by someone else, and the whole operation performed by someone who took possession of his hands, and did it for him. Very Remarkable!

Lorries rush through here down to the coast. Houses shake as they go by. In the Red Cross everyone is on call to go if the casualties are high. Thank God, so far they are not.

A Runaway Horse was racing along this week, having abandoned his cart long since, when a Police Van came in the opposite direction. There was no time to get out and seize the horse; but as it was galloping past him the policeman bellowed through his loudspeaker . . . Whoa! Whoa! Behold, the horse pulled up peaceably and was led away. Good work!

A visit last week from the Scottish soldier I met in the Park. He called to tell me he was to go on a course at Nottingham. Gave him a glass of ginger wine – he nearly drank the bottle. His sister is Mahri, a Gaelic name. He knows no one in London, so I was pleased to befriend him for an hour.

Our potatoes are poor in quality, and new ones are only for millionaires. Carrots have been 4/6d per bundle in Notting

Hill. They are to be controlled. Peas and beans are 3/– per pound. Shops can sell them easily at these prices. Grapes, they say, are £4 per pound.

Sunday, 18th These last three days have been one long Air Raid Alert, and we have had little sleep. Must get some tonight if I am to work in the day. So I have decided to come and bed down on the Sanctuary sofa. It is on the ground floor. I do not mind the guns, but the shrapnel danger through my skylight in the flat makes me hop out of bed to the door.

These Robot Planes go on after daybreak, which the old raids never did. I could hear the wretched thing travelling overhead at 6 a.m. They did not fall on us – but they fell on someone. Our guns barked out and spat and fussed until they had gone. They travel quickly and on Thursday night were low over Kensington. In fact everyone of us was perfectly convinced the thing was exactly three inches above the roof.

Nothing is said on the wireless or in the papers except . . . Southern England! That is us – and we are all fed-up.

Monday was our fire-watch. Mrs Hoare light-heartedly remarked: 'I don't think there will be any more air-raids.' And in my heart I agreed with her. But not a bit of it! Hitler has still got a sting in his Nasty Tail. At 4 a.m. we were amazed to be roused by a Warning. We all got up. In 20 minutes All Clear. Just as I had bedded down another went. I sat on the steps. It was just getting light. Mr Bendall reported to the Street Leader.

In the morning much discussion, for no one knew about Robot Planes. Cannot remember all the events of Thursday night. We had little sleep. I was in my flat – something trundled across the sky. In the morning nothing on the wireless, and we felt injured – as we needed the sympathy of our friends! On and off all day we had Warnings and gunfire. One Robot fell in Tooley St in the City. One of the women from our Printing Works rang up to say at Eltham they had had a terrible night – all her windows and doors blown out. It all pointed to Kent.

By Saturday we all felt very cheap. I longed to go and see the Invasion pictures, but did not feel equal to cope with queues – so went to a local Cinema and saw a little. All through we had across the screen – Air Raid Warning. Then All Clear. Three times. But the audience was in a light-hearted mood and laughed aloud. We had not learned then to take the Robots seriously . . .

Went to cheer up Auntie. She was not well and had slept little. She had heard something had fallen on St Mary Abbots Hospital. All night long they came. By dawn I could not believe it could continue. But it did. So got myself a cup of tea. Did jobs. Later felt sick from lack of sleep, and to the sound of the Brains Trust dozed off. Later went a walk. Felt better in the air. Every other person carrying a tin hat. Went along Marloes Road . . . great piles of glass marked the route. Heavy Rescue lorries were driving in and out gathering up the debris. All one roof of the Hospital gone . . . about 4 a.m. Saturday. One woman said twelve children were brought out dead. But I don't know, as my informant was too agitated to be coherent.

They may have to evacuate the Hospital. Many nurses killed. Heard another had fallen at Marble Arch, and in

Putney. As I walked back through the Park I pondered on these things, and decided to sleep tonight at the Sanctuary. London is in a chastened mood after the last three nights.

We have taken the Island of Elba, and are spinning up Italy. Last Thursday my bell rang, and it was my Scottish soldier, Jim Morrison. He had been ordered back from his Course, and was due for the Second Front. Gave him ginger wine, biscuits and a cigarette. He, as a seasoned soldier, thought he might be sent to some new invasion point. He did not mind . . . was not longing to go, but would see it through. I told him to come back and marry a nice Scottish lassie. A pity I did not take his Mother's address. She would have been glad to know I wished him god-speed. He promised to send me a card from France, and hoped to do the sights of Paris.

Kit called later. She could not get into the Proms, so drifted along to me. She hopes the Channel Islands will soon be free, and that her father will be with her.

I go on holiday to Chipping Campden next Saturday – if I can get there – Mother will join me. Have sent various parcels of food to the cottage in advance.

End of June 1944

JULY 1944

Sunday, 2nd The week before I went away I slept at the Sanctuary, and managed to get about five hours sleep every night. One can keep going on this. One night I was wakened by a light on my face, and thought it was the tail of the wretched thing overhead. But it was caught in the searchlights, and they travelled with it across the sky. To my fevered imagination, however, it seemed as if the thing was creeping up the front of the house, across the roof, and that it burst in the back garden. But in reality it was a mile away.

Monday, just as I had had lunch in the flat and was going to shop – a bumble sounded near. We all gathered in the front hall. Terrific explosion shook the house. We knew it was near – smoke and débris were rising. Obviously Church St. Feeling shaken I went out, saw police cars, ambulances and fire brigades tearing up Campden Hill Rd. All Notting Hill came out, and we thanked God we had escaped. It was on the bend of the Carmelite Church. Many killed and injured – any one of us might have been there. I go frequently.

A little cripple came to ask if we could send her away. A man had pushed her inside a public house as the bomb fell. She was only shaken but was unnerved. The authorities are on the spot so quickly, and the injured are attended to with amazing speed, everything cleared away, that one does not see the horrors. You only imagine it.

Went on like this all the week. We lost count of Warnings. However, we are so busy that we have little time to think about them. The papers call it the baby blitz. It is annoying to have it all the time. You just dodge out for a few minutes to shop. People are amazingly unconcerned – except the old. All the men think about is to get into the open and see one! But all London has slept dressed night after night. Tubes full to overflowing.

Did not buy my ticket to Chipping Campden in advance, as I thought I might not be here to need it! But we have all survived so far. War news is splendid. Americans on the point of taking Cherbourg. Others are rushing up the Italian Backbone.

Told my Poor People not to come while I am away if they can help it. But I expect there were emergencies. Saturday morning cleared my blankets at 6 a.m. and was nearing my door when the Sirens went. How long the road suddenly becomes! I could hear the bumble very near. I sprinted. It fell with a Bump at Shepherd's Bush. At 8 a.m. was ready. Looked round my little room, and hoped it would still be there when I returned.

Took a bottle of milk, some sandwiches and two hard-boiled eggs. How I came by these is not for the general public to know. Reached Paddington. Strolled about – a free woman for a whole week. Luxuriant thought! I cared not for bombs – I was on holiday. An enormous queue for S. Wales train, but my platform looked sparse. I was in front with hopes of a seat. My luck was out. First-class passengers only shouted a stern-looking official. By this time all seats gone. But I got a good corridor place by a window. When the train departed people were choking corridors and compartments as well.

Journey was delightful, notwithstanding that I stood all the way. A nice motherly old soul was next to me. On the other side a young married woman going to Hereford to see her husband on leave. Behind me an R.A.F. man. We all talked agreeably. Shared my milk and sandwiches with them, as they had further to go.

The little old soul was a fine character. She was 61, a cripple from the age of 3 to 16, being in one of Sir William Treloar's Homes. Result of a playground accident. She was taught a trade – a rare one for women – that of carpet making. It had been a great stand-by to her, and now she can make money renovating carpets. She works for all the big shops – they bring her the carpets, and she works in her garden. She married and has three fine children. Two boys in the Army. Her house is open to all soldiers and she writes 20 letters per week to Mothers. But she could not stand the Fly Bombs, and was going to friends.

Finally we drew into Campden. A complication – I could not get out of the train as it had over-run the platform. Looked a terrible jump to me. The Guard, however, was waiting to catch me, after I had struggled through the sitters and standers – the R.A.F. man following with my suitcase. Found the little bus, and very hungry arrived at Forge Cottage. Out of Bombs for a bit!

Very hot. Bernard Sleigh slung up the hammock. I dozed for a time. The bells chimed beautifully, and every time I opened my eyes I could see Campden Church Tower. We went to meet the family. They came in a hired car. An awful journey. Evesham bus full in Brum, and they had waited five hours for the next one! Cath brought her bike for me – hired a car at Bidford, picked Mother up at Evesham, and more dead than alive they were in Campden. Worn out – starving. Cath had to return at once. But we got tea, and soon restored Mother to herself.

Very pleasant week – though much rain. Lovely cycle rides. Italian prisoners interested me. They seemed very free – sounded Sicilian or Neapolitan from their accent.

Monday, 3rd Mother and I sauntered into a Sale in the garden of an old house. She adores a Sale. You note I frequently use the word saunter. Life in London is a breathless rush, so to move slowly and enjoy the movement is an enormous pleasure. We prowled round. Upstairs there were rolls of linen. Sheets! Having obtained a catalogue, we marked it. Unbleached – never mind. We sat around on various pieces of furniture, which were gradually sold beneath us. Prices horrified me. But the sun shone, and buyers were picnicking on the grass. We decided to bid up to £2 10s for the three old sheets. Blankets first. We ought to have been warned. Two fleecy blankets . . . they fetched £14 10s.

Then sheets. Many were patched. This made no difference. There was a mad desire to get them at any cost. A man was buying them all . . . said he could sell them easily. To

complete the story . . . those three patched unbleached sheets
. . . fetched £7 10s . . . But good luck had not deserted me, for
that very morning the dear Elsie wrote me that she would
spare me two . . .

Mother and I were sitting beneath a cherry tree eating
fruit, when a nice girl visitor asked us where we bought
them. We explained. She and her friend had missed the train
to Brum, and had sought in vain a cup of tea. It was 6 p.m.
and their spirits were low. I sympathized, and invited them
to the Cottage. As we were walking along two gentlemen
approached. Could hardly believe my eyes . . . one was my
History Professor, Sir Raymond Beazley. I spoke to him. He
knew me at once. He and Lady Beazley were staying near, and
I could see them.

Bernard Sleigh welcomed the girls, especially when they
betrayed an interest in Havelock Ellis, who is a friend of his
. . . All a great success . . . after tea and cake, and a booklet on
Havelock Ellis presented to them, they left over-joyed for the
train.

I had tea with the Beazleys at the house of Mrs Ralph
Heaton in Sheep St. All interested in my London life. Much
on the beloved Italy. Mrs Heaton's daughter is interned in
Germany. She is a sculptress, and was in France. Poor girl!
An intellectual treat was that Tea Party.

Cath arrived, having walked miles, as bus was full. She
dozed in the hammock. We bought strawberries, blackcurrants and red . . . believe it or not, poor sufferers in
wartime England. I brought some back to London, but had to
feed people with them on the journey, which was a difficult

one. Mother had gone back with Cath. At Oxford we all bundled out. A local train took us on to Didcot. Pouring with rain. Four deep on platform . . . waiting and waiting. An announcer indicated a train coming for Reading and London only. It had come from S. Wales and was already full. In fact in the corridor I could only stand on one foot – no room for the other! The door would not shut so one soldier had to get out . . . Arrived at last in London. Thankful! They could have left us at Didcot, and we could not have complained.

So I am back. Life is one long air-raid Alert, and things that go bump in the night. Not a whit better, really worse. Fetched my air-raid mattress – all the household is on the ground floor as in the Big Blitz. With the shutters closed we are as safe as it is possible to be, short of a direct hit. One listens fascinated to the Doodle Bugs passing over, holding one's breath, praying they will travel on, but feeling a wretched cad, because you know that means they will explode on someone else.

Our London Shelter in China Walk has had a bomb. The old place shook itself, and settled down again. But Mrs Johnson is not sleeping there.

Wednesday, 5th Florence has been declared an open city . . . and so is safe. Even the Germans could not murder anything so beautiful. Siena too . . . the French have entered in triumph. Warnings on and off these days. I am told City men undo the top button of their waistcoats when it goes, and button it upon the All Clear . . . thus they know what is going on. I have developed the floor technique. If you hug a pillow and let it take the weight of your body to some extent, you notice less the hardness of the floor.

One just before lunch. Saw our little yellow kitten listen intently as it neared us. Clutched him and prepared to dive under the desk. Great explosion – but it was a good way off. They aim at the workers – lunch time and going home, it seems. Again this evening in my flat heard the Thrum Thrum, pretty close. Saw it over Campden Hill – exploded near the Water Tower.

A Canadian soldier came to the office, had seen a bad one in Central London. [Plonk! one has just gone off now!] As he turned the corner it fell. He saw W.A.A.F.s working on a top floor who had foolishly put their heads out of the window, being drawn down by the blast. Bodies flew through the air and were killed on the pavement. Have heard from another lady in the same building. She ran for the stairs and was only shaken.

Very sorry for children who have to take exams in Air Raid Shelters, not able to concentrate after a bad night. Mr Churchill is to make a statement tomorrow. I feel Hitler, Goebbels and Goering are busily fitting incendiaries to the backs and fronts of the Next Lot – just to make it more difficult.

Thursday, 6th Real day of Summer – so less Doodle Bugs. Slept better. Mr Churchill says London is the chief target for the New Bombs. Interesting – for we did not know if we were the principal boy in this performance, or only one of the supporting characters . . . He tells us, as usual, the worst. We have to put up with them – until we have cleared the beasts from the French Coast. Casualties work out about 130 per day, killed more than wounded. This is high. It has been going on for three weeks.

Mother has taken in our old friend Mrs Harris. She was in Welwyn Garden City with her daughter, and could not stand them. Rene wired me, and of course, she is now in Brum.

Friday, 7th Today I really saw one. Walked to the flat as the Alert went. Half-way up heard a Thrum Thrum. A Platinum Blonde, the other side of the road lifted her head from reading a letter, and called out: 'Can you see it?' I replied 'no.' 'Come over here,' she shouted. And there, between the clouds, sure enough right over our heads, was a horrible black thing. It gave me a turn. The Platinum Blonde pursued her way, unmoved, still reading her letter. I regret to say I hastened my pace – though there is little likelihood, if it is directly above you, that it will fall on you. But it might have been rose petals for all the Platinum Blonde seemed to care!

Saturday, 8th A disturbed night. Turned in just before midnight. Dozing off when I heard two explosions. One Robot had dithered over this house for some time. I put my head beneath the nearest desk – and waited. It came. Terrific – as if in the back garden. House shook to its foundations – windows rattled in their sockets, but held. Got up, undid the shutters, found the yellow kitten asleep – but all intact. Slept little all night.

At 7.30 a.m. hastened up the road for a much-needed cup of tea, met a policeman – asked him about the All Clear. He had lost count. The robot was at Shepherd's Bush, next to the Pavilion, half a mile from us. Had a salad lunch with tomato. Managed to get half a pound – unique in the office. Felt addled from want of sleep, but determined to go out and see. Walked along Bayswater Road and saw the Coburg Court Hotel . . . it is still there, but all the rooms are scooped out – just like an egg when all the goodness has gone and the shell alone remains. Damage extends across the Park, where a little house belonging to one of the keepers is in a pitiable plight. Don't know when it happened. Went to Church St – all railed off at the bend and two policemen bar the way. Almost unrecognizable – every shop scooped out and blasted.

Turned along Gloucester Walk where they have had two. All that nice property uninhabitable. Desolation extends all round – windows gone. Returned sadly by Holland Walk, felt sleepy – so made myself comfortable on the divan, bound a scarf round my eyes and hoped my mind would let me sleep. It did.

Went round to Auntie Nell, who asked me to come with her to see Mrs South as she feared to go alone. We set off. Fancy! To walk from Kensington to Chelsea one has to think deeply in case one is killed en route. All passed off well. We took her some jam. She is 86 and scorns Fly Bombs.

The atmosphere of London has changed. Back into the feeling of the Big Blitz. Apprehension in the air. Buses half empty in the evening. Marked absence of people on the streets. Thousands have left, and many go early to the

Shelters. Children have been going in hundreds. Just one good piece of news – sausages are to have more sausage in them!

Sunday, 9th   Have come down to Sanctuary to write diary. Just heard fire engines pounding by. Perhaps it is not so bad as the Big Blitz, though it is nerve-racking to have it all day. But then the nights were wild with gunfire, and the great bombs came tearing and whistling down the sky, driving deep into the earth. These beastly things are only unpleasant if they explode near you. In the distance they don't sound much. Only you know some poor creature is beneath them ... everyone feels a prisoner in their own district.

But it is wonderful the way everyone carries on. Our milkman comes round as usual with his white pony. If he hears a bomb he looks round to see if it is in the direction of Wormwood Scrubs, where his family live; if it is not, then he tranquilly continues delivering milk. But it is no joke to be saddled with a horse and milk cart and Fly Bombs around. You can take shelter yourself, but you cannot take the horse in with you.

We have been helping one woman, dogged by ill-health all her life, who is trying to furnish a tiny room, as she cannot afford one already furnished. We had a marvellous response from our paper – both in money and kind. We send her out shopping – and she has been so happy about this. Has even forgotten Fly Bombs. She is not intimidated by Pontings or Barkers. She faced five distinguished gentlemen in the Carpet Department, who all rushed forward to serve her,

having no customers for their three hundred pound carpets
... Miss Fairman gazed at them and told them firmly she
could not afford large sums, but that she needed something
on her floor. Believe it or not, they produced a small piece of
lino, not new, which they let her have for five shillings. No one
else in all London can buy lino! When she has found a table
I have promised to have tea with her.

We are partly in Caen. Morning cold and wet – perfect day
for Doodle Bugs. Set off for the London Hospital to see
Auntie Mollie. Heard the unmistakable Thrum Thrum,
just as I reached cover. Two exploded while I was there, one
near enough to knock things off a bedside table. Auntie does
not worry, as she is on the ground floor and hopes to return to
Brede soon.

They gave out on the news about the Guards' Chapel.
Three weeks ago – that seems to be the system for announcing
places. A bad business. It fell at the Morning Service – a
Parade. About 150 people in the congregation and many
killed. Rumour has it that Princess Mary was there – she may
well have been as her son is in the Guards.

General de Gaulle is in Washington. How I hope he will be
a success with the President.

Monday, 10th Quiet night, felt refreshed in the morning.
But not quiet everywhere. Streatham, Thornton Heath and
Clapham are all in a more or less blitzed condition. Though
appreciably less Doodles are coming over. One did fall at
Shepherd's Bush on a mother and daughter known to us.
House caved in on them. They were taken to a Rest Centre,

and friends are allowing them to sleep on the floor. As yet not permitted to rescue any belongings.

Mother writes that thousands are arriving in Brum, from London. Arthur Bryant, spoke of the Invasion Plan. What Napoleon and Hitler had failed to do, we had done. He classed it as the greatest military operation ever undertaken. Not even a harbour on which to land the stuff! Well, when we are roused we can do things. Usually we are so infernally lazy.

Tuesday, 11th   More milk about now so many people have gone. Also cherries on view in the shops. Proms at the Albert Hall closed for the time being. Should not think Theatres are doing too well. A woman came over this morning with piles of children's clothing from Dalston – all washed. Most helpful.

Doodle Bugs have been falling all day. Notwithstanding I made an adventurous journey to S. Kensington to buy silks for a friend from the Royal School of Needlework. Weather grey and overcast. Mrs Hoare just returned from shopping, understood one had just fallen behind the Albert Hall. This was comforting! Rang the Needlework place, and they were still standing. Decided another was not likely to fall in the same place – so took Tube. But at South Kensington the Warning went. Many people looking apprehensive. Piles of glass being swept up. One seemed to have fallen near the steps of the Natural History Museum, which was cordoned off. V. and A. windows looked a mess. I hurried on. At the Royal School all windows out – and all goods put away. I congratulated the lady on being alive! She said a worse one had fallen at night on some service flats – plumb in the middle – and even the people in the basement were not dug out for days. A bad business.

She wished me a safe journey to Notting Hill, and I gave my hopes for her protection. Had to wait long at the station and saw the children's train. What a sight! Little boys and girls, Mothers and babies, gas masks, Teddy bears, dolls, queer parcels. All looked serious. They were off to a Main Line Station.

In the big shops like Harrods, Marshalls etc. they have roof spotters. When any Robot is heading in their direction a series of bells rings, and everyone – customers and staff – troop to the basement. Some shops have a flag, which goes on and off.

One waistcoat button man started off wrong – so his signal was reversed all day – so goes the story.

Wednesday, 12th The Food Office at Kensington has gone underground. It is a dangerous spot. Walked back – the big flats at Winchester Court seem shaved off. Mr Bendall brought back from the City – Tower Bridge – a piece of a bomb which fell near him. The Mother and daughter we help at Shepherd's Bush are to be sent away. They had a miraculous escape. The wardens shouted: Any help wanted? Mrs Thurston called back. The men had to lift the ceiling off Muriel's bed. Both were black from head to foot. A Spitfire was after this bomb, hit its tail, and the thing bounced round the Green.

Miss Ashton, one of our staff, was in a trolley bus when there was a shout: 'Get down all of you. Bomb falling.' Two buses full – everyone crouched beneath everyone else. It fell with a tremendous crash – their hearts stood still. Mercifully it was on an empty school.

The Golden Kitten is our local Fly Bomb. He rampages all over the office, upsets the wastepaper basket, and flings himself amongst the contents with Elizabethan abandon. Miss Moyes has ordered that he be brought up a strict vegetarian! Not in accordance with his ideas at all.

Now that people know the ropes a bit even the Open-Air theatre is picking up with audiences and struggling on. Notes of the last few days might be entitled – Reactions of a Timid Citizen to the Flying Bomb. But we are gathering courage. They are doing something to keep them away. The bombs are flying along a different track, which at the moment is not so near us.

Friday, 14th In Normandy they celebrated today the Fall of the Bastille in great style . . . so did General de Gaulle in Algiers. Roosevelt has accepted him. This time next year France will be free.

Another quiet night – shall risk going back to my own bed. Of course there have been terrible tragedies. A bomb fell on a queue of Mothers and children already bombed out, waiting to be served with clothing. Then a train packed with people had a narrow escape. The men stood with their backs to the windows to keep out the glass, while the women got as low as they could. On the platform everyone flung themselves down.

Some old folk should be put in the Eventide Homes we hear about. Two we deal with live in Public Shelters – they like them, the marshals are kind. I sent one a postcard and the warden delivered it to the old soul. This is Courtauld's Shelter near St Paul's. A popular one.

Sunday, 16th We think Hitler is considering something much more awful, which will break upon us at any moment.

Went to Radlett for week-end. They get plenty of Alerts, but the Spitfires leap into the sky and go haring after them trying to stop them arriving in London. I looked out during the night, but saw nothing. Fleets of bombers going to and fro filled the air with ear-shattering noise. It was nice to be in a comfortable bed, for a change, and not on the floor.

Lord Vansittart on Brains Trust about German democracy. He did not speak in a bitter way of the Germans, as I was led to believe. He pointed out that people can change e.g. Portuguese were once great explorers; the Swiss very warlike; so were the Vikings. But it took a long time. We do not want to wait too long until the Germans become pleasant neighbours. Joad behaved well. He knew he was with someone who knew more than himself.

Monday, 17th First night back in my flat and to my great indignation, at 5.15 a.m. the old wailer set up. How dare they? Found myself listening to the Thrum Thrum – Miss Lambart on the landing.

All horrified to read the Germans have bombed San Gemignano. All in spite. Heard the Service from Normandy with Monty reading the lesson and planes flying overhead.

Thus we sit at home and take part in a battle simultaneously. We are pegging on slowly – a case of biting off a morsel at a time. Russians are nearing borders of East Prussia.

Heard some of *Framley Parsonage*. Amazing how popular Trollope has become. It is because there was no income tax, no war, plenty of food and plenty of servants, in his novels! I love them and feel in another world.

Tuesday, 18th Slept soundly in my lowly bed – but there were explosions. It was a lively night from all accounts. One night I shall awake to find myself in the next world! One fell in De Vere Gardens. News does not pour in as in the Big Blitz days. Everyone keeps close to their own Rabbit Hole, ready to bolt down it immediately. I do not go out to see the damage, but try to snatch a little sleep after a bad night.

Had a bit of Camembert cheese today! Miss Jones' sister, a nurse, brought it back from France. Both historic and appetizing.

Wednesday, 19th Started at 1 a.m. and ceased neither by night nor by day! Woke wearily at 7.30 a.m. and trailed up the road. We lost count during the day. Mr Hillyard had one in the City. Various shops in Notting Hill are taking a prolonged holiday.

Auntie tried to cross the Park to Church on Sunday, but turned back on hearing a Warning. She hurried to the local Church only to find the vicar had ordered all the congregation to move under the galleries. How we adapt ourselves!

Thursday, 20th Night began badly. Composed my soul for the end twice! One barely scraped our roof – but everyone else thought the same. It fell at Shepherd's Bush. Could not find my torch – all the time the thing was coming nearer and nearer. Bumped my head in the dark. It is almost necessary to sleep with a torch in one's hand.

While Miss M. was dictating letters I made her move outside her room away from the glass. She stops up her ears, afraid of the blast sending her deaf.

An article on Count Ciano's diary. Evidently Edda has it, and has had copies made and sent to seven different places. She will publish later to vindicate her husband. It tells of Mussolini's paroxysms of rage . . .

Friday, 21st Far from good. Slept on and off for about five hours. Thuds on London all day. But at 8 a.m. the voice of the announcer was full of suppressed excitement, as he stated: the news is sensational. It was to the effect that some of the military chiefs had revolted against Hitler. The plot had been put down. Hitler had convinced the German people that he was alive by speaking to them round midnight.

All day we have waited for news. When men do such desperate deeds I can't think why they don't make sure they will succeed. Germany has cut herself off from Sweden and Switzerland.

People at Paddington and Kings Cross are having nerve-racking experiences waiting in queues. After an hour of standing there is the announcement: 'Take cover. Flying Bomb approaching.' What does one do? Stick it, or sacrifice that hard-won place in the queue!

Saturday, 22nd The Pig Breeder's son is fed up. He says Hounslow has had more than its share. They sleep in a surface shelter. He saw one the other night at tree-top height. Doubted it would clear the Shelter, but it glided on before the explosion. These bombs seem to make another war impossible. The finest Air Force in the world is no protection against them. By another 30 years they will have mastered the art of sending them to New York, and if we are too high-minded to use them we shall certainly be wiped out in a short space of time by enormous pantechnicons screaming through the air. It would be a matter of a week to wipe out London. The English will never be safe again. This will profoundly affect our lives after the war. Until this we did feel that behind a Cloud of Spitfires we could dwell serene. But this hope has gone.

I have not much further real hope for our poor old civilization. The brain of man has gone so far beyond his morals that the only thing to do is to scrap him and start again.

It is 11 p.m. as I write this. One has just passed over this house, much closer than I like. Been temporarily under the table. It has now dashed on to fall on some unfortunate folk.

Tuesday, 25th Not much authentic news from Germany. It would seem that Hitler will triumph over his Generals. But from neutral sources it is said they are not all caught – but are in communication with those of like mind on the Fighting Fronts. The Russians will go surging in on a thousand marching feet and give the Germans a taste of their own medicine. This is intended to sound vindictive. As the London taxi-driver said: 'Hitler should be killed by a Fly Bomb.' One rumour says the bomb blew off Hitler's trousers – a new pair had to be found to greet Mussolini! As Mr Churchill says – the Germans at this moment are killing one another. He has been to Normandy.

In the night a great explosion, caused by a Spitfire following it from goodness knows where, and exploding it over Hammersmith. The grandfather clock in this office never disturbs us in the day, but in the Dead of Night it is loud, and seems to give a terrible cough before it strikes midnight.

Don't like the sound of these rockets they are preparing for us. We are nearing Firenze – our soldiers are betting to be there before Saturday. I hope so. How thrilled they will be with those cobbled streets. Bernard Shaw is 88. I fear he is lingering too long. Why worry about money at his age? He cannot need it.

Saturday, 29th   A spot of excitement. No sooner had I reached my little flat than a Doodle came close in our direction. Roar grew louder. We sat on the stairs. It was losing height – but it passed over us. We took breath – heard the engine stop – and then the explosion. We understood it had cleared Campden Hill and dropped on that unfortunate Kensington High St. The next moment another came roaring over. Believe it or not – in the space of four minutes, four of those beastly things crossed our roof.

Had lunch and went out shopping, and to see where they had dropped. Milkman thought it was Phillimore Gardens. Later we heard opposite Pontings. They were commandering buses for ambulances. Then out came the truth – it was at the end of Holland Walk, had devastated Lyons Restaurant at corner of Earls Court Road . . . crowded with people for lunch. Went to look – shop unrecognizable. I make these full records, because people are undergoing a great test here. Some friends have just written me from the country that they had been rescued from the débris of their house in Westminster.

Crowds at Paddington today were the largest in living memory. They had to close it for 2 hours, and admit people in batches. Ban is lifted from Devon and Cornwall, and people are going there. I don't blame them. Just going to bed down. Trust to see the night through!

Smell of the lime trees in our drive is exquisite. Auntie Nell is convinced she will not live to see the end of the war. The end is hope deferred . . . we are always near, but it is not yet. [Note: She did not live to see the end.]

End of July Auntie has had a ring from East Ham Vicarage saying it has been blasted. They were all sleeping in the cellar. As the curate was in the drawing-room and they heard all the glass go, they rushed upstairs to see if he was alive . . . all this in the middle of the night.

The Americans have spied Pisa through their glasses. They are preparing a squad of engineers to straighten the Tower . . .

Listened to 'Country Magazine'. Discussion between Mr Street and another on the merits of scientific farming. He is all for science, and would not have a horse on his farm. The opponent drew a picture of the horrors of a scientific countryside – with no hedges, just charged wires. Spoke of Richard Jeffries who had described Clematis Lane and the wagons trudging along it . . . This would all be changed to a motor tractor wending its way between the aforesaid lines of wire . . .

The most exciting news is about the Italian Art Treasures. Major Eric Linklater entered a villa on a ridge a few miles from Florence to look at the city. He saw suddenly an Italian crucifix . . . gazing around, to his amazement he discovered Botticelli's *Primavera* stacked against the wall – also numerous pictures of Fra Lippo Lippi, Cimabuë . . . in fact all the treasures of the Uffizi! They had been sent out, it seems, padded with a few mattresses – a distracted Italian was trying to look after them. The Art Wardens of the United Nations were soon on the spot. Their breath was nearly taken away. This villa might easily have been bombed – no one was to know that all the Treasures of the Renaissance were inside. Until Florence is safe I doubt if these guardians will sleep at all.

End of July 1944

AUGUST 1944

※⇒⇒⇒ ❀ ⇐⇐⇐※

Tuesday, 1st There is to be a new system of Warning. The old wailer will still go on, but there is to be a Klaxon for imminent danger. Buses and trams must then stop and people can get off. We shall see how this will work.

I think the Russians will be in Warsaw before we are in Florence. The Germans are sheltering behind the glories of Pisa and Florence – just because they know we shall not shell them.

Wednesday, 2nd Fairly peaceful night, but did not sleep well. About 6.30 a.m. there was a terrific explosion – the house and windows shook from top to bottom. We have no idea where it fell – it must have glided a fair distance.

Mr Churchill's speech tonight as invigorating as usual. But he does not promise the Fly Bombs will stop until we capture all the sites. Nor does he say that we shall not have worse things over. It seems a race between our armies and the launching of the Horrible Things against us that will destroy whole districts.

A million people have left London. No wonder the trains have been crowded. I don't know how they have got them away. Certainly it is noticeable. We have plenty of milk now! Mr Churchill did not urge anyone to stay if they had not essential work to do. Unnecessary casualties are not wanted.

The Russians are nearing East Prussia. I feel that the moment the first Russian sets foot on East Prussia a thrill of horror will run through Germany.

Managed to get some kippers yesterday without queueing for them! This due to the million people leaving London. They have left a little fish for the rest of us. We are longing for some tomatoes. I have now gone on to Shredded Wheat and find it nice and refreshing.

Friday, 4th Just heard that those beasts of Germans have destroyed every bridge over the Arno in Florence, except the Ponte Vecchio – that after saying they would treat Florence as an open city. When I think of the Ponte Santa Trinità, which E. V. Lucas considered the loveliest span in the world, and that every bridge should be made like it so exquisite is its grace . . . Of course, if they leave the foundations I suppose they can build it up. Whereas if they had destroyed Ponte Vecchio no one would have known how the bricks went to make up those little shops. It is heartbreaking – and we do not know what else is in store.

We are all very tired as we get little sleep. Wednesday was a very sticky night. The air seemed full of horrors – they launched a record number, and there was damage everywhere. Last night the same. I began to doze off about midnight and then one of those wretched things approached . . . and so on.

Cooking my meal tonight between 6 p.m. and 6.30, there were six explosions – so someone was getting it. Whole evening a succession of Alerts. I have dozed a bit on my divan. News from Florence has depressed me.

The Channel Islands are to be evacuated, probably, by the Germans. Marvellous – and Kit must be in great spirits! The Americans are galloping on now they have cut out of the Cherbourg peninsula. But for us it looks rather a long way on the map before we can occupy those Launching Sites and give us some relief here.

People for Paddington trains have to queue in the street, but at Waterloo they managed to put them underground. Last week-end seemed to be the high water mark. One man at Waterloo was the amazement of all the railway world. He was queuing for the 5 p.m. train. They offered him to go on the one before – but he refused, saying that someone was meeting the 5 p.m. the other end, and on that he intended to travel. In vain did officials point out to him that he could wait at the other end. Not at all. Nothing would move him!

The police have raised the ban on our little Convalescent Home at Leigh-on-Sea. Miss Moyes is very pleased, and she has gone down to put it in order so that she can send people there. The trouble is the R.A.F. bring down lots of Doodles there and the noise of gunfire is terrific.

Saturday Bank Holiday, 5th A lovely day and I have got out a bit. Plums and apples have come to town. This is an event of great magnitude. I raised one pound in Notting Hill, and unable to resist I ate one apple in the street. Then I took a stroll along Church St and High St to get a clearer view of the damage. The weather was good and there seemed little likelihood of Doodles getting through.

Hornton St is a sight to see . . . an awful mess. Most of the houses looked deserted. As I neared the flat on my return I met Miss Brown. She had just returned from Portobello Market where she had found heaps of plums. So with another Old Dear we made a pleasant trip. Queued for twenty minutes and we got them. Two pounds of pink and two pounds of greengages. Also I bought a tiny rolling pin. It was the monstrous price of 2/6d. They were 6d before the war.

Went over to see Mrs King and Gretel, the harpist. They have a Morrison Shelter in the dining-room. It has a steel top. They feel safe inside it. Gretel is very like her father – reads the *Daily Worker*, and hates the financiers . . . But for the war she would have climbed high in her profession.

In the evening listened to Mr Shinwell, which I much enjoyed. Germans are withdrawing from Florence. Everyone terribly distressed about the Bridges. Just wanton destruction. The Rubaconte was the one Dante walked on. It is like crushing a beautiful flower to destroy Florence. Their guns, however, still command the City. The citizens will go mad if anything else happens. My part, where Poggio Imperiale School was, is on the South side, and on a hill. Perhaps people have taken refuge there. No mention of the Certosa and the monks there. They say no one dare show themselves on the streets, as it is certain death from German snipers.

A very quiet day and the armies are sweeping on. Praise be. Good night.

Bank Holiday Monday, 7th   A thunderstorm in the afternoon, accompanied by a collection of Doodles. In fact I did not know which was thunder and which Doodles! Had tea with Auntie Nell and we compared notes on the prospect of our outstaying the Doodles and their larger cousins which are due to come over. It is always best to envisage the worst, as Mr Churchill does. Then if it does not happen there is great relief.

Monday was lovely. Pleasant to be free all day. Went over to see the Ellis family in Wimbledon. Stood aghast at the station which has been practically destroyed. I learned later it happened at night when only a skeleton staff was there.

Doodles have fallen in a circle round the Ellis house. Window frames twisted and the house has been a mass of dirt and several ceilings have fallen – but they felt lucky it was not worse. Two friends, father and son, were with them. They had been completely bombed out. They all sleep in the re-inforced kitchen. Other people have been housed from time to time. There is much storing of mattresses and china that friends have salvaged from their wrecked property.

Glorious afternoon talking in the garden, which does Mr Ellis credit with apples, plums, raspberries, walnuts, pears and plenty of vegetables. I toured the bomb damage – really devastating, but remarkably little loss of life. But looking at the houses one could not believe anybody inside could have survived. But they did. They were under the stairs, or in shelters at the back, or Morrisons. All the schools in Wimbledon are closed. They held on for the children doing Matric – let them take exams in air-raid shelters, but the rest had to go. You could not cope with the situation, as the bombs fell day and night at all hours in such profusion.

Tuesday, 8th In Florence the Germans are sniping from the Tower of Palazzo Vecchio. From there they can cover the Boboli Gardens and the Piazzale Michelangelo. It seems they regret giving up Rome so easily, and are not going to do the same with Florence – art or no art.

The only amusing thing about it is that two sets of Florentines are fighting each other as soon as darkness sets in! One can see it – over the chimney pots and in the dark alleys in the good old Italian fashion, just as they did with rapiers and poisoned daggers in the Middle Ages. The modern Florentine expresses his feelings just the same. It is said they are bringing out old weapons put away for decades – probably from Garibaldi's time, and are getting at one another.

Anyway it seems not so easy to get the Germans out, and part of the city is short of water. People try to cross to the south. In this heat it must be awful without water.

One good story is that of an old cabby who tried to save his carrozza horse. The Germans have taken them nearly all. He struggled with it up the stairs, but it stuck half-way. The old man left it and it found its own way up! But now insists on looking out of the window. The Florentines are laughing as best they can at this story.

So sad about Warsaw. They are at their last gasp, and still the Russians do not come. The Poles always seem to start off on the wrong foot. We seem to be racing for Paris. Is it possible?

Friday, 11th Quiet night, but about 7 .30 a.m. a Doodle Bug hoovered our roof. It dropped I thought at Shepherd's Bush, because this house shook to its foundations. But they say it was Fulham.

Rumour hath it that the Germans have sent over some of their Super-bombs – but they have never arrived in London. Perhaps they hit Mars or Venus instead. I hope so. But the Swedes advise us not to under-rate what the Germans can do in this direction, for they can be fired from Belgium and even Germany.

It seems that Kesselring was over-ruled about Florence. He gave the Cardinal Archbishop of Florence a promise that the City would be unharmed. Owing to the Hitler Plot a rather more horrible Nazi is there now, and he gave the order about the Bridges. Their paratroopers are blowing up all sorts of things. Our boys can hear them.

Had to find lots of clothes this evening for one of our poor families who is being evacuated. They want to go into the country, but have no idea where until they are in the train.

Sunday, 13th Tried sleeping in my own bed last night for a change. I am tired of the office floor. A certain amount of activity . . . but I slept on until a quarter to ten – luxury indeed. A glorious sunset such as I have never seen in London last night. One of the Old Dears hiked me out and we climbed to the roof. Colours indescribably lovely.

Restful week-end. Read a biography of Dick Sheppard. I never heard him preach. Astounded he was so unhappy at school. But the most popular preacher in London could not keep his wife – she left him for someone else! Then the asthma – I am sure the doctors aggravated the disease with their drug treatment. They made him low in spirit.

Another book: *Missing Believed Prisoner*, is by a South African captured at Sidi Rezegh. Those awful marches through the desert with no food or water. The Camp with starvation rations. Then the Red Cross parcels and all they meant. I never realized it before.

Northern Florence is free, and the Food Relief people are rushing stores in by the tunnel which goes from the Uffizi to the Pitti. How often have I trudged that tunnel. It is dark and gloomy but strong. How thankful our men must have been to find it. When I used it I often thought how it could be of service in war . . . but I thought of small groups of men with swords! The Florentines rang the Great Bell from Palazzo Vecchio to let everyone know the Germans had gone! Fancy the old Vacca lowing again in a war. It seems the Partisans have been doing well. Disguised as Carabinieri they have kept up constant communication with the Southern bank – even having run a telephone across. Can't think how they did it. The population has been in cellars, of which there are plenty in Florence.

Mr Churchill is in Italy, and so is Tito. It looks as if they are going to have a front on Yugoslavia, and another in Southern France. Had tea with Auntie Nell, and we congratulated ourselves that we had survived another week. She goes to East Ham Vicarage to take charge. There she will sleep in the cellar with the rest of the household. On her return she is to make some Ginger Wine. I have given the sugar. We must have something for Victory.

Listened to *Berkeley Square*. Arresting play. One of those experiments in time that Priestley likes.

Monday, 14th Last night is what I call a dirty night. I was only awakened by explosions – some fairly near. Otherwise the News is of the best. Our Armies trying to trap the Germans, who are clever at getting out. The poor Poles in Warsaw. What an unlucky people they are. After struggling so hard, and then to get mown down. When the Russians are so near. We do not know the rights of it.

I see that Palazzo Pitti was used as a refuge by thousands of people during the siege. It is very strong. People camped out and put their pots and pans on the ducal tables. It would take a big bomb to penetrate that place. You can wade across the Arno at Ponte Santa Trinità – so why destroy the Bridge . . .

Wednesday, 16th Very busy. My Russian colleague away, and I have the responsibility of getting the Paper off, as well as keeping my own work going. The Printing Manager also away, and one staff. Poor Resti feared he would never get it printed for us to send off!

Fairly peaceful nights. Plenty of warnings today, but only one which made us all run for the stairs. It seemed very low, but it must have gone on a long way, for we did not hear it drop.

Just finishing Dick Sheppard's life. It seems he wrote to Hitler. Poor innocent! No reply. Then he thought he would tour foreign countries – Berlin, Budapest, Vienna etc. Nothing came of it. Could he not realize they would not have him! I am deeply sorry for his private sorrows. His indignation about St Paul's – the old Mausoleum on Ludgate Hill, as he called it – is illuminating.

Thursday, 17th Whatever took place in the night I knew nothing of it. I was too tired to bother. Lovely letter from Lucy. She has just got wind of the fact that Southern England is London. So she is anxious about Auntie Nell and me. Nice to receive such a sympathetic letter.

Doodles on and off all day. About 1.30 p.m. I heard one and urged Miss Ashton to defer going for lunch. We heard the explosion. They say it was Clapham and did much damage, falling on three buses full of people – but we are not sure. Someone who called at the office had to pass that way. She could not get through – but that was the rumour.

The news is tremendous. They can hear the Allied guns in Paris. Americans have taken Chartres, Dreux and Orléans, and knocked out 100,000 Germans. Whether they are prisoners, I don't know. In the south they are in possession of 500 square miles of France. Shall we be in Paris by next week . . . ?

I plan a visit to the Market on Saturday for plums. Got a few apples today. Also some teeny-weeny tomatoes. And one of the Old Dears brought me a pair of kippers. What a change they represent!

I gather Dick Sheppard was not entirely satisfied about Pacifism. Had he lived a few more years he would have changed his view like many of us! Like many popular men he was not happy. But he radiated love and kindliness and fun wherever he went. Sorry I never took the opportunity to hear him speak . . .

Sunday, 20th Splendid Doodle Bug day. It teemed with rain and there were a mass of Alerts. Kept hopping to the stairs with the other Old Dears. The things seemed to drop back and front of us. Once we saw the smoke arising from near the Albert Hall. Mr Bendall says that one fell in Hyde Park this morning. Had tea with Auntie Nell. She had been to St Peter's Church, which is quite near. The very near one made Auntie and many of the congregation get up in the middle of the sermon and retreat to the wall beneath the gallery. The preacher went on unmoved. Auntie cannot now tell Alerts from All Clears!

General de Gaulle has arrived in Cherbourg. What a day for him when he enters Paris in triumph! He has fought so valiantly and long. Frenchmen are proving themselves worthy of the name again. The Maquis have done better than anyone expected. The advance is colossal. The German Army in Normandy is Non-Est. The pocket is closed, and the remnants are fighting in a shambles – it is awful.

The Germans say we have crossed the Seine. Miles and miles of the South of France, quite undamaged, have fallen easily, and we are at the gates of Toulon and Marseilles – where the French inside are waiting to rise. Would you believe it!

We have dropped arms to the poor men in Warsaw, but I fear it has cost our men a lot – having to fly from Italy.

Cannot send my diary out to Lucy at the moment, as too many places are mentioned. Yet it is of no interest unless I do.

We are struggling to survive. Auntie has had a good week at East Ham Vicarage. They have real beds in the reinforced cellar, with sheets and pillows. Great luxury. She saw a Doodle over East Ham, but it went sailing on to Walthamstow.

We discussed the fate of civilization over tea, and were not too happy. These Robots have changed everything. The Germans can in the future, in complete secrecy under-ground, prepare in the years to come, more of such things, and launch them on an unprepared world. We shall be caught on the wrong foot again, given no time to recover, and then darkness will close down on us. I am sorry to be so gloomy, but really life is so different now that all earthly possessions seem to be of little importance. The treasures of the Past have been saved this time, but I feel it is the beginning of the Gotterdammerung. Man will perish under the machines that he has made.

I doubt if it will last my time and Cath's, unless something very different happens to the spirit of Europe in the next few years. Aren't we cheerful? We contrasted the joy of the Victorian era when men felt the world was getting better and better; it really seemed so.

Got the *Face Without a Frown* – Georgiana, Duchess of Devonshire by Iris Leveson Gower. This is the one with the magnificent hats. The author has made a splendid story out of it, though one would like to know much more. She was one of those charming good-natured people who come to a bad end through their own good qualities and trust in others. She had a good brain, and in modern times would have had a chance to use it. But in the 18th C. and born to great wealth she just wasted her time in aimless gambling and extravagant dress.

The luxury of life and the profusion of money is hard to imagine in these impecunious days. Hundreds of servants they had at every one of their big estates. It was like Cardinal Wolsey in his palmy days. Half the lackeys slept on a pallet under the stairs. But there was plenty of food, rough comfort and good comradeship among themselves.

Monday, 21st Today we nearly caught a Doodle Bug! It fell on the imitation Tudor Castle on Campden Hill. This afternoon at 3 p.m. I was busy sorting things for the Fair when a Doodle got nearer and nearer. The office was full of people and no one bothered. Having dived under desks so often and the Thing has been far away that I took no notice. Then I turned to run, but it dropped, and did the house shake and did we hear falling glass. Mercifully we were all right, but had behaved very foolishly. A bad cut from glass can be very nasty.

We ran in all directions to find out where it was. We mounted to the roof and just saw the smoke blowing away. Martin, Miss M.'s nephew, set off and brought back news it was Aubrey Road and Walk at the corner – Cressy House. Auntie Nell rang up at once as she realized it was near me. We also rang round. It gave us quite a turn. So I made some tea to settle us down.

Miss Ashton and I set forth on an expedition of enquiry. Most of the shops round Holland Park Tube station had lost their windows. We found the shell of the house. It used to have four towers. All that pretty property around is blasted. Mrs

Bennet, one of our voluntary workers, was in the baker's, and the owner dragged her to the back as the windows cracked right down.

I returned to my flat only to find I could not get in at the front door. The blast had blown off the lock. Two windows also gone. But my room was intact . . . the bomb had drawn the curtains right across. I gave a little prayer of thanksgiving that I had escaped again.

On Sunday Miss M. had a fearful journey back from Bath. They got in the wrong train and found themselves at Salisbury. There they discovered a train for Waterloo and leapt for it. An Alert was on in London. It was five minutes to midnight. The Tube was closed as it goes under the River, and always closes during raids. So by the light of one tiny torch the three of them struggled across Waterloo Bridge and down the Strand to Trafagar Square . . . only to find the tube closed for good. Miss M. was too tired to go further. So she and Mrs Hoare sat on the steps of St Martin in the Fields while Mr Bendall went in search of a taxi!

He wandered around for three-quarters of an hour. A man he met was directing lost soldiers to their hotels, and he was not very encouraging. However, he found one. The man demurred, as he had only enough petrol to get home. But with a heavy bribe he agreed to go as far as Holland Park. Were they tired! They had left in the morning at 8 a.m.

The bomb I said was in Hyde Park was at Queen's Way in Kensington Gardens. Lots have fallen in Regent's Park and hurt no one except once during the Open-Air Theatre performance. In Brixton there is so much damage that the authorities have told the people that if they have a kitchen just Call it Home, live in it – and be thankful!

Wednesday, 23rd It is a Great Day. Paris free again. I heard it first at 2 p.m., but on the 6 o'clock we were told with full ceremony. They played the Marseillaise. I stood to attention in my little room, and wept a few tears of thankfulness that France had been born again.

I am so glad they did it themselves. Now we await the great day when de Gaulle, the French, the British and the Americans all march in – and the nightmare of 1940 will be undone. What must Hitler be feeling!

To return to our unimportant little selves. Last night was bad. Warning at 4.30 a.m. . . . bomb approaching. It sounded menacing, so seizing my torch I crept under the desk. The engine shut off. I waited. With a devastating crash it came down and the house rocked to and fro. I got up, slipped on my coat. I feared for those at the top of the house, but could hear no cries for help. I undid the shutters to find the kitten. No sooner had I done this than another approached. Under the desk again. Believe it or not – six of them one after the other tore through the sky and crashed fairly near. But none so near as the first. The kitten was sitting bolt upright, every nerve extended. I comforted him. Then I heard Miss M.'s voice. I called upstairs. She was all right – but had been wakened by a blinding light in her room, through the black-out, and the Crash. However, it seemed we had escaped yet again.

It was in Portland Rd, just behind us, on a block of working-class flats. Most of the people were down the Tube –

and so there were only two deaths. Damage to property is awful. The blast extends for half a mile around. You lose your windows, if not your house. Hundreds are homeless as a result, because it is all such tiny property.

Today the sun is shining. We hope to have a less exciting night. I did not know last night if Auntie's flats had been hit – or if my own little place had gone.

Sunday, 27th What a week of happenings! But let us dispose of small things first. I slept in my own bed. A treat. We had had a good lull – and began to hope. But no such luck. Just before 7 a.m. a Jolly Old Doodle came singing towards us. We were all on the stairs as it burst. Smoke arising from Cressy Towers again. Then along came another. That fell in the Serpentine. After that I slept through sundry rumbles until 10 a.m. Blessed sleep!

Then had a rapturous day listening to all the great news coming through.

The Duchess of Gloucester has a little son. How glad she must be. I wonder if she will take the children to Australia.

A tin of mustard, I find, is over a shilling – just a moderate sized tin. Monstrous!

Saturday I turned on the French News, and the set nearly exploded all over the room with excitement. One French speaker after another shouting with joy at the tops of their voices.

General de Gaulle entered Paris at 7 p.m. on Friday. I had imagined him doing this on a white charger. But not at all. He is the head of the French Government and is to proclaim the

Fourth Republic. He is needed, so I suppose he leapt into a jeep and soon took charge.

Our Government on Friday announced that the ban was lifted from all the Coast towns – Imagine the British public getting this news for their breakfast! Everyone packed a bag at once, I believe, and made for the stations. It has been a mounted police week-end at Paddington – all in the sunshine. They would go – and again today. Victoria has been packed with people tearing down for a breath of sea air. And they deserve it.

I listened to the bulletin from Chartres Cathedral, where they were burying 30 men of the Maquis. Wonderful to hear the Service from that lovely place.

Went and had a Paris Tea with Auntie Nell and Mabel Lucy. We all wore our best frocks, and toasted General de Gaulle in ginger wine afterwards.

Yesterday was the real excitement in Paris. A Holiday and 200,000 people gathered in the Place de la Concorde. General de Gaulle re-lighted the flame over the Unknown Warrior. Then the German snipers left began to fire from the Hotel Crillon at the crowd. The B.B.C. man, Robert Dunnet, was there among them and recorded it all.

We could hear the chatter of the people, the rattle of the tank fire, and Dunnet, nearly incoherent with excitement, trying to find out what was happening and describe it to us. It was thrilling. People crawled for shelter under the tanks that were firing up to the hotel! Dunnet got behind his recording car for safety, but the crowd did not break and fly. Some Red Cross people got on a balustrade and kept order, and moved the people away. A great hole was made in the Hotel Crillon as the car was taking records. You could hear the gendarmes speak, and Dunnet break into a little French, and an English girl beside him helping him to describe the scene.

This was exciting enough. But there was more to come.

We were switched over to Notre Dame where de Gaulle was to come for the Te Deum. Masses of people were in the Square and the Cathedral. He arrived – firing broke out. We could hear it. Then just as the man was saying that de Gaulle was on the steps of Notre Dame the thing snapped off! What happened was that with the firing a surge of people broke upon the announcer, split the cable, and he was hurled to the ground. He just picked himself up in time to see the General go in. Firing then broke out there. But he never hesitated for a moment. Amid a hail of bullets de Gaulle walked the length of Notre Dame.

The announcer said it was the bravest thing he had ever seen. Throughout the Service the firing continued. Women sheltered behind pillars, under seats – but the Mass continued with the General standing and the Maquis trying to find the sniper in the galleries. Then he walked again down the aisle amid a second rain of bullets. But not one touched him. What a scene! One priest was screening a child. Masonry was hurled about – but the French did not move.

Monday, 28th   On all fronts we are sweeping on – but I expect soon we shall have to go slow a bit. It cannot all be jam.

Plenty of Doodles all day. We can dimly hear the Klaxon. It is supposed to go Three for Danger, and One for All Clear.

But I cannot say I have grasped it. Mr Hillyard says no one in the City seems to take any notice of it, and unless a Doodle is actually flying into your face you do nothing about it! Aren't we getting tough!

Have been trying to help one old woman with her room. She has but one, which was blasted, and the ceiling is partly down, and she fears the man above may descend on her with all his belongings. So she sleeps in the Shelter, and only cooks her meals in the room, with one eye, so to speak – on the above. The landlords have so much to do they cannot cope with everyone. I am to have a word with the surveyor and hear definitely from him whether the room is safe or not. No one takes any notice of the old woman's complaints, and it is only because I state very firmly that I am speaking for a philanthropic society, and threaten to ring up the Council, that we can get anything done. We pay the old woman's rent – but are withholding it for the time being.

Wednesday, 30th   Great pleasure of a visit from Kit. She rang up to say she was dining with her distinguished cousin, but would like to see me and rest a bit in the flat. She has been approached by the B.B.C. to be one of Six to broadcast to the Channel Islands as soon as they are free. It is a great honour. She is allowed 100 words. She has sent it to them and awaits instructions. I should love to hear it – she will let me know the time, if possible. The Channel Islanders are hanging on to the wireless every hour, hoping for news of the German evacuation.

The Golden Pussy Cat, known for short as Little Doodle,

does a blitzkrieg all over the office. He and Mr Hillyard ended up with overturning a vase of flowers with all the water on to his papers. All hands to the rescue in mopping up. But Little Doodle thought this was all part of the game, and had to be forcibly removed to the other office. He is very popular with everyone, as you can see.

Thursday, 31st Went along to Kensington Food office today, and with a Warning on, such a small journey takes on something of an adventure, as the Food Office is in such a hot spot. It is all in a Shelter. The Warden on duty and everyone listening. I could hear nothing, so returned on the bus. All Clear went as I reached Notting Hill.

London has a glut of coal at the moment. This is due to the million people who have left London, and also to the fact that the thousands who have been blitzed have nowhere to store coal. So people like us have our deliveries easily. It is the same with the milk. At the moment there is plenty.

I had occasion to go to the dentist. The Chair is in front of a huge window. As soon as the Alert goes he puts up a portable shutter and all goes well. Otherwise it would be too nerve-racking to be drilling a tooth with a Doodle Doodling overhead, and liable to drop. This happened while I was there.

Kit's sister lives at Epsom Downs. There they bring down 50 Doodles in an hour! Just imagine if the whole 7,000 sent had reached London! It would have been flat and no mistake.

End of August 1944

SEPTEMBER 1944

»»»» ❋ ««««

Friday, 1st Marvellously quiet day and night. Our capture of the Fly Bomb coast is telling immediately. Tonight the Canadians are in Dieppe.

The plan to bring the Sanctuary kitten up as a vegetarian is failing dismally. I brought in Mr Hillyard's ration, and the Little Doodle came bounding into the office, and never rested until he had located it. I hurried upstairs to the Fridge. Anyway Mr H. gave him a bit, and did he enjoy his little self!

Sunday, 3rd The end of five years of war!

How well I remember that first Sunday. I was living in Kensington Park Road in a lovely big room. Saturday I had been called to the First Aid Post, and spent the night there. We expected air raids any moment. There was a terrible thunderstorm. I returned to my room at 7 a.m., worn out and tumbled into bed. At 11 a.m. I was awakened by the first siren. I jumped out of bed, expecting to see the sky filled with German aeroplanes and bombs dropping fast upon us. That was to be – but not yet.

It is all incredible and unbelievable. Here we are with the end in sight – and we are intact. The silence at the moment is uncanny. After listening to sirens on and off all day and all night for ten weeks, it seems strange without them. Have we finished with them?

Have had some good eats this week. Our house agent is letting us buy tomatoes. Mr H. had some nuts – pecoes – sent him from Washington, and he gave me a lot.

Received a p.c. from Mrs Ellis in Wimbledon. They were bombed out of their house last Monday. Just escaped with their lives. How thankful I am! I have spent such happy times in that house. I was there August Monday and we all felt this might happen. The Bombs had been so close, and like murderers, tend to return to the scene of the crime.

To hear the words Battle of Germany beginning. What a thrill!

We have all got friendly in my Flat residence due to the Fly Bombs. The Old Dears have lost their pernickity ways, and as we sat on the stairs, not knowing whether the bomb was going to drop on us, we became very much a band of brothers.

The peace of these last few days passes belief. I have been out twice today, and never had to listen for danger. Went with Auntie Nell to Church. Along the Flowery Walk we passed the time of day with a lovely tabby cat. Roses were all out. The Church was full of uniforms . . . W.R.N.S.; A.T.S. and officers. The preacher was the Rev Naylor, Assistant Chaplain General to the Forces. He made us laugh. The story was as follows: A man on Tower Hill addressing the crowd in religious terms, was heckled by a grimy looking man, who called out: 'We have had Christianity for 2,000 years, and look what a mess the world is in!' The preacher replied: 'Yes, and we have had water for two million years, and look at your face.'

Mr Morrison's speech at Manchester was good. He insisted on giving the poor old British a bit of praise.

Friday, 8th   A whole week I have slept in my own bed. Said Good-bye to the Office Floor and thanked it for its kindly treatment of me during the past ten weeks.

Tonight, however, at a quarter to seven, a Terrific Explosion rent the air, followed by a low rumble. I nearly leapt out of my skin. No Warning on. So it could not be the new secret weapon. Perhaps it was an explosion at a munitions factory, or a bomb of long delayed action. All the Old Dears much upset . . .

Victories every moment! Brussels and Antwerp on Monday. This time the poor old British got there first. To hear the Highland Pipers over the radio, in St Valery, was cracking.

Everyone now knows our sufferings over the Fly Bombs, and we have received praise and commendation, which has given us much satisfaction. I tell Barishnikov he does not play fair. He takes credit for all the Russian victories, and now for being a Londoner. He just lives in a halo of glory from dawn to dusk.

We are pleased the Queen Mother of Belgium defied the Germans and locked herself in, refusing to go to Germany. There was a picture of her and her servants doling out wine and sandwiches to the British boys.

The second story told by the preacher last Sunday was as follows: A soldier in the Desert approached a Padre and asked him to say a Burial Service over his chum, Joe. 'Where is he?' asked the padre. 'In the truck. I have brought him from . . . I could not leave him without a Christian burial,' replied the soldier. The padre looked in the truck. 'I can't see him,' he remarked. 'Oh,' was the reply. 'He's been sitting beside me. I kept him near me until I could bury him properly. He was a real chum.'

Mercifully Auntie Mollie left the London Hospital some time ago. For a Fly Bomb fell on the Cambridge Ward where she was. It killed two patients, and injured some nurses.

Monday, 11th Wonderful week of freedom. It is like being released from prison. We have wallowed in our liberty of movement. Full account of it all has just been published. Wonderful the care and foresight shown by the authorities. Long hours of watching and hard work that has been put in – not to mention lives lost. The poor pilots – bombing the Pas de Calais again and again.

Went to the Cinema. Enjoyed *The Four Feathers* with Ralph Richardson. Also the News with pictures of the Germans being marched through Moscow. The expression on the faces of the Generals as the population glared at them . . .

Auntie Nell and I took the bus to see Mrs South. Church St is at last open to traffic. They must have shored up the buildings. Pathetic to see. Mrs South far from well. Later took a walk near Holland House. One can get a view of it now, for the Fly Bomb destroyed the hall. Trees are all blasted. The ghosts of Charles James Fox and Lord Macaulay have possibly been around to look at it.

Good news goes on. We have liberated Luxembourg and sang the National Anthem of our smallest Ally!

Wednesday, 13th We have heard a lot about the big explosion heard all over London on Friday night. There is nothing about it in the papers . . . word is just going round. But we fear it is the V2 which has arrived. On Tuesday morning about 6.15 a.m. all London was aroused from peaceful slumber by a further terrific explosion, bigger than the last, in that the murderous rumbles went on after the explosion.

I had been fast asleep. There was no Warning. I felt sure it was no Gas Works exploding, as we thought when we heard it on Friday. It was something the Germans were sending over! It is the great topic of conversation as soon as people meet. But neither radio nor newspapers speak. But we feel if many more come the truth must be told. Rumour says this last fell on a motor factory near Kew. Many were killed. It is all hush-hush. They seem to be Rockets which drop from the stratosphere. You may be out peaceably walking and one drops. Nice prospect!

I was dreaming of robots last night. Dozens of us in a room – all with a Fly Bomb attached to our shoulders waiting for them to go off!

Kit has recorded her Channel Islands broadcast. A nice young man took charge. He watched from a glass window and counted the time. How thrilled her father will be!

Tuesday, 26th I have been to Brum for a week. But to return to Friday, Sept 15th. At 4.15 a.m. another mysterious terrific explosion. It quite unnerved me, and I could not sleep again. We gather it had fallen at Staines – or in that direction. The

Pig Breeder had felt it badly at Hounslow. All Londoners were looking at one another as if they had a disgraceful secret to hush up. We all have a covert look – a dreadful secret – a skeleton in the cupboard.

Saturday I set off for Paddington at 8.15 a.m. Had to queue a long way round. Just as we were half-way another huge explosion rent the air. We, waiting, looked at one another – another!

Got a seat and was only an hour late. They have been doing some painting and distempering at home. There are no workmen, so you just do what you can yourself. A programme was arranged for me of taking down the Blackout, mending cushion covers, sheets and towels. You can buy none of these things, so I interspersed such good work with seeing a few friends.

The sun shone, and the garden looked very nice. They do not expect any more raids. There are lights on the Hagley Road. After five solid years of blackness what a joy to move without a torch. The spiders have been having a lovely time, and are rather sorry the war is nearing a close.

Had tea on Tuesday with Elsie and Neville, and he told me as much as was allowable about the super supers on London. I was comforted to learn that the Government do know where they are coming from. They are said to be fifty feet long and five feet wide. Like an enormous Pencil . . .

All the week the liberation of Holland has been going on, but it has not been so easy as Belgium. Our airborne men are in a tight corner.

Returned to London – mobs of people – but got a corner seat!

End of September 1944

OCTOBER 1944

❦ ❦ ❦

Sunday, 1st Very dark in London when I arrived back. I had to follow other people's torches, as my hands were full. Just as I reached my door and was fumbling for the key that Wretched Siren went and a Doodle came racing along. I got to my room – but quickly made for the stairs. We all thought we were for it. But No – it travelled on. What a welcome back!

Busy week – all my poor people trooped in in large numbers. Went to see Auntie. She looked very washed out. It is still very dark in the streets here.

We have had a bit of a jolt this week in that our Airborne Army has had to retreat from Arnhem with losses of so many splendid men.

Have had good luck with a Library book. Managed to get *Where Love and Friendship Meet* by Mrs Belloc Lowndes. It is the later story of the Belloc family, and presents the French in a most attractive light.

Monday, 2nd Had tea with Mary Bewley in a nice top flat in Queen's Gardens off Leinster Terrace. She told me the story of a friend who was at a Lord's Cricket Match when over came a Fly Bomb. All the players flattened themselves out and expected the worst. The thing after circling round came to earth in Regent's Park.

Went on to see Dr Remy. We talked of Carola and their honeymoon. How she had danced at her wedding reception. I must tell her when I see her after the war is over how I enjoyed hearing about it. We decided that a lot of money is not essential to the enjoyment of life; but that friendship and goodwill are.

We have had Churchill's speech to cogitate over. He is not sure the war is not going into 1945. He bucks up the French and the Italians. He resents any comparison between Hitler and Napoleon. As usual full of good sense.

It seems that one of our Fortresses with a full load of bombs, instead of dropping in the North Sea as it should have done after the crew had baled out, went gallivanting all over England, including the Midlands and right to Liverpool. All the sirens went – sirens they thought would never be used again! Fighter pilots dashed into the sky after it, but after circling over the city, it headed for the Atlantic – where presumably it fell. What a mercy!

We are in the Sixth Winter of this wretched war. Would you believe it!

Sunday, 8th   Still a few Doodles about. Thursday evening, just as I was passing the police station, the siren wailed out. So I made a hop, skip and a jump down the road, and got in just before the creature came over. They say the Germans are dissatisfied with the New Super Rockets. They are not sufficiently terrifying. You are dead before you know anything about it. Whereas Doodles are bad for morale. You can hear them coming . . . So now they intend to try something else. So there will be no peace for London and the South until the Germans are totally defeated . . . and that will not be this side Xmas. Poor Dutch!

Death of Wendell Wilkie. Rather unexpected, but I do not think he would have been much our friend. He was brilliant; but those whirlwind tours of his served no purpose but to expose his own ignorance.

Dare not take down Black-out here. They say London is blacker than ever. Lovely week-end with Kit. Reached Watford about 1.30. She had a sumptuous repast for me. I dozed in front of her fire. She is passionately interested in Polar exploration, and had a book on Dr Wilson. I skimmed through. There were nice allusions to Uncle Tom. He says Captain Scott was quick-tempered.

We cycled over to Radlett as the morning was nice and bright. About six miles – a glorious run. I do love cycling. It is the nicest mode of progression, except a horse. Anne and her friend made us welcome. Came back through a glorious park. Near the exit, however, there was a notice: If you see the red flag do not advance beyond this point. No prams and no bicycles. A good thing Kit did not know about this, or we should never have ventured. Lovely walk with coal-black cows, undulating parkland and a glorious stone house.

Sunday, 15th Kit had a Quince Tree, laden with fruit. We gathered some. Very rare in England. We put one in an apple tart – should not want too much of it. I told the Old Pole about it – he was much interested.

No bombs much. They say they are mostly in North London which is having a bad time. We have alerts, but are thankful for the general slackening off.

Mr Churchill in Moscow. He is a one. He is having a great round with Stalin, and is trying to do something for the Poles. The banquets they are having are terrific . . . sit for five hours! They all went to the Ballet and the whole house cheered them.

It is Autumn and the leaves are turning. Terrific gale during the week which tore the leaves off here.

Discussion the other night between Lord Vansittart and Barbara Ward, and others, on Germany. He agreed with the Belgian Prime Minister that Germany produced Hitler, not Hitler Germany. Hitler was just an expression of the country. The others tried to bring in German Liberals – and said it was difficult to fight machine guns. Vansittart said there were no machine guns in 1914. Somehow I agree with him. Though in Napoleonic times the Germans were regarded as a pacific people, while the French were the war-mongers. Anyway it is the Germans we have to deal with.

I have felt for some time that after three months and more of Fly Bombs, I wanted some new experience of an exciting nature. So I fixed with a friend, who seems to know every hotel there is, to go to the Dorchester for tea. We knew we could not afford a dinner. I have so often longed to enter the best hotel in London. So garbed in my best, I stepped forth. We turned first into the Grosvenor, but it said 6/6d, which we thought beyond us a bit. And we did not want to dance. So we entered a great soft carpeted lounge in the Dorchester, and sank down into some nice armchairs in an alcove.

A distinguished looking waiter asked us if we wanted tea – in which case we must wait until 4 p.m.

We smoked and looked round. A few people drifted in. A naval officer had drink after drink, and seemed worried. The little page boy in buttons came hurrying in with a message. Perhaps he had been let down.

At 4 p.m. a very inferior tea was served to us. Sandwiches, thin and beautifully cut, but the insides had no flavour of any kind at all. I think it was just soya bean. Waiter then appeared with a tray full of cakes and pastry – we were allowed two. They were awful. The cups were plain white – I expect all their own were broken. The lounge filled. Several officers. One private. Finally a society beauty swept in. She was in black, with feathers in her hat. Seeing no corner seat she flowed back to the centre of the room, nearly knocking a man over. They sat down and soon were both absorbed in newspapers. Obviously a husband and wife.

At a quarter to five we asked for our bill, and felt lucky to get out at 4/6d each, for a tea the like of which I should have been ashamed to serve in my flat. But I had had tea at the Dorchester, and that is another ambition satisfied.

Had a lovely stroll back through the Park, as I considered we could not afford the bus. I prepared a very nice dinner . . . chops, potatoes and tomatoes. For cocktails – Auntie's own ginger wine. For sherry – Government lemon squash, and for port – more ginger wine. All much better than the Dorchester would have provided!

Glorious to think that Athens is free. The wireless nearly burst itself this afternoon quoting all the ancient Greeks on Hellas.

Sunday, 22nd Rocket Bombs have certainly fallen on some-where this week. The other night at 11 p.m. just as I had left the Sanctuary, I had a strong feeling that one was on its way. So keen was the impression that I hugged the wall all the way and thought to myself – Well, I can't do anything except go on. So I went on. Just by the police station a blinding light filled the sky – like for a flashlight photo. I was blinded by it . . . 50 seconds later I heard the explosion. But it was at least ten miles away. What it must have been for the poor souls near it, I dare not think.

Lovely parcel from Lucy. A tin of tongue, which I am putting by for our Victory supper. Auntie Mollie has given me a nice velvet frock, scarcely worn. Very kind for the price of clothes is preposterous. They ask £14 for the most ordinary-looking garments.

Monday, 30th Rockets are increasing in number. From hearing one or two per week, we now hear several in a day – and there are all those we do not hear. Very unpleasant. Still nothing is said in the newspapers about them. Up and down the country no one knows except a few people. They are obviously getting the range of London better. Grrrrr!

A Fish and Chip shop has opened in Notting Hill. A great boon to lonely bachelors like myself. I have informed all the others.

Lots of entertaining for me this week-end. Marie came. I had changed into my elegant Rest Gown, which is most useful. Then Kit came bringing extras for the supper party. For I was to entertain her distinguished cousin, Major

Gallienne, who was coming to my humble flat straight from the War Office.

I do not entertain members of the Secret Service every day, so I was a bit nervous. But all went well. Kit brought chops and greens. I made pastry. Aunt Winnie had sent some small apples, but I cooked them – peel and core. Then tore them limb from limb. We made custard. Major Gallienne came punctually. He is twenty-nine and is, of course, a Channel Islander. After the meal embellished with Auntie's ginger wine and the Government's lemon squash, we sat around the fire and talked.

We got round to religion. We found ourselves in the presence of a young man who has thrown overboard organized religion, even to the extent of any idea of a future life. Kit and I gave him a run for his money. I made tea, and showed them Bernard Sleigh's piece of linen showing his Map of Fairyland.

At 11.15 our visitor thought he had better go, and though we were all enjoying the talk very much, I thought so too. I did not want a series of notes from the Old Dears about my late nights. So with whispered instructions to them both to creep down the stairs, and not breathe, I said Good-bye.

Kit returned and we soon bedded down – leaving the place rather like a bomb site. In the afternoon came Barishnikov with his daughter Alexandra. She is very Russian-looking. I liked her. He has lent me a book called *I Married a Russian*.

End of October 1944

NOVEMBER 1944

❈

Monday, 6th Poor Holland . . . we are pegging away at it. Slept very badly. At 3 a.m. a fearsome report. Lay waiting for the next Gas Main to drop – that seems to be the name for them. I dozed off – and then came another. At 8 a.m. felt cheap and made some tea. Then a Doodle came along. We did have a dose.

I developed a terrible stiff neck, so had to wrap myself up, close the window and sleep it off – Gas Mains or no. Heard later one fell at Ealing – it exploded in the air and ended on a Recreation Ground. But another at Wapping did a lot of damage. The Doodle fell on a Residential hotel at Purley.

There has been a lovely moon. I should like to see the Abbey and St Paul's so, with clouds racing overhead.

Saturday went to the Ballet – *Les Sylphides*. Had seen it years ago at the Coliseum with the Russian Ballet. The next was a new one – *Miracle in the Gorbals*. This is a Glasgow slum. Did not care for it much. Then *The Quest* – part of Spenser's *Faerie Queen*. St George, Una and the Saracens etc. Also the House of Pride and the Seven Deadly Sins. Splendid.

Behind me was an artistic egoist with lots of hair. He had three ladies with him. During the interval he informed them that in England he understood there were three million surplus women. He was corrected to one million. However, he persisted, adding, 'It will teach you to appreciate us the more!' The elder lady thought for a second, and then remarked in some wonderment – 'The thing is – what is there to appreciate?' A good answer.

Went to see poor Auntie Mollie in the London Hospital. Her leg is not making progress. She is depressed. Petticoat Lane was doing a roaring trade as I passed.

Thursday, 16th What a wonderful time Churchill has had in Paris. Apparently the French admire us very much. That is a great tribute because they are the most critical of people.

Walcheren Island has been captured, and the Rockets seem to be less, but on the days before we had lots. They were using them up! Now we hear they are coming from The Hague, and Resti says from the Harz mountains.

On Sunday morning going to see Auntie I found Petticoat Lane barricaded off. One had dropped on Friday, early afternoon, and had done horrific work. Auntie Nell on the same errand had missed it by a shade – just a few moments. When she reached the London Hospital they were taking in the casualties. Auntie Mollie looked very poorly.

I Married a Russian has charmed us all. An educated English girl fell in love with a Russian scientist at Cambridge, Cavendish Lab. She married him and arrived in time to enjoy the First Five Year Plan! How they suffered from cold, hunger, bugs and lack of every comfort! She wrote these letters home to her sister. Things got better. She escaped from Kharkov as the Germans entered. In a few minutes you learn more about Soviet Russia than in years of newspaper articles.

It is very cold. The Little Doodle is the pin-up boy of the office. He has a piece of fur he imagines is a mouse, and chases it all over the desks. We are frightfully busy for the Christmas Fair.

Sunday, 26th Thank heaven the Fair is over for another year! Total £1,400. It is miraculous. On my Rubbish Heap, the Caledonian Market, I took £105. And not a thing on it worth sixpence, as Barishnikov announced.

I had been given a moth-eaten stag's head, with broken antlers. Everyone laughed, and said I should never sell it. So I put it on the Stall as a mascot. Mr Hillyard screwed up some of the insecure parts. At 3 p.m. there strode through the hall a young R.A.F. soldier. He walked straight up to my mascot, put his arms round it, and said with rapture: 'Oh, I like that. How much do you want for it?' I could not believe my own ears! He informed me engagingly that he was going to be married, and wanted to furnish the flat. And so he buys the most useless thing he could have! I laughed much. So I priced it at 2/6d . . . Marvellous! Then I fetched from behind the stall two ancient Victorian pictures in good frames. 'Luvly' pronounced the young man and his damsel. I then bethought myself of a bombed out dressing mirror, the shelf for which remained. The young soldier's face shone with delight. He was handy, and he could use it. So for ten shillings away they went in triumph. I verily believe they considered the flat half furnished.

The other incident was a sad one. Miss Cameron suddenly appeared at 1 p.m. on the Saturday, looking white and shattered. She sank into a chair. A Rocket Bomb had dropped in Holborn, and the casualties were terrible. She was blown over and spent several unconscious minutes. I rushed to our First Aid cupboard and measured out a little precious brandy; then others fetched her cups of tea. Miss Moyes remarked that but for the Grace of God, it might have fallen on 3, Lansdowne Road, and all our Christmas Fair customers. We put her to bed. This is the second time Miss Cameron has been in the street and seen horrors. You cannot take shelter from a Rocket.

End of November 1944

DECEMBER 1944

⟫⟫⟫ ✳ ⟪⟪⟪

Monday, 4th One Friday morning a Rocket fell at Eltham. A woman in our Printing works had arrived when the phone rang for her to return home at once. She rushed back. Her home was in ruins, but her mother had survived. And so we go on. Rockets fall on the Just and Unjust impartially. We get little news, but many are dropping in the country around.

Very busy week sorting clothes for people, some of them evacuated. I am glad to help them – but one does get tired of the sight of old clothes! Saturday I got real depressed – I had not had a week-end to myself for three weeks. So I ate a meagre lunch, had a snooze, a bath, changed every stitch I had on, put on my best bonnet and shawl and went out. Saw Mabel Lucy and explained how thankful I was to get a change of society.

My Swiss colleague came to supper. It makes a mess of my meat ration, but he does enjoy it so much. He stole downstairs at 11 p.m. But now the Old Dears know me, I do not worry.

Went to the Hospital. Found Petticoat Lane had partly re-opened. Great crowd round someone selling hot chestnuts. How the soldiers love this Market! Auntie was better but still in some pain.

Mr Churchill was 70 the other day, so everyone has been telling him he can have an extra ounce of tea! His daughters were with him for breakfast.

A grand show with the Home Guard. I heard the King in the evening. Also Princess Elizabeth launching the ship.

Thursday, 7th A few Incidents! One Rocket the other night fell straight into the Thames. It just missed Waterloo Bridge and the Strand. What a Splash! One does not like to think what would have happened if it had touched the Underground which goes near there.

My Red Indian Chief friend has been heard of. He was at Lily Dale Camp.

A notice about the spread of dry rot in London. Due to lack of paint and years of bombing.

Went down to Kensington food office. Lots of old folk signing on for their extra ounce of tea. It makes a lot of difference. Officials were very patient with their slowness.

A Hansom Cab is seen periodically doing duty round here. I gaze at it with great satisfaction. I never rode in one. They had just gone out when I had money to do such things. We also have two taxis . . .

Thursday, 14th I am losing count of the bombs. I don't see how we shall escape. Tuesday night at nearly eleven, I was clearing up the letters, when a Terrific Explosion rent the air. I can only remember clinging to the person next to me, and being semi-conscious for seconds. Windows seemed to bulge in – whole house shook from stem to stern. It was close.

Mr Hillyard and Mr Bendall rushed out as soon as anyone could move. They could hear falling masonry and there was a strong smell of sulphur. We learned it was the end of Lancaster Road. Streets full of people. Poor old women with hair down their backs and scarcely anything on . . . Old men looking shaken and worried. Two of our friends held their torches for the rescuers until the mobile searchlights arrived. It is all poor property down there and the devastation was terrific. Later Miss M. went down as we had people there on our list. Men were busy repairing mains. Women were wandering about trying to get kettlefuls of water.

Then Mrs Smithers, who was due to come and help, rang up to say she had been clearing débris all night. A bomb had fallen eight houses away. She and her husband were aroused by glass falling all over their bed. All the doors and windows blew in.

Mrs Johnson, warden of our G.W. Shelter in Lambeth, rang up to say the place was once more blasted. Her husband was away. It was so cold with all the windows out! Then she saw a man with piles of black stuff on his shoulder, who asked her if she was in trouble. 'Indeed, I am,' responded Mrs J. 'Well, then I might as well begin with you,' was the response, and he began patching up the holes. How they will hold a Christmas Party there for old people we do not know – however they are persevering.

When one bomb dropped my hair slide flew to the other side of the room. They all tell me that my hair obviously stood on end! I am not surprised.

Had dinner with Dr Remy on Saturday. I gave him a

history of the Four Georges. As they were Germans he was interested. Needless to say they did not receive many bouquets from me. He sat on the only chair, while I curled up in his fur coat, as usual. There are lights on the Bayswater Road now. I did not use my torch either way.

Terrible troubles in Greece. I support Mr Churchill. It is obvious you cannot have everyone wandering about with guns in their hands, doing what they like. It seems akin to the Wars of the Roses.

Tuesday, 19th Very busy all the week with the Poor of the Parish. We continue to add to the numbers we help. All the old folk came Monday and Tuesday. Wednesday and Thursday for the Mothers and children. Not easy without any toys.

If I write that we have not had a Rocket in our – so to speak – Back Yard, for several days, sure enough one will drop tonight. So it is best to say nothing. Mrs Smithers phoned us details of her bomb. Twelve people were killed. Every slate is off her roof. Her chimney is cracked. They used Rescue Dogs to find the people. They had a miraculous escape.

I must say Good-bye to everyone until after Christmas. Merry Xmas to all – and a Happier New Year.

Thursday, 28th Very different from last year, when we had no Second Front. Our sixth war Christmas. News temporarily not so good. But food easier. We all managed to get a plum pudding.

Up to the last people were coming for money, clothing,

toys etc. It was joy to see the gladness on their faces as they received the things. We have had dozens of thank you letters for money sent by post.

I was warned that on Paddington station at 4 p.m. they were queuing for the 6.10 p.m. to Birmingham. Resti then kindly came with me to help me with luggage. We were obliged to circle the streets outside, streams of us, but eventually we reached the main line station. Here throngs were moving in all directions at once, with luggage. I eventually found my queue – twenty abreast and one hundred deep! Was I right – yes, a likely looking man informed me, for the 6.10. I waited for one hour and forty minutes. Packed solid. People seemed to be standing on my feet, or resting their luggage on them. I could dimly feel my own stuff, but had lost hold of the handle, and feared someone would mizzle my Xmas Pudding.

The announcer called out Cardiff and Swansea. Many people grew restive. At 'Have your tickets ready' – the Welsh were roused to frenzy. Somehow they got out – but others were too tightly wedged to move. Next to me was a paratrooper. He looked so weary I ventured to ask him if he came straight from the front. He said he had and was dog-tired. I offered him a cigarette. He just shook his head. So I left him alone.

At 6.20 p.m. there was a move. Everyone bent down with renewed exhilaration to seize their luggage – and with a mad rush we swept on to the platform. The train for Birmingham was in!

Of course, by the time I got there it was full . . . I struggled on down. My rubber boots seemed to slither all over the place. I felt I could do no more . . . But I put my head despairingly in a carriage . . . 'Is there one seat?' Yes . . . was the welcome reply, and a soldier lifted my case and basket. I sank down exhausted. The bliss of that moment. I had got in.

It seems that the Services had been let in by a back entrance, and they had been comfortably seated for some time. The poor paratrooper need not have stood, had he only known. Beside me was a naval boy and his W.R.E.N. wife. They both went to sleep in each other's arms the whole journey. A businessman and I had a good natter on Russia. I arrived an hour late.

Dr Hillier was waiting patiently on the station. Cath had been over to Campden to fetch Bernard Sleigh and his cat. She carried a fowl for Xmas in one hand, and the cat under the other arm. He was the admiration of the bus, having amber eyes, being all black but for a white tip on his tail. He is reputed to amble alongside Bernard's bike when he goes to his allotment, and return curled round his neck. Such an animal must be treated with great respect, and he was.

Sunday morning, Xmas Eve, we were roused to our great astonishment by a siren. Could not credit it. I thought – How they follow me! Everyone said simultaneously – Vere's fault. Poor Cath had to don her uniform and go forth into the cold night with my torch. Bonbon, the Honoured Guest Cat, most astonished at these goings-on in the middle of the night, began prowling round the room. In his wanderings he upset my breakfast tray with milk, tea-pot, cup and saucer, which were on a table. What a mess! Poor Bonbon looked at the floor with deep concern.

The All Clear went. Cath and others had turned up in an amazed state at the Post – one warden darted in full of good intentions, but minus his teeth! No authentic news – but possibly a few Fly Bombs!

Had tea with Elsie and Neville, but he refused to divulge the facts. There had been damage and casualties. Elsie opened one of her cherished tins of pears and cream. Neville belongs to the School of Wicked Financiers. They make wars. You have only to read the *Financial Times* and you know when the next war will be . . . and when it will end. As a result of his studies he gave the following prophecy! The war will go on all through 1945 to Christmas – unless it ends in March. This is orful!

After that the Japanese war will be nothing. The Wicked Financiers will finance both sides. So if you have no money you cannot fight a war. We drank to the confusion of Neville's prophecy in excellent sherry!

Xmas breakfast very nice – all my gifts had been picked up on my Caledonian Market. I cooked the dinner. We listened to the King's speech. Then fog descended on our world. It continued. I feared for my return to London. The train came in like a ghost in faint outline. I got my One Seat. Reached London an hour and a half late. Bakerloo out of action, but found an Inner Circle and thankfully reached my flat at 11 p.m. House very cold. No hot water. It seems Brum had had the coldest Xmas since 1892!

Mr Churchill flew to Athens on Xmas Day. The Greeks seem even more undisciplined than the Italians. The German counter-attack still on . . . how far are we from our happy dreams of the war being over!

Sunday, 31st Icy winds are blowing. Have had a lovely long letter from Chief Os-Ke-Non-Ton. He writes from a Wigwam on the shores of a frozen lake. There is an old swan skidding about on the ice. He says he feels like an old swan himself, is lonely and longs to come back to England, which is a home to him. Such a friendly letter. I long to entertain him in my Notting Hill wigwam for supper – as he has often entertained me.

Seagulls are flying around. I put out some modest bits of breakfast for my sparrows, but heard a great tramping to and fro on my roof and much argument. Seagulls were making off with it, flying around in a world shrouded in mist.

Lights can now be seen after dusk. This is a great help. Heavy white frost each day. We are supposed to save gas, but I regret to say I put on my fire when I wake to warm the place up. Fancy being in a bombed house with makeshift windows!

A few Rockets – but not near us. Frequently I wake up in the night and am surprised to find myself alive – because if you pass over with a Rocket Bomb you would never know until you came to – on the other side of life!

End of the Year 1944

THE YEAR
1945

'And a hard time we had of it'

'O sweet and blessed country'

*'Here is the man who marshalled
the English Language and sent it into battle
when we had little else.'*

'And the Heart of the Eternal is most wonderfully kind'

THE MAIN EVENTS
OF THE WAR
IN 1945

1945

	29	German Army in Italy surrenders
	30	Suicide of Hitler
May	2	Russians complete capture of Berlin
	3	British recover Rangoon
	5	German Forces in West surrender
	8	Victory in Europe Day. Final German surrender
	13	*Great thanksgiving service in St Paul's Cathedral*
May–August		United States Air Offensive against Japan
June	21	Conquest of Okinawa completed
July		Potsdam Conference
August	6	Atomic bomb on Hiroshima
	9	Atomic bomb on Nagasaki
		Russians invade Manchuria
	10	Japanese ask for Armistice
September	2	Final Japanese surrender

JANUARY 1945

Tuesday, 2nd   Sunday I decided to invite a few Old Dears in to toast the New Year. It was just Ginger Wine, and Christmas Cake sent me from Northern Rhodesia by Lucy. We drank to England and Victory.

Listened to radio. Heard the bells of Malines Cathedral. Then from a family in France suffering from the cold. Also one in Holland. Finally the Watch Night Service from St Paul's. Just as all these wonderful sounds were coming over the air, behold, I heard a Rocket drop. Just to remind us that there are unpleasant things still around, and that the war is not over.

It has been thunderingly cold. I have woken up every morning with my nose half frozen, and though we are urged to save gas and electricity, I have had to put my gas fire on to thaw the room a little! Was roused this morning at 3.45 a.m. with a terrific crash, fairly near. I registered strong disapproval, and dozed off again. Hammersmith way they say.

New Year's Eve I heard a Channel Islander give vent to his feelings . . . He had been having a drink or two . . . I'm a Channel Islander, he shouted . . . and the Channel Islands are still under the Germans. I was born and bred there . . . He ran all the words into one. Kit would have sympathized with him.

I must remind Dr Remy that in times of crisis central heating breaks down. They would not now be shivering in Paris if they had a few open fires like those in England.

Barishnikov is under the weather and has been for a long time. I have felt compelled to give him my butter ration. This is the height of virtue.

Thursday, 4th So many Rockets falling tonight that I do not feel like going to bed. Never had such a night of them . . . five in our area. The warden rang up from our Night Shelter in China Walk, Lambeth and said the place was more or less wrecked. They had a soldier from Antigua with them, and were in the only room where the ceiling did not come down.

They have come over here to sleep, and looked like arrivals from a shipwreck. Mrs Johnson really ill, and I do not wonder. They have had to leave the place – just packed a few things and came – too worn-out to bother further with anything.

Miss M. and Mrs Hoare, who so seldom go out, were at the cinema to see *Henry V*. Nice treat for them with Rockets falling, and to return to learn our own Shelter was wrecked.

Mr Hillyard keeps comforting me by saying we cannot all get killed. But it is all unnerving. With Doodles I could dive under the table. I think I shall venture back to my flat to sleep. Being at the top of the house, one can take a slide down to the street.

Snow is falling. Great fire in the sky.

Monday, 8th Am expecting another Rocket at any moment. They say one has dropped on the Bakerloo line. The *Daily Mail* is getting fed-up, and thinks the farce of Southern England might be done away with. Or we could send a few secret weapons on them for a change.

Miss M. has been to see the Shelter. She realizes it could not be used again. It is being emptied, and the stuff is to come to no. 5 for storage. She will re-open as soon as a suitable building is found. They say 100 people were killed that night in Lambeth, so the escape of the Johnsons is remarkable.

Nice letter from Helen Neatby in Uganda. She has bought a car and met a Hippo.

By special dispensation I can go to the London Hospital to see Auntie Mollie on a Sunday. She looked brighter, and ate the apple I was able to take her.

I am struggling with the *Brothers Karamazov*, but do not find myself at home with any of the characters. Must read something about Dostoevsky.

A baby chimpanzee has been born at the Bristol Zoo. We had an interview with its parents. A great event – as few are born in captivity.

I must record the finale of my Mother and the Pig Bin outside our gate. There seems no one to empty them. So annoyed was Mother that she went herself to the Council, and waxed so indignant that the man, I think, hung on to the counter for support, and then said: 'Madam, I will fetch the bin away myself.'

Friday, 12th The snow is quite a few inches deep. It may have slowed down the Rockets. Very slippery – I go gingerly up the road in the dark.

I have been impressed with this awful book, called *I Was Hitler's Maid*. Barishnikov and Resti think it is true. Very depressing. I felt that when a great European country can give itself over to such an evil system of government, it is time mankind perished from the earth. Worse than anything in the Ancient World. We are fighting 'evil things' as poor Mr Chamberlain admitted. It would be better for us to die one by one, and let the Nazis rule over a nation of tombstones, than that they should ever conquer us.

Dr Remy was interested in the book. I read him extracts when he came to have a meal with me. He considered it quite authentic.

Also am reading *Berlin Diary*, by Shirer, an American war correspondent. Our public men come out very badly in the years before the war. *The Times* man never had his stuff properly reported . . . so we went headlong down to disgrace and near annihilation – saved by a very few.

Wednesday, 17th Warsaw has fallen to the Russians! Unexpected and wonderful news! We could scarcely credit it. Barishnikov went dashing in to Resti. We tell him he speaks as if he had done it himself. But he loves to score off Resti and . . . the Swiss Army and Navy.

They say all the guns of Moscow were banging away in unison. I cooked my supper with much elation, after standing to attention for the Polish National Anthem. I suppose the war will end like this. Now it seems to be going on for ever and ever and ever. Then suddenly one day it will cease – and we shall not be able to believe it.

Oranges in Notting Hill today. Not unpacked, but I could return. I spread the good news. We have a Disagreeable Greengrocer round here, and Barishnikov is always baiting him. He is determined to get some oranges out of him. He goes in every two hours to annoy him . . . B. can see the cases of oranges in the shop. But at my shop I was served for three ration books . . . with five oranges. I looked doubtfully at these lovely Jaffas – but how to divide five oranges among three people! I begged humbly for one more . . . he considered and caved in. I departed much elated.

Then we found Resti had had none. I lifted my voice in the office, and Mr Smee, one of our voluntary workers, offered to go round. Barishnikov told him to try the Disagreeable One for fun, as legally you cannot refuse oranges if the book is from Lands End. Gruff and Grum surveyed the ration book, and said it was not in his district. Mr Smee regarded him cheerfully . . . 'How observant you are. You ought to have been a detective, not a greengrocer.' At this the oranges were hastily weighed. He obviously thought Mr Smee was a plain-clothes detective – and he does look like the Head of the Police Force, being tall and authoritative. We were all delighted.

I could not help thinking of Warsaw in 1939, and the despairing awful broadcast from the poor Mayor, who said he was speaking for the last time – and he hoped that the stand they had made helped a little. I suppose he has perished in

these intervening years. The Poles have fought most bravely –
even the Germans say so.

Thursday, 18th Terrific gale blowing today. It will pick off the
rickety roofs. Not so many bombs during the last few days.
Read more of *Berlin Diary*. He writes in the terrible year of
1940 – now it is all going in reverse. What a struggle it has
been! His observations are all on the side of England; but as
defeat follows defeat, he keeps wondering what we are up
to and when it is going to stop. So did we, of course. His
descriptions of Paris under the Germans must be most
interesting to those who know it well.

Mr Churchill has made a great speech in the House, and
wiped the floor with some people. I have backed him from the
start over Greece. Cannot think how people have the
effrontery to be against him – unless their information is
better than his – which it is not. But he is profoundly hurt at
what has gone on.

Monday, 22nd Russian advance into Germany. We hang on to
the News and just gloat and gloat. After the dismal Christmas
news it is lovely to feel the nutcrackers are beginning to work
at last.

Shirer says the Germans did not want war in 1939. They
were quite willing to have everything without war – but war
they did not desire. Dr Remy always says this. He met Lord
Haw-Haw several times. He avoided him as a traitor, but once
they were side by side in an air-raid shelter, and he had to
speak to him. Haw-Haw hates Jews and capitalists – and so
threw in his lot with Germany.

Had a Salad Tea with Auntie on Saturday . . . and even obtained some Fish and Chips for lunch. The snow was quite thick. It was a pretty scene – the Church with the broken steeple, the moon riding over the clouds, the snow clinging to one side of the trees and outlining all the twigs. I tried to imagine I was in Moscow.

Listened with great interest to the play *Love on the Dole*. It ran for a long time in London. Very sad and true – though I was not much in touch with social conditions then.

Long day indoors on Sunday. Glorious! Found the *Observer* rather critical of Churchill, which I don't like. I realize more and more what we owe him – it is only in the future it will come out. Were it not for him I should not be writing this diary – but should have long since been adorning a Concentration Camp.

Mrs Johnson gave me further details of her feelings when the Shelter was bombed. They felt the blast wind round the building three times. The first made them unconscious for some seconds, but next they felt the building falling to pieces around them.

The Russians go pounding on. Is it possible that the next bound will land them in Berlin?

Monday, 29th   It seems possible that the Germans in despair will withdraw men from the Western Front, and so enable the Americans and British to flow in, and so enter Berlin from one side, as the Russians enter from the other. How Hitler must be chewing up the mats in Berchtesgaden these days! I should not like to have to take his coffee in to him!

We have had a fair amount of bombs at all times of the day and night. Do not know where they have been dropped, but to be bombed out in these bitter days must be Hell on earth. They have opened the Emergency Coal Dump in Kensington, and people can take along their prams, etc, and buy coal. Not before it is time. I had an old woman in today, and gave her money to go there without delay.

Every day seems colder than the next. At the Hospital today, Auntie had to put my hands in bed and thaw me out.

What a desert Warsaw looked as the Russians entered. No one there. They say there are plenty of Millionaires in Moscow now. They have villas by the sea. They pay Hollywood salaries to their stars.

The case of Elizabeth Jones has shocked every welfare worker in the country. She is aged 18, and has ended up with a conviction for murder. She has a nice face, and at school was popular. The women police have orders to round up these young girls and see what they are doing.

End of January 1945

FEBRUARY 1945

❊

Thursday, 1st This is written under a great shadow. Auntie Nell is seriously ill and is in St Charles' Hospital. Her life hangs by a thread.

She was quite well on Sunday when I had tea with her; but on Monday evening she felt sick and giddy and went to bed. The Doctor said her heart was not in good condition. Miss Topsy phoned me, but said I could do nothing. On Wednesday she was much worse. It was obvious she was seriously ill. He ordered her to Hospital. She was quite sensible and asked if Miss Topsy could not nurse her. The answer was No. So this dear kind soul helped Auntie in the ambulance. They phoned me that it was not good.

I sent Mother a card. They said I must go at once. I flung on hat and coat and went to the Hospital. There the Sister interviewed me, saying she might as well tell me that they did not think there was the slightest hope. She was too weak to operate, though they were giving her a blood transfusion. There she lay behind a screen. She looked ill and grey, but opened her eyes. She was most surprised to see me. She has no idea she is so ill, and talked of an operation tonight. It is femoral hernia. I whispered to her the news that the Russians were rushing for Berlin, and the old spirit flashed out in her joy. She was too tired to talk . . . so I kissed her and came away.

I felt very blue as I left her. Found Miss Topsy in Auntie's flat. Neither of us could bear to think we should not see her bobbing about in it, full of enthusiasm over something. Aunt Winnie is coming from Brede tomorrow. I phoned East Ham Vicarage.

At 10 p.m. Miss Topsy phoned me that they were to try the operation and on this ray of hope I shall try to sleep.

The Rockets are still dropping on London. A fearful Wonk at 4.15 a.m. and another mid-day. The Thaw has set in, and everyone has had burst pipes. One was pouring gallons of water into the street near us all night long.

Sunday, 18th   It is some time since I have written my diary. Since the beginning of February unforeseen events have crowded on me, and I have been overwhelmed with business, sadness and worry. Nothing less than the sudden illness and death of dear Auntie Nell.

For the family it is like the passing of the chieftain. She had made herself the Head of the Clan, and living in London all relatives from abroad could make her home their Headquarters. The Chieftainship was sometimes a little overpowering; but if anyone of us was in trouble it was Auntie Nell to the rescue, and she would do anything to help.

Personally it is a terrible loss, as her flat has been my second home for so many years. I have seen her nearly every week, except during the bad blitz, when she was away. Latterly we have been in constant touch – facing the ups and downs of good news and bad. I am stunned for the time being. However, she died in the plenitude of her powers. No trouble to anyone. On the contrary she was still rendering acts of service all round.

We had a Memorial Service for her at St Peter's, Bayswater. About 35 people were present. It was beautifully taken by her very dear friend Canon Morris Hodson, and his wife played Handel's Largo, Auntie's favourite piece of music.

I am now absorbed in the business of giving away her bequests, and arranging for the storage of the furniture until Aunt Vere returns from Kenya. Auntie Mollie is still ill in the London Hospital, and Aunt Winnie has the house at Brede to keep going. However, we are being helped.

It is strange that bombs are still dropping on London. East Ham Vicarage was blasted the day Auntie died. Similarly Cicely Lucy's house at Golders Green. So far we are intact here, but a bomb fell on Shepherd's Bush during the week – this is the next village to Notting Hill. Thank God that was one dear Auntie Nell did not hear, for they frightened her very much, far more than she ever let me know. She was proud and tried to keep a brave front, and we did our best to keep one another's spirits up. But they wore her down, and lowered her resistance to illness. That was why she went so rapidly.

We are pushing the Germans from our side – and the Russians are doing it from the other. It is like Giant Nut-crackers. They may have to retire from Italy. But it is all a long time. I had prayed earnestly that dear Auntie would survive to the peace. We had planned such a Party – she and I. We were to put on our best frocks, and drink the health of England and

Mr Churchill in great style. But now that little Party will never take place, and Lucy will not see her again – nor Aunt Vere, to talk over all our experiences and the dangers we have escaped.

I shall not be able to record any more Tea Parties. No more Salads that she knew so well how to concoct. No more ginger wine and apricot jam that she used to make with such joy. I buried her with the Rose of England – One she always wore to go to National Services. It looked so lovely and appropriate on her. I found it in her Jewel Case.

While I was making that awful journey to the Coroner's Court I saw all round Pontings queues of women. I was told it was sheets. The Government had released some, and so short is everyone that women were outside the shop at 5 a.m. Not hundreds, but thousands. Police were controlling the queues. Some of the happy buyers got in my bus . . . loaded.

I got into conversation with a woman expecting her husband back from the Middle East after 3 years. She was scouring the town for a fowl, as he seemed to be expecting turkey and mince pies. The latter she had, but . . . (while I am typing this Two Rockets have fallen . . .) I suggested a place in Notting Hill. I hope she got one. Well, we all plod on our weary way.

Sunday, 25th Difficult to keep up my diary with so much correspondence about Auntie Nell. But I feel better in myself, and I can grapple more. Went to see Auntie Mollie, and she is walking down the Ward with two sticks. She looked happier and brighter.

Went on to East Ham Vicarage. What a scene of desolation! They have had a miraculous escape. The last rocket was as near the Vicarage as makes no matter. Only the fact that it is a well-built square old house did it stand up to it. All around is like the City . . . Desolation.

We are 18 miles from Cologne, and the Russians are closing in on Frankfurt – but the Germans are not beaten yet. I am tired and can write no more. Good night everyone.

End of February 1945

MARCH 1945

***** ❋ *****

Sunday, 4th Bombing has stepped up this week after a few days lull, when we thought they could do no more. Rotten. The other night awakened by an Alert – very unusual. A Rocket fell about 11.15 p.m. Then in the night someone rang my bell. This was astonishing, but mercifully I was so tired I disregarded it. I thought it was all part of a nightmare of which I was the victim. In the morning, on comparing notes with other residents, I found mine was not the only bell rung that night.

Very busy with two remaining Aunts. One leaving Hospital, and the other coming up for business and to take her sister home.

These bombs are in Northern England as well – and I expect in the Midlands. Even at this stage of the war we are having raiding bombs, rockets and fly bombs – all over at once – I jolly well think we have had enough. I am fed up. Aunt Winnie was alarmed at our Bumps in the night.

Saturday, 17th This is my last week-end in Auntie's flat. The removers come in on Thursday. Bombs still about. One fell just as one of my little birds was eating on the window sill, and he nearly flew into the room, he was so startled. Another as I was leaving the office at 11 p.m. It nearly threw me into the middle of Ladbroke Grove. All the earthquake blasts which follow the explosion are terrific. They go right through you, and I continued my way shaking all over. Even in bed I begin to tremble all over – so great is the shock. I have had enough. There seems no end to it, and a great weariness of spirit overtakes me at times.

Anyway the Spring is here and that is a great comfort to us. The almond blossom is on the trees, and the yellow forsythia is flaming on the bushes – not to mention the hawthorns that are getting a covering of delicious fresh green.

Auntie is to stay in Hospital longer in order to have an eye operation. I was just thinking of her when I heard the unmistakable buzz-buzz of a Fly Bomb. I retreated to the corridor. We are so experienced now with these beastly things that everyone came out, complete with suitcase. We heard it explode. Another well-trained Old Dear was knitting in the corridor on her floor – waiting the All Clear or The End!

I must record an interesting discussion on the League of Nations, in which Gilbert Murray told a story about tradition. One of the reasons why the League failed was just this. The Americans do not seem to understand that to build up tradition takes time. A College in U.S.A. put up the following notice: It is the tradition of this College that students do not walk upon the grass . . . this tradition will begin on Monday.

I cannot get Dr Remy to see that the British Constitution has tradition behind it. These gim-crack constitutions, made to measure and all correct in theory, do not usually survive more than 20 years. Anyway we have learned, as someone said, that you cannot prevent war by running away from it – so many English people thought you could.

It is St Patrick's Day, and our little Golden Pussy was wearing a bright green ribbon. He looked so sweet, as green as his colour. He nearly exploded with pride.

A little tiny theatre called The Gateway near here, in Chepstow Villas, presents excellently acted little performances. Have seen one by Clemence Dane, called *The Way Things Happen*. Another *The Silver Cord* by Sidney Howard.

Sunday, 18th Learned that a water-main had been struck, though it was a bomb I did not seem to register, I was so busy packing up to leave Auntie's flat. No water for the next few hours . . . Kit and her sister are coming for a few hours to picnic in the flat after attending the first half of Bach's St Matthew's Passion at the Albert Hall. It was a treat to have them. They wished the little place were mine! We discussed our general fed-upness with bombs. Flo said what a joy it was that, having a child, she was able to go up to Lake Windermere without offending her conscience.

I then set off for the Hospital. Poor Auntie did not seem very well. She was all bandaged, and I fed her with her Tea. Then I went on to Chelsea by Cheapside and Smithfield, where the bomb fell last week, with great loss of life. I was thankful to reach dear Mrs South and have tea. She looks very strained.

We have crossed the Rhine. All to the good, but I should have been much more pleased if they had taken Holland.

There was much good sense in Churchill's speech. He

does not think we can make a new world with a stroke of the pen. I am all for Beveridge – but not for no work for anybody, with young men in fancy shirts just rushing about expressing their selfish selves!

Palm Sunday, 25th Weather marvellous all the week. Hottest day in London in March for half a century. The sun blazed down from a sky of cloudless blue.

The armies are getting on fine. How glad we shall be when they get the Dutch coast. Then the bombing may stop. But when we are in a pessimistic mood we feel there will never be an end, and that the Germans will launch them to the last from the last German mountain! However, one hears now such names as Worms being captured, and the Palatinate cleared.

A bomb fell the other morning in the Great West Road, straight on the Packard works and the Pyrene factories. Not far from us as the crow flies. My removing man had a brother there, who said it was awful. Petrol caught fire, explosives went off. Then there was a Fly Bomb at the bottom of Leinster Gardens near Whiteleys.

A sad moment when I saw dear Auntie Nell's well-loved furniture carried into storage from the flat. I have brought away all stores of food, and can hardly move in my own flat for bottles and jars.

Mabel Lucy has been turned out of her flat, but as she was going to live in Stratford-on-Avon anyway, she does not worry.

Wednesday, 28th It seems to be victory all along the line. Fighting in Frankfurt and soon the Americans will take the city. Why the Germans keep on fighting God only knows. There is a Hitler Götterdämerung. Perhaps he will not die, but be swallowed up in a cloud of fire and be a legend ever after like Frederick the great Emperor! Anything may happen at the moment.

A notable place was demolished the other day. It is the Whitefield Tabernacle in Tottenham Court Road, with a direct hit. [We did not realize this at the time, but it seems to have been the last bomb.]

End of March 1945

APRIL 1945

✦

Tuesday, 3rd This unhappy war seems drawing to a close, and it may soon be that we shall hear the last bomb drop. We were amused the other day at the way the newspapers had to camouflage the bomb in Hyde Park. It had fallen, they said . . . on a piece of waste ground . . . that it had destroyed one or two Army Huts in Southern England, and had blown out the windows of an hotel and a cinema . . . Behind this description lies one of the most famous spots in London. The Soap Box Orator's Corner at the Marble Arch. The hotel was the Cumberland. The Cinema – the Regal. It also took windows in Park Lane and Edgware Road. No one would suspect such well-known place names from . . . 'waste ground in Southern England.'

I have been away for a few days. Did not hear bombs for two days before I left, and they are demolishing the street surface shelters. But we must be on our guard about rejoicing too soon.

My journey not too bad. Queued at 4.30 p.m. for the 6.10 to Brum. Soon we were twenty abreast. I read the morning paper in which it stated that we were winning victories. It was lovely not to depart to an orchestra of Flying Bombs, or the menacing rumble of a Rocket. Everyone looked happier. Then at last we were loosed upon the train and we all ran – hundreds of us. I got some idea of how the Bethnal Green disaster got out of hand. Even this was unpleasant for a few moments. I found a last seat in one carriage, and sank down to breathe sighs of thankfulness that I had done it once again.

Another wartime journey and perhaps the last!

Dr H. met me as usual. Found the family in session including all the Cats. There are three kittens! My sister has named them as follows. Stalin – because he is always before schedule – climbing etc. Roosevelt – because he feels he is important. Winston – because he never minds being mentioned last. Anyway we had the pleasure of the three lolloping all over the house during Easter. The Mother did nothing but chat to them and to us all the time. I could not hear myself speak at times owing to her enthusiasm over these babies. She kept drawing our attention to them. When I cleaned the carpet sweeper they fell in and out of it, and covered themselves with dust. They played fortifications round my legs – Alas, Hélas, and all other sounds of woe – my silk stockings were rent in more than one place.

Went to see various friends with Mother. Mrs Harry Duffell. Her niece and husband, Colonel and Mrs Cole were there. The former remembered my father. We thrashed out Russia and our debt to her. We considered it about fifty-fifty.

Then to see Mr and Mrs Philip Styles of the Birmingham University History department. He has edited the County History of Warwickshire. I was able to pass on a little information about the connection of the Lucy Family with the Mill at Stratford-on-Avon. Philip stated definitely that the Mill owner came up with the idea of claiming Charlecote, and the Lucy of Charlecote would have been glad to have a connection proved. But certain vital papers were missing – the family say during the Civil War. They were Royalists, and ruined by the war. Charlecote Lucys were for the Parliament.

As a background to all this the rush into Germany continues. I prayed they were getting into Holland – I did not want to return to more bombs.

Thursday, 5th Russia has declared she is no longer neutral with Japan. So that is another nail in Hitler's coffin which is nearly made – it only remains for him to be put inside it.

We have had no more bombs.

Auntie Winnie is in Rye Hospital with a scalded leg. I don't know what to do with my aunts – one after another they fall by the wayside with various accidents. Trudged over with a suitcase for the one in the London – but where will she go with her sister out of action?

Story about fraternization. Strict rules in Germany about it. It works well with regard to the military, but it is difficult when our soldiers contact women and children. One English officer scowled hard for three days at the damsel who was doing for him – only to discover she was an unhappy Pole, far away from her own country!

And our soldiers cannot resist giving the German children rides in their jeeps up and down the village street.

We are conquering Hanover . . . one's mind goes back to George I, who longed to die there, and kept urging on the coachman . . . Osnabrück, Osnabrück. And now we enter it as conquerors.

My journey back to London was uneventful until I reached Paddington when the handle of my suitcase came right off . . . mobs of people about . . . it was heavy, and I had a basket too. A nightmare to reach Ladbroke Road. I nearly broke my arm. Poor Vere! She was in the devil of a mess, but preserved a heroic exterior, and no outside person would have known of her sufferings.

We thought the war might have ended over the week-end, but it seems a bit stiffer everywhere. The Russians are mopping up Vienna. The Austrian Resistance are doing all they can to get the Nazis out. This told me by an Austrian refugee . . . Alas her English pronunciation is execrable, and she never stops talking . . . until I am ready to scream and wish the Austrian nation and its troubles in Hades. Poor Soul, I am sorry in my heart for her. She has lost all her relations. But I cannot forget that Hitler is an Austrian.

Have heard from a young British soldier that the Germans he is guarding are most docile. They have weeded out all the truculent Nazis, and all the map-reading brainy ones, and he is left with a residue of 17- and 18-year-olds, who are like sheep. The Italians, he says, are much more temperamental.

In Occupied Germany the white flags come out by the dozen and every burgomaster hastens to make himself agreeable. All seem glad it is over, and they don't mind the Americans and British at all. They are people with a dual personality – the Bully and the Serf.

Monday, 9th Prunus trees are out and they are lovely. Listened to wonderful broadcast all about Mulberry, Phoenix, Whale and Gooseberry. We made it and thought of it. We are very clever – when we have to be! Otherwise we are too lazy. I hope those people who shouted so many years for a Second Front, listened too – and were ashamed.

I must record that in Brum over Easter I had an ice cream – the first I have tasted for years. Neville interviewed a cow, who promised the cream; then a farmer's wife said she would make it. His sister gave him a tin of pears – and this wonderful concoction was produced for his wife and me at our Luncheon Party. He had been doodling about in his room for ages, and Elsie did not know what he was up to. Just grand!

No more bombs for more than a week. No one knows what it means to us to go to bed in peace, and not take leave of all our possessions, and wonder if we shall wake up in pieces, or with the roof collapsing on our heads, unless they have lived with it. Having a vivid imagination I have constantly visualized these things, and wondered which one would happen to me.

I shall be able to fetch out my Venetian glass goblet – that has been put away for so long. All this uncertainty of life has gone on for so long now that it seems we had lost all sense of security at all. It was either fire bombs, or shells, or doodles or rockets. All have pursued us in turn. Poor Auntie Nell, she suffered so much. How she would have gloried in our present freedom.

Met Mrs Wickham Steed the other day in the dyers and cleaners. I do love his broadcasts, and wish I could hear more.

Lovely to hear Italian pronounced correctly and with such loving care.

Went to Hospital to see dear Auntie Mollie. I hope for the last time there. Came back via Chelsea and Mrs South. She is 87, and as young as anyone could wish. We talked of my family which she has known nearly all her life.

Wednesday, 11th No Bombs! No spuds either! Went up to my precious Fish and Chip shop – plenty of fish, and he would fry your potatoes if you brought them! We shall have to go on rice – and this is getting scarce.

My Orange lady was in an angelic humour. Gave them to me without a murmur. The trees are fresh and green. We are fanning over Holland, but the Germans are still fighting.

Friday, 13th It is a Black Day for all of us. President Roosevelt died yesterday very suddenly. What a shock when I hopped out of bed this morning, and found the *D.T.* all in Black, and the terrible announcement. I shed tears. It will make it harder for Mr Churchill. They got on so well and Stalin is of a different mentality, and a hard nut to crack.

Anyway, so many thanks to you, Mr Roosevelt, for all the help you gave us, and the way you worked to save us in those dark and lonely days of 1940. The House of Commons adjourned today on Mr Churchill's suggestion – the first time in English History it has done this for a foreign statesman. That shows the debt we owe him.

Another bit of information – this regards the Mona Lisa, and other pictures of the Louvre. They were passed around in France. The Resistance always sent news through to the R.A.F.

in London as to where they were. So they were never bombed. Wonderful.

The Americans are 15 miles from Berlin! Perhaps then they will declare the end of the war. But it came for us here when the last bomb dropped.

Monday, 16th Just had the good luck to hear the first speech of the new President. I am sure we are going to like him personally. He is very humble about himself, and seems to be a man of sincere faith, and asks God to help him in his great task. He has not the force of Roosevelt, but his one idea is to follow in the late President's footsteps, to whom he looks up as one of the greatest of men. He stressed the responsibility of America in the new world order.

The matron of the London Hospital broadcast last night. Such a sweet feminine voice, yet she must be a woman with plenty of character to hold such a post. Hers, she said, was the largest voluntary Hospital in the country, and had received direct hits.

Very tired, so walked through the Park on Saturday morning. No daffodils, but the lime trees were superb. A small child of three was standing in front of Queen Victoria very worried because she could not see her feet!

Went to the office later and did some work, but every time I bent my head over the desk waves of nausea passed over me, and I had to give up. Lay flat on my back in the little flat and began to pull round. It is reaction after all these years of war and constant bombing. I must get into the fresh air as much as I can.

Auntie Mollie, after a bad journey, has now joined her sister in Rye Hospital.

Friday, 20th How wonderful to write that we are all racing to Berlin. How often have we dreamed about it during these awful years! Yet it never seemed possible it could come true.

But we are stricken with horror at the awful revelations from the Concentration Camps. The dead and dying found in great heaps on the floor . . . Dirt and misery unspeakable. Not only neglect, but acts of outrageous cruelty on a gigantic scale. It is no use the German people saying they did not do it. They allowed such people to come to power, and cheered them when they were winning. Now they disown them. Naturally! They are losing. That is the German all over . . .

I hope the terrible films taken by the Americans will be shown all over the land, especially in the Universities, where students are inclined to be above such low physical details, and merely look for the Causes far back in History. There were Germans coming away, and the expression on the faces of the women showed nothing of humiliation or shame. Master Race, indeed!

The Funeral Memorial for Roosevelt was a great Service at St Paul's. I was somewhat amazed, though, to hear Mr Churchill referred to as Roosevelt's lieutenant! It was just as much the other way about. Mr Roosevelt never stood up to the Desperate Situation that Churchill did, when he had to forge a new weapon from nothing, with the enemy at our Front Door. Only the Navy between us and the Germans. He is always so modest that there is danger of people taking him at his own valuation. However, Mr Roosevelt was the greatest friend we ever had in our hour of need. But Churchill gave him time, and in so doing saved America, Russia and ourselves.

The black-out is to end on Monday. I now possess three torches just as we do not need them any more! For six years we have been tormented with them. The First Ice Creams are back. Not good, but the shadow of better things to come!

Monday, 23rd   Went down to Sunningdale yesterday. Glad to be speeding out of London. Trees seemed so fresh. The men in the carriage were reading their papers with great satisfaction. John Englishman was pleased. How often has he had to stomach bad news – so galling to his pride! But today the Russians are in Berlin and the long dreary years are drawing to a close. Everyone of us, perfect strangers though we were, felt a vibration of acute satisfaction.

Miss Wise and I had a lovely day. The laburnums, red and white may, azaleas and rhododendrons were all out in the beautiful house in which she lives. Such a treat to relax. I sat in the window of her lovely room – not a building in sight. All houses of big financiers in this part – not the charm of farms and cottages. During the Big Blitz they had one Great Event . . . a dog fight between Poles and Germans just above them, and those blighters dropped 90 bombs in an area of a few miles. Mercifully they fell mostly in gardens and fields, but the local inhabitants thought it was the Day of Judgment – at night.

Saturday I set to work to spring-clean all Mr Hillyard's

Filing Shelves. It extends from ceiling to floor. Five years accumulation of dust and soot. A good man and true – Mrs Yirrell by name – agreed to come and help me. From 7 p.m. to 11 p.m. we toiled and moiled – I got blacker and blacker – I upset the Vim. Never mind, we persevered until it was finished. Were we tired! I was almost unrecognizable from dirt. Hoped for a nice bath– but on arrival at the flat, water was cold . . . Anyhow I had a great sense of virtue.

There are no Soap Flakes. I suppose they are all being sent to swab down those awful Concentration Camps.

Princess Mary must be anxious about her son. We hear the German prisoners are getting better food than we are. The very idea!

Wednesday, 25th   We are actually allowed to lift the black-out. But it seems to make us all nervous when we see the lights streaming forth from the house! We have been so well trained after all these years that we still have the feel of the chains that have bound us for so long. When I went up the road the one place from which light streamed bravely out was my police station. I should think they had on every one in the building. But in London generally we are not going to be rushed. We still find it hard to believe the need is over.

However, the Speaker has had the joy of kindling the Lantern of Westminster Tower once more, to show that Parliament is sitting. He has been longing to do this.

I was amused to hear that the Germans in Berlin are making full use of their Undergrounds. The Russians have suddenly found German soldiers emerging behind them out of the ground! So they turned suddenly and captured the station. They trundle guns down, and have them on the platforms ready for the next train to arrive in! We might have had to do the same.

Poor old Pétain is standing trial. He is 89. I wish he would just die. King Leopold of the Belgians is due to cross the frontier. Some people think he will never be King again. I have no theories about it.

Friday, 27th My own black-out is down! What a lovely event to record! I have torn it down, cleaned the paint underneath, and washed the curtains. I do look nice. Hip! Pip!

The Russians and Americans have met. Germany is cut in two. Goering has resigned with heart trouble, and we have bombed Berchtesgaden – good and proper. Just imagine that after all the dismal events I have had to record in this diary for so many years, I can really put down such wonderful items of news!

It is difficult to reconcile the docility of the average German with the inhuman brutality of others. Now they obey our orders just as they obeyed the Nazis. Are they just flabby robots? And the worst of them – Brutal Thugs? Certainly, Kramer, the commandant of Belsen looks criminal – and so do the women who had charge in the camp.

It seems almost impossible to make the Germans understand they are responsible for the Concentration Camps. They just have no public conscience. Each man for himself always. Yet they are full of conceit about themselves.

It seems Mussolini has been arrested at the Swiss frontier.

He was storming with rage. The Americans call him one of the Greatest Flops in History. This seems an apt description. How different from the man with whom I shook hands! I can see him now – full of strength and vitality and ambition – unbending graciously before the English Miss!

My aunts still seem full of trouble. But they are not the only elderly folk falling about. The hospitals are full of them.

We are getting more milk. This helps a lot. Also eggs.

Monday, 30th The amazing news is that Mussolini is dead. The Italian partisans of N. Italy have taken him prisoner while he was snooping into Germany. They tried him then and there – shot him and Clara Petacci – and hung their bodies in Piazza Loreto in Milan. So that is the end of him. In the short diary I kept in Italy – unhappily I did not continue with it – I kept asking what would be the end of him. I knew it would be a bloody one. And here it is at last.

I am thankful the Italians have done something themselves. A resistance against the Germans. They have not just been intimidated by the Gestapo . . . but have suffered and sacrificed, and so the world does not despise them.

I lay awake a long time last night thinking of all we have been saved from in this country. Think of the French. A British agent told us the other day how he had organized Resistance. He had been passed from one to another, had been fed and hidden by simple people who had risked themselves and their families for the honour of France. He returned recently to the village. Alas, nearly all had disappeared. One or two members of a family were left, but others had met a fate not to be thought of.

Here we have been bombed and bombed until we are weary of it, but we have not been called upon to see our families arrested, nor do such deeds of danger. These French were just clerks and shopkeepers – and they were not intimidated by the Germans.

It is this that makes us despise the Germans. There is no similar Resistance there. It is useless for us to drop parachutists to organize them. They do not lift a finger to throw off the chains that bind them. Only a foreign army can do it – then they just obey the foreign army. Yet other occupied countries – with people not so clever as the Germans, have never for one moment accepted domination.

Snowing today. The vagaries of the English climate are truly astonishing. The air is thick with rumours. Bernadotte, descendant of one of Napoleon's marshals, is mentioned as being in touch with the Nazis.

Saturday night went and had a Binge. Waited in the hall of the Strand Palace Hotel for my friend, as obedient as any German. Then the Lounge door burst open, and Mrs Renton came tearing out to say she had been keeping a table for ages. I reminded her of my habitual timidity in the stately portals of hotels. We had tea. Great fun to watch the people. Much better than the Dorchester. Later we had dinner. Beside us were a lady and a boy. We watched the dancing. We ate roast pigeon. The lady opened conversation. She and the boy had just returned from Australia, and she was full of admiration for all we had endured. We welcomed her back. She wished she had never left. They both looked forlorn and sad. Her eyes full of tears, she explained – 'I have come back to much tragedy – my husband has left me.'

Dr Remy came and had tea. I was uncompromising over the Germans. We have all been so shocked over the pictures of the Concentration Camps that we can hardly contain ourselves. Not to mention our starved prisoners – while the Germans here are living on the fat of the land! Geneva Convention indeed. Fiddlesticks!

Well – we have been saved by Mr Churchill, and there is not a man, woman or child in this country who does not owe him a debt we can never repay.

Bad shortage of potatoes. I use them a lot, as I cannot be bothered to cook much else. The Old Pole is good. We have had three nice oranges each.

Dr Remy is disgusted at the good treatment we have given Hess and Von Papen. 'Why don't they have to queue up with their tin mugs like other prisoners?' he demanded.

The dear little boy, Clive, who lives opposite, delighted me the other day. I met him skipping along to school by his Mother, and also following them was a nondescript little tabby cat! 'Oh, yes,' they explained, 'he always comes.' Believe it or not, as I followed the trio up the hill and across the road with my eye, the Cat was galloping alongside! Cats are not usually so fond of little boys.

End of April 1945

MAY 1945

✺

'The strife is o'er, the battle done
Now is the victor's triumph won'

'And they who with their leader have conquer'd in the fight'

Monday, 7th The war is over. They say tomorrow is V.E. day, and that Mr Churchill will speak at 3 p.m. and the King at 9 p.m.

And so it all ends, and the long nightmare I have recorded in these pages is finished at last. All we can say is thank God. I can now go to St Paul's, or the Abbey, represent dear Auntie Nell, and give thanks for all the family in different parts of the world for this great deliverance. We have been spared the worst in this country. We have not had to take part in a Resistance Movement, nor see German soldiers marching through our streets, nor had to be rescued by our colonies.

According to rumour Hitler, Goering and Goebbels are dead. We do not know. The Germans have been giving themselves up in millions. It is quite incredible.

Victory in Europe Day, Tuesday 8th Today we have been celebrating! Thunderstorm in the night. No one slept much

587

for excitement. But the sun shone warm, and it has been a Glorious Day.

Kit and I reached St Paul's about 11 a.m. One service was in progress, but another was soon due to begin. All through I continued to give thanks for our great deliverance. We had a splendid view of the Lord Mayor of London walking down the aisle, and his Chain of Office seemed to glitter with diamonds. The Choir sang the *Te Deum*. All the little boys were back. We sang all three verses of the National Anthem with great firmness, confounding their politics with tremendous enthusiasm.

Lovely and warm outside. We thought of the wonderful fire-watchers the Cathedral has had. They held their own Service. I remembered that Sunday when I walked past it, smoking ruins around, and a few weary firemen gathering their apparatus together.

We sauntered down to the River, and ate our lunch above the Temple stairs, near the *Discovery*. Carefree after so many years of anxiety. Then along to Westminster and Whitehall. We stood in Parliament St. What a squash! The buses scraped within an inch of us, and the horses of the mounted police rubbed their flanks against us.

Precisely at 3 p.m. Big Ben's chimes told us the moment was about to begin. All traffic stopped. The mounted policeman wiped the sweat from his brow. All was still. How wonderful to be standing in Whitehall, in the shadow of the House of Commons, listening to That Voice which had steered us from our darkest hours to the daylight of deliverance. No words can express what we owe him. He mentioned the Channel

Islands to tremendous cheers. Kit was thrilled that they should be specially mentioned on such an occasion. She has not heard from her father for eleven months.

By now we were exhausted with heat and standing. Heaps of people on bicycles. There was a tandem – Mother, Father and Baby. Spectators were horrified at the position of this tiny mite, with a great bus towering above it – but the baby did not worry. We reached Downing St with a great effort. But I could no more. We had heard him speak.

The tube at Trafalgar Square was impossible of entrance, so we walked along Pall Mall. Cars passed us with people riding on the hoods and the bonnets. Everyone was just letting themselves go. We were glad to get to the flat for a cup of tea!

In the evening we had our own party. We were quite a United Nations. A Russian, a Swiss, a Channel Islander, a Scot-cum-Welsh and me, a true-blue English Midlander. We had ersatz champagne. Tinned grapefruit. Salad. Tongue. Tin of crayfish – and a Plum Pudding. All of us had been saving these viands up for a long time. All Beautifully prepared by Miss Cameron. It was in Barishnikov's garden flat, which is bigger than mine. We had lovely coffee, and then he produced his pièce de resistance, some 1898 port . . . or some such date. We drank numerous Toasts . . . Churchill, Stalin, Auntie Nell, Kit's father in Guernsey . . . then the men drank to us.

We listened to the radio, and just tuned in to the moment when Mr Churchill came out in his Siren suit and conducted *Land of Hope and Glory*. He was wearing a black Homburg Hat. What a lad! He was cheered to the echo. God bless him!

They all returned with me. We saw the Sanctuary flood-lighting . . . It was decorated splendidly with flags. It looked fine – and many people were looking at it. We had tea at my flat and waited for the Midnight News. Then they crept downstairs, and Kit and I were glad to bed down.

[The diary continued for many years but one postwar quotation is needed here]

Wednesday, 16th To return to other matters. I was very amused at the rescinding of the bill against Gloom and Despondency. Now it is not against the law to be gloomy or despondent. So great was our danger in certain years that we were forbidden to look miserable. Now we can be as unhappy as we please! Freedom is returning.

'Sing to the Lord with cheerful voice'

Winifred VERE HODGSON was born in 1901 in Edgbaston, Birmingham, where her widowed mother ran the family home as a boarding house. Vere, named after an uncle who was the marine biologist on Captain Scott's ship, read History at Birmingham University, taught first at the Poggio Imperiale, the former Summer Palace of the grand dukes of Tuscany which had been turned into a 'rather select girls' school' (Mussolini's daughter was a pupil), and later on at a school in Folkestone. From the early 1930s she helped to run a local charity in Notting Hill Gate. Vere kept a diary from girlhood onwards and in 1976 edited her 1940–45 diaries for publication as *Few Eggs and No Oranges*. After her retirement she went to live in the village of Church Stretton in Shropshire, where she died in 1979.

If you have enjoyed this Persephone Book why not telephone or write to us for details of our other titles, in print and forthcoming?

PERSEPHONE BOOKS LTD
28 Great Sutton Street
London EC1V 0DS

Telephone: 0171 253 5454
Fax: 0171 253 5656
sales@persephonebooks.co.uk
www.persephonebooks.co.uk